FDR'S BUDGETEER AND
MANAGER-IN-CHIEF

FIFTEEN CENTS   JUNE 14, 1943

TIME

THE WEEKLY NEWSMAGAZINE

Boris Chaliapin

HAROLD SMITH, DIRECTOR OF THE BUDGET
Czars may come and czars may go, but he goes on forever.
(U. S. at War)

VOLUME XLI   (REG. U. S. PAT. OFF.)   NUMBER 24

FDR'S BUDGETEER AND MANAGER-IN-CHIEF

Harold D. Smith, 1939–1945

MORDECAI LEE

SUNY P R E S S

Published by State University of New York Press, Albany

For information, contact State University of New York Press, Albany, NY
www.sunypress.edu

Library of Congress Cataloging-in-Publication Data

Name: Lee, Mordecai, 1948– author.
Title: FDR's budgeteer and manager-in-chief : Harold D. Smith, 1939–1945 / Mordecai Lee.
Description: Albany : State University of New York Press, [2021] | Includes bibliographical references and index.
Identifiers: LCCN 2021024216 | ISBN 9781438485331 (hardcover : alk. paper) | ISBN 9781438485348 (pbk. : alk. paper) | ISBN 9781438485355 (ebook)
Subjects: LCSH: Smith, Harold D., 1898–1947. | Roosevelt, Franklin D. (Franklin Delano), 1882–1945. | United States. Bureau of the Budget—Officials and employees—Biography. | Budget—United States—History—20th century. | Finance, Public—United States—History—1933- | World War, 1939–1945— Finance—United States. | United States—Politics and government—1933–1945.
Classification: LCC HJ2051 .L398 2021 | DDC 352.4/80973—dc23
LC record available at https://lccn.loc.gov/2021024216

10 9 8 7 6 5 4 3 2 1

In grateful appreciation for two decades at the
University of Wisconsin–Milwaukee and its terrific
Golda Meir Library. A professor could not want for more.

Contents

Illustrations

Abbreviations

AA   Administrative Assistant, formal title of the six presidential aides authorized by the 1939 Reorganization Act. Also a generic personnel category for a staff aide to a senior federal executive.

AP   Associated Press (news wire service)

APSA   American Political Science Association

APSR   *American Political Science Review*

ASPA   American Society for Public Administration

BOB   Bureau of the Budget (renamed Office of Management and Budget [OMB] in 1970)

BS   *Baltimore Sun*

CCPA   Committee for Congested Production Areas

CR   *Congressional Record*

CSC   Civil Service Commission

CSM   *Christian Science Monitor* (afternoon newspaper published in Boston)

CT   *Chicago Tribune*

CwP   Conferences with President, HDSP

DFP   *Detroit Free Press*

DM   Daily Memoranda, HDSP

DR   Daily Record, HDSP

EO   Executive Order

EOP   Executive Office of the President

FDRL   Franklin Delano Roosevelt Presidential Library, Hyde Park (NY)

FY   Fiscal Year. *Note*: The traditional fiscal year in the American public sector starts on July 1 and ends on June 30 of the next calendar year. FYs are titled by the year they *end* in. For example, FY 1941 started on July 1, 1940, and ended on June 30, 1941. In the 1970s, Congress bumped federal fiscal years forward by a quarter, beginning on October 1 and ending on September 30. Most other governments retained the traditional fiscal year.

GPO   Government Printing Office (a federal agency, formally part of the legislative branch)

HC   *Hartford [CT] Courant*

HDSP   Harold D. Smith Papers, FDR Library

LAT   *Los Angeles Times*

NDAC   National Defense Advisory Commission

NRPB   National Resources Planning Board

NYA   National Youth Administration

NYHT   *New York Herald Tribune*

NYT   *New York Times*

OCD   Office of Civilian Defense

OEM   Office for Emergency Management (agency in EOP)

OES   Office of Economic Stabilization

OFHDS   Office Files of Harold D. Smith, Central Files, OMB Records, Record Group (RG) 51, National Archives II, College Park, MD

OOI   Office of Information, BOB 1941–51, Central Files, OMB Records, RG 51, NA II

OPM   Office of Production Management

OWI   Office of War Information

PACH	Public Administration Clearing House
PAR	*Public Administration Review*
PCAM	President's Committee on Administrative Management
SPAB	Supply Priorities and Allocations Board
UP	United Press (news wire service)
WHM	White House Memoranda, HDSP
WP	*Washington Post*
WPB	War Production Board
WS	*Washington Star* (afternoon newspaper except on Sunday, when it was published in the morning)
WSJ	*Wall Street Journal*

Preface

It was November 1944. President Franklin Roosevelt had just, incredibly, been reelected to an unprecedented fourth term. As was the custom for presidential appointees, Budget Director Harold D. Smith submitted a pro forma letter of resignation. This routine act derived from the traditional political custom giving a reelected president a clean slate to reconstruct and revitalize his administration in preparation for a new term in office.[1] FDR promptly rejected Smith's offer. He wrote back: "I would no more accept your resignation than fly by jumping off a roof. You are essentially persona grata and doing a grand job. If you talk any more about resigning I will act. A Marine Guard from Quantico will be stationed at your side during every minute of every twenty-four hours. Enough said!"[2] That was not the first time FDR had complimented Smith. When declining an invitation to attend a Bureau of the Budget (BOB) staff party two years earlier, he wrote, "Your three years of service as Director of the Budget may not have added to your life expectancy, but I can assure you that your faithful work has increased mine."[3] Yet Smith has become a largely forgotten figure in contemporary history.

The motivation for this book was curiosity and proximity. The curiosity came from hearing so much about Smith during my doctoral studies in public administration in the 1970s at Syracuse University's Maxwell School. His writings about the importance of budgeting seemed to be reprinted in so many anthology textbooks and on nearly every course reading list. Then he seemed to largely disappear from literature. I wondered about that. The sense of proximity came from running across him so frequently in my previous examinations of some of the other original entities of the new Executive Office of the President (EOP), which FDR had created in 1939 based on the recommendations of the Brownlow Committee. Without any particular grand design, I had profiled the Office of Government Reports and its director, Lowell Mellett (2005); the Liaison Office for Personnel Management and its head, William McReynolds (2016a); and the Office for Emergency Management and its officer, Wayne Coy (2018a). In all three cases, the close working relations that these three officials had with Smith stood out as one of their key levers of power. Their names appeared regularly in Smith's daily calendars for meetings, phone calls, and working lunches. If Smith and BOB were working on something relating to their jurisdictions, whether these be budgets, reorganizations, executive orders, or the like, Smith made sure his EOP counterparts would always be consulted. Generally, if any had a major reservation, Smith and BOB would hold off on any final action until their concerns were dealt with. I wanted to know more about him and the agency he had molded nearly from scratch. Again, I wondered why he seemingly became largely overlooked in the more recent literature. With this inquiry into Smith and his BOB, I have now unintentionally profiled the leaders of four of the six original units of FDR's Executive Office of the President. The other two were the White House Office (consisting of the six administrative assistants [AAs] to the president who were expected to have a passion for anonymity) and the National Resources Planning Board (NRPB). The former entity would be impossible to profile because it was not an *agency* and had no head or director. It was simply the organizational identifier and budget salary line for these presidential aides. The workings of the latter agency have been relatively well covered in the historical literature, in particular by Clawson (1981).

The list of archival sources in the bibliography identifies the collections cited in the text. I also greatly benefited from answers to my queries from the Luther Gulick Papers at the Newman Library of Baruch College (NY), Archives and Special Collections of American University's Library (Washington, DC), Archives of the National Association of Manufacturers at the Hagley Museum and Library (Wilmington, DE), National Agricultural Library (Beltsville, MD), Burling Library Archives at Grinnell College (IA), Still Pictures Branch of National Archives II (College Park, MD), and the University of Wisconsin–Madison's University Archives and its Steenbock Agricultural Library. I was also fortunate to have four outstanding research libraries close by: Main Library of Northwestern University (Evanston, IL), Memorial Library of the University of Wisconsin–Madison, the downtown branch of the Milwaukee Public Library, and the Golda Meir Library of the University of Wisconsin–Milwaukee. Information professionals are the custodians of history and protectors of knowledge. Historians could not succeed without them. So many helped me that, regretfully, I cannot name each one individually. However, several went so beyond the call of duty and had a never-say-die attitude that I must acknowledge their special help. I benefited from the advice of Martha Schiele, Director of the EOP Library. Even though the library is closed to the public, she cheerfully answered several of my inquiries about her holdings, which included the collection of the BOB/OMB library when the EOP library was created in 1977. Grateful appreciation to Kristen Carter, Supervisory Archivist at the FDR Library, for sharing a digital file of the Harold Smith Papers slightly in advance of posting it online.

My thanks also to Professor James Pfiffner of George Mason University. Jim is a fellow Badger, in both meanings of the state's nickname. We're natives of Wisconsin and graduates of the university's flagship Madison campus, although we didn't overlap there and only became acquainted decades later. He read the entire manuscript with a fine eye for detail and made dozens of valuable suggestions, as well as saving me from what would have been an embarrassing blunder. He is the best one could ever want from an academic colleague.

As has become almost routine, my thanks to all staffers at SUNY Press and particularly to Senior Acquisitions Editor Michael Rinella. His encouraging demeanor is a salve for calming nervous authors, especially those who worry a lot. I consider myself fortunate that this is my fifth book with Michael. In general, authors cannot hope for a better home than SUNY Press and its staff.

Finally, a note on the dual referencing style used here. Generally, parenthetical citations are concise for references to published material, while archival and journalistic sources (especially when the latter are not bylined) are briefest when referenced in endnotes. Therefore, as a pragmatic convenience, this book uses both citation styles depending on the category of the source. The seventeenth edition of *The Chicago Manual of Style* (2017) permitted flexibility in referencing style: "As long as a consistent style is maintained within any work, logical and defensible variations on the style" are acceptable (§14.4). My thanks to SUNY Press for allowing me to use this style again, as it did with several of my previous books. Also, a caveat about capitalization. In the 1940s, "government" and "federal" were routinely capitalized in official documents and the press. Less consistently, so were "budget" and "executive branch." I realize that copyediting guidelines generally permit changing the case of a word without violating the precision of a quote. Nonetheless, I opted to retain the capitalization, even though it is archaic.

As always, notwithstanding the help of so many people, any mistakes in the book are mine alone.

Introduction

When Harold D. Smith headed the US Bureau of the Budget from 1939 to 1946, the media considered him an important news figure. He was on the cover of *Time* magazine in 1943. Seeking to convey to its readers his stature in the war effort, the cover's subtitle explained that "czars may come and czars may go, but he goes on forever."[1] Having the distinction of appearing on the cover of *Time* says much about his importance. But this was hardly a one-off. Smith gave the commencement address in 1941 at his alma mater (Kansas) and his speech was broadcast live on a national radio network.[2] He was occasionally depicted in political cartoons as an important news figure, including the *Washington Star* and the *Chicago Tribune*.[3] In 1943, Walter Lippmann, probably the most influential columnist of his day, came to Smith's office for an off-the-record interview. They talked for an hour.[4] *Life* magazine ran a picture of Smith as a member of FDR's "party" and *Newsweek* profiled him.[5] In 1942, after giving another speech on a national radio network, the periodical *Vital Speeches of the Day* printed the text in its next issue (Smith 1942e). He was a guest on a long-running educational radio series called the *University of Chicago Round Table* (Smith 1941e). His out-of-town speeches were often covered as national news.[6] In 1941, when reporters wrote about FDR's most important and influential advisors, he was routinely included.[7] Four years later, that was still the case. A weekly newsmagazine went so far as to say that, next to the president, Smith was "perhaps the most powerful man in the Government."[8] Another way to measure his importance from the media's point of view is from a recurring feature in the *New York Times* called "The Day in Washington." It summarized key news developments from the capital that were covered in separate articles in that day's paper. From 1939 to 1946, Smith was mentioned in it forty-seven times.[9] The *Washington Post* ran a slightly different directory of daily news highlights called "The President's Day." Smith appeared in it nineteen times from 1939 to early 1942.[10] Front-page news is another metric of media importance. In 1942, Smith appeared twenty-one times on the front page of the *Washington Star*. He also wrote articles in the mass media, including the *Sunday Magazine* of the *New York Times* (Smith 1946a), a nationally syndicated column for the Sunday newspapers (1942a), and two articles in the monthly *American Magazine* (1945d; 1946b).

Even though Smith was part of FDR's administration, some pro-business voices viewed him positively. The president of the US Chamber of Commerce wrote the foreword to Smith's 1945 book praising him (Smith 1945a, v–vi). A columnist for *Nation's Business* wrote that Smith "is making a big reputation as a competent administrator."[11] In 1943, *Fortune* magazine praised BOB's record of "invaluable service" and recommended strengthening it by expanding its field service and increasing its jurisdiction over the civil service.[12] The Government Spending Committee of the National Association of Manufacturers invited him to speak to a dinner meeting.[13] Smith led a BOB effort to reduce the number of questionnaires that federal agencies sent to businesses. Conservatives routinely praised him for his success at doing so.

Smith's professional colleagues and peers also thought highly of him. In 1939, at the founding meeting of the American Society for Public Administration (ASPA), he presented a paper at the concurrent annual conference of the American Political Science Association (APSA) (Smith 1939). A year later, ASPA members elected him as the organization's second president, succeeding William Mosher, dean of Syracuse's Maxwell School. After Smith's term ended, some of his successors continued to be major figures in the new profession, including Louis Brownlow, Luther Gulick, and Leonard D. White. Two colleges awarded him honorary doctorates for his professional accomplishments, American University (DC) and Grinnell College (IA). On the 125th anniversary of its founding, Allegheny College (PA) invited him to give a commemorative lecture to its business school (1940a). Smith was also invited to speak to conferences of many professional and practitioner organizations, including a conference of state and local finance officials in the South (1941b), Society for the Advancement of Management (Smith 1944c), Municipal Finance Officers Association (1944d), American Municipal Association (1941f), Council of State Governments (1942b; 1942c; 1947), the American Road Builders Association (1944b), and the National Tax Association. During WWII, the National Municipal League described him as "an outstanding exponent and example of management brains in government."[14]

Smith's Conception of Budgeting:
Apolitical, Non-policymaking, and Anonymous

Smith influenced the cultural norms of the profession of public budgeting. He said that a budget director should be an apolitical expert who served the chief elected executive through neutral competence rather than politics. Other important values he asserted relating to his role included that he was *not* a policy maker, was relatively unimportant regarding non-budgeting issues, and had a low public profile. He repeatedly stated these values through the mass media. *Time* magazine's cover story attributed to him four essential operating principles that contributed to his success. They included that "he must have a 'passion for anonymity'" and "must stick to his administrative duties, leave policy to the politicians."[15] The central focus on a budget director being apolitical was frequently echoed in media coverage of him. For example, in 1941, a popular magazine for women explained that "when the President required a man who was a scientist rather than a politician," he picked Smith.[16] In a front-page profile in early 1943, the *Wall Street Journal* explained, "His engineering background gives him a scientific and non-political outlook on government. And it is in a detached, scientific manner that he tackles problems about him."[17] The same month, a syndicated columnist quoted him as describing BOB's organizational culture as "detached, objective, [and] critical."[18] A few months later, a feature article in the *Saturday Evening Post* described Smith as "the business manager and efficiency expert" for FDR.[19] When Smith announced in mid-1946 that he was stepping down as BOB director, an editorial feature in the *Detroit Free Press* praised his career because he "proved what a non-political expert can do in a non-political office."[20]

Smith also routinely declared that he did not make policy and that he was not important when it came to non-budgeting aspects of the government. After FDR announced his intention to appoint Smith as BOB director in 1939, Smith said in an interview with a national wire service that, like his role as Michigan's state budget director, the federal budget director "does not make policy—and should not be popping off" about it.[21] Four years into the job, he was still saying the same thing. Downplaying his role, in a media interview "he calls his job 'housekeeping.'"[22] The issue came up in several congressional hearings. In 1940, a senator asked him, "Do you consider your organization as a policy-making organization?" Smith replied, "It is not. The Director of the Budget does not make policy. It is up to the President and Congress to make the policy" (US Senate 1940c, 19). A few years later, he walked it back, but only ever so slightly. He conceded, "We do deal with what I call a minor area, or a secondary area of policy, but we do not originate policy" (US House 1943b, 286).

Incongruously, much of the media coverage of Smith emphasized his dislike of publicity and being a public figure. A 1941 profile said that "Smith has shied from the public spotlight. He has too many secrets to keep to make public appearances."[23] A different profile a few months later declared that "Mr. Smith sincerely prefers the background, and is one of the few officials around Washington who really has a passion for anonymity. In fact, he was in the capital a couple of years before many folks realized how much weight he really carried in the inner circle."[24] The American entrance into WWII did not change those depictions. A business columnist observed that "Smith shies from publicity."[25] A reporter's book about Washington said that Smith "shuns personal publicity" even though he was accessible to reporters (Childs 1942, 85). Another book that year said that Smith was "little known to the public but has tremendous influence as the President's incorruptible right-hand man for purposes of internal administrative coordination" (Kiplinger 1942, 334–35). The next year, during yet another interview with a reporter for a profile, he displayed a sense of humor about the incongruity of it all. "He said the worst thing that ever happened to him was to get trapped into this interview."[26]

Review of the Literature

Given the central role of BOB in federal operations, Smith occasionally appears in public policy-focused literature in modest and passing roles and usually in neutral and descriptive terms. Examples from the twenty-first century include civil defense (Roberts 2014), arms production (Koistinen 2004), Social Security (Gibson 2003), Japanese internment (J. Smith 2003), and social welfare (Williams and Johnson 2000). Smith also has bit parts in many biographies, such as those of FDR (Daniels 2016; Burns 1956), Harry Hopkins (Sherwood 1950), and Paul McNutt (Kotlowski 2015). As would be expected, Smith is often referred to in the literature relating to operational matters that touched on BOB's portfolio, including reorganization (Arnold 1997; 1998; Pemberton 1979; Polenberg 1979), budgeting (Dame and Martin 2009; Kahn 1997), FDR's managerial style (Wann 1968), and the managerial presidency (Pfiffner 2020; Grunes 2011).

General textbooks in public administration that had multiple editions document Smith's importance and then his gradual disappearance from contemporary relevance. In the 1948 edition of his textbook, Leonard White (who would have known Smith through ASPA) wrote that "under the leadership of Harold D. Smith, it [BOB] developed into the principal staff agency of the Federal government" (1948, 62), that Smith and the bureau now had "considerable influence" (63), and that Smith's view of the role of BOB was "a radical reorientation" from that of his predecessors (261). In the last edition of his textbook, White mentioned Smith much more briefly but continued praising him for having "transformed the character of the Bureau" (1955, 62). Pfiffner's multi-edition textbook referred to Smith in the second edition (1946, 365n7, 373n4, 379n14).[27] Smith disappeared from later editions. Dimock and Dimock's first edition praised Smith as "a new kind of administrative leader in America." They described him as having "fine human qualities and deep sympathies" and that he "had a distaste for preliminary or unfruitful, controversial conferences and often avoided them, but when he moved, he did it decisively and effectively" (1953, 210). However, he disappeared from later editions. Budgeting textbooks also present a similar arc of Smith's rise and, then, gradual fade out in pedagogy. Burkhead praised "the transformation of the Bureau of the Budget" that Smith engineered (1956, 293). The first three editions of the long-running textbook series *Public Budgeting Systems* cited Smith's role in expanding the concept of budgeting toward program planning (R. Lee and Johnson 1973, 103–04; 1977, 66; 1983, 68). However, the reference was omitted beginning with the fourth edition in 1989. Smith is wholly absent from several other major multi-edition budgeting textbooks, including Lynch (1979; 2017) and Gosling (1992; 2016). On the other hand, a few twenty-first-century budgeting texts approvingly flagged Smith's writings (Willoughby 2014, 1, 20–21; Mitchell and Thurmaier 2017, 196) and a reader for public administration students republished a tribute to his professional contributions (Holzer 2000, chap. 2).

Smith also stood out in writings by public administration and political science faculty. Some praise came from people who worked with him during the war. After the war, when they returned to the academy, they continued to think well of his record. For example, in late 1946, Harris praised Smith in *APSR* for remaking BOB into "one of the most important administrative developments in recent years" (1946, 1140). Gulick (a quasi-academic) began praising Smith even before the war ended. In *APSR*, he flagged for readers that "the influence of the Director of the Budget was also of great importance." For example, BOB "made an extraordinary contribution not only in orderly budgeting, but also in management and organization" (1944, 1176). In his Alabama lectures after the war, Gulick praised BOB's central role when it "brought the facts together, stated the issues and alternatives, and pressed for agreement at the highest levels and for decisions by the President" (1948, 51). He listed BOB as among the five "best organized offices in Washington during the war" (103). Similar assessments came from faculty who weren't in Smith's immediate network. Lepawsky wrote that, during the war, "Smith carried a heavy part of the responsibility for integrating the activities of governmental administration and industrial management." As a result, he was "in a strategic position" to provide useful observations about the real world of public administration (1949, 199).[28] In 1953, Waldo wrote that Smith had "a distinguished career in governmental fiscal affairs" (305). Burns's biography of FDR's wartime leadership described Smith's "gifted leadership" of BOB, making the agency "the President's biggest single staff resource" (1970, 452).

The modest literature on BOB/OMB as a federal and presidential agency also praises Smith and characterized his directorship as "an exceedingly creditable term of service" (Hobbs 1954, 29). Berman's history described him as "truly one of the unheralded administrators in the history of American political institutions" (1979, 14). Mosher's comparative study of OMB and GAO said that "probably the most influential of all budget directors down to 1981 was, and remains, largely unknown outside of the government—Harold D. Smith" (1984, 175n7). In another study of OMB, Tomkin described Smith as BOB's "visionary" director (1998, 33). Burke's comprehensive examination of the institutionalized presidency noted that BOB under "Harold Smith, was much more significant than it had been with Smith's predecessors" (2000, 11). Dickinson and Rudalevige provided a positive and in-depth examination of Smith's role during FDR's presidency, concluding that he was "dual-hatted," in that he developed BOB as a center for neutral competence in public administration, but also that he provided political advice to the president (2007, 19). An overall assessment of OMB noted Smith's contributions in the areas of management, legislative clearance, and neutral competence (Bose and Rudalevige 2020). Daniels declared that "Smith became the most important single civilian administrator in Washington" (2016, 14). Finally, in observance of the agency's centennial, Pfiffner emphasized that "Directors Harold Smith and James Webb [Smith's successor in 1946] led BOB during the 1940s, the only era of the budget bureau in which the management function was highly valued and power-ful" (Pfiffner 2020, 14). This string of complimentary observations in the research literature have largely established and maintained Smith's sterling reputation in budgeting and public administration.

Rationale and Scope

From the preceding literature review, the plain question is: What did Smith do to earn such praise? He has been depicted as something of a role model and pioneer for the then-rising profession of public adminis-tration and, within it, the specialty of government budgeting. Such high standing and reputation is in contrast to the absence of significant research literature examining in detail his actual record and work. There have been no in-depth reviews of Smith's professional life or biographical accounts.[29] Similarly, Smith's public assertions of his professional values have not been juxtaposed with his actual working record. What came through loud and clear in his normative statements and observations was that, in his view, budgeting was an apolitical expertise, that it did not involve policymaking beyond strictly budgetary considerations, and that it should be a relatively anonymous and behind-the-scenes role. Starkly put, did he practice what he preached? Or was this an artifice of a public persona that hid more than it revealed? A detailed examination of his record and activities as US Budget Director can examine the accuracy of his professed professional principles.

To accomplish these goals, this inquiry is a de novo investigation into Smith's record at FDR's BOB. These chapters rely largely on bedrock primary sources, such as archival documents, federal publications issued at the time, and other contemporaneous sources. Reliance on secondary sources and post hoc sources was held to a minimum. Original and primary sources of accounts of his work were less colored by hindsight and later perspectives—even if Smith's papers are somewhat biased because they came from him. An important qualifier about the scope of the book is the focus on Smith's professional service as FDR's budgeteer and de facto manager-in-chief. It is not a history of BOB from 1939 to 1945, although Smith's leadership of the agency inevitably includes some aspects of the bureau's operations. Nor is it a comprehensive history of the major public policy issues of his time, rather only discussing them in the context of his role and involvement. Some of the themes to be explored include what he did and how he did it. One prism entails examining more closely the values he stated to the media that were central to his approach to budgeting: being nonpolitical, limiting his policy involvement to budgetary issues, and seeking low public visibility. How accurate were these claimed professional values? Another prism is whether he functioned exclusively in a staff role, limited to offering advice to the president, or if he was also the de facto line manager of the entire executive branch who directly supervised all manner of administration, implementation, coordination, and operations.

Sources and Methodology

Harold Smith's Papers

Franklin Roosevelt hated memos for the file. He liked to do business verbally, in person, and without any formal written record (Breitman and Lichtman 2013, 314). That way, he could change his mind if he wanted to without any documentary proof that he had done so. (Which he often did.) History is lucky that Smith felt compelled to ignore that. After every meeting with the president, Smith would go back to his office and dictate a summary of the meeting, particularly the subjects he brought up and the guidance FDR gave him on how to handle each matter. It was not that Smith was particularly eager to violate Roosevelt's operating etiquette. Rather, for the Bureau of the Budget to be the president's central management agency, Smith's staff of specialists needed to be informed of precisely what Roosevelt's guidance or policy was. After dictating his summary of a meeting, his secretary would cut up the document into the discrete policy decisions FDR had made. Based on the assignments and specialties of each BOB staffer, she sent them a copy of the meeting summary that related to their responsibilities.[30] This was not only more efficient than Smith having to talk to each of them individually, but it gave the staff a more textured understanding of what the president wanted (and did not want). With a written record of Roosevelt's desires, each staffer could not only implement the directive but also, as time passed, be able go back to it when necessary to be sure of what the administration's policy was.

History is the unintended beneficiary of Smith's diligence in constructing BOB to be the president's central management agency. One can track issues rising to the policy or political agenda, how FDR sought to handle each, and how BOB proceeded to implement presidential guidance. Smith's summaries of meetings with FDR are sometimes more than dry policy history or budgeting information. They also track FDR's ebullience and moods. For example, in early 1941, Smith asked for a brief meeting with the president to finalize some details for a reorganization of the defense production mobilization. When he was finished, he expected to stand up and leave. Instead, Roosevelt was in a talkative mood and recounted a luncheon he had just had with Interior Secretary Ickes about Ickes's desire to move the US Forest Service from USDA to Interior. From there FDR segued to the trees he had planted at Hyde Park and about woodworking. "The President was evidently relaxed and wanted to talk about something unimportant. General Watson [the appointments secretary] came in and said that I had promised not to take more than five minutes of the President's time. The President told Watson that I was not taking the President's time, but he was taking my time."[31] On another occasion, Smith had asked for another short meeting. By coincidence, FDR was about to have his hair cut. Smith recounts, "[The president] suggested that I talk to him while he was getting his hair trimmed. One of the White House colored servants came in with barber's equipment. The President was put on his wheelchair and the hair cutting operation began back of the President's desk in his office, with the rug rolled back." Smith quickly covered the business at hand. "The President chatted along about one thing and another of a current nature, while he was getting his hair cut. . . . The President seemed quite unconscious of the fact that the barber was working on him, as he chatted, but would screw his face to one side as the trimming job went along. When it was over, I bowed out with a goodnight, having spent about 45 minutes of which perhaps less than 15 were needed for the immediate business I had to clear with the President."[32]

Two weeks after Pearl Harbor, Roosevelt invited Smith and assistant director John Blandford to join him for lunch at the White House. They welcomed the opportunity because it meant a relatively solid and uninterrupted hour to talk. They covered nearly a dozen issues, in each case briefing FDR on what each specific issue was and getting his feedback and instructions.[33] In mid-1943, at the end of a long substantive meeting, Smith told FDR that he had bought a farm in rural Virginia and was spending his free time there. FDR promptly told Smith of a food popular in central Europe that came from deer meat. Perhaps it could become popular in the US as well? It was an amusing anecdote and indicated Roosevelt's far-ranging mind and memory. Getting back to his office, Smith commented, "I think the President gets a good deal of relief from these conversational excursions into subjects about which he needs to take no responsibility."[34]

A more somber account came from Smith's first meeting with Roosevelt in 1944. FDR was in bed, seeing few visitors, ostensibly down with the flu. Smith had not seen the president for over a month because he had been away at the Teheran summit meeting with Stalin and Churchill. According to Smith, "[The president] seemed worried and worn out. I have never seen him so listless. He was not his usual acute self." Smith noted that in the past he occasionally had had meetings with the president in his bedroom, "but never so groggy." In fact, in the middle of reading a draft of his annual budget message, it looked like he had nodded off. Either he was just exhausted from the long trip and the flu, "or else that Admiral McIntire had doped him heavily in order to keep him quiet."[35] One FDR biographer cited Smith's account because it so tangibly conveyed Roosevelt's decline (Hamilton 2019, 204). Historians are fortunate that Smith was such a detail-oriented and organized person and willing to disregard FDR's general ban on memos for the record. His papers at the Roosevelt Presidential Library are a fount of information. However, they were not his *office* files. Rather they were limited to four series:

Daily Memoranda (DM): These extend from April 1939 to December 1940. Smith dictated what he did that day. Because these are dictations (and he likely rarely proofed them), they sometimes contain garbled phrases, names, and titles. His daily memorandum for Labor Day in 1939 included in the middle of the text a notation "(End of cylinder)." Clearly, he was speaking into a Dictaphone that day. However, it is possible that due to the holiday, no secretarial staff were present to take his routine dictation and therefore, as an exception, he used the Dictaphone that day.[36]

Conferences with President (CwP): These summaries cover Smith's entire BOB service from 1939 to 1946. Immediately after meeting with President Roosevelt (or Truman), Smith usually dictated what they had covered and what directives the president had given him.[37] Smith sometimes brought with him to these White House meetings BOB's assistant director (Blanchard, Coy, Appleby). On those occasions, the assistant director often dictated the meeting summary.[38] Occasionally, Smith did not dictate a summary of a meeting. For the busy year of 1941, his secretary kept a separate record of "Conferences with the President—Not Dictated."[39] Her list covers twenty-six meetings. In some cases, her summary of the subject of the meeting (if she knew) indicated that it was relatively minor and brief. For example, on January 9, 1941, Smith took some letters of appointment to the White House for the president to sign.

White House Memoranda (WHM): This series covers Smith's entire BOB service, 1939–1946. These are memos submitted by Smith to the president between meetings or as follow-ups to meetings. The collection appears to be incomplete, largely consisting of substantive and informative documents, rather than cover memos to paperwork for the president to sign. These memos rarely have a subject line in their titles and therefore can only be identified by date.

Daily Record (DR): These records extend from spring 1940 through 1946. These are Smith's office calendars maintained by his secretaries, usually Miss Marie Johnston. In many cases, they are little more than post hoc listings of his appointments and phone calls that day. His secretaries rarely sat in on his meetings and did not routinely listen in on his phone calls. This is clear because they sometimes marked items with a question mark when they were not sure precisely what the subject of the meeting or call was, how to spell the person's name, or what the person's link to Smith was. She often could figure out what the subject of the call was, although sometimes she guessed, either by noting what they "probably" talked about or placing "(?)" after listing the likely topic. Smith's practice was in contradistinction to Treasury Secretary Morgenthau's standard operating procedure. He had a stenographer sit in on all the meetings he hosted and listen to his calls in order to create a verbatim record of each. Amusingly, during Smith's first few months as BOB director, Morgenthau's secretary was not sure what his full name was. She identified him as "Donald C. Smith."[40]

While not consistent, some entries in the daily record are quite detailed, probably if he asked that she sit in to hear his side of a phone conversation and then to type up what he said. In a phone call from John Blandford, Smith's former assistant director who was then head of the federal housing agency, Johnston quoted Smith telling Blandford "to keep his shirt on," that is, to calm down.[41] On rarer occasions he asked her to listen in on the conversation and then to prepare a detailed summary of it, particularly what the other person said and what they agreed to do (or not do).[42] Less frequently, she inserted her own characterizations of the comings and goings. For example, she described a BOB official who "sauntered in for a moment, then sauntered out."[43] On another occasion, when Wayne Coy arrived for a meeting with Smith, Smith was still on the phone. Coy "entered and waited on the side lines."[44] When a senator called Smith to inquire into the status of a decision about an airline matter, Smith frankly replied that so many people were involved in this issue that "God alone knew what the answer would be." According to Johnston, "That satisfied the Senator. He seems to have trust in Him."[45]

Even though voluminous and detailed, the archival collection of Smith's papers nonetheless needs to be treated with care. Their strengths are that they were dictated, summarized, or drafted shortly after the events they narrated, sometimes the same day. They were fresh and nearly instantaneous records. They reflected how things looked at the time. The weakness of Smith's records is that the narrator presented his version of what happened. Therefore, he was likely to put himself in the best possible light rather than using a confessional perspective or depictions of his actions negatively or critically. The exception to this general caution about his papers is the daily record. He did not author it and probably did not see what Johnston listed. As a result, the information in them was the least likely to be skewed from a personal perspective, although Johnston appeared to be utterly loyal and dedicated to him. Nonetheless, even with that caveat, her lists of phone calls made and received, visitors, and meetings were all factually based in an elementary sense, in that they truly occurred and that the subject matter was usually based on her own direct knowledge.

The National Archives II site in College Park (MD) is the depository for agency files. Some records from BOB are included in Record Group (RG) 51, of the Office of Management and Budget. Within it was a small collection of Smith's office files (OFHDS), evidently mostly from his later years there. Nonetheless, they were somewhat helpful in rounding out material omitted from his papers at the FDR Library. Smith had only given two historical interviews before he died in early 1947. Robert Sherwood interviewed Smith for his book on Roosevelt and Hopkins (1950, 72). Sherwood deposited his research records for the book at Harvard's archive. Similarly, Herman Somers interviewed Smith for his book on the Office of War Mobilization and Reconversion (OWMR) (1969, 67n34). He later donated his research notes for the book to Yale's archive. Oddly and sadly, both collections are missing those interviews.[46] Finally, Smith was surprisingly prolific. Excluding media coverage, he created a relatively large corpus of published matter reflecting his views. For his BOB years, there are about thirty items, such as speeches, addresses, articles, and radio appearances (see bibliography). In addition, he testified dozens of times at congressional public hearings. Those meetings usually included his prepared statements, reports he submitted during or after the hearing, as well as his answers to questions.

Historical Research Methodology: Triangulation

For this de novo inquiry into Smith's BOB record, the focus must be on primary sources and minimal use of secondary sources. A key benefit of using original sources is that they are based on what was known at the time and are not distorted by hindsight or later developments. These sources provide a sense of history *in the present tense*, as it unfolded, without any foreknowledge of what would eventually happen. As a kind of raw history, this conveys how things looked and felt at the time. It is history in slow motion. In particular, there are two seemingly inexorable tendencies facing historians that need to be consciously prevented. First, historiography needs to avoid imposing a sense of inevitability or "rightness" to the eventual outcomes. Foner's history of the three post–Civil War constitutional amendments on slavery emphasized the distortions of hindsight. "In retrospect the abolition of slavery seems inevitable, a preordained result of the evolution of American society." Rather, "like all great historical transformations, it was a process, not a single event. It played out over time, arose from many causes, and was the work of many individuals" (2019, 21). Second, history needs to avoid smoothing out the jagged edges of events and contradictory developments. In explaining his approach, a biographer of Gandhi emphasized a conscious effort to "reconstruct these arguments as they unfolded at the time, regardless of how they have subsequently been interpreted, projected, or (as is sadly often the case) distorted" (Guha 2018, xiii). Two twenty-first-century histories of the WWII era provide good models for re-presenting familiar history by recapturing this kind of "in-the-moment" perspective. In his history of Great Britain's prewar appeasement policy, Bouverie sought to "write a narrative history which captured the uncertainty, drama, and dilemmas of the period" (2019, xii). Similarly, Lelyveld's recounting of FDR's last year cautioned that "because we read history backward, we know the answer" (2016, 11). That can lead to a kind of backfilling approach, which is heavily biased due to such foreknowledge.

For a historical research methodology, the triangulation research approach is particularly apt (McNabb 2018, 46, 379, 417–18; 2021, 280, 366; Eller, Gerber, and Robinson 2013, 354). The goal is to identify primary materials that are wholly independent of the other two. With them, a historian is able to reconstruct a chronology of events, sometimes day-by-day, even hour-by-hour. One source might confirm what was presented in another, might fill-in lacunae of the other sources, and might even contradict the other sources. In this way, historical triangulation can recreate a rich and textured narrative of developments and events (Lee 2019c). For this study, the three sources for the triangulation methodology were archival materials, contemporaneously published official government documents, and journalism.

First, archival sources included Smith's papers (discussed earlier). Diaries and office files of other major participants were also helpful, but only if authentically contemporaneous. These included the diary of Interior Secretary Harold Ickes and the transcripts of Treasury Secretary Morgenthau's staff meetings and phone calls. The publication of post hoc and edited diaries or memoirs are suspect. Second, official government documents, such as reports, formal messages from the president to Congress, congressional committee reports and hearings, proclamations, statutes, and the like, all are accurate of what they purport to be. As print materials, they cannot be amended after release or publication. Like archival documents, they are the raw stuff of history. In particular, the US federal government has often been described as the largest publisher in the world, with a flood of materials issued by the Government Printing Office (GPO). Third, self-evidently, journalism is a mediated recounting of events by observers. Nonetheless, it represents how things looked at that time to the reporter. Newspaper coverage conveys that moment. The reporter did not know how things would turn out or what eventually ended up being important or minor. Excepting (unleaked) activities behind closed doors, media coverage indicated the media's sense of importance, however flawed.

Structure of the Book:
Chronology of Smith's Public Service Career

A chronological structure is very helpful in trying to reconstruct events as they unfolded and based on how they looked at that moment, without the omniscient tinting of retrospective hindsight. The first two chapters cover his initial year as BOB director, beginning with his focus on reorganization in spring and summer of 1939, then pivoting to preparing the president's FY 1941 budget during the last quarter of 1939. Given that this pair of chapters examine his first-time experiences with these responsibilities, they are necessarily quite detailed in order to convey what the job of BOB director entailed. The subsequent chapters are by calendar year. They similarly present in-depth examinations of Smith's activities and views, in particular in the context of rapidly changing circumstances, political or otherwise. In rough chronological order, these included the initial war events in Europe and Asia (1939–1940), FDR's declaration of a limited state of emergency (1939), his gradual mobilization of armament production and military preparedness (1940), the presidential election (1940), his declaration of an unlimited state of emergency (1941), Pearl Harbor (1941), each of the war years (1942–1944), another presidential election (1944), and FDR's brief fourth term (1945).

The focus of each chapter is on relatively new activities or issues that call for significant detail and discussion. These chapters seek to avoid unnecessary repetition of subjects discussed in detail in preceding chapters or routine activities of BOB. However, Smith had four recurring annual events: preparation of the budget for the next fiscal year, drafting the president's budget message, participating in the budget briefing for the White House press corps (FDR called it a "seminar"), and congressional appropriations hearings for the president's proposed budget for BOB itself. Even though they occurred on a permanent and fixed cycle every year, they were often quite different and distinctive from previous cycles, usually due to external events and developments. Therefore, every chapter will discuss them but with particular focus on what differentiated them from the preceding year. The concluding chapter identifies some of the recurring themes of Smith's career as FDR's budgeteer. In particular, it suggests that Smith may deserve the moniker of having been Roosevelt's *other* assistant president.

Chapter 1

FDR's "Great Reorganizer," April–July 1939

The federal Bureau of the Budget was created in 1921 by the Budget and Accounting Act.[1] This new law was the outcome of a fierce decades-long effort by good government and public administration reformers during the Progressive era to improve and professionalize the management of government at all levels. The push for organizing government around an executive budget focused on the need to integrate the operations of semiautonomous agencies and bureaus into a more coherent executive branch, to provide a comprehensive plan to fund government priorities, and to strengthen the power of the chief elected executive vis-à-vis the legislative branch (Kahn 1997; Rubin 1994). The new Bureau of the Budget was organizationally within the Treasury Department but was accountable directly to the president. In its early years under presidents Harding, Coolidge, and Hoover, BOB was a small agency that focused on accomplishing *efficiency*, the term used for cutting government spending, a favorite goal of conservatives. The bureau also worked closely with the US Bureau of Efficiency to identify further cost savings (Lee 2006b, 105–12).

Roosevelt's BOB Directors, 1933–1939

When New York governor Franklin Roosevelt campaigned for president in 1936, he said he was a fiscal conservative and that he wanted to balance the federal budget. Based on that campaign commitment, conservative congressman

Lewis Douglas (D-AZ) accepted FDR's invitation to be his budget director. At first, he was able to pursue the goal of cutting government spending. But Douglas disagreed when FDR eventually committed to deficit spending in order to reverse the effects of the Great Depression. Douglas also disagreed with the increasingly liberal tilt of the New Deal. By mid-1934, he concluded he had to resign on principle. FDR tried to talk him out of it for fear of the political repercussions, but Douglas insisted. He resigned in late August (Zelizer 2012, chap. 7). However, Douglas retained his respect for FDR as well as his commitment to the Democratic Party. Therefore, he refused to speak to the media about why he resigned and refused to be used by Republicans to bash FDR. On September 1, his wife told a reporter on his behalf, "He has promised President Roosevelt not to say a word. It was agreed that the President would do whatever talking might be done."[2] The next day, Douglas spoke directly to a reporter but did not go any further than his wife's comment the day before: "I told the President that I would make no statement, and I am determined to do the courteous thing."[3]

FDR quickly appointed Daniel W. Bell, a longtime senior civil servant at the Treasury Department, as acting BOB director.[4] One of the reasons for the quick action and the selection of an insider was the pressing and fixed timetable of federal budgeting. In the fall of a calendar year, BOB and a president received budget requests for the following fiscal year from agencies. They would review the requests, adjust them up or down, and then finalize a comprehensive executive budget to reflect the president's priorities. In the first week of January, a president submitted his budget to Congress. Congress then had six months to act on the budget proposal before the beginning of the fiscal year on July 1. (Sometimes Congress missed the deadline.) Traditionally, all funding bills begin in the House of Representatives. (This traditional practice parallels the Constitution's *requirement* that taxation bills must begin in the House.) Therefore, the House Appropriations Committee and its subcommittees (largely based on departmental jurisdictions) would hold hearings on the bills comprising the president's budget request and then recommend (usually) revised versions. Once passed by the House, the same process would occur in the Senate, though the Senate Appropriations Committee often acted as a court of appeals for the president and departments to request revisions to the House version. All this while the clock was ticking toward the end of the current fiscal year and the beginning of the next.[5] With Douglas resigning in late August, FDR needed a replacement who could hit the ground running and not mess up the now-pending "high season" of BOB budgeting. Bell fit the bill.

Appointing Bell as acting director reflected in part this need to avoid any delay in BOB's preparation of the next budget (for FY 1936) as well as giving FDR more time to consider a longer-term appointment. Another factor in giving him the acting title was Bell's status as a civil servant. If he accepted a permanent appointment, he might have to forfeit his participation in the classified civil service and his eligibility for a federal pension. By serving as *acting* director, Bell did not have to resign from the civil service.[6] There was no legal limit on how long a person could serve as acting BOB director. As it turned out, Bell was there until 1939.

Beginning in 1936, there was another reason to keep Bell as acting director. FDR wanted to reorganize the executive branch. If a reorganization were to alter BOB's status or role, then having an acting director in place might make it easier to replace him with a permanent successor. In part, there was a good government reason for FDR's general interest in reorganization, such as bringing like bureaus together under one roof, such as the Bureau of Lighthouses and the Coast Guard's life-saving boat stations. This focus on efficiency also appealed to conservatives who believed reorganization would reduce duplication and thereby cut federal spending. However, for FDR, the issue was improved management. This was an emphasis on operational *effectiveness*, rather than money-saving *efficiency*. In particular, Roosevelt wanted to strengthen a president's ability to manage the executive branch, getting more centripetal leverage to counteract the centrifugal tendencies of autonomy-seeking bureaus. Knowing he would be busy running for reelection in 1936, he appointed the President's Committee on Administrative Management (PCAM) to devise a comprehensive reorganization plan that he could pursue in 1937, assuming he was reelected. Its members were Louis Brownlow (chair), Luther Gulick, and Professor Charles E. Merriam. FDR released the PCAM report in early 1937, asking Congress to approve it. The report emphasized the importance of a president having the central management tools a chief executive needed to fulfill his constitutional duties. It identified three staff roles for what it called administrative management and that were essential to accomplish this: budgeting, personnel, and planning (Lee 2019b). The report argued that central management agencies for these three functions needed to exist, to have strong legal powers, be under the president's direct supervision, and be located in the executive office (US Senate 1937a).

The two-year political fight over congressional adoption of the PCAM reorganization report does not need to be recounted here in detail.[7] However, one side effect of the reorganization fight is that FDR largely froze any actions on management and personnel matters that might subsequently be affected by reorganization legislation. He, of course, did not know in early 1937 that it would take two years to pass the bill. For example, he had been hoping to move some of the auditing powers of the General Accounting Office (GAO) into the executive branch. (GAO was a legislative agency.) Therefore, while he was waiting, FDR declined to appoint a new comptroller general. In case a reorganization bill would indeed reshuffle some of GAO's powers, FDR did not want an incumbent in place (for the fixed term of fifteen years) who could claim that no changes could be made during his term (Lee 2018b). In this context, retaining an acting director of BOB had the same rationale: it froze the status quo of BOB's leadership pending the outcome of the reorganization fight in Congress.

A side story of the reorganization fight was that the subject of presidential control over BOB was not controversial. After all, the 1921 Budgeting Act had already done so, merely keeping BOB formally as an entity within the Treasury Department. Moving BOB out of Treasury and into a presidential office was minor and not in the gunsights of the conservative reorganization opponents on Capitol Hill. As a result, some of the more detailed recommendations that PCAM made about strengthening BOB in staffing and funding could be separated out of the reorganization fight and dealt with outside that politically hot arena (Morstein Marx 1945, 683; Neustadt 1954, 653n41). Another reason this specific proposal was not controversial related to the politics of reorganization. When FDR announced the creation of PCAM, the skeptical conservative coalition on Capitol Hill wanted their own study and by a more reliably middle-of-the road (even conservative) source, the Brookings Institution. The Brookings report became the underlying and legitimizing source for political disagreement with PCAM. However, Brookings similarly endorsed strengthening BOB (US Senate 1937b, 125–28). In that context, in April 1938, FDR sent a message to Congress asking for an increased appropriation to BOB for FY 1939 of $132,000 (US House 1938a). The House Appropriations Committee approved it and folded it into an omnibus supplemental funding bill it was working on (US House 1938b, 28). The Senate agreed and FDR signed the increase into law on June 25, 1938.[8] Even the *Chicago Tribune*, which reflexively opposed FDR in its news coverage, tepidly agreed it was a good idea.[9] By February 1939, as part of the funding cycle for FY 1940, Bell reported in detail to the House Appropriations Committee what he had done to reorganize and strengthen the agency with the additional funding (US House 1939a, 936–55). Another initiative Bell took to strengthen

BOB, irrespective of the reorganization fight, was to increase and expand BOB's library (Lee 2016b, 89).

In all, Bell probably needs to be seen as much more than a caretaker director. Besides strengthening BOB institutionally, he actively oversaw the annual budgeting process and routinely met with FDR to confer with him and obtain presidential decisions. Based on FDR's office logs, Bell met with him 218 times between 1934 and 1939, roughly 40 times a year.[10] However, for Bell, running BOB was an unpleasant experience. It is possible that as a longtime civil servant he was never fully comfortable with FDR's fluid and improvisational governing style, let alone policy reversals, ambiguity, misdirection, and keeping his options open to change his mind. Bell likely preferred the smoother and predictable bureaucratic due process embedded in Treasury's standard operating procedures. In terms of his substantive policy views, he was a budget-balancing conservative. One pro-business reporter said that Roosevelt's spending proclivities "became so distressful to Mr. Bell—or so it was reported—that he asked to be relieved of his responsibilities."[11] Revealingly, Bell's experience was so negative and unpleasant that when the nascent FDR Library asked him in 1948 to write up his reminiscences of working for FDR, he declined. Nine years and a world war later, he replied that the memories were still "liable to be too personal to me" (Lee 2016b, 101n31). Nonetheless, Bell's nearly five years in the BOB hot seat deserves credit and recognition. Many people did not last that long given FDR's competitive administrative style, a kind of governmental version of survival of the fittest. Bell may not have enjoyed it, but he certainly served FDR's needs in the long interim between permanent directors.

Looking for Mr. Smith

After the bruising two-year fight, in the spring of 1939, the president could see that he was finally about to receive from Congress some limited reorganization powers. He signed it into law on April 3, 1939.[12] It permitted him to submit reorganization plans to Congress. Unless Congress passed a legislative veto rejecting a plan within sixty days (no amendments were permitted, it was an up-or-down vote), the plan was enacted. A key and often-forgotten detail was that the legislative veto required both houses to disapprove a reorganization plan. If only one house voted it down, the plan would still go into effect. (The law also had a long list of congressional sacred cows that were excluded from any reorganization plans.) FDR was raring to go. At last, he could do some of what he had been thinking about when he established PCAM in 1936.[13]

If Roosevelt was on the verge of having reorganization powers, it was also now time to have a permanent budget director to plan and implement the details of the reorganizations he (and Brownlow) had in mind. The new reorganization law would also finally permit the president to strengthen his central management tools to oversee the government. This new institutionalized presidency would put the BOB director at the crossroads of all manner of public administration in the executive branch. FDR needed someone who had face cards for all these arenas: reorganization, budgeting, legislative clearance, executive orders, and management. In anticipation of signing the reorganization bill, FDR started putting out feelers for the right candidate to replace Bell even before the reorganization bill reached his desk. Roosevelt asked Treasury Secretary Morgenthau to quietly seek appropriate candidates.[14] Given that BOB was formally a subunit of Treasury and that Bell was a Treasury civil servant, it was a good place to start. Also, Morgenthau took seriously assignments the president gave him. He was opinionated and argumentative, but a request from Roosevelt needed to be fulfilled, if only because FDR had a good memory and was detail oriented, and therefore was likely to ask him about it in a later meeting. Morgenthau and Bell conferred with Brownlow. As head of PCAM, Brownlow would have a good sense of the upcoming scope of reorganizations and the skills necessary to prepare and implement them. In addition, as the director of the Public Administration Clearing House (PACH) at the University of Chicago and his long-standing role in promoting the professionalization of public administration, Brownlow had an exceptionally large network of acquaintances (Lee 2020). To avoid promoting gossip and rumors, the three met in an out-of-the way office in the basement of the Treasury building. According to Brownlow, "their office staffs knew nothing about our meeting." Morgenthau said he was looking for someone "of a general city-manager type who had experience and had proved his skill in administrative work, especially of a budgetary character, but who had not been an active partisan politician." Brownlow recommended two: Smith and A. E. Stockburger, who had been a city manager in California and a state budget director (1958, 414).

Morgenthau also talked on the phone with Frank Murphy, the new attorney general. (He had just been defeated running for a second term as governor. When Murphy won in 1936, he appointed Smith as his budget director.) Morgenthau told Murphy, "Confidentially, the President authorized me to look around for a successor to Danny Bell, who wants to come back and do the regular work in the Treasury. . . . And in looking around, we've been checking all over, we've run into Harold Smith." What did Murphy think of him? "He's very good. He's a conservative, careful fellow, great integrity, has during the past two years done about eight men's work instead of one." Murphy also recommended Weldon Jones, who had been on his staff in the Philippines as auditor and financial advisor.[15] "They are both sound, but Smith is sound, careful, and in exact budget work maybe he's had a little more experience."[16]

A few years after becoming BOB's director, a profile of Smith in the *Saturday Evening Post* lightheartedly claimed that Smith "has risen from nowhere" to become FDR's budgeteer.[17] That, of course, was an exaggeration. By 1939, Harold D. Smith had established himself as a professional public administrator, good government reformer, and budgeteer. A native of Kansas with an amorphous interest in public service, he graduated with an engineering degree from the University of Kansas in 1922 and received a master's in municipal administration from the University of Michigan's recently established graduate training program. Returning home, he was a junior staffer at the League of Kansas Municipalities from 1925 to 1927, serving mostly as a traveling consultant to league members on such issues as zoning and urban planning (Lee 2020). That led to an offer to revive the Michigan Municipal League, which did not have any salaried staff. He led the Michigan league from 1928 to 1937, successfully growing the league in membership, finances, staffing, services (such as a municipal purchasing co-op), and publications (Lee 2021). After Murphy was elected governor in 1936, he sought a nonpolitical expert to be his budget director. Based on Smith's reputation at the Michigan league, he invited Smith to serve in that position. Given the Great Depression, it was a tough time to try to manage a state's finances and balance the budget. Despite occasional criticism, Smith was largely viewed by members of both parties in the state legislature and the media as a nonpartisan budgeteer who provided credible information and knew state government in detail. Murphy was defeated in 1938 by the Republican incumbent he had beaten two years earlier. The winner asked Smith to stay on, if only because he seemed to be the only person in state government who knew the state's finances in detail. This decision by Murphy's Republican successor added to Smith's nonpolitical and nonpartisan reputation.

Morgenthau and Bell decided to bring Smith to meet with the president and let FDR decide. According to Smith, Bell kept after him for nearly a month to come to DC "to talk about a job" without ever specifying what job it was.[18] Smith agreed to come. First, he met with Morgenthau, who tentatively offered him the BOB job. Then Bell took him next door to the White House and they met with FDR for fifteen minutes on February 1, 1939.[19] According to Smith, Bell introduced him to the president and FDR said, "So you're the Smith I've been hearing about. I wanted to see what you looked like and you've passed muster." Then Bell said to Roosevelt, "But I'm afraid, Mr. President, that he has a lot of bridges to burn behind him in Michigan." Roosevelt wordlessly reached into his desk and handed Smith a matchbook. "You'd better start burning," he said. That was the end of the meeting.[20] Smith walked out of the White House utterly baffled. "Turning to Dan Bell, he fingered the matches, [and] asked: 'Say, did he give me a job or didn't he?' "[21] Perhaps FDR simply wanted to meet him and decide later? Bell said he *thought* that the president had asked Smith to take the job. If that was the case, Smith told Bell, "I hope you won't rush me on this—that is a week or two weeks. I've really got a lot of strings" to deal with. Bell said that would be fine. Still, it was an ambiguous situation. Morgenthau met with FDR on February 3, mostly to talk about economic policy. He raised the question about Smith. Yes, said Roosevelt, I want him to be BOB director, go ahead and "offer him the job." Morgenthau then called Bell and said, "The President has confirmed your impression and that you are authorized, definitely, to offer him the job. . . . Give him a good sales talk." Bell said he would. Based on Smith's earlier request not to be rushed, Bell told Morgenthau he would give Smith until February 20 to decide.[22] Smith eventually said yes, telling friends he "could not afford to refuse" the president.[23]

Within days, there were rumors about it, perhaps a not-for-attribution leak by Murphy.[24] On March 6, Smith confirmed to AP that he "may" become BOB director.[25] Predictably, at his next regularly scheduled press conference on March 7, reporters followed up, asking FDR, "Have you offered any federal post to Harold G. [*sic*] Smith of Michigan?" "No," said FDR (Roosevelt 1972, 13: 175). For Smith this must have been all very confusing. Had he fundamentally misunderstood the apparent job offer? Had the president changed his mind? Roosevelt, who was notorious for denying something when he wanted to, may well have wanted to wait for a more propitious time to make the announcement. It is also possible that he parsed his answer by taking the question literally. It was technically accurate that *he* had not offered the job to Smith. FDR had authorized Morgenthau to authorize Bell to do it. It is also possible that he slightly misheard the question. Finally, the next day, the White House announced

Smith's appointment with an expected starting date of April 15.[26] Smith sounded relieved after the confusion. "These last 48 hours have been very peculiar. . . . I can't understand the reports that came from Washington yesterday. It may have been that the President was stalling for time and some correspondent misinterpreted his statements. The whole announcement was forced in the first place, since it wasn't to have been made until later."[27] Now that the appointment was official, Smith was willing to speak openly to the press. He mentioned three goals that were immediately on his mind. First, from personal experience he said there were "administrative conflicts" between federal grant programs and states. He hoped to improve coordination and cooperation to reduce that. Second, he wanted to expand BOB so that it could exercise stronger budget control over the executive branch. The problem, he said, was that "too many budget offices . . . seek to set an economy example to other governmental departments by limiting themselves to small budgets. The result is . . . that while the budget office is saving $20,000, some other department is spending $10,000,000 with no control by anybody." Finally, he said a person in his role "does not make policy—and should not be popping off" about it publicly.[28]

A nationally syndicated columnist summarized the reaction in Washington to the appointment. "He is quiet, unassuming, a family man, good at figures—and is very definitely non-political and non-partisan in his attitude. Consensus of informed financial opinion approves his selection as an astonishingly good one."[29] Morgenthau conveyed nearly the same thing. In a private meeting on tax policy before Smith started, he said, "I don't consider him a political Director of the Budget." A staff member echoed the observation, that Smith "himself said he didn't consider himself a political Director of the Budget."[30] An article in the monthly magazine of the US Chamber of Commerce praised the appointment because "Mr. Smith has a record of efficiency in budgeting Michigan's finances."[31] A few weeks after starting, the media quoted Smith as saying, "The President himself told me he didn't want me to 'yes' him against my better judgment and I don't intend to."[32] In all, Smith was presenting himself as the epitome and embodiment of the new profession of public administration. He did not make policy, he only implemented it. He was apolitical, a civil-service-style technocrat. His goal was to strengthen spending controls over the sprawling federal executive branch to achieve major economies rather than piddling ones. He would stand up to the president and insist on the principles of sound management and public administration, not politics.

Breaking in the New Guy, April 1939

Smith was sworn in on Saturday, April 15. The timing indicated how eager FDR was to get started on reorganization as well as to make news for the big Sunday papers. Murphy accompanied Smith to the Oval Office. Amusingly, there was last-minute confusion about who had legal authority to administer the oath of office. FDR suggested he could. After all, he was president! However, as attorney general, Murphy "made a curbstone ruling that the President did not have such authority." Then Murphy ruled himself out, too. They quickly located Frank Sanderson, the White House auditor, and he did it. Indicating his interest in the fly-speck details of government, FDR also asked if the signed commission of appointment (a legal document) should be handed to Smith before or after taking the oath (Emmerich 1971, 77).[33] After they were done, Roosevelt turned to the media observing the ceremony and said, "They might describe Mr. Smith as 'the great reorganizer,' in view of the fact that he will have immediate charge of the government's reorganization."[34]

Figure 1. Smith taking the oath of office, April 15, 1939. *Left to right*: FDR (holding appointment commission), Attorney General Frank Murphy, Smith, White House auditor Fred Sanderson. Credit: Associated Press Images. Used under license.

Smith landed in the eye of a tornado. The new legal process for reorganization, three years in the making, had just been signed into law twelve days before. Now, with Smith in place, Roosevelt was eager to start using his new powers "with his customary rapid pace" (Brownlow 1958, 415). He wanted Smith to begin drafting the first reorganization plan *immediately*. Smith plunged in to prepare the first reorganization proposal, tentatively scheduled for submittal to Congress by the end of April, as well as everything else on his desk that was urgent—and that covered just about everything.

Smith was the new kid on the block. In the capital's highly competitive hothouse of political power, cabinet secretaries and Capitol Hill pooh-bahs were ready to test him, perhaps exploit his newness to assert and grab power. In fact, that happened ten days after he was sworn in. A congressman called to get final approval for the federal government to buy land adjacent to Arlington Cemetery to preempt any development on it. He claimed that the War Department and the National Capital Park and Planning Commission (chaired by FDR's uncle, Frederic Delano) had already signed off on the purchase. Smith carefully said that he would be glad to look into the status of the project. It did not take long for him to find out that Bell already had rejected the idea given the exorbitant asking price and that any adjacent development would occur no matter how big the cemetery was. Smith, also carefully, double-checked with the president, who agreed, saying the price was "highway robbery."[35] No rube was Smith. Given how gossipy politicians are, the story would surely spread quickly. The new sheriff in town was as detailed-oriented as his predecessor, if not more.

Another test came with the release of the first reorganization plan eleven days into Smith's incumbency (discussed later). The plan transferred from the Commerce Department to the incipient National Resources Planning Board (NRPB) an obscure unit called the Federal Employment Stabilization Office. In an effort to ridicule FDR and Smith, and rub raw the still-touchy subject of reorganization, someone leaked to a reporter that this office no longer existed. Congress had defunded it a few years earlier. The administration was so stupid! It did not even know that the office no longer existed! It was about to become the laughing stock of Washington, another example that (big) government was incompetent. Smith did not panic. He personally talked to the reporter and calmly said that the congressional authorization for the existence of the office still was on the books. Therefore, the transfer meant the new planning board would inherit some statutory powers to exert as needed.[36] Unspoken was an even more important detail. The conservative coalition liked to claim that central planning was an effort at collectivism, practically the same as communism. Therefore, when the time came, conservatives opposed any statutory authorization for NRPB and wanted to kill an agency that was based only on an executive order. With the transfer of the stabilization office to NRPB, the administration could defend the agency as having statutory responsibilities and that it was not merely based on an executive order.[37] Congressional opponents of planning would have to pass a law to deauthorize this executive branch duty if they wanted to undermine NRPB's legality.[38]

At the other end of Pennsylvania Avenue, congressional appropriators were also breathing down Smith's neck and testing him. As discussed earlier, in 1938, the House Appropriations Committee had approved a large increase in funding for BOB in order to reorganize and strengthen it. Now, in the spring of 1939, just two weeks before Smith's appointment was announced, committee members said they were getting impatient. The committee's report on the Treasury funding bill for FY 1940 (beginning on July 1, 1939) warned BOB:

> With no little concern, the committee has taken note of the numerous increases, both in number and amount, occurring in the various Budget estimates submitted for the operation of the Treasury and Post Office Departments in the fiscal year 1940. Economies in all governmental operations should, and must be, had. While it is realized that the increased personnel made available to the Budget Bureau . . . could not be appointed in time to be effective in the preparation of the 1940 Budget, the committee does wish it understood that is [*sic*, it?] shall expect results to flow from this revitalized Budget agency and is confident that measurable economies may be anticipated when the Budget for the fiscal year 1941 is prepared. (US House 1939b, 10–11)

It was the political equivalent of a shot across the bow to whoever would be BOB's director in 1939. These powerful appropriators were laying down their explicit expectations about what the president's FY 1941 budget proposal to Congress, due in January 1940, needed to include. Smith had to deliver on that expectation or be deemed as failing their good faith and proactive support for strengthening BOB and increasing its funding.

At the same time, Smith quickly learned the breadth of FDR's knowledge of the government and his interest in just about every detail. On his fourth day on the job, he met with FDR and other senior officials to discuss a new relief message and appropriation. During the meeting, "the

President showed a remarkable grasp and memory of the whole chain of events connected with the development of the relief administration from the beginning" of his presidency. He then asked for an authoritative report on relief for American Indians, saying he thought his administration had been more helpful on that subject, "citing from memory some figures of a past Administration."[39] A week later, they met to discuss the details of the second reorganization plan. Back in his office Smith dictated a summary of the meeting and an observation: "The knowledge of the details of the Federal establishment on the part of the President impressed me during this conference as being nothing short of amazing."[40] The next month, Roosevelt told Smith he had reviewed a proposal from the State Department to send a woman from the Library of Congress to advise a South American country on setting up its own national library. He said that, for example, the project's budget for her wardrobe was too high. "The whole conversation could not help but amuse me that the President of the United States should take time out to discuss the details in connection with an individual assignment. He said that the whole matter irritated him, that he had written a long memorandum to the Department of State."[41] Smith also got a foretaste of FDR turning to him as a kind of all-around administrative problem solver, even for non-budgetary matters. A member of the Civil Service Commission (CSC) had written a blistering letter to the secretary of war about the department's noncompliance with the executive order requiring all cabinet departments to appoint a qualified personnel director. The letter was copied to the president, who promptly referred it to Smith "to straighten out." Smith later dictated for his daily summary his impression that this non-budget subject "is the sort of thing that I did a good deal of for Frank Murphy in Michigan and it looks as if the President might be trying me out on this one."[42] He was right. Years later, he told a colleague that he indeed had become FDR's "Mr. Fixit" (Hess and Pfiffner 2021, 24). His apprenticeship was over. Time to deliver.

Reorganization Plans I and II, April–July 1939

Smith's timing for beginning at BOB was lucky in one respect. Coming into office in April was the low season for budgeteers. Congress was wrapping up passing appropriations bills for FY 1940 so that departments would have their budgets in place for the beginning of the fiscal year on July 1. Then, serious budgeting for FY 1941 would not begin at BOB until September when departmental requests would be reviewed by BOB's Estimates Division (including what they called budget "hearings").[43] So Smith had about four months when he could focus more on the non-budget roles of BOB, particularly, in this case, reorganization.

Five days after being sworn in, Smith and Brownlow had initial drafts of the first batch of reorganization orders to submit under the new law along with the presidential message to Congress that would accompany it. They met with the president on April 20 and on Sunday, April 23.[44] He went carefully through the drafts, making specific suggestions and comments. For example, he knew that conservatives wanted proof that reorganization would lead to economy, that is, spending cuts. Therefore, he asked that the message specify that savings should be tracked based on each agency's overhead administrative expenses, not their total funding. By excluding program costs, the percentage of savings would appear bigger. It would also help by focusing attention on consolidations of duplicative staff services (HR, budgeting, etc.) in previously separate silos, rather than line activities. The message and plan were sent to Congress on April 25, Smith's tenth day in office. It was a major proposal, including pulling several agencies together to create the Executive Office of the President; consolidating disparate welfare and human service units into a Federal Security Agency (FSA) (conservatives opposed creating a cabinet department of public welfare because that could be seen as institutionalizing a permanent federal role in relief and welfare); merging construction-oriented agencies into a Federal Works Agency;[45] and pulling together most credit and lending agencies into a Federal Loan Agency (US House 1939c). Regarding BOB, besides transferring it from Treasury to EOP, the plan also abolished the Central Statistical Board, an independent agency, and transferred its functions to BOB. This strengthened BOB's central and managerial role. In all, this was a major reshuffling of the executive branch and it gored many oxen, particularly departments that were losing bureaus and independent agencies that were losing their autonomy. A leader of House conservatives, Congressman John Taber (R-NY), promptly introduced a resolution to veto the plan. He said it was "an attempt to coerce Congress" into a de facto conversion of the temporary alphabet agencies into permanent ones.[46] It failed on a lopsided vote and the plan, known formally as Reorganization Plan I, was scheduled to go into effect on July 1.[47] Smith walked over to the Hay-Adams hotel to have a drink with Brownlow and Merriam to celebrate. He said, "Brownlow, who has worked three years on reorganization, admitted that he felt like a new man. He was very happy over the result."[48]

The president, Smith, and the rest of the reorganization team quickly pivoted to finalizing a second reorganization plan. The day after releasing the first one, Smith and Brownlow had lunch with FDR and talked for nearly three hours. "He O.K.'d certain proposals, left others for later discussion and indicated he wanted studies of certain other proposals."[49] More long meetings with the president were on May 3, 6, and 8.[50] At the last meeting, he read the draft, "made several minor changes and then wrote in longhand several paragraphs which he wanted added to the message."[51] With that, he said he was done. Smith went back to his office, had the final version of the message with FDR's changes retyped, and then walked back to the White House to hand it to Stephen Early for submission to Congress on May 9.[52] Reorganization Plan II was more complicated than the first and therefore less appealing to the media to cover. (In turn, media disinterest meant publicity-hungry pols on Capitol Hill intuitively understood that investing time and effort criticizing the plan would not likely pay off with any substantial coverage.) Plan II mostly involved transfers of bureaus between departments. (Interior was the big winner.) FDR also consolidated all official representatives of the federal government abroad into a unified Foreign Service. This meant Commerce and Agriculture Department attachés were now part of the Foreign Service. The message again repeated the politically attractive claim that the approval of the plan could lead to a savings in administrative expenses, in this case about $1.25 million (US House 1939d, 6).

Smith's intense work with FDR and a small handful of trusted advisors (like Brownlow) was done in secret. There were no consultations with departmental secretaries, no heads-ups, no sign-offs, no negotiations. Roosevelt knew that if word leaked out what he was considering he would be inundated with efforts by the losers to change his mind, whether by his cabinet secretaries, their allies on the Hill, or special interest groups that liked the status quo. When the president felt compelled to call in a Senate and House leader about this, he emphasized the importance of confidentiality. As these legislators were leaving the White House, a reporter naturally asked them what was in it, but "neither revealed details of the plan."[53] The first woman in the cabinet, Labor Secretary Frances Perkins, came to Smith's office to complain about rumors she was hearing, and *why wasn't she consulted?* Smith inwardly sighed because he "could not tell her" what was going on. "About all I could do was try to look pleasant, and listen to her story."[54] A week later, they talked on the phone. This second conversation was even more uncomfortable for Smith because "the President had asked us not to discuss the moving of the Employment Service with her." Smith "could only politely listen. On the whole, it was rather embarrassing. . . . I tried my best to placate her."[55] Similarly, when USDA Secretary Wallace asked to meet with him to submit the department's ideas for reorganization, Smith already knew he did not agree with those (self-serving) suggestions, remarking, "Although I did not tell the Secretary as much."[56] After Treasury Secretary Morgenthau tried to influence an upcoming reorganization plan, Smith sighed to his diary, "[This incident was] one of many examples I have noticed around here recently of Cabinet Officers unwittingly, or otherwise, sabotaging the President's program of reorganization." For Smith, these experiences reinforced the importance of confidentiality in reorganization planning.[57] Congress did not exercise a legislative veto over Plan II and it also went into effect on July 1.[58]

However, for Smith, reorganization work did not end when Congress approved each plan. At BOB, the heavy lifting was just beginning. First, for political reasons, he had to make sure that the president's claim of savings on administrative expenses would actually occur. One approach was to freeze hiring temporarily; another was to control overall spending.[59] Second, there were endless bureaucratic details that had to be ironed out as part of the implementation of the two reorganization plans. For example, to smooth the meshing of the US Employment Service and the Unemployment Compensation office (two closely related but previously separate activities), he detailed two BOB staffers to work on site full-time to handle the scores of policy, management, organizational, and personnel details for a successful consolidation.[60] He kept in close touch with other staff who were handling other aspects necessary for implementing the reorganization, including Donald Stone, now head of the new Division of Administrative Management, and Wayne Coy, temporarily detailed to BOB before moving to the new Federal Security Agency (Lee 2018a, 48).[61] An important roadblock was that the Reorganization Act excluded the CSC from any reorganization plan. However, FDR thought he could bypass that. There was a vacancy on the three-member commission and he asked Smith to find a replacement who would consider himself as part of the president's team. That kind of de facto White House liaison on the commission could greatly assist in accomplishing the PCAM goal of central personnel management, along with budgeting and planning. Smith spent large amounts of time canvassing for the right person. He submitted two finalists to FDR, who tentatively preferred Arthur Flemming from American University. But there was still one more detail. The federal law required the CSC to be bipartisan and the current two members were Democratic appointees. Was Flemming by chance a Republican, he asked Smith. Smith checked and he was. FDR nominated him to the commission. Flemming greatly improved coordination between the administration and the commission on HR policies (Lee 2016a, 64–67). No detail was too minor to think about nor to involve FDR, who relished such a role in decision-making. What about the letterheads of the agencies within the incipient and unprecedented Executive Office of the President? Which detail should be in larger lettering: the name of the agency or its membership within EOP? A presidential executive office was so unprecedented and so meaningful in terms of bureaucratic power that Smith consulted with FDR several times about that. FDR wanted the emphasis on EOP as a presidential office. Furthermore, should they be within the White House telephone exchange and use the White House mailroom? Smith preemptively apologized to the president for bothering him about that. Roosevelt disagreed, saying "he considered that a very important detail to the effectuation of the reorganization" and he agreed on all steps Smith mentioned that would emphasize how close these EOP agencies were to the White House.[62]

The (reorganization) dust had not even settled yet when FDR said he wanted to start working on Plan III while away on vacation. Smith said the working list he was keeping was now "nearly three close-typewritten pages of items." He suggested that the president indicate "where he wished the emphasis placed."[63] (As it turned out, due to pressing international developments, Plan III was delayed until April 1940.) Brownlow was mightily pleased with Smith's work on the two reorganization plans. He described Smith as having "characteristic adaptability and great ability, [and] then became, in fact as well as in theory the captain of the team, so far as organization of the executive branch was concerned" (1958, 416). Smith had become, just as FDR declared when Smith had been sworn in, his "great reorganizer."

The Kind of Budgeteer FDR Wanted:
A Man for All Seasons

Besides serving as the lead person on reorganization, Smith spent much of his time during his first half-year at BOB shaping the agency to reflect his vision in terms of its structure, personnel, and mission. These were the early steps in his long-term goal of reestablishing the bureau as an elite presidential agency of apolitical budgeting professionals. They served the institutional presidency, irrespective of who actually was president, his partisan affiliation, his ideology, or his governing style. In a sense, Smith was seeking to accomplish for presidential budgeting what the founders of public administration and city management wanted for the entire American public sector: neutral experts and civil servants who were isolated from politics, were not affected by election results, and who sought to accomplish the goals established by the elected branches of government in the most efficient and professional manner possible.

A month after he began, he briefed the president on what he was doing to strengthen BOB's capabilities. He mentioned that he was hiring the Public Administration Service's (PAS) Donald Stone to run the new Division of Administrative Management to promote improved public administration in the executive branch and he was trying to recruit John Blandford from the Tennessee Valley Authority (TVA) to be BOB's assistant director. FDR knew both, approved of both, but was skeptical Smith could pry Blandford away from the TVA Board.[64] Generally, Roosevelt responded, "we were wise in taking immediate steps to strengthen the Budget Office."[65] To facilitate the staffing-up of BOB, FDR agreed to send a message to Congress about permitting the early release during the fiscal year of appropriated funds (US House 1939e). Indicating a desire for a collegial and open culture, in his second month as director, Smith sent a memo to all BOB staff inviting suggestions for improving operations of BOB and then was pleased with the ideas they submitted.[66] He also had several extensive meetings with the senior staff of the Civil Service Commission to be sure that the recruitment and selection procedures of the commission reflected what Smith wanted and that the salary ranges for the senior staff were appropriate.[67] That was, of course, only the first step to hiring first-rate people. He visited the budget office of Virginia's state government in part to see if any staff there should be recruited and to spread the word to their counterparts in other state budget offices of job openings.[68] In particular, Smith insisted on personally interviewing finalists for BOB jobs. This, of course, was time consuming, but he did it to assure that the agency would have first-class employees. It was Smith's "desire to go over each appointment in the Bureau with a fine-tooth comb in order that few mistakes be made."[69] He also preferred only hiring from the outside men for junior positions, such as recent college graduates.[70] That way they would be trained in-house and be inculcated into the new BOB culture before moving up the ladder. In addition, these younger staffers could quickly take up some of the more mundane and ministerial paperwork that up to now was burdening the short-handed senior agency officials.[71] Despite Smith's efforts, it was slow going. By mid-August, BOB had a staff of 70, with authorization for 110.[72]

Another priority for Smith was to expand the mission of BOB. He wanted it to be more than a narrowly defined budget agency. Rather, he wanted it to be the de facto management consulting and research firm for the executive branch, akin to what PAS was to public administration around the country (Lee 2017). PAS was more than a model; he raided its staff for senior positions at BOB, including Stone to head the Administrative Management Division and Bernard Gladieux to work on reorganization and regionalization.[73] In late May, he was hoping that FDR would "use the Budget Office as his administrative arm in seeing that the proper organization pattern is worked out" in federal agencies.[74] Indeed, a few days later, FDR specifically directed Smith to get involved with a troubled agency. He was delighted by the assignment because it was "an opportunity to demonstrate in practical terms what it means to render assistance to the President in matters of management."[75] By mid-June, Smith was comfortable enough with such a role that he told the head of an agency that "it was the desire of the President to use the Budget Office as a third party in ironing out various difficulties" in management and operations.[76]

Smith also took the first steps to assert BOB's and EOP's primacy in fiscal policy planning. He complained about the continuing conservative policy on taxing and spending that Morgenthau held, advocating a balanced budget just as persistently as Smith's predecessor, Douglas (Zelizer 2012, 147). Smith, exasperated with Morgenthau and Treasury's dogmatism regardless of the state of the economy, took some steps so that the nexus of economic planning could imperceptibly and gradually shift to the nascent NRPB.[77] He attended what felt to him like interminable meetings on spending and economic policy hosted by Morgenthau,[78] some consisting of an informal troika of Morgenthau, Marriner Eccles of the Federal Reserve (an early Keynesian), and Smith; sometimes more of a quadriad, with Delano (of NRPB). They met with FDR in early June to present a supposedly consensus paper and recommendation on fiscal policy (Blum 1965, 38–39).[79] It was a mishmash of their differing views, papered over to have a semblance of unanimity but breaking no new ground, except Morgenthau finally getting the hint that FDR had shifted back to deficit spending.[80] Smith concluded that there was a "lack of economic planning in the Government."[81] A reporter got wind of the meeting and called Smith about it. Smith, still unclear what kind of media role FDR wanted a BOB director to have (or not have), agreed to talk, but he prohibited any direct quotations. The resulting wire service story accurately stated that Smith believed the administration needed to have a unified taxing-and-spending program and that there was a need for it to be led by a central economic planning office.[82] A few days later, Professor Merriam invited Smith for dinner with Beardsley Ruml, an economist and statistician, formerly at the University of Chicago and now a senior finance officer in the private sector. Ruml made a strong argument that Keynesian economics was valid and that it should guide the administration's current economic policymaking.[83] Smith was convinced not only of the essential rightness of Keynesianism, but also that the administration needed to adopt it as its basic fiscal policy. Furthermore "this must be done immediately under the [direct] supervision of the President in a much more neutral atmosphere" such as BOB, rather than the doctrinaire conservatives of Treasury.[84] Smith proceeded to create a Fiscal Division at BOB but was unable to appoint anyone to head it for lack of finding the right candidate so far.

As for FDR's view on Smith and BOB's public profile in the media, that gradually became clear. Roosevelt did not expect Smith and BOB to have a passion for anonymity, the explicit role PCAM set for a president's new six administrative assistants (AAs), positions that were also approved in the Reorganization Act. Smith raised the subject with the president. Smith told him, "I would be happy if he indicated to me that I was not to talk to the newspaper men. He seemed to feel that this was not practical."[85] For Smith that was a signal that if the situation called for it, he could do media relations, but not routinely. For example, powerful Senator Richard Russell (D-GA) called to ask if Smith would permit the senator to release to the media a letter Smith had written Russell about overspending in a pending agriculture appropriations bill.[86] Smith did not hesitate to assent.[87] In another case, FDR noted the continuing attacks by the conservative coalition on increases in federal spending, pinning it all on him. The president "seems to feel that Congress and the newspapers of the country were hanging the whole matter of spending upon the Administration, whereas the Congress had increased the appropriations some 260 million over the [president's] Budget [request], and in addition, had committed the Government to new activities which would increase subsequent budgets."[88] He asked Smith to prepare a document with this information and release it to the press. Without any reluctance, Smith agreed to do it. Again, however, he followed the practice of being the source of the news, but permitted no direct quotations. The tabulations received a modicum of coverage.[89]

Some of the press coverage in Smith's early months at BOB indicated how broad the reach of the bureau was into the details of federal operations and how minutely it was involved in even seemingly minor questions. Some of that power came obviously from its power of the purse, but another major lever was the bureau's legislative clearance role. Every bill that an agency or department wanted Congress to act on first had to be reviewed by BOB. There were different shadings of positive recommendations vis-à-vis a president's program, going from strong to weak to neutral. A negative recommendation, "not in accord" with the president's program, generally doomed the bill. Similarly, the bureau would make recommendations on bills reaching the president's desk, first, collating recommendations from the affected departments and then adding its own independent judgment if he should sign or veto them. Some examples from Smith's initial months demonstrated this extensive oversight of the executive branch. He rescinded the policy that civil servants had to obtain permission from their supervisors before applying for positions in other agencies.[90] Smith approved a request for additional funding for the DC government's welfare department.[91] He recommended that Congress allocate a quarter of a million dollars to Commerce Secretary Hopkins for an "appraisal of the larger problems that affect the commerce and industry of the country."[92] Smith weighed in on a controversy over unemployment compensation taxes for employers in DC,[93] supported funding for a study of a cross-isthmus canal in Nicaragua,[94] and endorsed funding for the new Council of Personnel Administration.[95] Perhaps the most striking example of the breadth and depth of BOB's power throughout the federal establishment was a front-page story in the *Washington Post*. Smith had signed off on amendments to the District of Columbia's lunacy commitment law.[96] This was not the kind of topic one would expect a budgeteer to weigh in on. But it was for Smith's BOB. The Bureau of the Budget was a kind of Bureau of All.

An Apolitical Budgeting Technocrat?

All theories and professional protestations aside, it was impossible for a budget director to be neutral politically. Budgeting by its nature was a political, ideological, and partisan activity. Smith tried to propagate the view that all a budgeteer did was implement, as efficiently as possible, policy decisions by the elected class. But this was a mirage. The preceding example of Smith's media relations regarding Congress appropriating more than the president had requested was to make a *political* point. Yes, one could argue that the substance was a dry factual report, but it was simultaneously a deliberate political act to influence public opinion in favor of the administration.

Behind the scenes, Smith was never reluctant to mesh his political observations and budgetary technical expertise. For example, he told Interior
Secretary Ickes that a congressional investigation of the National Labor
Relations Board (NLRB) was likely to discover what Smith already knew,
that NLRB "was a terrible administrative mess and that it was the one thing
that was likely to blow up in the face of the Administration" (Ickes 1954,
687). Regarding the reorganization that shifted the US Employment Office
from the Labor Department to the new FSA, he emphasized to Stone the
political as well as managerial importance of a smooth transition. If that
could be accomplished, "the President would probably not have occasion
to hear any further complaint, or have any further pressure brought to bear
on him from labor groups."[97] He told the deputy head of the US Housing
Authority that there was a political danger of its program expanding too
fast. An agency should "not get ahead of its support and, consequently, roll
[sic, roil?] up opposition to the extent that there would be a reaction to it
as so often happens under too enthusiastic prosecution of programs with
desirable social objectives."[98]

Politicians from Capitol Hill, whether friends or opponents of the
administration, knew the importance of a budget director. Smith routinely
got calls and personal visits from them about their pet projects, desires for
federal funding, and concerns that BOB's legislative clearance office might
release a negative recommendation about a bill. In May and June, his first
two full months at BOB, he had scores of calls and visits. For example, in
his second week on the job, Senator Burton Wheeler (D-MT) called to talk
about funding for a TB hospital on an American Indian reservation.[99] The
next week, the congressman from Detroit called because he was concerned
BOB would not support funding to buy nearby land for a naval aviation
training base.[100] A few days later, a California congressman called asking
for funding for a Coast Guard station in Monterey.[101] On May 11, 1939,
a congressman called about federal funding to expand a national park in
his district (even though federal policy at the time was to accept donations
of land, but not pay for land purchases) and a senator wanting funding
for a dam on the Mississippi.[102] A few days later, a Virginia congressman
wanted approval of a $10,000 study of pink oysters.[103] A Florida senator
wanted BOB, in its legislative clearance role, to recommend to Congress
passage of a bill to mint a special coin to commemorate the restoration of
St. Augustine.[104]

In June, a congressman from the state of Washington wanted to know
if BOB would give a positive recommendation to a bill on payment levels for

irrigation projects.[105] A senator came to Smith's office to lobby for changes in the reclamation law, particularly about adjusting contracts (i.e., charges) by the federal government to users.[106] Rabid racist congressman John Rankin (D-AL), who never hesitated to criticize the administration about race relations, called to ask for a federal contribution to the Chickasaw-De Soto Memorial Commission.[107] On June 10, a Texas congressman called about building more dams in Great Plains states, a member of the House Committee overseeing the District of Columbia called to lobby for more federal funding for the district, and the secretary to a Senate leader called with a head's up that the senator wanted to talk about the Cumberland Gap National Park.[108] A senator and two congressmen from the state of Washington came to his office to protest the bureau's negative recommendation regarding a bill to pay several attorneys $30,000 for their fees for handling claims submitted by Indian tribes.[109] A senator called to tell Smith of his unhappiness that the bureau recommended against changing a legal formula on federal funding to DC.[110] A congressman from upstate New York wanted to know what he needed to change in a bill FDR had vetoed (based on a BOB recommendation) to fund a bridge over Niagara.[111] A Minnesota congressman came to talk about disaster relief after a cyclone, and one of the state's senators called about the same thing.[112] For each caller and visitor, Smith either tried to explain the bureau's position or promised to find out what it was. He also tried to convey that, if possible, he would try to help find a solution or to reconsider the bureau's stance. He was always trying to get to yes. This record is certainly not that of a dogmatic or purist bureaucrat acting as if he was above politics and not deigning to talk to self-serving, parochial, and grubby politicians. Smith intuitively understood his need to serve the best interests of his elected boss—including considering the larger political implications of dissing these pols. Occasionally he had to tell a congressman that it was highly unlikely that a reconsideration would reverse BOB's view. A representative from Louisiana had proposed a bill for $100,000 for a survey for a Natchez-Trace Parkway. BOB looked into it and then issued a negative report, saying it was not in accord with the president's plan, a recommendation that usually doomed a legislative proposal. The congressman called to request reconsideration of that recommendation. Smith politely agreed to do it but conveyed it was not likely to change the bureau's position. "Our not-in-accord letter was not a perfunctory matter, that we had already given the problem due consideration and that the President had *definitely* said he did not want piece-meal development of the national highway-parkway system until there was a complete survey and plan."[113]

Similarly, cabinet secretaries routinely called or visited him to promote their departmental agendas, complain about their budgets, and seek positive BOB recommendations on their legislative proposals. Politics was always in the background. A leak to the press from a dissatisfied official could turn a small matter into a big story about conflict within the administration or make the president look bad. FDR's political enemies were ready to pounce and exploit any executive branch matters that could weaken Roosevelt politically. Smith treaded carefully. USDA Secretary Wallace called to lobby for more funding for the Farm Security Agency in his department.[114] Smith met with Attorney General Murphy and FBI director Hoover to hear their plea for money.[115] A few days later, the AG did an end run by asking FDR directly for the money. Murphy reported to Smith the president "was favorable"—an ambiguous answer. FDR said he wanted a BOB report on the subject before making a final decision.[116] At a meeting about which new construction projects to fund, Postmaster General Farley told Smith that approving new post offices in underserved Long Island and Westchester County (NY)—heavily Republican areas—could redound to the political benefit of the president.[117] The (acting) secretary of the navy called to talk about getting more office space.[118] Commerce Secretary Hopkins called to push for presidential approval of a housing census—requiring money, of course.[119] As he did with senators and members of Congress, Smith always agreed to hear them out and listen fully to their complaints. Some expounded at great length, especially Labor Secretary Perkins, about reorganization. In one of those longer phone soliloquies, she even intimated a political threat. If an item she disagreed with were nonetheless to be included in a reorganization, "there would be severe repercussion. She also said that the removal of the Employment Service she considered a slap at her and that she wondered how many more such slaps she would be justified in taking."[120] The potential of resigning—and noisily—would be a significant political hit to Roosevelt, even if it was wholly irrelevant to a purist budgeting technician. Smith clearly understood he was more than an apolitical budgeteer. Being aware of and responsive to the best political interests of the president was naturally part of his job. In all cases, he promised cabinet secretaries that he would look into the matter, learn more, and get back with what he found or decided. Smith also routinely had personal contact with heads of lesser federal entities, such as the independent agencies, regulatory commissions, District of Columbia government, and judges. Everything was very important, at least to the people wanting to bend his ear. And everyone knew how important this low-profile and practically anonymous bureaucrat really was.

Beyond these federal officials, all manner of other self-interested private citizens wanted to talk to him. Smith seemed to have a (relatively) open door policy of seeing outsiders or talking to them on the phone. He did not want to become isolated in his office shuffling paper. He also knew that public complaints about him could only go in one direction: the president. For example, he met, ate with, or chatted on the phone with the head of the American Institute of Accountants,[121] an official of the Minnesota Highway Department,[122] Brookings Institution Board of Trustees,[123] dean of the University of Michigan's forestry school,[124] the head of LA's electric power utility,[125] representatives of the labor union of civil servants,[126] the directors of the Council of State Governments and the Association of Tax Administrators,[127] the head of the North Carolina Municipal League,[128] miner's union president John L. Lewis,[129] head of Pan Am airlines Juan Trippe,[130] political scientist James Fesler,[131] and civic leaders from Youngstown (OH).[132]

Smith's Behind-the-Scenes Politics

Of all the people he interacted with during this early period, Smith developed the closest relationship with Interior Secretary Harold Ickes. This was perhaps a surprise, given Ickes's reputation for argumentativeness, sulking, curmudgeonly behavior, inserting himself into political issues that were outside his department, and commenting publicly on just about anything. He was hard to work with and seemed constantly unhappy and complaining. On the other hand, he was honest to a fault, micromanaged his department and PWA to keep out political corruption and cronyism, and symbolized a connection between the two Roosevelt presidencies. As a reformist, good government, and politically active attorney in Chicago, Ickes had supported the progressive wing of the Republican Party. For example, in 1911 Professor Charles E. Merriam, who had been elected to a term on the city council (from the university's neighborhood), ran for mayor against the Democratic machine's candidate. Ickes was active in Merriam's losing campaign. In 1912, Ickes was a prominent supporter of Theodore Roosevelt's insurgent campaign against his too-conservative successor, William Howard Taft. Roosevelt's third party was informally called the Bull Moose Party and Ickes proudly wore the Bull Moose label for the rest of his life. Smith was a kind of opposite-world Harold. He was quiet, undemonstrative, calm, and methodical. He tried to avoid arguments, breaking off relationships, or publicly criticizing someone. In his first year at BOB, he rarely talked to the press and had a very low public profile. During the planning for the reorganization, FDR met with Brownlow, Merriam, and Smith. They knew Ickes would like what he gained in the plan but would obsess about what he was losing. According to Brownlow:

> Then turning to Smith he said, "You know, if I may address Dishonest Harold, Honest Harold has a peculiar trait. He is as honest as he is reputed to be, but he is like an honest cop patrolling a city market. He won't let anybody steal a peanut, but every once in a while he will reward himself with an apple here or a banana there as a tribute to his own honesty. Thus it is with Harold Ickes. He won't let anyone else take a bureau away from him, but he will be glad to pick up one or two if convenient in order to maintain his strict honesty." (1958, 419)

Smith apparently took no offense at the jocular remark, likely understanding FDR's lighthearted characterization was not in malice. Instead, FDR was trying to make a point comparing Smith's pragmatism and flexibility—which was similar to FDR's working style—with Ickes's rigidity and pious self-regard. (Smith did not even mention this comment in his summary of reorganization meetings with FDR.)

The first time Smith and Ickes met reflected their opposite personalities. According to Smith, while working on the reorganization, "Ickes is obviously a little grumpy because he was not appointed [Public] Works Administrator in addition to his job as Secretary of the Interior. I saw him at the White House yesterday morning and he looked plenty down-cast. When I shook hands with him, about all he seemed able to do was grunt."[133] Ickes's version confirmed that encounter.

> Smith introduced himself to me but I didn't catch his name and I really didn't know who he was until I got back to the Department and asked [Assistant Secretary] Burlew to describe him. It was only at the end of the conference that I suspected it might be Smith. Later I was to learn, through Tom Corcoran, that he [Smith] felt that I had snubbed him and he felt it deeply because he had always looked up to me from old Bull Moose days.[134]

It was not an auspicious beginning to a working relationship, let alone a political and policy alliance. Ickes immediately realized his blunder and that it had the potential of creating permanent rupture and vendetta from a powerful BOB director. He invited Smith to come to lunch.

> Smith is a serious-minded man, as well as being serious in demeanor. He is not impressive in appearance, but he seemed alert and I have been told that he has real ability. I made haste to assure him that when I had met him at the White House I hadn't gotten his name and did not know who he was. We had a pleasant luncheon.[135]

Smith's version paralleled Ickes's:

> I had lunch with Secretary Ickes in his private dining room in the new Interior building. It was the first time I had been in the very sumptuous quarters. . . . The incident [at the White House] was just a little amusing to me and there was nothing personal on my part because I realized Ickes was feeling let down because he was not appointed the new Works Administrator. Ickes apologized all over the landscape for his performance prior to our lunch. It seemed to disturb him greatly. He said that although he had met me before he did not recognize me as Budget Director, and that he was a little hard of hearing anyway. I tried to put him at ease by adopting that 'think nothing of it' attitude. We had a very delightful luncheon, and I think it did a great deal to bring about better understanding. Ickes is really a grand person and had a tendency to get a bit too agitated about matters, and has perhaps too much of a proprietary attitude toward his Department.[136]

From then on, they got along grandly even when they disagreed. Smith and Ickes lunched again in July[137] and in August.[138] Certainly, they were policy wonks and could discuss in depth various policy proposals. However, the key was when Ickes was able to get beyond Smith's careful apolitical façade. During these lunches he discovered Smith's politics. After the July luncheon, Ickes was surprised to report: "From what I have learned first hand, he is a real liberal."[139] He apparently was so gobsmacked about it that after their next lunch in August, he felt compelled to make the point again in his diary. Smith "is a liberal," he delightedly repeated.[140] No, it was not a mistake the first time. That meant Smith could be a political ally in the constant White

House wars between the various ideological factions of the administration and their counterpart wings of the Democratic Party. For example, Smith and Ickes both supported public power, a concept that for-profit electric utilities were crusading against without letup.

After Merriam had arranged for Ruml to give Smith a confidential briefing on Keynesian economics (mentioned in the preceding section), Smith used his private dictation to reveal his political views, this time on economic policy:

> It was my feeling that the New Deal was an expression of economic and social forces that had been gathering momentum at least since the 1920's, if not before, and that actually the Federal Government had embarked upon a radically different fiscal policy than that employed in this country heretofore, but that there had been no efforts to define or to limit that fiscal policy, or describe it in a manner that would make it clear to the country generally. It seemed to me that the President essentially was a budget-balancer, and an adherent to old fiscal schemes, but that gradually he had come to a realization that something had to be done and slowly was being pushed into a new conception of the role of the Federal financing in the national economy.[141]

Perhaps Smith's most political act in his first year at BOB was talking to a private citizen from Michigan who was thinking of running in the next election as a Democrat against Congressman Clare Hoffman (R-MI). Hoffman was one of the most rabid anti-Roosevelt conservatives on Capitol Hill (Lee 2005, 106, 198–99, 224n12). Smith did not know the potential candidate from his own years in Michigan, but was nonetheless willing to talk to him.[142] Smith may have been a political cypher publicly and professionally, but his dedicated service as FDR's budgeteer was based not only on Smith's efficiency and expertise in budgeting but also because Smith *agreed* with FDR politically, too. In this case, Smith was willing behind the scenes to help knock off an anti-Roosevelt congressman or, at least, not have a free ride and instead give him a run for his money.

≈

In his first few months as BOB director, Smith had successfully established himself. First, as mandated by the president, he became the "great reorganizer" of the federal government. He quickly prepared the two formal reorganization plans that FDR submitted to Congress and then Congress approved both (i.e., did not veto them). As a result, Smith had shepherded a major reshuffling of executive branch entities into a somewhat more coherent organizational structure. He also oversaw the establishment of the Executive Office of the President (EOP) as the centralized management arm of a president. It included shifting BOB to be under a president's direct supervision, along with establishing nascent EOP entities for personnel management and federal planning. Smith also began building up BOB institutionally so that it could better oversee budgeting and spending. He strengthened BOB's roles in legislative clearance, economic planning, and management improvements for executive branch agencies. Now for the hard part, his first budget.

Chapter 2

War in Europe, Empowering BOB, and First Budget, July–December 1939

War Worries and Federal Spending, Summer 1939

By the time Smith began at BOB in April 1939, military tensions in Europe had already been going on for more than a year. Hitler's Anschluss of Austria occurred in March 1938 and the infamous Munich agreement to give him the German-speaking parts of Czechoslovakia was signed in late September 1938. In mid-March 1939, a month before Smith's swearing in, Hitler invaded and took over the rump of Czechoslovakia. In reaction to Hitler's violation of the Munich agreement, France and Great Britain quickly made public commitments that they would go to war with Germany if it attacked Poland. It was in this context that Smith began managing the federal budget. President Roosevelt was trying to steer a middle course between isolationists and internationalists. His political and policy solution was a gradual increase in national military expenditures and procurement. Nicely, these increases in spending also had the economic effect of stimulating the economy and creating jobs.

As soon as he began at BOB, military issues were crossing Smith's desk and coming up in his conversations with FDR. In late April, he signed off on legislation from the Army for "gradual forced retirement" of the bulge of WWI-era officers who were not likely candidates for further promotions and instead were "over-age in grade." Getting them to retire would "open up avenues for promotion of younger and more aggressive men." Important to Smith, it was not very expensive in terms of expenditures.[1] A few weeks later, he talked to FDR about a navy training program for aviation cadets and the president agreed to it.[2] Given the increases in appropriations to the Army and Navy, the two civilian departments and counterpart uniformed services were expanding in personnel and would need more office space in the capital. Roosevelt supported building two new federal office buildings in the district for them.[3] (This also had the advantage of opening up more space in the State, War, and Navy Building just west of the White House for the president's six new AAs and the EOP's central management agencies.)

Another idea was to bulk up reserve holdings of strategic war materials. The concept was very popular with Congress, particularly members whose states and districts would benefit from increased federal buying of natural resources. Congress sent FDR a bill authorizing $100 million for that. When discussing whether to sign it, Roosevelt told Smith it was too much money, that he would prefer something in the range of $10 million. In particular, a smaller appropriation would likely prevent pressure to buy domestic manganese. "He said that our manganese not only costs more but is not nearly as good as that which can be purchased elsewhere."[4] A few weeks later, the president convened a meeting of senior military advisors and Smith to discuss how much was needed. They agreed he would request an appropriation of $25 million.[5] They also agreed in principle to obtaining strategic war materials through a barter system. "The President indicated that he believed that a great deal could be done along this line."[6] An agreement with the United Kingdom (UK) to swap US surplus holdings of cotton for rubber was quickly made by Ambassador Joseph Kennedy. This was especially appealing to southern politicians from cotton states, a depressed commodity in the Great Depression. (A reminder that Great Britain was not at war with Germany in mid-1939.) At a follow-up meeting on this project, FDR said "he would draw up the budget for this in pencil on my [Smith's] memorandum to show how he would distribute the purchases between the various materials."[7] In late August, Smith approved the War Department's proposed allocations for procuring strategic materials.[8]

Smith and Roosevelt also conferred on increased spending for topographic mapping of the US because it would be useful in a time of war to identify likely new locations of natural resources. As usual, FDR had some views on the subject. He did not support requesting additional funding from Congress for the immediate future, saying that current funding should be adequate. He asked Smith to be sure that, given how many federal agencies were involved in mapping, a program be well coordinated between them to avoid duplication and competition. They discussed that maps created by the Army Corps of Engineers were done with less cash outlay than by Interior's US Geological Survey. Finally, he did not support an effort to finish mapping the entire country; rather he wanted it focused "where it is most needed by the War Department and others."[9] In late June, with the end of FY 1939 ten days away, Smith brought to the president a request by the Coast Guard to expand its presence in Alaska. Under normal conditions, Smith would have felt comfortable making the decision. However, these were not normal times. He felt he "should clear the matter personally with the President since," Smith noted, "he knows and is able to evaluate the national defense element [of the request] better than I." Smith was aware of the increased spending implications of this and other related matters. Compared to the president's original budget plan for that fiscal year, they would likely bust the budget: "I am afraid that a good many crimes against the Budget are being committed in the name of national defense."[10]

The pace of defense-related budgeting and organization continued with the start of the new fiscal year (FY 1940) on July 1. The Navy, now in the midst of expanding and building ships, wanted to increase its authorized staffing by twenty thousand people. The president phoned Smith to approve only an increase of three thousand for the Navy plus two hundred more for the Marine Corps.[11] An Alabama congressman sought to have a new federal munitions plant built in his district, but FDR agreed with Smith that it should be located in the TVA service area where the supply of electricity was more abundant.[12] Smith had several conversations with a representative of the food canning industry. The industry was still weak economically and wondered if it could—on its own—start producing a strategic stockpile of canned food to be available exclusively for government purchases. No federal spending would be required at the front end of the effort. Smith encouraged him to pursue it with other more appropriate officials.[13] In late August, Smith felt the not-yet-approved idea "had taken on new importance in the view of the European situation."[14]

Hitler Invades Poland and
FDR Strengthens BOB, September 1939

Over the summer, Brownlow and Smith worked on a plan for FDR to bring EOP into active existence (based on Reorganization Plan I that had gone into effect on July 1) so that the managerial agencies around the president would be in place and in full operation in order to assist with the emergency related to the European war.[15] Such an order was needed to provide an authoritative list of what agencies would be in it, their names, their missions, and the relationship between EOP agencies and the White House. Given that EOP was unprecedented, everything would need to be spelled out.[16] In late July, Smith met for several hours with the three members of (now expired) PCAM (Brownlow, Gulick, and Merriam) and Herbert Emmerich, who had been a senior PCAM staffer (Lee 2016a, 30).[17] They decided they would need at least several weeks to prepare a draft for discussion with FDR.[18] Smith updated FDR in mid-August that the draft still was not done and that they would submit it to the president in a few weeks.[19] Later that month they shared their draft with Roosevelt. Typically, he read it carefully and made several changes. The executive order was finally done and ready for promulgation on August 29.[20] However, FDR had not signed it before September 1, 1939.[21]

Hitler's invasion of Poland on September 1 was not a bolt out of the blue. In late August, Roosevelt returned from a vacation a few days early "on account of the European crisis." He promptly decided to hold off on approving a relatively routine BOB plan for funding a temporary congressional-executive economic council "until we knew the answer as to whether or not there was to be a European war."[22] By late August, everyone around the president was monitoring the increasing likelihood of a European war.[23] Up until now, Roosevelt had always conducted business with Smith in person and through dictated notes. Indicating the quickening pace of work, Roosevelt telephoned Smith several times to handle some urgent items.[24] When Smith met with the president on August 29, their conversation was interrupted several times by urgent phone calls and to listen to foreign broadcasts about the latest developments from the radio on his desk.[25]

By now, FDR was also thinking about the possibility he would need to declare a state of emergency and wanted to be sure this would fit with the draft of the EOP executive order that Brownlow and Smith were preparing.[26] Neither Brownlow nor Smith were particularly happy with its emerging form in the president's thinking. Smith commented flatly that parts of it were not "sound administration."[27] During these planning and drafting meetings, Roosevelt insisted to this small cadre of men who were working on this order and related documents that "nothing should be said about the contents of these Orders or even that the Orders were being prepared. . . . The President mentioned certain people who are publicized as knowing everything that goes on in Government, and cautioned that under no circumstances should they know about this."[28] It was more than every politician's dislike of leaks and desire for surprise news. For example, his comments applied to more than just the executive order itself. In this case, FDR wanted to avoid agencies taking preemptive and parochial actions that would narrow his flexibility and possibly reduce the comprehensiveness of multiple documents, policies, and decisions he was preparing in reaction to events in Europe. Smith speculated that FDR was hinting at his unhappiness with the attempted fait accompli from the War Department when it had appointed a War Resources Board while the president was away on vacation. Roosevelt had successfully maneuvered to make it irrelevant, but he did not want a repeat to occur (Lee 2005, 60–65).[29]

One of the hysterical accusations flung at FDR during the reorganization fight in 1937–1938 was that he wanted to become a dictator and that reorganization would permit him to do that. Politically, things got so bad that the president even felt compelled to issue a statement denying that he wanted to be a dictator (Lee 2016, 53–55; 2005, 38).[30] In that context, the creation of EOP, as a centralization of a president's managerial powers to oversee the executive branch, remained a touchy subject. For FDR, Hitler's invasion of Poland and the declarations of war by the UK and France on Germany provided a context to justify the mobilization of EOP without triggering a full-blown version of the usual political criticism from the conservative coalition. In a flurry of public activity, on Friday, September 8, he signed a proclamation declaring a limited national emergency "for the proper observance, safeguarding, and enforcing of the neutrality of the United States and the strengthening of our national defense within the limits of peacetime authorizations" (Roosevelt 1969, 1941: 488–89). He also announced several other actions to expedite American preparedness.[31]

That day, he also signed Executive Order 8248 creating EOP so that "the President will have adequate machinery for the administrative management of the Executive Branch" (Roosevelt 1969, 1941: 490–91). However, he delayed releasing it publicly for a day, instead aiming for the large Sunday newspapers. In the press release accompanying the order, he carefully stated that EOP was being created "with the concurrence of the Congress" and that the new entity entailed "no new powers, no new duties, [and] no additional responsibilities." He also justified EOP because the presidency "must be molded into a compact organization . . . so that the flow of work will be speedy, smooth and effective. Only after this has been accomplished will the President have adequate machinery for the business-like handling of his job" (Morstein Marx 1947, 17). The text of the executive order laid out in detail the specific tasks FDR was assigning to BOB. Besides its traditional budgeting activities, he formalized its non-budgeting powers, including:

- "Conduct research in the development of improved plans of administrative management, and to advise the executive departments and agencies of the Government with respect to improved administrative organization and practice.

- "Assist the President by clearing and coordinating departmental advice on proposed legislation and making recommendations as to Presidential action on legislative enactments.[32]

- "[Provide] consideration and clearance and, where necessary, in the preparation of proposed Executive orders and proclamations.[33]

- "Plan and promote the improvement, development, and coordination of Federal and other statistical services.

- "Keep the President informed of the progress of activities by agencies of the Government . . . to the end that the work programs of the several agencies of the Executive Branch of the Government may be coordinated and that the monies appropriated by the Congress may be expended in the most economical manner possible with the least possible overlapping and duplication of effort" (Roosevelt 1969, 1941: 492–93).

In addition, given the unprecedented nature of the entities within EOP, the executive order proactively addressed any potential claims of autonomy and independence by those agencies from BOB, their ostensible coequal in EOP, not their overlord. Roosevelt explicitly assigned BOB the power to oversee the budgets of the other EOP agencies similar to its traditional role vis-à-vis executive branch agencies and departments (Roosevelt 1969, 1941: 495–96). Finally, when FDR had reviewed the draft executive order, he wrote in a new assignment for the extant state offices of the incipient Office of Government Reports (OGR) (replacing the National Emergency Council): "To report to the President on the basis of the information it has obtained [from its field service] possible ways and means for reducing the cost of the operation of the Government" (Roosevelt 1969, 1941: 494).

Smith was unhappy about that, thinking the task was more appropriate for BOB and could be a justification for BOB to have a field service, one of his long-term goals. However, he decided not to make an issue of it (Lee 2005, 216n7).

Media coverage of the reorganization latched on to a quote by FDR's press secretary Stephen Early when he briefed the press on the new executive order on Saturday, September 9: "It is out the window for the much heralded and celebrated creatures of imagination. We have heard and read about the brain trust. Here's an emergency. Here's an executive order. I do not see any place for those we previously heard about." In that political context, FDR was impliedly leaving behind the New Deal's focus on recovering from the Great Depression and shifting to national defense and the need to manage it well.[34] Pragmatically, it was an irresistible and distracting spin for a politics-obsessed White House press corps that usually considered stories about public administration and management to be boring snoozers. For Smith, he now had his updated marching orders.

Preparing the President's FY 1941 Budget, September–December 1939

It is a tautology that budgeting is the main job of a government budget office. Even though Smith had spent part of the year in recalibrating BOB's mission to encompass a much broader spectrum of federal operations, the budget was still its most prominent and traditional assignment. The last quarter of the calendar year was BOB's "high season." In a macabre kind of way, Smith was as lucky about the timing of the traditional budgeting season as he had been regarding reorganization. Hitler's invasion of Poland on September 1 and Stalin's on September 17 occurred just as BOB was about to begin constructing the president's FY 1941 budget plan. Beginning in mid-September, the staff of the estimates division received departmental requests, reviewed them intensely, held in-house hearings, and developed recommended estimates. Toward the end of the year, BOB's director would meet with the president to review the estimate for each department, pose some questions for FDR to decide, and then finalize that agency's budget. Now, with the beginning of BOB's in-house development of the budget for FY 1941, the European war situation and the president's pivot to increasing defense could be baked into the estimates, whether an agency asked for it or not, or even if it would be submitted to Congress as one integrated budget or as two, with the second specifically about increased defense costs due to the war abroad. No matter. This would not be a *war* budget, only one to strengthen America's defenses while retaining its neutrality status.[35] By the first week in January, when the president's budget request would be submitted to Congress, the budget needed to be a coherent whole, reflecting the European events that began on September 1 and the administration's gradually shifting priorities as well as secular economic conditions.

In the typical Washington obsession with politics, 1940 was an election year and all developments in Washington orbited this key event. FDR would be finishing his second term and, based on the precedent established by George Washington and observed by every president up to now, FDR would be in the last year of his presidency. In that context, his budget would not be seen as a political and reelection plan. Instead, usually, political attention would shift to potential candidates in both parties. Based on these historical patterns, the underlying justifications for the president's FY 1941 budget would not be fraught with attacks and accusations that it was a reelection budget. However, FDR would not play according to Hoyle. In the first half of 1940, he said repeatedly he had not decided if he would run for reelection and, in fact, he might. Politically, that froze nascent campaigns by Democratic candidates seeking the party's nomination. It also meant that the FY 1941 budget request submitted to Congress in January 1940 might be a political document that would put him in a favorable place politically for an unprecedented campaign for a third term. Even when deciding in December 1939 whether to include in the budget an item as small as redecorating the White House residence for a new occupant or for inauguration costs could be interpreted as FDR's political signals. Therefore, he pointedly asked Smith not to include them in the budget and instead to remind him late in the 1940 congressional session to send Congress a supplemental budget request for those kinds of items.[36]

Even though this was his first annual budget with Roosevelt, Smith assumed it would be a major and time-consuming effort for the bureau, including needing the president's frequent input on all major decisions. Based on his interactions with FDR so far, he knew that the president was detail-oriented, was well informed about the federal executive branch, had extensive views on federal operations, and wanted to be involved at great specificity in the development of the budget. To convey what this budget preparation entailed, here is an overview of Smith's budget-related work during the quarter.

Roosevelt's Role

The multi-step process for budgeting under Franklin Roosevelt reflected his personal presidential style of being directly involved in decisions, his willingness to consider appeals from his tentative decisions, and all manner of public policy that was embedded in the budget. Also, given that this was his first budget, Smith wanted to be sure he understood FDR's views and would not make decisions on the president's behalf. Some examples of Roosevelt's budgeting style included these descriptions by Smith. (To reduce the clutter of too many notes, these passages mostly are from Conferences with the President [CwP].)

October 16: One-hour meeting to obtain general budgeting guidance on about a dozen issues. The president "took up our issues one by one in order to give us an indication of his thinking":

- He generally wanted departmental budgets "held at the present level and below if possible."

- He wanted to delete any new public works projects in part due to improved economic conditions. With nonfederal construction spending up, he did not want federal projects to trigger higher prices for materials and workers. Referring to the novel Keynesian economic perspective, he said, "If the [public] works theory was a good one . . . it should mean that work would be curtailed in periods of advancing prosperity."

- "He took the sheets representing a summary of requests and did what he called 'rule of some' [*sic*, thumb?], marking them up. This gave us an indication of a stiffer attitude toward the Budget."

- He wanted to keep increases in new defense spending down to about $300 million.

At the end of the meeting, "the President indicated his liking for dealing with budget problems."

October 25: Smith related to FDR his conversation with Secretary of War Woodring. Smith had told the secretary that the president's guidance for new Army spending in the defense package would be $120 million. In reaction, Woodring strongly objected that the figure was too low. After hearing this, "the President did not seem willing to revise his figures upward."

November 15: Smith presented BOB's recommendations for the USDA budget. "The President seemed quite pleased with the cut we were suggesting for his consideration. He not only approved them, but cut very much deeper. He jokingly said that I should go to the head of the class. . . . He said that he was willing to take all the blame for it. He cut further some of the research bureaus, much below our recommendations."

November 27: Smith flew on an army bomber to the Georgia White House. When he arrived, he joined the president for lunch and then they had a three-hour meeting.

- "The President okayed the budget for the Panama Canal Zone very much as we had developed it," including some increased spending for strengthening canal defenses to be included in the "B" budget.

- "The budget of the Department of Justice [DOJ] he cut back in total below last year." Smith defended some increases requested by the department and recommended by BOB, but FDR insisted on doing this for Anti-Trust Division, FBI, and Murphy's pet project of a crime prevention bureau. "The President wanted to be consistent and not undertake any new activities, even if laudable ones." Smith particularly advocated for more money for Bureau of Prisons. "This the President recognized and was inclined to take our judgement as to the needs of the prisons." At the end, "he went down through all of the items individually using his rule of thumb [of about 1 percent] to see how much money he could save. When he found that he did not quite get the amount below last year he indicated what the total should be and asked me to distribute the remainder."

- "He went over the Treasury [Department] in some detail . . . cutting the Treasury rather generally, despite the fact that the staff of the Bureau that had examined the Treasury felt that some increases were necessary. . . . He cut out new vessels for the Coast Guard and trimmed the Coast Guard budget in a number of places. He felt that the larger vessels which they proposed should be built by the Navy, if at all. . . . Furthermore, the new ships could not be built in time for emergency patrol duty." At the end of the discussion, FDR jokingly said that when Bell was BOB's acting director, he never brought in proposals to cut Treasury's budget.

When the meeting was over, Roosevelt drove Smith back to the airport in a car that was modified to be driven solely by use of hands.

December 14: Smith presented proposed budgets for all EOP agencies, including a sheet with several options for BOB such as status quo or major increases. For the latter, Roosevelt joked, "I will close my eyes and mark it." He approved expanding BOB without much discussion, saying, " 'Now don't you argue with me about this.' I replied I never argued after I had won my case." Laughing, Roosevelt told a (probably exaggerated) story from a few years earlier when Morgenthau asked for money for a new project. FDR approved it, but then Morgenthau kept making his case. FDR slightly reduced the sum. After that happened a few times, Morgenthau got the message and stopped talking. Smith told his diary, "If the President did not get some fun out of his job I don't know how any President could live under the pressure."

There were several loose ends that Smith needed FDR to act on. For the Bureau of Fisheries and Biological Survey at Interior, "we felt he should relax this item at least $50,000 of the $100,000 cut he had proposed. To this the President agreed." Earlier, FDR had decided to cut the Immigration and Naturalization Bureau by $500,000. Smith recounts, "We had made a very thorough study and determined that the falling off of immigration was a rather small factor at this time in the work of the Bureau, and explained this to him in some detail. However, he was very reluctant to change this cut. After some argument he finally said, 'Will you settle for $400,000' "? The last major item was a written protest from Navy CNO Stark of the personnel ceiling of 152,000. Roosevelt took Stark's letter from Smith and "wrote across the bottom of it . . . that the 152,000 figure would have to stand; that he would not authorize its increase. The President's note at the bottom of a document in a situation of this kind closes the issue and saves us no end of trouble in the Budget Office."

Dealing with Agencies

When conveying FDR's decisions to agencies, Smith usually faced strenuous pushback regarding cuts—usually those made by the president. Smith always tried to explain the rationale for the decisions, sometimes promised to revisit the cuts with Roosevelt, and never opposed an agency head threatening to appeal to the president directly. For example (to reduce the clutter of too many notes, most in-house meetings are in Daily Memoranda [DM]):

November 1: General Hines, head of the Veterans Administration, complained about the cuts to his budget. Smith told him that Roosevelt "had trimmed on the general theory that General Hines was doing a good job and that he knew where to cut. General Hines indicated that he was not as good as the President thought." Smith promised BOB would look into a few of the specific items that were cut.

November 14: Upon a restudy requested by VA, BOB slightly increased the agency's budget due to a demonstrated need for medical facilities in Baltimore and Philadelphia. Did the VA want to appeal to the president the other cuts to its budget? No.

November 23 (Thanksgiving): Smith accepted some USDA suggestions for revisions of FDR/BOB budget cuts, but noted, "In some cases we made no adjustments whatever. There was a general reaction that the Department of Agriculture should have set up its program in terms of priority. This the Department has never been willing to do, but always insisted that its budget request represented the minimum. This is quite in contrast to other executive departments and does not sit very well with the Estimates Division."

November 29: The Federal Communication Commission (FCC) submitted a memo to the president protesting its approved budget, even though it had gotten a $300,000 increase. "I pointed out that the President had already passed upon his budget and had considered all of the issues." The Federal Power Commission also protested its budget and lack of staffing for an interagency Federal Power Committee, as well as no funding for a proposed new power plant construction program. "I explained the situation—that I had cleared this with the President, and that he was not disposed to change the budget. . . . That under the circumstances, in the frame of reference under which we were working as given by the President there was nothing we could do."

December 5: Smith met with the chair of the Social Security Board who was protesting budget cuts. "I told him that we would have the staff refigure the matter and if there was anything seriously wrong I would try to make adjustments. Later in the day I called him to inform him that the staff had developed nothing new. . . . I also felt that in light of my experience in taking these matters back to the President for adjustment that there would be little chance of getting the amount increased." Smith assured the official that BOB would support an increase during the fiscal year if the record proved a specific activity was underfunded due to the volume of work. The official "was not satisfied and inferred he might like to take the matter to the President, which I indicated I had no objection to his doing. Later, however, he called and indicated he would take a chance and leave the figure where it is now."

Estimating Revenues and Drafting the President's Budget Message to Congress

Finishing with the president's spending plan did not complete the budget. The other side of budgeting was estimating revenues. At this point, Treasury Secretary Morgenthau believed he held the trump card. His approval was necessary for the revenue estimates to be included in the president's budget proposal to Congress. And the draft of the president's budget message to Congress could not be completed without plugging revenue figures into it. Beginning on December 19, the fight with Morgenthau over revenue estimates for FY 1941 came to a head. As an economic conservative heading a department that was, understandably, conservative financially, Morgenthau's routine role was the requirement that Treasury submit revenue estimates. The early skirmish in this battle had occurred on October 3. Now that the new Reorganization Act permitted a president to have six administration assistants (AAs), in July he quickly appointed Lauchlin Currie, an economic aide to Fed chair Marriner Eccles, as his AA for economic and financial matters. This gave the president independent economic assessments uncolored by Treasury's ideology or Morgenthau's personality.

On October 30, Currie had said Treasury's preliminary revenue estimates were about $300 million too low. This discrepancy was a political and policy problem. Politically, lower revenue estimates had the effect of increasing the amount of deficit spending in the budget. That would be an attack point by the conservative coalition. Policy-wise, the discrepancy gave Morgenthau enormous leverage to try to get FDR to lower spending and, generally, to be catered to.[37] For several meetings in the fall, Morgenthau invited Smith to attend discussions about final revenue estimates. At those meetings, the secretary tried to pump Smith for information on what was going on with the budget, but Smith always claimed that he had no information to contribute to the discussion. Indeed, Smith wanted higher revenue estimates to reduce the deficit. According to Ickes's diary, Smith's motivation was driven by both policy and politics. Ickes claimed that Smith conveyed to him (Ickes) that he wanted more optimistic figures "to make a better budget showing."[38] At this point, the difference between the final Treasury estimates and the White House was about $200 million. Politically, that was still a lot of money.

December 23: At a meeting with Smith and Currie on December 23, in exasperation, FDR said he would put in his budget a revenue estimate that was higher than Treasury's and that he would explain in his message why there was a difference. This had never happened before and would humiliate Morgenthau by marginalizing his supposed central role in budgeting. (It would also delight the conservative coalition by showing some cracks in the administration.) After the president made that decision, Smith went back to his office and told Bell. Smith argued that the discrepancy between the two figures only amounted to about 3 percent of the total. Was it worth Treasury's and Morgenthau's embarrassment over such a relatively small amount? Furthermore, economic forecasting was not as precise a field that a 3 percent change was inviolable. Changing an estimate by 3 percent would be little more than rounding up slightly. Bell and Morgenthau folded. After they left, Smith noted, "The President dictated and I took in long hand several pages of suggestions for the Budget message."

December 27: In a two-hour meeting, FDR reviewed the draft of the budget message. He "seemed to be very well pleased with the draft but dictated a number of paragraphs which he wished to have inserted."

December 29: A final two-and-a-half-hour meeting to review the budget message included Currie, Morgenthau, and Bell. As usual during budget meetings, Smith brought Blandford, his deputy. "Since I did not work on it [the cover message] in detail, much of the credit goes to Blandford and Lauchlin Currie. The latter was inclined to make a point of his contribution with the boss throughout the discussion."[39] At the end of the meeting, FDR asked Smith to bring him the page proofs as soon as they were ready so he could review the message one last time.

December 30 (Saturday): Smith brought the page proofs to the president. They met at the residence (the second floor of the White House), rather than the Oval Office. Smith wanted to be sure to call "his attention to certain minor changes" from the previous day's version. Roosevelt "suggested a few although minor additions" and then said he was done and that Smith could release it to GPO for printing. He asked Smith to bring him the publication version by Tuesday to help him prep for the annual budget briefing with the press on Wednesday, also the day he would send it to Congress. When Smith got back to his office, GPO staffers were waiting to get the final approved version of the message. He asked them to get a copy of the printed version to him by Tuesday to give to Roosevelt.

With that, Smith was done (at least in terms of *preparing* the budget). Looking back at the end of the day, he was pleased but tired. "No one who has not had the opportunity to go through the assembling of the budget of the Federal Government can have any conception of the pressure under which one must work from the fifteenth of September until the third of January when it must be submitted to Congress. It is probably the most important document in this country, at least so far as its impact upon the social and economic as well as political life is concerned." It was a fitting, if grandiose, tribute to the work involved. The budget was 1,038 pages (US House, 1940a) and Smith had met with the president twenty-four times. He was exhausted. On New Year's Day, he stayed home for his first entire day of true leisure since September. But even on a day off, he admitted he "spent several hours" preparing for questions as soon as the budget would be released.[40] It was his version of a busman's holiday. After all, now it was time to go public. For Congress, the annual budget process had not yet *started*. Smith would need to pivot to the next step in enacting the president's FY 1941 budget.

Meanwhile, Back at the (Smith) Ranch: A De Facto Manager-in-Chief of the Executive Branch

Smith's early professional goal had been for a career in city management. After half a year at BOB, he was increasingly seeing his role as the federal counterpart to a city manager. He was the de facto coordinator of the executive branch in his role as highest-ranking professional public administrator in the federal government. And no one else was doing that. In a sense, FDR had been his own coordinator until now. However, this was increasingly impossible with the war in Europe. In addition, the concept of creating EOP was to perform something along these lines, even though none of its five agencies had that explicit duty. With BOB expanding in size and scope under FDR, Smith now had the standing, capability, and stature to perform in this general management role.

For example, regular BOB business did not stop during budget season. Smith was spending about half his time on non-budget matters, such as making final decisions about clearing proposed legislation from agencies.

Many related to his public administration responsibilities, including repercussions of the recent reorganizations. In particular, Smith was often frustrated with officials who did not consider public administration as worthy of their attention. They often ignored the organizational aspects of problems facing them as well as possible managerial approaches that were necessary for solutions. He confidentially complained about New Deal in-house fixer Tommy Corcoran who repeatedly focused on the personalities and politics of people in a particular dispute, rather than any organizational factors at play.[41] Similarly, AA Currie only focused on the substantive policy area and "when he has a problem [he] thinks in terms of the individual rather than in terms of organization."[42] When he attended a dinner honoring the first of his predecessors, Charles Dawes, Smith was surprised that Dawes's after-dinner comments "referred in some detail as to how he had handled coordination of the Government's activities. It seemed to be more or less on a personal basis rather than on a basis of sound organization."[43]

Some problems were post-reorganization tremors. Smith was surprised at the crude approach to public administration taken by Paul McNutt, head of the new FSA. McNutt had experience as governor of Indiana and then US High Commissioner to the Philippines, yet he botched efforts to pull together the formerly autonomous bureaus into his new agency. "There was often a tendency on the part of people who had no great experience in administration and no sense of feel so far as administration goes to conclude that there are simple answers."[44] He was equally exasperated with Labor Secretary Perkins for how she was trying to deal with problems in one of her department's bureaus. "This is another example of where someone has gone ahead without seeing all of the steps in advance."[45] He was also frustrated by a public and political post-reorganization war between the Civil Aeronautics Board (CAB) and the Air Safety Board that, in his view, was merely an "organization problem."[46]

Some of Smith's concerns were based on what he considered central and permanent principles of good public management coming from his own career and from the Brownlow Committee report: separating politics from administration, separating policymaking from a nonpartisan and apolitical civil service, and central presidential management of the executive branch through the three staff functions of budgeting, personnel management, and planning. For example, after a problem with agencies fighting, sometimes the resulting political compromise was for an interagency committee to be in charge of all matters related to that topic. "I am not very enthusiastic about committees with administrative responsibilities. I feel that the administrative responsibility should be definitely lodged with the Secretary of the Department."[47] Similarly, he opposed an effort by a bureau to restore its pre-reorganization independence from USDA. As a principle, "the President was absolutely opposed to independent agencies" and so was Smith.[48] Also regarding USDA, Smith felt that program delivery at the local level was poorly coordinated between bureaus engaged in related programs. "It is my impression that much needs to be done to unify the Agriculture program at the county level."[49] This was no mere drive-by or offhand critique. In the second half of 1939, Smith met repeatedly with Guy Moffett, who directed Rockefeller funding in public administration, about Moffett's idea of an extreme version of intergovernmental relations. Moffett wanted to fund an administrative experiment that would truly unify program delivery, rather than merely coordinate vertical administrative siloes. The conception was a true unification at the local level of program services from all levels of government: federal (all departments!), state, and county. Smith was intrigued.[50]

Another early principle of public administration was the importance of public reporting, namely, the obligation of government agencies to report routinely to the public-at-large about agency activities (Lee 2003; 2006a). When he headed PWA, Ickes had allocated some PWA money to build a radio studio on the top floor of the department's new building.[51] Then, Reorganization Plan I partially recreated PWA into a new Federal Works Agency and stripped Ickes of his role. That meant the radio studio was no longer under Ickes's oversight. What to do with it? The issue of the administration enhancing its PR by having its own radio studio could be politically controversial with the conservative coalition and the press. It needed to be handled gingerly (Lee 2005, 94–95). After checking with the president, Smith approached the problem in as low-profile a way as he could, to avoid triggering political attacks. He arranged for an interagency committee, chaired by OGR's Mellett, to develop a noncontroversial policy on the use of the radio studio by federal agencies.[52] However, in this case, Smith was doing more than decluttering a post-reorganization org chart. He strongly believed in the importance of public reporting as a core aspect of public administration. Smith had promoted doing this when he headed the Michigan Municipal League and he continued to support it at BOB. At a meeting about the studio with Mellett and others, Smith noted, "They seemed quite pleased at my understanding of the need for information service such as this that would get the picture of governmental problems out to the public. We discussed the problem of governmental reporting generally." Smith also told them that the members of the committee "should be chosen who have a personal vital interest in the over-all problems of governmental reporting in order that the committee may not be just another committee but a rather vital force in this field."[53] Smith further demonstrated his personal commitment to public reporting in a paper he read in December at the annual conference of the American Political Science Association (APSA). He declared that one of BOB's duties was "translating the annual budget into terms which are more easily understood by the citizen. . . . Perhaps a primer of Federal finances might present through charts and other graphic means, a picture of where the taxpayer's dollar goes and of services performed for him by his Government" (Smith 1939, 17–18). For Smith, public relations was an integral component of public administration.

Even when preoccupied with the budget, Smith continued his effort to strengthen BOB institutionally with the goal of building up the agency's "esprit de corps."[54] He continued the practice of personally interviewing candidates considered for hiring, sometimes liking them, sometimes not. After several interviews with younger federal employees with about four to five years' experience, he came to a sour conclusion: "I am somewhat alarmed, however, in finding how narrow are the interests of some of these young people . . . and have been doing more or less routine, repetitive jobs. They read almost nothing but the newspapers, take part in no out-side organizations, do little or nothing in the way of hobbies and . . . do not seem to be conscious that they are traveling in a very narrow groove." He hoped that a revised CSC process for qualifying applicants for budget examiners and management analysis positions would finally give him some better choices.[55] He found it particularly hard to hire qualified candidates for the Administrative Management Division. Even though it was "swamped" with work and needed additional staffing, "it is difficult to find people in this field who do not need to be led around by the hand."[56] Nonetheless, by the end of the year he was quite satisfied by the improvement in the bureau since April. When a presidential aide called to remind him of an assignment from FDR, Smith lightheartedly, but in earnest, replied, "This Office was so efficiently run that the first reminder was quite sufficient."[57]

Trends in Smith's early BOB work (chap. 1) continued in the second half of the year: FDR's deep involvement in all matters federal and Smith's quiet but clear political commitment to Roosevelt. At their many meetings, the president was curious about nearly everything and eager to contribute his guidance. In these one-on-one conferences with Smith, Roosevelt suggested that the governor of Puerto Rico (a presidential appointee) should have three staff assistants and enumerated what their precise portfolios should be: fiscal coordination, public works, and welfare.[58] He marked on a map of Alaska the locations where he thought new landing fields should be built.[59] FDR suggested that the Post Office sell annuities as a form of retirement savings.[60] Regarding VA hospital construction and costs, "the President had a good grasp of the problems and felt keenly enough about it to revise our [BOB's] letter and dictate one of his own."[61] Roosevelt strenuously opposed the suggestion from the Army that he approve buying the existing civilian airport in Mobile (AL) to serve as a new air base. Smith then restudied the proposal carefully and eventually agreed that buying the airport was the best solution for the Army's needs and the price being asked for the land was reasonable. Nonetheless, the president still disapproved it. Finally, General George Marshall, the Army's chief of staff, and Smith met with FDR and answered his detailed questions about the plan. After an extensive discussion that answered his concerns to his satisfaction, Roosevelt was persuaded to change his position and he signed the approval documents on the spot.[62] When discussing hunger and federal food surpluses, he recalled a practice in Paris where leftovers from wholesale fresh food markets were sold at the end of the day at a special location and at half price to people in need. Perhaps the federal government should encourage the same practice? Doing that would reduce the current role of the federal government as middleman: collecting agricultural surpluses and then distributing them.[63] FDR was also concerned about the increasing number and scope of federal reclamation projects. He said they should be limited to creating arable land for the resettlement of farmers from the dustbowl or farmers who had been dislocated due to federal construction projects (such as the TVA dams). Roosevelt was convinced that too many reclamation projects tended to benefit large farm owners instead of serving farmers with small holdings. He wanted to stop that.[64] Nothing about government bored the president. He wanted to be in on everything.

Professionalizing Public Administration

A central management principle emanating from the reorganization related to the normative role of EOP agencies. This went to the heart of the emerging doctrine in public administration that there were two distinctly different roles in the executive branch: line and staff. Public administrators in line positions ran agencies; they were high up in the pyramidal hierarchy and were in charge of delivering a government service. On the other hand, staff services entailed advising the line administrators. Staff roles had no power over anyone else; they were not part of the chain of command. Rather, they exercised expertise such as personnel, accounting, and budgeting to help the line manager run programs as efficiently and effectively as possible. The concept of an executive office serving the chief executive elected officer was to be a wholly staff role, as were the duties of the president's six new AAs.[65]

Notwithstanding the instances when Smith seemed to be evolving into the de facto general manager of the executive branch, he was insistent on the dogma emphasizing the difference between line and staff. The latter should only be confidential advisors to the president. EOP agencies—especially NRPB—should not permit themselves to be co-opted by serving on various ad hoc committees created to resolve administrative and policy issues through bureaucratic compromise. As a voting member of such task forces, NRPB would be taking a position and becoming an advocate *to* the president for whatever other agencies agreed to. As a result, NRPB would no longer be staff, it would be line. Smith insisted that EOP agencies represent themselves as, at most, neutral nonvoting observers on committees and task forces. That way, they would reserve their advice on any recommendations or reports coming up from line agencies to the White House. Staff should make their views known only to the president and his direct advisors. Smith also felt that way about his participation in the task force Morgenthau had convened earlier in 1939 on economic policy. He regretted his early active role in meetings and gradually asserted to Morgenthau and others that in his staff role Smith was merely the president's observer. Being careful, Smith made sure FDR agreed with him on this line-staff distinction, particularly policy roles of EOP agencies.[66]

Similarly, Smith also felt that FDR was not utilizing his new AAs properly. They were supposed be *staff* advisors and troubleshooters for the president. They should handle discrete problems that a president would refer to them. Then their recommendations should go back to the president. Smith was quite annoyed when AAs permitted themselves to be co-opted by executive branch agencies, particularly those trying to reach the president through the back door and, crucially, undercutting BOB's monopoly on communicating with the president about budgetary and managerial issues. For example, Smith thought Currie was "out of turn" when he became a de facto lobbyist for the Commerce Department to the president and, similarly, when James Rowe did the same for the FCC.[67] Brownlow disgustedly reported to Smith that William McReynolds, who had been at Treasury and now was the AA for personnel management, was still referring to Morgenthau as "boss" and continued to accept assignments and perform errands for him. When Brownlow gently chastised him for doing that, McReynolds claimed he really had severed his service to Morgenthau, but Brownlow was very skeptical that was accurate.[68] Smith was inclined to believe Brownlow was correct, if only because of the way Morgenthau continued to treat Smith even after Smith moved out of the Treasury building. Smith was also disturbed that the president's appointments secretary did not seem to understand that AAs (and EOP agencies, for that matter) were in-house staff advisors and should have priority access to Roosevelt. Instead, Watson seemed to be keeping them at arm's length, the same way he treated requests from politicians for meetings with FDR.[69]

A key manifestation of Smith's active interest in public administration practice and research related to the promoting of professional associations for practicing administrators. Initially, the only such venue in Washington was the local chapter of the Society for the Advancement of Management.[70] He participated in several meetings and attended a few others.[71] After leading a roundtable presentation on reorganization, Smith "did not feel that [their] discussion was well organized or particularly helpful."[72] The organization and members did not seem to be quite the perfect fit for Smith's goal of elevating the practice of *government* management as a profession. Smith's overriding effort at professionalization was to help found the American Society for Public Administration (ASPA). The central rationale for such an organization was the assertion that the Governmental Research Association (GRA) was not serving such a purpose. Before going to DC, Smith had been a member of the Rockefeller-funded Committee on Public Administration of the Social Science Research Council. The idea to fund a study to justify the need for an organization separate from GRA began there and had Smith's support throughout. Smith was convinced that there was a "science of administration" and he wanted a more appropriate venue than GRA to "bring together people interested in the scientific aspects of governmental administration."[73] Day-to-day practitioners were just too busy and therefore an organized and high-quality research effort was needed. The culminating event was going to be a showdown at GRA's annual conference in September in Princeton (Lee 2014). Smith encouraged his federal colleagues to attend and planned to give a talk at the conference, but he had to cancel at the last minute due to FDR's actions during the first weeks of the European war.[74]

In preparation for the founding of ASPA at the APSA annual conference in Washington in December, Smith encouraged his staff to attend planning meetings and he kept in close touch with Brownlow and Mosher

on developments.[75] Smith personally helped inaugurate the new organization with a nineteen-page conference paper on "The Role of the Bureau
of the Budget in Federal Administration" (1939). He discounted the old
paradigm of central budget bureaus as exclusively focused on cutting
spending. Rather, after Reorganization Plan I and the September executive order, BOB's role was broader. Yes, it sought economy and efficiency,
but it also sought to improve government management, oversight of the
federal executive branch, control tools for the president, economic policy
planning, and quality research. Smith's view of BOB was that it was the
central crossroads of everything happening in the federal government. In
addition to its executive branch and presidential roles, BOB should serve as
an expert advisor to congressional appropriations committees, not just the
chief executive. His speech was considered news.[76] Similarly, the founding
of ASPA at the APSA conference was also news, including Smith's leading
role in it.[77] Smith was not only pleased with the specific results but also
stimulated intellectually by the concept of professionalizing government
management. On one of the evenings of the conference, USDA Secretary
Wallace gave an after-dinner speech and Smith was seated at the head table.
After it was over, Smith invited some attendees to his home to continue the
conversation. They talked until 2:00 a.m.[78] This was the kind of high-level
management theorizing he sought.

A Minor Public Figure

Smith stayed largely in the background, making only occasional public
appearances and cautiously talking to reporters. For example, on November 2,
he gave a talk to the annual conference of the American Municipal Association in Chicago, a group he had been active in while heading the Michigan
Municipal League. He expressed his opinion that urban planning "had gone
to seed" because it now mostly focused on physical elements of cities and
had downgraded consideration of human needs.[79] He also called for more
centralized research about government to improve municipal management
and for increasing intergovernmental cooperation.[80] As a public speech, it
was open to the press but garnered minor interest.

     When he was working on the budget, Smith was generally tight-lipped
with the media about the tentative decisions the president was making. For
example, in mid-November he wanted to tamp down rumors swirling around
DC about how much the budget would increase military spending. He
agreed to talk on the record to an AP reporter, including permitting direct

quotes. Smith said the rumors were "wild" estimates and that the budget planning would reflect "common sense" decision-making and would resist "extravagant" increases.[81] Later that month, the White House made a PR effort to spin a line that the upcoming budget was economy minded, that is, cut spending.[82] That always played well to deflect the ongoing attacks of the conservative coalition that FDR's spending was out of control and a danger to the republic. Given the secrecy with which Smith was working, with minimal effort, Press Secretary Early was able to generate headlines like "White House Puts Economy to Fore," and "Roosevelt Sets Economy Goal." Those stories mentioned Smith's role without quoting him.[83] He was directly quoted in only one story, blandly saying, "cuts are being made on some items."[84] He was equally cryptic about his flying visit to the president in Georgia in late November. The day before his trip, "he declined to comment on the budget situation."[85] When he landed, he merely said the effort to cut spending "is a whale of a job."[86] After the meeting, when FDR drove him to the airport, there was a press scrum clamoring for comment. Smith blandly said, "we continued pruning operations on the budget" and then referred reporters to put their questions to the president, idling his car at the end of the runway.[87] The well-publicized event made Smith a minor news celebrity. The Sunday *New York Times'* weekly news quiz posed this question (sixth of twenty): "On his trip South last week President Roosevelt talked with Harold D. Smith and Marvin H. McIntyre. Who are these men?"[88]

Nonetheless, it is inaccurate to assume Smith never talked to reporters. He occasionally took their calls. For example, on November 13, he talked on the phone with a reporter from AP and on December 7 talked to two reporters, but each time he did not speak on the record.[89] However, Smith agreed once to be interviewed for a human-interest profile. The column asserted that "this blond, blue-eyed, soft-spoken, fortyish fellow would be one of the last you'd take for a budget boss." The column recounted his background as a farm boy in Kansas, his training to be an engineer, and then career shift to government management. According to the profile, he was a practical and modest man who made furniture in his woodworking shop in his basement and cut his children's hair. Then it cutely noted that his "children must show how far a city planner will go. The two older have the same birthday two years apart. The next two have the same birthday five years apart."[90] To his diary, Smith sighed, "I despise this sort of thing, but it seems a part of the job."[91]

Politically, 1939 was a tough year in terms of world developments and Smith's effort to carve out his role in the administration. In an interview, he made a coy comment that his philosophy was that "men who want to be administrators should leave politics alone." The reporter quickly informed the reader that this was accurate: "He has."[92] But Smith promptly contradicted himself when relating a dinner party conversation. When asked about his politics, he said, "I don't rightly know. You see, I'm a Republican, but I get around to voting Democrat so often."[93] In private, Smith was even more explicit to the president of his political loyalty. He told Roosevelt that he hoped the president would indeed run for a third term.[94] Smith was juggling the insistence of public administration professionalizers that budgeting was an apolitical activity with his explicit agreement with FDR's political, economic, and social priorities. Notwithstanding this discrepancy between his public and private political values, he nonetheless felt he had worked hard and accomplished much in 1939. However, 1940 would not be any easier.

Chapter 3

Spending, Reorganization, Defense, and Third Term Campaign, 1940

Capitol Hill and the FY 1941 Budget, Spring

The president sent his budget to Congress on January 3, 1940. His cover message reflected the themes that Roosevelt and BOB had honed for three months: holding down routine spending, maintaining adequate economic stimulus to continue overcoming the 1937–1938 recession, additional (separate) funding for defense, and taxes to cover that new military spending. FDR also included a short section on public administration in his message. He said that reorganization had permitted some economies in spending for FY 1941, which he called "reduced rations." He estimated this had saved $11 million and was deducted from agency base budgets. He also said that further saving would occur "with further readjustment in the machinery and business practices of the government." However, Roosevelt felt that his central management agencies were in "a condition of undernourishment." For that reason, he was recommending "making a modest investment" in their budgets and staffing. This would "in future years pay large dividends," by improving management and having the in-house expertise for further efficiencies and spending cuts (US House 1940a, xiv). Before releasing the budget to Congress and the press, FDR hosted his usual annual budget "seminar" for the White House press corps. Knowing the complicated detail involved in a budget and wanting to convey the plan's larger themes, he routinely held a press conference on the budget. The contents were embargoed until the public release of the document, thus giving reporters some time to digest it and write their stories. This was Smith's first experience with the tradition. About a hundred reporters attended and the press conference lasted about two hours. Roosevelt "answered a great many questions offhand, and only occasionally was it necessary for me or anyone sitting with him to supply information. . . . At no time did the president seem to be at a loss for information, although occasionally we supplied details."[1] Smith spoke only three times, briefly adding supplementary details (Roosevelt 1972, 15: 28, 31–32).

In his December speech at the founding of ASPA, one of Smith's relatively novel points was that BOB should be a source of expertise and knowledge not only to the president but to Congress as well. He was hoping that as appropriations bills went through their respective subcommittees, BOB could be called on to answer questions, explain certain details, and follow up with other issues on the minds of the members. However, generally, the traditional separation of powers doctrine largely walled BOB off from the House Appropriations Committee. In his view, "this process must in its very nature be a joint enterprise of the Executive and Congress" (Smith 1939, 17). In an effort to kick-start this unorthodox relationship, in late 1939 Smith had conversed with the chief clerk of the House Appropriations Committee. He said that there were several management-related items that BOB had inserted across the board into the budgets of executive branch agencies. Perhaps the committee leadership would want to be briefed on these horizontal issues given that they would come up in the budget of every vertical silo? After discussing it with senior members, the clerk told Smith they agreed to receive such a briefing. Smith, Blandford, and Estimates Division director Martin went to the Hill on December 30 to meet with the committee's leadership, including the chairs of the subcommittees that handled individual agency budgets. Smith described the BOB effort to institute consistent and across-the-board policies on administrative promotions, standardizing shift hours at federal hospitals, operations of departmental personnel offices, and the transfer of agency positions that had been funded by relief and other emergency economic appropriations to regular annual funding bills.

A few committee leaders were interested, but some were not. Congressman Clarence Cannon (D-MO) was the second most senior member of the majority party on the committee (and would become a long-serving chair beginning the next year). Regarding the BOB plan to standardize civil service promotions, "Mr. Cannon did not seem to understand that our proposal was based upon the merit system; that is, even if money were allotted according to our formula for promotion purposes a person who was not worthy still would not be promoted. Cannon seemed to feel that somehow or other the proposal was giving the Administration power which he apparently felt it should not have."[2] One could practically hear Smith sighing inwardly that closer cooperation between BOB and the House Appropriations Committee was not going to be easy and went against the committee's long-standing culture. Nonetheless, in September he submitted to the House Appropriations Committee BOB's plan for a unified and comprehensive federal policy on salary advancement in the civil service (US House 1940i). He had timed it so that the subcommittee chairs would be able to consider it before the beginning of their FY 1942 hearings. If they ended up concluding it was a good idea, they could then insert the policy into each of the individual appropriation bills they would begin handling in December. On the other hand, the chair of the Senate Appropriations Committee, Alva Adams (D-CO), seemed to be much more willing to consider Smith's offer. Adams confessed that the committee was thinly staffed and that most of the information and knowledge about agency activities largely came from public hearings. Hearings were not particularly helpful for comprehensive consideration of an agency's budget plan, given the routine sparring that happened between members and agency heads or between members with opposing interests. Also, the culture of the appropriations process was that hearings were largely adversarial, with members probing for weaknesses and having a tendency to focus on small items.[3] Finally, given the congressional tradition that funding bills begin in the House, the Senate committee's role had evolved historically into a court of appeals for agencies unhappy with the House version. This reactive role limited the committee's consideration to the agenda of the agency instead of a de novo consideration of the president's proposed budget. Starting cautiously with Smith, Adams suggested trying to identify some policy areas for BOB to provide the committee with reports and information.[4]

In the meantime, Smith wanted to have more comprehensive knowledge of what the current interactions between BOB and Congress were. He asked all agency staff to keep records of all contacts and requests for information from the Hill. That would give him a better sense of how Congress was currently using the expertise the bureau had. In fact, he had no idea how much or how little contact there was.[5] However, there was a limit to such interbranch cooperation. In January, Senator James J. Davis (R-PA) introduced S. 3140 to transfer BOB to the legislative branch, somewhat parallel to what the Bureau of Efficiency had been until 1933 (Lee 2006b). He felt that any budget office attached to the executive branch would inherently reflect the self-serving perspective of agencies. Congress needed to have an independent and expert office to provide it with objective information about agency programs and spending. "Only in this way can Congress know whether it is justified in increasing or decreasing appropriations. . . . There is no harder task to perform than to liquidate Government bureaus once they are set up. Congress could do so with justification under this proposed bill," he said.[6] Davis then sent a letter to the president asking for his views on the bill. Naturally, Roosevelt and Smith were against it. It would undo everything they had accomplished so far. Smith prepared two versions for a presidential reply to Davis's inquiry. One was brief and the second was longer and the "snottiest."[7] FDR signed the latter. The bill was routinely referred to committee and never heard from again.[8] But the idea was hard to kill. When it came up at another appropriations hearing in late 1940, Smith publicly argued against it. He said, "Both groups might be going into a department, one after the other, and I think that would probably result in a great deal of confusion. I think it is possible [for BOB] to funnel the information in such a way that you would get the same result without the confusion" (US House 1940c, 786).[9]

For the FY 1941 budget, a few of the subcommittee chairs were eager to get a head start on their hearings. They asked Smith to convey, confidentially, the proposed budget for the agencies under their jurisdiction before January 3. One was the subcommittee that dealt with the annual independent offices appropriation bill. It covered agencies that were not within any cabinet departments and that had statutory authorization. BOB's hearing was on December 19, 1939 (US House 1939f, 1–23). It was a relatively routine session. Smith had a prepared statement that he read, subcommittee members asked some questions (sometimes repeating each other), and Smith either replied on the spot or promised to submit subsequently his answer for insertion into the transcript of the published hearing. Some questions focused on what was different from last year, a routine approach for an incremental budgeting process. For FY 1941, it was the creation of EOP (and the transfer of BOB from Treasury into it) in Reorganization Plan I and the transfer of the central statistical board to BOB. A minority party member asked for a detailed submission of all employees of the bureau, their titles, personnel classification, and salaries. Smith had that information at hand and offered to give it to the member (impliedly, keeping it out of the published record of the hearing). He demurred, saying Smith should hand them to the stenographer. Another minority party member wanted to know about the internal decision-making process in the Estimates Division. Smith said he would be glad to discuss it, but also (showing his thorough preparation) said it would not be different from the testimony by his predecessor a year earlier.

Smith emphasized two themes, one on the record, one off. The former was his effort to persuade the committee that BOB could do a better job if it had a permanent field staff as well as funding to send DC-based estimates staff to inspect agency projects. He felt that this would greatly improve BOB's ability to judge more directly the merits (or lack of) regarding any agency's program. In the latter, he recognized that the culture of government budgeting included that a budget office should set an example by holding down costs and staff. He said this expectation hampered the ability of a budget bureau to have in-house capabilities to do its job. Therefore, the request for FY 1941 included a substantial expansion of the bureau, its staff, and its budget. Smith said this was necessary to implement the missions that the president had assigned BOB in 1939 in Reorganization Plan I and the September executive order implementing it.[10] As the conversation was off the record, there is no transcript of how subcommittee members reacted to it. Smith was also showing some of his political chops by doing it this way. He conveyed that he understood the legislative touchiness of talking openly and extensively about spending increases. With no transcript, there was nothing to flag attention to this highly sensitive political topic. The general expectations of the House membership-at-large was that this committee's raison d'être was to cut spending. The subcommittee would not want to highlight this to other members when such an action contravened its own supposed mission. Smith was doing them a favor and that is probably why they agreed to let that part of his testimony be off the record. No transcript, no criticism.

Nonetheless, given that the subcommittee had increased BOB's budget even before Smith succeeded Bell (chap. 1), it largely continued to strengthen the bureau. With the exception of deleting $21,400 for additional statistical personnel, the committee approved the other increases requested by the president. The committee report said that this was important for "building up in the Bureau of an investigative staff of sufficient size to go into the field and make a study at first hand of the various activities on which it must pass. Additional funds are also provided for studies of governmental organization, procedures, and methods of operation" (US House 1940b, 5). Smith then needed to appear before the counterpart committee in the Senate. On January 25, 1940, he testified before the Senate Appropriations

Committee's subcommittee for the Independent Offices bill. The members did not have any major concerns about the increase in BOB's budget and, eventually, concurred in the House recommendation (US Senate 1940a). Most of his testimony related to funding the nonstatutory EOP agencies, NRPB and OGR. He made a particularly strong argument for the benefits of those agencies having field offices, laying the groundwork for an eventual request for a BOB field service (US Senate 1940b, 20–27).

Smith did not have much to do with congressional consideration of all the other appropriation bills for FY 1941. As a general matter of practice, Smith enunciated the principle that a BOB director "did not appear before the Committee unless requested to do so by the Committee or the President."[11] Secretaries and agency heads were obligated to defend loyally the president's budget request at their hearings. In a few cases, Smith got involved in the congressional consideration of the budget behind the scenes, such as during the consideration of the DOJ bill regarding a transfer of the probation office to the courts and funding for a departmental personnel officer.[12] Another time, also in private, he was involved with funding a liaison officer to be included in the budget of the High Commissioner to the Philippines.[13] Smith was also conscious of the political implications of the president's new budget plan for FY 1941. For example, in January, Senator Arthur Vandenberg (R-MI), an isolationist, sent a letter to Smith asking for comprehensive summaries of *all* Navy costs, including recently approved spending and plans already approved for its future expansion. Smith knew that "this material will undoubtedly be used by the opposition for political purposes," yet acknowledged "an obligation to present the facts as carefully as possible."[14] As in his media relations in 1939 (chap. 2), here was another example of how Smith tried to juggle simultaneously the principle of apolitical public administration with his support of FDR's policies. He was trying to balance his commitment to apolitical budgeting while being a team player in the president's administration. In this particular case, apolitical won out, at least as it played out publicly.

The "Great Reorganizer," Part 2: Plans III, IV, and V, April–June

After Reorganization Plans I and II went into effect on July 1, 1939, Roosevelt and Smith wanted to continue the project. Plans I and II had focused on *inter*departmental transfers. Neither had addressed *intra*departmental matters, such as merging separate units within the same department. Smith and FDR assumed the latter would be less controversial politically because these were zero-sum movements, with no department on the losing end of a reorganization. In January, Smith requested all departments submit their proposals.[15]

As it turned out, the proposals from agencies were somewhat slow in coming in and were sometimes not a good fit for what Smith, as FDR's designated Great Reorganizer, was looking for. Smith viewed this round as "a kind of clean-up job" following the 1939 reorganizations. Once it was done, the only things remaining "would amount to perfection in detail" of what he had accomplished in his first year.[16] However, reorganization was not a purely apolitical management activity. Politics were never far from the surface. For example, at one of their planning meetings, Smith asked Roosevelt if the idea to abolish the posts of comptrollers of customs at Treasury should be in the tentative draft or should be dropped. The president "indicated that he had a big question mark in the back of his mind concerning the political significance of this proposal at this time. He felt that it might develop a great deal of opposition in Congress." FDR also declined to propose converting the Maritime Commission into an agency headed by an administrator, rather than a board. He acknowledged that this was a good idea from the viewpoint of public administration, but that "the time was inappropriate and felt that it might stir up the animals too much and doubted the wisdom of any action."[17] He meant its *political* wisdom.

BOB submitted to him its draft for Plan III in late January.[18] Roosevelt conferred with key members of Congress about it.[19] They gave their input on what would likely be controversial and what not. In particular, they recommended a legislative tactic of slicing up BOB's plan into several different proposals. Any reorganization would likely draw opposition from somebody, usually stakeholders (and their allies on the Hill) who liked the status quo. Therefore, the grander the reorganization plan, the more opposition it would draw. Better to water down the opposition by submitting a few skinny plans.[20] Also, BOB had some ideas for a few more interdepartmental changes, a bird of a different feather politically. Back to the drawing board. By mid-March, Smith felt they were nearly done. He ended up with three lists: "those we could recommend without hesitation to the President and those that required somewhat further study and those that had been studied sufficiently that we felt should not be recommended because of no net gain."[21] He then met with FDR and showed him the lists. "The president okayed nearly all of our suggestions." Smith, again, was impressed with FDR.

"He has such a vast detailed knowledge of the Government. With a new president we would have had to have taken from a half an hour to an hour of discussion on each of the proposals submitted."[22] Roosevelt sent Plan III to Congress in early April relating to intradepartmental matters and a few weeks later Plan IV regarding interdepartmental changes.

Plan III consolidated several units in the Interior Department to create the Fish and Wildlife Service, in the Treasury into a Fiscal Service, and in USDA into a Surplus Marketing Administration. Politically, these were considered "relatively uncontroversial" and had no serious opposition.[23] The savings were only $150,000, but Roosevelt argued that even if a plan "resulted in no administrative savings at all," he "should still consider them

Figure 2. Smith in his office in the Executive Office Building, February 1940. Credit: Harris & Ewing Collection, Prints and Photographs Division, Library of Congress, LC-H22-D-8367.

worthwhile in view of the increased effectiveness of administration that will result." In a Rooseveltian flourish, the plan abolished the Recorder of the General Land Office because it was "a relic of the quill-and-sand-box period in the transcription of land records. Its duties can readily be absorbed by the regular civil-service personnel" (US Congress, 1940d). There were no major objections on Capitol Hill and the plan went into effect on June 30, 1940.[24] The interdepartmental transfers in Plan IV were of many relatively small entities (US Congress 1940e).[25] For example, given his dislike of independent agencies outside of cabinet departments, Roosevelt bulked up FSA with several small entities, including Howard University and Freedman's Hospital (Lee 2018a, 265n26). Again, like Plan III, the savings were modest.

However, one proposal in Plan IV was very controversial. It moved the Civil Aeronautics Authority (CAA) from its status as an independent agency into the Commerce Department. To interest groups who liked having their own little agency (in this case pilots and the aviation industry), this was abhorrent. They did not want anyone to have any supervision over their agency, any obligatory coordination with other like bureaus, let alone the grubby paws of control from a politician, the secretary of commerce. Even worse, it was Harry Hopkins, a do-good social worker and supporter of big government. In a relatively typical Washington brouhaha, the issue was conflated into a debate over claims the reorganization would degrade aviation safety and the independence of crash investigations. The conservative coalition was delighted to be alarmed by FDR's power grab. (Not only was it an election year, but Roosevelt had not yet announced if he would run for an unprecedented third term.) It was a choice, one conservative congressman said, between "Pilots or Politicians."[26] Influential *Times* columnist Arthur Krock wrote that "the President has sought steadily to get the power of purse and personnel over independent agencies. . . . [If approved] CAA reports to Congress must pass through the filter of Mr. Hopkins, and there will be a barrier between Congress and the regulation of air service."[27] Senator Pat McCarran (D-NV), who thought of himself as the czar of federal aviation policy, was opposed to anyone impinging on his fiefdom.[28] The *Times* editorialized against it after someone leaked to it the confidential study of the idea by BOB's Division of Administrative Management.[29] Some other headlines from the time capture the political excitement: "Hubbub over Civil Aeronautics Board,"[30] "President Strikes Back on CAA Shift,"[31] Attorney General "Jackson Holds Shift Will Leave C.A.A. Still Free,"[32] "President's Order No. 4 Stirs Bitter Controversy,"[33] and "Air Bureau Battle Started in House."[34]

This controversy was the epitome of the clash between apolitical public administration and vested-interest politics.[35] Roosevelt and his allies argued that good government was an objective and nonpartisan enterprise. They said that reorganization would help cut duplication and costs (efficiency) and/or would improve the quality of management in the executive branch (effectiveness). At this point, the new American Society for Public Administration was only a few months old and its founding was treated as signaling a major advance in improving government management. For these reasons, Smith became the point man and spokesperson for the administration on the CAA reorganization. If the justification for this particular reorganization (or any other) was that it advanced sound management and organization, then the advocate for it would appropriately be the nonpartisan budget director and, as depicted by the president when Smith was sworn in, the *expert* in reorganization. Duking it out in the political arena of the capital was not Smith's métier, but he tried his best. He helped draft a statement released by FDR on April 30 explaining the BOB recommendation.[36] Then, on May 2, trying to clarify Plan IV, he wrote identical public letters to the secretary of commerce and the head of CAA detailing what the reorganization did and did not do.[37] Roosevelt started his May 3 press conference by bringing up the issue and releasing a letter from the attorney general to Smith confirming that the plan was legal—contrary to the claims of critics (Roosevelt 1972, 15: 309).[38]

The House rejected the reorganization plan, 232–153. The roll call consisted of all Republican members and seventy-seven conservative Democrats. It was now up to the Senate. The Reorganization Act of 1939 required a vote by *both* houses to reject a reorganization plan. Trying to save the situation, Senator James Byrnes (D-SC), an ally of Roosevelt, quickly convened a hearing of his Select Committee on Government Organization. Smith tried his best to make his case on the merits and the facts (US Senate 1940c, 1–29). His prepared testimony included defensive comments such as the "mistaken conception" and "confused allocation of functions" of the status quo, "so much misinterpretation" of the BOB recommendation, and that "existing multiplicity of agencies outside of the regular Executive establishments . . . hampers the complete coordination of all governmental activities." He concluded by saying that "in place of the existing three agencies whose relationships are confused, and whose functions to an extent overlap, the reorganization plans substitute two agencies whose duties and jurisdictions are so defined as to carry out the distinction which Congress clearly intended—the separation of regulatory and administration functions."

Some committee members then witheringly questioned Smith. They bored in on the minutiae of public administration. How would CAA budgets be handled? What powers would the secretary have in such situations? Did all public reports have to be cleared with the secretary before release? They argued over what the phrase "related routine management functions" meant. It was not until near the end of Smith's appearance that conservative Harry Byrd (D-VA) brought up the subject that supposedly unified conservatives: Would it save any money? Yes, said Smith, $220,000 a year. The ranking Republican on the committee, Charles McNary (R-OR), bored in on two relatively abstract, but controversial, principles. Given that the reorganization plans came from the president, did Smith "advise him to make this transfer?" Smith replied, "I do not think I am at liberty to say." Here was an early application of the doctrine of executive privilege, the claim that anything said between presidents and their advisors was confidential and constitutionally protected. Then McNary asked about what public administration called the politics-administration dichotomy. "Do you consider your organization as a policy-making organization?" No, Smith replied, "It is not. The Director of the Budget does not make policy. It is up to the President and Congress to make policy." This went to the heart of the orthodoxy of the early tenets of the profession, namely that bureaucrats only implemented policy; they were not participants in its adoption or enactment.[39] The media covered Smith's testimony extensively. A sub-headline in the Republican *New York Herald Tribune* summarized that "Smith, Budget chief, evades responsibility query," while the *New York Times*' more neutral sub-headline synopsized that "Smith and McNary clash over who drew up Roosevelt plan for transferring agency."[40] The archconservative *Chicago Tribune* quoted Democrat McCarran as confident that the Senate would reject the plan.[41] The event was of such heightened press interest that AP moved on its national wire a photo of the three senior members of the committee during the hearing. One caption described them as "deep in thought" while another said it was a "study in senatorial expressions."[42]

The floor debate was the climactic event. The *Times* described it as a "bitter debate, at times marked by invective" from Senator McCarran. At one point, he tried to interrupt Majority Leader Alben Barkley (D-TN), who "shouted" back that he refused to yield the floor.[43] The presiding officer ruled McCarran out of order. During the roll call, McCarran challenged some of the pairs (of senators who were present but declined to vote to counterbalance absent senators). His objection was also ruled invalid. The newspaper said that the administration had exerted heavy pressure to sustain the president. In the end, the Senate voted down the rejection of Reorganization Plan IV by a vote of 46–34. The *Times*' analysis of the roll call was that most members who were up for reelection in November voted against the president, while members in the midst of their six-year terms sided with Roosevelt.[44] The roll call was considered so significant politically that the *Times* published it in full.[45] Smith's relief was palpable, saying, "We were very much pleased" by the result because—trying to get back to his apolitical public administration role—"we considered this proposal a considerable step forward."[46] It went into effect on June 30, 1940.[47]

In reaction to Hitler's invasion of Western Europe on May 10, Roosevelt decided to recommend one last reorganization just before Congress adjourned for the summer. On May 21, he asked Smith to prepare it quickly and Smith gave him the paperwork the next day.[48] In his message, FDR said, "The startling sequence of international events which has occurred . . . has necessitated a review of measures required for the Nation's safety." Therefore, he submitted Reorganization Plan V to move immigration and naturalization from the Labor Department to the Justice Department. This move, he acknowledged, would not be necessary "during normal times." However, given the impact of the war on immigration applications, he wanted it to be "closely integrated" with the other duties of the Justice Department, such as the FBI (US House 1940f).[49] Privately, the president told Smith explicitly that he wanted the reorganization because he was concerned about "fifth column activities" by supposed legal immigrants.[50] Roosevelt acknowledged in his message that the plan would not save any money. Another problem was that Congress's planned adjournment of this floor session was less than sixty days away, the legal window for Congress to veto a reorganization plan. Waiting the full sixty-day period would push implementation the Plan V to the next floor session. FDR did not want to have to wait that long. Given the situation, no one in Congress objected to the plan and no one objected procedurally to adopting a joint resolution permitting the plan to go into effect before the sixty days had expired.[51] Here was an indication that, notwithstanding the isolationists' fervor and the politics of the upcoming presidential election, no one on Capitol Hill wanted to be seen as weakening the national defense, in this case from aliens. The plan went into effect on June 14.[52]

Congressional approval of these three reorganization plans did not mean Smith's work on the subject was done. There seemed to be no end to the details BOB had to attend to for full implementation of the personnel, budgetary, and other routine management matters of those reorganizations.[53] That the plans would take effect at the end of FY 1940 was a convenience for bookkeeping and other records, permitting a kind of de novo status for the affected units effective the first day of FY 1941. Smith was especially attentive to the CAA transfer. Once its transfer to Commerce was approved, there were several high-level resignations and the media was ready to declare the transfer the cause of the implosion of the agency. Acknowledging the "unfavorable publicity," Smith rationalized that the transfer had merely exposed internal tensions.[54] He claimed that "the transfer merely gave play to the forces that had developed out of previous bad organization, arrangements that gave ambitious personnel an opportunity to grasp for positions."[55] In mid-August, he was still working at it. He was facing numerous "difficulties" with the agency: getting the CSC to reclassify CAA positions, pursuing an internal reorganization, frustration with Secretary Hopkins for not taking charge, and dissatisfaction with the army officer appointed to head it.[56] At the end of 1940, when testifying on BOB's budget for FY 1942, Smith was asked how much money the three reorganization plans that year had actually saved. As of December 31, he reported, $599,331 (US House 1940c, 756).

There were other minor reorganizations in 1940 that did not invoke the legal requirement of submitting a presidential reorganization plan to Congress. In those instances, Smith and BOB had smaller roles. They included the internal reorganization of the Navy that was recommended by the secretary of the navy directly to Congress because it might require *statutory* changes and a reorganization of the budgeting process for the District of Columbia.[57] The long-running reorganization story of the year was one that did not happen: the transfer of the US Forest Service from USDA to Interior. Smith generally was for it but had interminable meetings and phone calls discussing it. There was intense lobbying for and against it from within the federal government, from Congress, and from affected special interest groups. Roosevelt finally asked Smith for the paperwork to submit the plan to Congress. Then he changed his mind after he met with several powerful members of Congress who opposed it. FDR knew it would be a donnybrook. He was not sure he would win and preferred not to lose. In the end, he never signed the paperwork. There were likely several other factors, including the growing importance of defense versus routine public administration as well as not wanting to face (exaggerated) political attacks claiming that the transfer out of USDA showed he was anti-farmer if he ran for a third term. Ickes kept lobbying for it after that, but it was all for naught.

Strengthening BOB

Smith and his staff were very busy in 1940, whether due to the defense emergency or routine business. Smith was conscious of how significantly the workload had increased. A few weeks after submitting the president's budget plan to Congress, Roosevelt said he was surprised to see Smith at a meeting. Showing awareness of how hard BOB had worked on preparing the budget, FDR assumed that Smith and other BOB staff could take some time off for well-deserved vacations now that the budget was in the hands of Congress. "I told him that there were too many problems around here to leave," Smith said and then lightheartedly added, "and Mrs. Smith told [me] that I had run out of money."[58] Six months later, when he was routinely at work on a Saturday afternoon for the seemingly endless meetings and paperwork, he noted to his diary, "the pressure of work is such that long hours are necessary to keep up with the job, to say nothing of getting ahead of it."[59] In particular, making final decisions about legislative clearance for bills that agencies sought to introduce created a "considerable volume" of work and was "becoming particularly heavy."[60] He also had the never-ending job of trying to impose order on a preternaturally disorganized administration (and president). When Interior Secretary Ickes directly lobbied FDR for more soil conservation funding (at the expense of USDA), Smith was so mad he was "crabbing about" Ickes to a friend.[61]

Smith dedicated much time in 1940 to recreating BOB in his image. For his new Fiscal Division (to develop fiscal policy—that is, taxing and spending—for the federal government), he hired German émigré and early Keynesian Gerhard Colm as a senior economist[62] and J. Weldon Jones (who was in the Philippines working for the US High Commissioner) to head the division.[63] He also created a new position of legal counsel and recruited Edward Kemp from the Justice Department to fill it.[64] For personnel matters, he hired Edgar Young to be the bureau's personnel officer. Young's responsibilities covered the routine scope of HR, including proper classification of bureau personnel (for rank and salary), working with the CSC to certify lists of potential employees who were qualified, and processing new hires.[65] At midyear, there were still fifty positions that Congress had funded but had yet to be filled. Smith continued to insist on personally interviewing finalists, but he confessed, "Interviewing personnel is occupying a good deal of my time."[66] The next month, he expressed frustration: "We are having a time finding top-notch people on the list" from the CSC.[67] In September, he tried to break the logjam with an hour-long conference with Young,

Blandford, and Lawton (Smith's AA and the de facto business manager of the bureau) on how to solve it.[68] He also explained to Congress that one of the reasons for the delay in fully staffing the bureau was because BOB "must have a large percentage of mature people, larger than would be true in other bureaus and departments of the Government" (US House 1940h, 376). These were not entry-level positions for recent college graduates. Overall, for FY 1941, BOB was authorized to employ 223 staffers and Smith sought another thirty-five slots for FY 1942 (US House 1940c, 739).

To promote personnel stability at the top of the agency, he wanted to convert the assistant director position to a civil service status. That might help recruit and retain highly talented people because it would assure job security and help depoliticize BOB. Everyone, except Smith, would be in the classified service. Being careful, he checked with the president before doing that and FDR approved it.[69] However, it never came to fruition. Blandford, Wayne Coy, and then Paul Appleby were all at-will appointments. Roosevelt continued demonstrating his confidence in Smith. He sent a presidential message to Congress requesting an increase in the bureau's base budget of $50,000 (US House 1940g). The president also approved an allocation of $100,000 from his discretionary emergency defense funds to strengthen the bureau's abilities regarding defense. With that new money, Smith created a temporary unit within BOB. He viewed it as "a new type of organization for dealing with the situation."[70] It would be responsible for overseeing the vast increases in spending that were now occurring in the military and in materiel procurement. He described it as "an outside check on the performance of the defense agencies."[71] This new office also would attend to issues of organization and management in the defense sector. For Smith, this was a shrewd strategic decision to create it as a temporary division. Its spending and staffing would be segregated from the ongoing work of the bureau. Then, when the war would be over and there would be clamoring from Congress to cut spending, he could eliminate the temporary bureau and oppose any cuts in BOB's base budget and staff.

The president showed his public support for BOB and Smith in other ways, too. On June 26, 1940, he signed Executive Order 8455 requiring departments and agencies to submit reports and updates on public works construction to BOB and NRPB. This was followed by Regulation 1, issued by Smith and Delano, his NRPB counterpart, providing more specific guidance on the procedure to implement the executive order and the form and content of these agency reports (Pearson 1943, 32). Two months later, Roosevelt signed Executive Order 8512, creating a comprehensive accounting, auditing, allocation, and apportionment system for federal spending. It was designed by Smith (and others) to give BOB more reliable and up-to-date information on departmental and agency expenditures on a monthly basis. A journal for the accounting profession praised it because, finally, the federal government could "keep central summary accounts from which statements could be prepared showing the financial operations and condition of the government as a whole" (Morey 1942, 80). Smith made an unusual effort at media relations to explain the importance of this reform, calling five reporters and lunching with another.[72] He said that the order was "the most important move toward improvement of public reporting and budgetary control since the adoption of the Budget and Accounting Act of 1921."[73] His effort at proactive PR resulted in wire service coverage, including attention from the *Wall Street Journal*.[74] Later that month, Smith issued an in-house directive with more specifics on how BOB should prepare to implement the executive order.[75] Then, working with Treasury and GAO, the other central financial agencies, they jointly issued a bulletin with specific guidance to all federal entities on implementing the executive order.[76]

During the spring and summer, Smith "began the practice of sending Budget investigators into the field making examinations of the budget problems" they faced at work (US House 1940h, 374). For example, at the beginning of the summer, L. C. Martin, the head of the Estimates Division, left for a month-long trip to visit some of the big-ticket items that his division would have to judge come the fall.[77] The examiner for the War Department visited military posts in the South and Midwest to see physical conditions of structures and transportation equipment. Others visited VA hospitals, naval shore stations, reclamation projects, and field operations of the Social Security Board (US House 1940h, 375). By the end of the calendar year, BOB staff had spent 665 person-days doing field inspections out of town (US House 1940c, 729). Smith himself tried to set an example by going on a few such inspections, including to CAA's lab in Indianapolis,[78] the Brooklyn Naval Yard,[79] the Coast Guard Academy in New London (CT),[80] and the Naval Academy in Annapolis (MD).[81] He also made a point of touring some of the federal installations in the DC area, including the Government Printing Office,[82] the Bureau of Printing and Engraving,[83] the Coast and Geodetic Survey,[84] Bolling airfield,[85] and the Washington Naval Yard.[86] In September, Donald Stone, head of BOB's Administrative Management Division, presented an updated summary of how Smith (and he) conceptualized this revitalized BOB. Speaking at a GRA conference, he said that an anachronistic concept of budgeting had focused on cutting spending and maintaining accounting records. Now, budgeting had evolved into an instrument of policy (including fiscal policy) as well as a method of improving administration. The real test of a budgeting office should be "the extent to which it helps the chief executive develop a suggested program of action for the consideration of the legislative body—and, subsequently, the aid which it renders the chief executive in facilitating the economical and effective execution of the program."[87] It should also focus on PR by disseminating "to the citizens information concerning the work of their government."[88] Stone concluded by stating, "The job of the Bureau is to help implement management all the way up and down the line; and . . . the Bureau is essentially a servicing rather than a controlling, restricting, negative agency."[89] Here was a cogent depiction of the vision that Smith and Stone had for the profession of public budgeting, circa 1940.

Emerging as a Public Spokesperson for the Administration

Smith may not have been a good fit for the gladiatorial cut-and-thrust of political combat that he had faced regarding CAA's reorganization. Nonetheless, throughout his career he recognized the importance of public communication as an integral part of public administration. In 1940, he occasionally traveled to give speeches and routinely talked to reporters in the capital. Smith was relatively circumspect about the speech invitations he accepted. He had a relatively narrow sense of his brief, namely, that he should largely limit himself to two subjects: federal budgeting (and related fiscal policy) and public administration, including his early career specialization in municipal government. When OGR head Lowell Mellett asked Smith to give a talk to a housing conference, Smith demurred, wondering about "the appropriateness of the Director of the Budget making such a speech."[90]

Within a few months, he gradually loosened up. In April, he gave three speeches out of town, the first was to a lay audience on civics and urban planning, while the other two were relatively dense presentations to specialized audiences on economics. On April 4, he gave a talk in Flint (MI) on "Your Civic Responsibility." Smith was the keynoter at the local chamber of commerce's annual convocation for local public officials to discuss improving government. He said that democracy depended on citizens being actively involved in social groups to promote the betterment of their locality. Unless there were activist groups interested in public policy, there would be a "civic sleeping sickness." Only through the active involvement of individuals and civic groups could "government planning bodies" do a good job of reflecting public priorities and interests. Recognizing the varying interests of such membership groups, he recommended that each city have a "citizen council" made up of a representative from each group. This would serve as a venue to hash out public needs and present consensus proposals to relevant governmental planning agencies for consideration and adoption.[91]

The second speech was at Allegheny College's business school and focused on the federal budget (Smith 1940a). In particular, he addressed the standard talking points of conservatives. Yes, the budget was big, but too big relative to what? The accusation was being made in a vacuum, lacking any substance or context. He quickly reviewed some of the things that the federal government did, implicitly challenging conservatives to specify what programs and services they would cut. Another routine accusation was that the federal workforce was bloated and should be cut, too. Excluding the military and mailmen (as they were called in those days), firing everybody else would only cut the budget by 10 percent. Most federal spending was through grants and aids to farmers, veterans, and the unemployed—not to bureaucrats. Similarly, conservatives attacked spending on research as a "frill." Well, it was only 1.5 percent of the budget and resulted in concrete benefits. Finally, he addressed the insistence on a balanced budget. To do that, the federal government would be obliged to ignore the business cycle, of people being unemployed and farmers unable to make a living. Smith advocated Keynesian economics, arguing that federal spending should increase during recessions and depressions to offset the harm falling on people. The speech garnered minor press coverage even though AP reported it.[92]

Later that month, speaking to the Detroit Economic Club, he addressed some related issues (Smith 1940b). If federal spending was going up, as conservatives claimed, then that meant the US budget director was "a fat, lazy, watch-dog slumbering peacefully while burglars jimmy a safe marked 'the treasury.'" To demonstrate how closely budgets were examined, he detailed the process of the budgeting "gauntlet" that happened first in BOB and then in Congress. Nothing just happened without anyone noticing. Rather, the instigation of increased spending often came from special interest groups. If proposals for increased spending "were properly labeled, an illuminating list of interests would be identified." He also emphasized, as he had in his congressional testimony, that a budget director did not make policy, Congress and the president did. Using some of the same examples of conservative attacks that he had used in his Allegheny College speech, Smith put them more explicitly in a political context. "Now that a campaign is under way you will hear much of this sort of talk. Since campaigns in many ways tend to confuse rather than enlighten," he wanted to be sure the audience had basic awareness of federal budgeting. Another contentious political issue was defense spending. Isolationists claimed it was either unnecessary or provocative. Surely, Smith argued, "at least a moderate strengthening of defense is imperative in view of the kaleidoscopic events which now shake the world." Again, his speech attracted little national media attention.[93] Even though these two economic speeches were not political events and Smith was tiptoeing around controversial political matters, they were nonetheless public justifications of the rightness of FDR's policies. They implicitly promoted public support for his reelection—assuming Roosevelt decided to run.

As in 1939, Smith routinely talked to reporters when they called him. Sometimes he would decline to say anything on the record, sometimes he gave them budget information but did not agree to be quoted, and—less frequently—he spoke on the record. The reporter who called him the most often was Irving Perlmeter, a staff correspondent for AP whose beat included BOB. Another frequent caller was Jerry Kluttz, who wrote a daily column aimed at a readership of federal employees for the *Daily News* (and, beginning in December, the *Washington Post*).[94] Smith developed a relationship of trust with them and was a bit more open than his usual caution with reporters. For example, when Kluttz called him about rumors Smith or Blandford were about to be appointed comptroller general, Smith waved him off the story, saying the rumors were pure speculation and not based on anything concrete.[95] On August 1, Perlmeter "dropped in for some news."[96] Smith tried to accommodate him. The next day, AP moved on its national wire a story "President Asks Funds for Refugee Children," quoting a formal letter from Smith to Congress.[97] A few weeks later, Perlmeter called for the latest presidential allocations of defense funds.[98] Later that day, AP ran a story, "F.D. Allocates $10,000,000 for Defense Workers." The story cited Smith, but contained no quotes.[99]

This cautious media relations policy made Smith a minor news figure, particularly to news consumers in the capital. Headlines of some stories mentioning Smith in January (a particularly budget-heavy news month due to the submission of the president's annual budget) included "Claim 5,000 Off Payroll,"[100] "Seeks Tax-Refund Money,"[101] "Treasury May Tax Agencies,"[102] and "Budget Chief Warns Agencies to Train for Less Spending."[103] Often he was named in stories that were based on FDR's daily schedule, such as "also meeting with the president" or "in the group that met with the president." Smith seldom worked proactively to be in the news. He held a rare news

conference in August to brief the DC press on the details of his plan to
reorganize the role of the DC municipal government vis-à-vis BOB (alluded
to in the reorganization section).[104] Sometimes reporters dropped by to
talk to him without an appointment. If he could, he would accommodate
them. For example, a reporter from International News Service wanted
some up-to-date information on appropriations and Smith gave it to him.[105]
When a reporter from the weekly newsmagazine *United States News* called
for authoritative numbers on new defense spending, Smith had to frankly
caution the journalist about "the difficulty of making careful estimates at
this time."[106] Smith also knew media coverage could easily turn negative,
either personally or about policy. For example, on October 22, he agreed
to brief Robert Kintner (who cowrote a syndicated column with Joseph
Alsop) on the defense program, particularly federal reports and statistics
about it. Smith knew it was "difficult to get a story over completely." He
warily assumed the eventual column "is going to be critical, which is the
danger of this sort of thing because it disturbs our relationships," that is,
Smith's ongoing behind-the-scenes work with multiple agencies involved in
this.[107] He was right. The column indeed was critical, implying that accurate
statistical reporting was a mess, but gradually improving. "Better late than
never," they opined.[108] Oddly, the column made AA Currie look good,
although he played a marginal role in the matter. (He allegedly forwarded
a presidential assignment he received from FDR to Smith.) Washington
politicos would infer that Currie was either a source for that column or
perhaps an ongoing leaker to these columnists. Media relations in DC was
often a lose-lose proposition for senior officials like Smith.

Budgeting and Organizing for National Defense, May–October

The Nazi invasion of Poland in September 1939 had, as promised, triggered a declaration of war by Britain and France. They mobilized their
armies and placed them largely behind the Maginot Line. However, they
took no significant offensive actions, leading to its derogatory appellation
as the Phony War. In reaction to the invasion, FDR had declared a limited
national emergency, increased defense spending, strengthened the military,
and expanded production of armaments and other materiel. In relative
terms (of what came later), this period in the US was one of gradual and
modulated developments.

Everything changed on May 10, 1940. Hitler invaded Belgium and Holland aiming toward France and the British Expeditionary Force (BEF). Roosevelt sprang into action. Two days later, he convened a meeting with the senior officers of the army, leadership of the War Department, Treasury Secretary Morgenthau, and Smith. FDR suggested that, comparable to the post-WWI concept of naval parity or a fixed ratio between the US and foreign navies, maybe the US should have a similar policy for airplanes vis-à-vis the Luftwaffe. He pushed for a goal of producing fifty thousand planes a year, a number he practically plucked out of thin air. (A reminder that the air force was then part of the army.) The usual bickering occurred. Smith left the meeting with the conclusion that General Marshall "was the only one who knew what he was talking about."[109] Two days later, FDR told Smith that he wanted similar augmentation of the Navy's budget.[110] On May 16, Roosevelt addressed Congress and requested an additional appropriation of $1.1 billion for defense, beyond the significant increases in spending already approved in late 1939 and early 1940. Indicating the national mood (even though it was an election year), he was cheered fiercely by members of both parties. According to the *Times*, "rarely, if ever before, has Mr. Roosevelt received such an ovation." It was "a demonstration of national unity in a time of international crisis."[111] There were, of course, endless implementation details that Smith worked on, such as gearing up the Civil Service Commission for the large increases in hiring civilian workers for the naval yards, enhancing acquisition of strategic materials, and tighter regulation of immigrants (the latter through Reorganization Plan V).[112]

Then Roosevelt turned his attention to an organizational structure to handle this quantum jump in the mobilization and production of armaments. It will be recalled that to implement Reorganization Plan I (in 1939), after Hitler invaded Poland, FDR signed an executive order establishing EOP and included in it a stand-by agency, an Office for Emergency Management (OEM). Now he wanted to bring that into effect. On May 25, he signed an administrative order (a new category of a presidential document that was a subset of an executive order) mobilizing OEM (Lee 2018a, 28–29). Brownlow, Smith, and McReynolds had a round robin of meetings to implement the details.[113] Eventually Roosevelt settled on a somewhat confusing and awkward structure. Using the WWI law authorizing a cabinet-level Council of National Defense, he would reconvene the council for one meeting solely to approve creating a National Defense Advisory Commission (NDAC). It would be a kind of exoskeleton of the executive branch for all arms production and related matters. This encompassed practically everything the federal government did except the military services, including construction, employment, production priorities, infrastructure, food, transportation, and job training. NDAC would not have any explicit legal powers, would not have a chair, and could not give orders to the military. Nevertheless, it would be expected to organize an effective mobilization of arms production. The membership included blue-ribbon businesspersons such as General Motors CEO William Knudsen, railroad executive Ralph Budd, and US Steel's board chair Edward Stettinius. Coming from the liberal side, labor leader Sidney Hillman, liberal economist Leon Henderson, and consumer advocate Harriet Elliott balanced them out.

FDR appointed AA McReynolds as NDAC's secretary and liaison to the president as well as putting him in charge of the new OEM. Neither Smith nor Brownlow liked this organizational structure because it was vague, messy, and confusing—nothing like the orthodoxy of sound organization they advocated. But they knew they had a clientele of one and they had to yield to the president. Roosevelt announced it at a press conference on May 28 and convened the first meeting of the commission on May 30, Memorial Day (Roosevelt 1972, 15: 383–94; 395–407). Smith attended the commission's first meeting and renewed his acquaintance with Knudsen. (They knew each other from Smith's Michigan days.[114]) Next came Smith's efforts to address the multiplicity of cascading and related issues, such as the complicated splintering of federal programs for industrial job training, reductions in nondefense spending to offset some of the military increases, coordination of federal mapping activities, and bureaucratic fights over pilot training.[115] These organizational events were taking place against the backdrop of stunning events in Europe, including the German Ardennes offensive to surround the BEF and most of the French army, the Dunkirk evacuation, and the gradual collapse of the French government. On June 20, the president announced that he was appointing two senior Republicans to head the military departments: Henry Stimson as secretary of war and Frank Knox as secretary of the navy.[116] That such eminent Republicans would accept his invitation to serve helped reinforce the message that the defense mobilization was neither contrived (as isolationists and pacifists claimed) nor political. Two days later, France surrendered. Smith attended White House meetings leading to a further presidential request that Congress appropriate another $5 billion for defense.[117] (For the reorganization of NDAC into the Office of Production Management in late 1940 and early 1941, see chap. 4.)

Administration and (Some) Politics:
Running BOB While Roosevelt Was Running for a Third Term

About two months after the Nazi invasion of Western Europe, the other shoe dropped. On July 16, Roosevelt announced he would accept nomination for a third term. For Smith, the ostensible apolitical budget director, this meant navigating his role while the president was away actively campaigning for reelection. Certainly, there was little change in the mundane (if that is the word for the federal government under a limited national emergency) and the daily business of BOB: funding, organization, investigations, presidential declarations (executive orders and proclamations), and legislative clearance. Smith now had much less direct contact with the president, about once a fortnight. Over four months, they had eight relatively routine and quite short business meetings: July 30; August 22 and 24; September 5, 12, 14, and 24; and October 18.[118] FDR also called him from Hyde Park on August 30.[119] When NDAC members met with the President to fill him in on their work and obtain guidance, Smith attended as an observer, but did not participate in the conversation.[120] At a one-on-one meeting with FDR on September 24, besides extensive discussions about funding defense, the topics they discussed included cotton crop failures in Louisiana, recruiting the best candidate to head the selective service system (i.e., the draft), creating a Columbia Valley Authority (comparable to the TVA), coordination of intergovernmental relations and services, and social security. At the end of the meeting, Smith commented to his diary, "I am always impressed with the volume and scope of matters which the President must attend to."[121]

Smith's last working meeting with Roosevelt before the election was on October 18. That was also the same day FDR announced he was *beginning* his active campaign. The president asserted that all his public activities from the Democratic convention in mid-July to mid-October were not political and not as a candidate running for reelection. Rather they were appearances as president and commander in chief at a time of a national defense emergency.[122] Given the enormous stakes at hand, of trying to be reelected to an unprecedented third term, Smith was quite surprised by Roosevelt's mien that day. He noticed that FDR "has his usual pleasant disposition. If there was anything going wrong in the world of a disagreeable nature, you would not guess it from the President's manner."[123] Tiptoeing closer to politics, Smith attended a speech Wendell Willkie gave at the National Press Club in mid-June (about two weeks before he won the GOP nomination).[124]

It was packed, with about a thousand Washingtonians, all curious about the Republican phenom.[125] On August 24, Smith met with Howard Hunter, deputy head of WPA. The topic of the meeting, as listed on his calendar, was "(Wendell Wilkie [sic])."[126] An hour later Smith and AA McReynolds met with FDR for forty-five minutes. Oddly, Smith did not dictate a summary of this conference with the president, as was his usual custom. His daily record lists the subjects of the meeting as "housing, various national defense matters, etc."

Other stray fragments hint about politics. Earlier in the summer (before FDR declared), Smith had a brief meeting with the president to work on a message to Congress requesting additional defense funding. Roosevelt seemed to wave him off, saying he felt the message draft was OK. But Smith insisted that the president take a closer look at it and consider it in the broader context of overall war developments, rather than as yet another in a long series of requests for additional military appropriations. Smith felt "the President was underrating the importance of this message, especially since it was coming just prior to the Democratic National Convention."[127] Roosevelt acquiesced and later that day they had a two-hour session to revise it, with FDR inviting Hopkins to participate in the redrafting. After the Democratic Convention, USDA Secretary Henry Wallace, now also the vice presidential nominee, gave a speech at the National Press Club. Smith attended, wondering how Wallace would do. He later commented that Wallace "gave a very good extemporaneous speech. . . . Wallace is not a good speaker, but impressed the group with his sincerity and the substance of his speech. He gave what he had to say a rather sound, philosophical basis."[128] In another case, Smith forwarded to FDR a clipping "that may amuse you." It was about a vendor of campaign buttons who "was no slouch in developing sales incentive."[129]

Smith's most explicit campaign involvement occurred in late October. At one of his infrequent meetings with Roosevelt, Smith told him that the political situation in Michigan seemed relatively negative. Smith had gotten a letter from Murray Van Wagoner, the Democratic nominee for governor. (They were acquainted because Van Wagoner had been the elected state highway commissioner when Smith was Michigan's budget director.) Van Wagoner reported that the campaign for the Democratic ticket in Michigan was in very poor condition. He urged Smith to convey a message to FDR that a presidential visit to Michigan would be a good idea.[130] Roosevelt replied to Smith "that he could not do it. He did indicate an interest, however, as to why" Van Wagoner felt that way. "I told him that I had no notion as to why this had happened, and he asked me if I could do a little checking for him. This I promised to do."[131] Getting back to his office, Smith asked an aide to check with Supreme Court justice Frank Murphy, the former governor, and ask if he knew what was going on. Murphy called him back.[132] Smith also talked to AA James Rowe about it twice. (AAs were exempt from the Hatch Act ban on political activities by federal employees.) Smith then filled in Hopkins, too.[133] For three days, Smith contacted people he knew in Michigan to get a sense of the political situation there. He then sent a memo to FDR summarizing what he found out. He reported that the presidential reelection campaign in Michigan "has been very quiet" and that "the national ticket is not getting as much play as it might on billboards, etc." On the other hand, from the opposition, the "third term argument is being used with some effect in press and on billboards, accompanied by reference to the Constitution and George Washington. No effective answer is made." Similarly, "unpleasant, unfriendly reception accorded Willkie at factories under C.I.O. influence has revived memories of the 1938 strikes and radical activities" and that "fruit throwing has evoked a reaction sympathetic to Willkie." Also, the "Democratic State Chairman has handled legal matters for utility interests" and it appeared that he was quietly supporting Willkie by not boosting Roosevelt. There was even a rumor that Van Wagoner's supporters had a secret "understanding" with the reelection campaign of Republican senator Arthur Vandenberg to support each other. What to do? Smith recommended that the national campaign office "send some outsiders into Michigan" to boost FDR's reelection.[134]

The next day, Murphy called Smith. Murphy said that from his own discrete contacts he came to the same conclusions Smith had stated in his memo to FDR the day before. He said that "the State Democratic organization is doing almost nothing on behalf of the President, and that there is no spark of New Deal leadership in the Democratic crowd."[135] One of Murphy's sources was Michigan's WPA director, Abner Larned, who happened to be in town. Murphy suggested Smith contact Larned to hear his observations in more detail. Smith did. He invited Larned to come to his office to talk. Before he arrived, Smith called AA Rowe and suggested he join them to hear what Larned might say. Larned was a successful businessperson and Republican who also was a supporter of the social reforms of the New Deal. His appointment as WPA state director reflected these unusual qualifications. However, after years of Republican accusations that WPA was little more than a Democratic patronage machine, Larned and his counterparts in the other states were now prohibited by law from any direct political activity. Nonetheless, Larned hoped FDR would be reelected. During a two-hour meeting, he told Smith "the campaign in Michigan is a thoroughly local one and that it could not be more local if it were a campaign for the election of constable. . . . The State Democratic crowd is doing very little for the national ticket." The only major national surrogate sent by the Democratic National Committee to Michigan to campaign for FDR was a recent visit by New York City's Mayor La Guardia (originally elected to Congress as a Republican). Larned also said that, as the Democratic candidate for governor, Van Wagoner "is saying very little about the President and the New Deal because he wishes to draw Republican votes, which are necessary for his election." Larned repeated the rumor that "Van Wagoner has a hook-up with the Republican bosses" who were focusing on reelecting Vandenberg. After hearing all this, Smith picked up the phone and called FDR's political aide Marvin McIntyre. Smith told McIntyre that he had some important information from a visitor about the status of the Michigan campaign. McIntyre asked Smith to bring Larned over to his office right away. Smith did. Later that day, after Larned got back to his hotel, Smith called him to follow up and find out what, if anything, had transpired or had been decided.[136] In this instance, Smith had clearly crossed the line of the apolitical principle that there should be a strict separation between professional public administration and politics.

Preparing the President's FY 1942 Budget, September–December

Presidential election or not, FDR to be reelected or not, annual budgeting must go on. BOB's high season for drafting a president's budget plan usually started in mid-September. Smith tried to carry on, with a business-as-usual attitude. However, this time, there were some significant differences from the previous year. First, this would be Smith's second budget with FDR. Smith now had a better sense of Roosevelt's general decision-making approach to budget decisions. He did not need FDR's guidance for those matters. Second, Smith had now mastered the mammoth federal budget and, with that previous experience, could handle more matters in-house with a greater confidence that he was usually on the right track. Third, FDR now had more confidence in Smith's budgeting decision-making and did not feel a need to micromanage the process quite as much as he had the previous year (chap. 2). As discussed in the preceding section, Smith's personal meetings with the president to draft the budget were infrequent during the campaign. Even during a few relatively long business meetings on September 24 and October 18, Smith did not raise *any* budget-related issues. At the end of the October meeting, Smith told FDR "that I would not bother him until after the election, if I could help it, but that there were a number of rather fundamental issues that I was holding back for discussion later when he had more time."[137]

Beginning in October, the Estimates Division held its hearings on agency budget submissions, but Smith rarely attended them, waiting for his involvement later in the process.[138] Smith personal participation in preparing the FY 1942 budget occurred during BOB's Board of Review sessions, when estimates staff presented their recommendations to the senior leadership of the bureau for finalizing BOB's decisions, subject only to changes by the president. The Board of Review began meeting on November 4 and continued almost daily until December 18. On Election Day, November 5, Smith was attending a daylong session on USDA's budget.[139] Smith's first post-election appointment with FDR was scheduled for Tuesday, November 12, a week after the election. However, Roosevelt was so busy he "failed to see the President."[140] Instead, they met the next day for thirty minutes to go over BOB's estimates so far.[141] A week later, they had a two-hour meeting to cover recommendations for USDA, Commerce, TVA, and several other agencies.[142] On November 27, they went over the estimates for the Navy, Labor, and Treasury.[143] Indicating how advanced the budget preparations already were, on the day after Thanksgiving AP ran a story that BOB now projected that given earlier tax increases federal revenues in FY 1942 would cover all expenditures by the civilian side of the executive branch. In that artificial sense, it was a balanced budget. However, defense expenditures were *not* calculated into that statistic.[144] On December 17, Smith, Blandford, and the president had an extensive meeting. They discussed the overall picture of the budget so far and reviewed their final recommendations, "which had been handled during his absence." Without making any changes, Roosevelt then "approved our action and initialed the [budget] sheets."[145] News coverage of this meeting described it as part of the "final conferences" on the budget.[146] By the week of Christmas, FDR and Smith were largely done with the budget itself and were drafting the president's message to Congress.

At a news conference on December 27, Roosevelt roughly confirmed that he would be recommending about $10 billion in defense spending for FY 1942 and therefore that he was cutting nondefense spending "to the bone."[147] A few hours later, AP moved a detailed story on the specifics of the budget, based on information it had obtained "authoritatively." It stated that the $10 billion for defense would be "double that of the current year, and easily the largest since World War days."[148] Smith had talked to AP's Perlmeter that day after the press conference and after his meeting with Roosevelt, so it is likely he was the source.[149] FDR might have suggested Smith make the leak, perhaps to set the stage for his Sunday night fireside chat on national security. The leak helped dominate the news agenda over the weekend, helped soften the blow of such an unprecedented peacetime appropriation for defense, and heightened public interest in tuning in to the radio broadcast. It was a historic and memorable talk. Roosevelt discussed the recent Axis aggression, why it was a threat to the US and to the hemisphere, why Britain continuing to hold out against the Nazis was of direct benefit to the US, and how stronger American defenses and aid to allies would help keep the US out of the war. In his peroration, Roosevelt called for America to become "the great arsenal of democracy" (Roosevelt 1969, 1940: 643). He also made a passing reference to his December 20 announcement that he planned to reorganize NDAC. In the fireside chat, he said he wanted "a more effective organization to direct our gigantic efforts to increase the production of munitions. The appropriation of vast sums of money and a well coordinated executive direction of our defense efforts" were essential to this national security mobilization (642). The specifics of that reorganization would be finalized after the turn of the year.

Promoting Professional Public Administration: APSA President, December

In those final hectic days of finalizing the budget, Smith was in something of a hurry. He wanted to finish the budget message and any last-minute changes to the budget itself because he had committed to attending the annual joint ASPA/APSA conference in Chicago on December 28–30. During the year, Smith continued to be active in both ASPA and APSA. For example, he served on a committee of APSA to review the relationships of political scientists to the "real world" of government. Chaired by Professor Joseph Harris, the committee submitted its report to APSA's leadership council at the conference. It called on political scientists to make a greater effort to be relevant to government and to offer their expertise to practitioners. The report noted the "undue emphasis" on publishing for faculty seeking promotions. Instead, "departments should take into account the research and public service activities," too.[150] During the conference Smith also was a discussant at a panel on "The Problem of the Public Debt: Should the National Debt Be Limited?"[151]

Smith's major presentation at the conference was in a symposium on EOP, sponsored by the three members of PCAM, Brownlow, Gulick, and Merriam. Leaders of each EOP agency presented papers summarizing the work of their agencies. Smith's paper was titled "The Bureau of the Budget as an Instrument of Management." As presented, it was a twenty-three-page paper, released in mimeograph form by BOB. The second issue of *PAR* then published all the papers of that symposium, with a shortened title of Smith's paper, "The Bureau of the Budget" (Smith 1941a). He reviewed the history of BOB before EOP and then presented in detail the organization, structure, and record of the agency during his directorship. Smith analogized BOB and EOP as the governmental equivalent of a person's central nervous system (114). Similarly, EOP in general and BOB in particular provide "a system by which information can be collected, classified, compared, and transmitted for decision by the Chief Executive" (115). He concluded by saying that the definition of success for the bureau would be by "playing an essential role in the process by which democracy meets the challenge of a complex world" (115). Then, at the annual business meeting during the ASPA track of the conference, Smith was elected by the members to be president for the next year, succeeding William Mosher, its first president.[152] (Gulick was elected vice president.) This election was a major confirmation of Smith's seminal role in the rise of the profession, the coalescing of a new national association divorced from GRA, and the vision of ASPA as uniquely spanning the worlds of the academy and practice. It was a public signal of Smith's importance, not just internally as BOB director, but also externally as the epitome of the new profession and discipline.

Chapter 4

Neither War nor Peace,
plus Business as Usual, 1941

Organizing the Arsenal of Democracy, January–May

After the November election, Roosevelt quickly pivoted back to presidential business, finalizing his FY 1942 budget proposal to Congress (chap. 3) and restructuring his emergency defense organization.[1] The weaknesses of NDAC's complicated, confusing, and cumbersome structure had gradually became apparent in the second half of 1940. The commissioners sometimes had competing and conflicting missions. Without a chair, no one had the standing to resolve the disputes. In addition, NDAC's secretary, AA McReynolds, had no expertise in the economic and industrial issues at hand, nor did he have an interest in trying to assert power over the commissioners. Besides, he already had a full-time job as head of EOP's Liaison Office for Personnel Management (Lee 2016a). Roosevelt did not mind messy org charts and in fact liked it when conflicts had to rise to him for resolution. That is what a president was supposed to do, he felt. Nonetheless, NDAC was a *political* success. It embodied the importance of national defense in the election year without being seen as pro-war, the way isolationists sought to depict Roosevelt, nor as a threat to free enterprise, as conservatives constantly accused him.

With the election behind him and the worsening situation in Europe, FDR wanted to strengthen NDAC, though he was not sure exactly what he wanted. On Saturday, November 30, Smith raised the issue. He said that in the process of developing NDAC's budget for FY 1942, he had inevitably come into "some valuable information as background for adjustments in the defense organization." The president agreed, saying that Knudsen, NDAC's commissioner for production, had recently given him a report and chart with his own reorganization suggestions. Roosevelt handed them to Smith and asked him to study Knudsen's ideas and then, in reaction, submit what BOB would now suggest for reorganizing NDAC. FDR said he was inclined to keep NDAC, while somehow elevating and strengthening Knudsen's power as commissioner for production and Donald Nelson's power as commissioner for procurement. Roosevelt said he was leaving in one and a half days for a post-election vacation and would be glad to have Smith's memo to take with him to review and reflect on.[2] It was a rush job. Smith worked on it all day Sunday until 1:00 a.m.[3] On Monday morning, December 2, he polished it and had it typed; then he rushed to Union Station to hand it to a White House staffer just before the train pulled out at noon.[4] At their first meeting after Roosevelt came back from vacation, Smith wanted to pick up where they left off. FDR said "he had not had an opportunity to study [the] report" while away and asked Smith to summarize it orally. BOB's recommendation was to elevate the commissioners for production and procurement to "directors" of production and procurement, making them senior to the other NDAC commissioners, with more power, leverage, and autonomy. In reaction, the president said that his thinking was evolving and now he was inclined to have four senior people. In addition to directors for production and procurement, he wanted them to have two coequals, for price control and for labor. He wanted "a check" on production and procurement, which inevitably tilted to the perspective of business. He would counterbalance them with two New Deal liberals with leftish views on economic policy and labor rights in armament factories. That led him to think that NDAC was outdated and could be abolished in toto. He also felt that the new structure would need a stronger, activist presidential agent to oversee it. FDR said he wanted to shift the focus of the new entity to OEM. He would then appoint an aide to be in charge of OEM and subsidiary entities within it. Smith said he would prepare a new draft encompassing the president's ideas.[5] It was another rush job, with the president asking for it in two days.

On Friday, December 20, Smith recommended creating an Office for Production Management (OPM) headed by a director. Three division heads would report to the director: purchasing, priorities, and production.[6] FDR tinkered with it a bit, saying OPM should be run by a board consisting of a director, an associate director, the secretary of war, and the secretary of navy. He would appoint an aide as liaison between OPM and the White House. Later that day, Smith asked Brownlow for his reaction to FDR's latest iteration. Brownlow stressed clarifying that the four-member board headed OPM, not OEM.[7] After meeting with NDAC on December 20 to present his reorganization intentions, Roosevelt held a press conference to announce them (1969, 16: 372–83). He described the experience with NDAC as a "study period, and [we] had learned thereby of certain needs" for managing the defense emergency. He would create an Office for Production Management with Knudsen as director and Sidney Hillman (the labor leader, NDAC's commissioner for labor) as associate director. This reflected FDR's desire to balance business and labor. Furthermore, to link OPM more closely to the needs of the military, a Priorities Board would consist of those two and the secretaries of the two military departments. They would make all final decisions. Nelson would be under Knudsen and Hillman as head of purchasing. Other senior OPM officials would include (from NDAC) Leon Henderson for price controls and Edward Stettinius for raw materials. To reduce potential confusion about the new structure, he showed the press an organization chart BOB had prepared showing the structure of the proposed OPM.[8] As for the remaining NDAC silos, they would continue with the current commissioners. Roosevelt also said at the press conference that OPM would be within OEM. It sounded complicated. However, it represented Roosevelt's firm principle that there would not be one person as a dictator for the defense mobilization, which was what business, conservatives, and the military wanted. Such an approach implied a marginalization of the president himself. That would not do, certainly not for Roosevelt. He said it explicitly at the press conference. No "Czar or Poobah or Akhoond of Swats." A president's constitutional duty as chief executive was absolute and he could not—and would not—delegate it to anyone.

Smith was standing next to him at the press conference and the president turned to him several times when talking about EOP and OEM. He asked Smith to remind him what else was in Reorganization Plan I and the executive order operationalizing EOP. Smith said he could not recall. Then a few minutes later, FDR again turned to Smith about the reorganization and executive order:

ROOSEVELT: "Have you got it there, Harold?"

SMITH: "I haven't Mr. President."

ROOSEVELT: "Never mind, it had very broad powers." (16: 374–75)

Even though FDR was *announcing* it, he had not yet signed any paper-work. He said it would take a little time to translate his decision into an executive order. He expected to sign it after Christmas, maybe in about eight to ten days. Now for the hard part: nailing down the details while different centers of power maneuvered behind the scenes to frame the order in their favor. It became a classic tripartite power struggle. Business wanted a corporate executive with full and unfettered managerial power to run the entire defense mobilization. Labor wanted its own representative to check any moves by the business leader to degrade labor rights and subordinate labor to management. Finally, the armed services submitted a plan that would give them direct control. Over the next two weeks, there was end-less lobbying of the president and his staff about what to do. Smith was caught in the middle, having his own ideas about what "sound" organiza-tion should look like, but loyally determined to prepare the paperwork precisely as FDR wanted.

As a form of bureaucratic and political warfare, leaking started. The Washington Merry-Go-Round column reported quite accurately about the fights going on behind the scenes.[9] Smith complained to Press Secretary Early that "too much information was getting out to these reporters."[10] The Secret Service was asked to investigate and identify the leaker.[11] Prompted in part by that column, at his press conference the next day, reporters asked FDR when he would release the OPM executive order. After all, it was now past Christmas and a week after his December 20 announcement. Roosevelt said it was still "being worked on" and vaguely expected to finish "in a few days." The leaking continued. On New Year's Eve, the *Wall Street Journal* reported on its front page that business had won. The executive order would give Knudsen full power over the other three leaders FDR had listed as coequals in his press conference: labor's Hillman, and the secretaries of the two armed services.[12] Later that day, at another routine press confer-ence, reporters asked Roosevelt if the executive order would give "increased authority" to someone to handle fights over decentralization of facilities and factories. FDR replied that a policy about decentralization was inherently controversial and therefore a fair resolution was not due to anyone's *cur-rent* lack of authority. Then another leak. On New Year's Day, the *Times* reported that the latest draft completely disempowered Hillman and labor into an advisory role, with Knudsen becoming the "coordinator general of the whole defense machinery."[13] A few days after that, columnists Alsop and Kintner reported that "New Deal factions end truce with row over defense set-up."[14] Pro-labor New Dealers in the administration were horrified and pulled every string they could to get the president to reconsider. It got so bad that FDR could not even have an uninterrupted half hour to work. For New Year's Eve, he and the first lady invited some friends for dinner and then to toast the new year. One of the invitees was Sidney Sherwood, McReynolds's assistant NDAC secretary. Sherwood's mother was a friend of Roosevelt's mother and he was an ally of the more liberal first lady. After dinner, the president retired to his office to work until it was closer to midnight when he would rejoin his guests. Eleanor Roosevelt whispered to Sherwood that this was the perfect moment for him to see the president alone and to make his case (that she shared). Sherwood knocked on the door and entered. He hurriedly tried to argue against the apparent final draft of the executive order. He said, "There is a concerted effort to supersede you, your administration, and the government itself by 'big business.' Their intent is to set up a Director General of Defense whereby 'big business' can have complete control of the Defense Program and gain back what it thinks it has lost under your administration." FDR replied, "I know it. . . . Don't worry, Sidney. I haven't signed the order yet" (Lee 2018a, 33).

Smith was stuck in the middle of all this. Beginning on December 21, he had multiple meetings with his in-house reorganization team, the Justice Department, and Brownlow, all trying to divine a structure that would conform to Roosevelt's hazy idea, but also with the basic principles of good public administration (and legality). The external principals, Knudsen, Hillman, Stimson, and Knox, sent their representatives to meet with him and have input into the evolving draft(s). It seemed like a round robin of consultations without end.[15] Smith met with FDR on December 31 and showed him what he had come up with. The president went over the draft and then gave him instructions for additional changes. One of the issues was about the respective duties and powers of the OPM director general (Knudsen) versus the associate director general (Hillman). For example, FDR wanted all division heads to report to both, not just to Knudsen. That would make Hillman the de facto coequal to Knudsen or, at least, in the chain of command between Knudsen and the division chiefs and therefore unignorable.[16] On January 3, Smith showed Roosevelt another draft that precisely reflected their December 31 conversation. However, he also brought another version that he said "had the advantage of greater simplicity and the further advantage of playing down the apparent anomaly with respect to administrative organization."[17] FDR kept both versions, saying he would confer with Knudsen and Hillman. He also gave copies to the two military secretaries. Everybody was pouring over it with a fine-tooth comb.[18]

On January 6, FDR told Smith that Knudsen and Hillman were satisfied with the draft and therefore would Smith please give him the formal paperwork to sign. Smith replied that the package would entail an executive order, an administrative order, and two orders from the Council of National Defense (the statutory vestige from WWI that FDR had used to create NDAC). In that case, Roosevelt said, please clear the administrative order with the four principals.[19] For Smith, one more lap around the track. Finally done, on January 7 the documents were delivered by Smith to the White House for the president to sign and announce at a press conference that day.[20] Executive Order 8629 created the Office of Production Management (OPM) as a unit within OEM. It would be run by a director general and an associate director general, *both* direct appointees of the president, and the secretaries of the two military departments. OPM's duty would be "to the maximum extent compatible with efficiency . . . to increase, accelerate, and regulate the production and supply of materials . . . and to insure effective coordination of those activities" with the rest of the federal government. The director general was to accomplish these goals "in association with the Associate Director General." This implied that the director general could not make decisions without the approval of the associate director. OPM would have three divisions: production, purchases, and priorities. Finally, Roosevelt created within OPM a six-person Priorities Board to serve as an advisory body. Four members (including the chair) appointed by the president, plus the director general and associate director general. Its duty included taking "into account general social and economic considerations and the effect the proposed actions would have upon the civilian population." This was apparently a hint about inflation, cost controls, labor rights, and minimizing disruption to daily life (Roosevelt 1969, 1940: 689–92).

The administrative order elaborated on the powers and duties of OEM as an EOP agency. It was to "advise and assist the President in the discharge of extraordinary responsibilities imposed upon him by any emergency arising out of war, the threat of war, [or] imminence of war." It was to liaise and coordinate with other EOP agencies and the executive branch about such emergencies. Thinking ahead, Smith also included a post-emergency duty "to facilitate a restoration of normal administrative relations." To avoid ambiguity or autonomistic tendencies in the executive branch, the administrative order also explicitly stated that OEM would encompass NDAC, the Council of National Defense, and (the new) Defense Communications Board (Roosevelt 1969, 1940: 693–94). At his press conference releasing the executive and administrative orders, Roosevelt said that the four officials (Knudsen, Hill-

man, Secretary Stimson, and Secretary Knox) would make "policy" while
Knudsen and Hillman would "carry it out" as managers. He analogized the
relationship between the four and between the two as partners in a law
firm. While each partner had some discrete specializations, major decisions
could only be made by all the firm's partners together. Reporters persisted
about the status of Knudsen versus Hillman. Was Knudsen unequivocally
the "single, responsible head" of OPM? FDR parried that Knudsen and
Hillman were jointly "a single responsible head" of the new agency (Roosevelt 1972, 17: 52–62).[21] It was clear as mud. Smith had tried to smooth
out the administrative and managerial details, but the heart of the concept
was Rooseveltian, a temporizing compromise, straddling a conflict, and not
resolving it definitively or authoritatively. Still one more final detail to go.
On January 9, Smith gave Roosevelt the paperwork formally appointing the
officers of the new OPM.[22]

It turned out that this change in the organization of the nonmilitary
side of national defense was merely the opening round for a nearly never-
ending series of modifications that FDR made in the component parts of
OEM. In fact, that was the whole point. OEM was not a statutory agency
and therefore Roosevelt could tinker with it at the stroke of a pen, simply
by signing another executive order. He liked the flexibility and fluidity
that this approach to public administration had. He could do whatever he
wanted whenever he wanted. Whatever the circumstances called for—be
they organizational, personnel related, crisis related, political, or reflecting
external developments in the war. He was not handcuffed by a law passed
by Congress, necessitating going back to Congress every time he wanted
to change something. Smith was his loyal scribe and official recorder,
implementing what the president wanted, while keeping him within the
guardrails of legality and reflecting the rudimentary principles of good
public administration.

A few days later, Roosevelt signed an executive order prepared by
BOB to create within OEM an office to coordinate defense housing (for
people migrating to jobs at new defense factories). From March to May,
he signed more executive orders drafted by BOB creating more entities
within OEM, including the National Defense Mediation Board and the
Office of Price Administration and Civilian Supply. With other paperwork
that he requested from Smith, in April FDR appointed a liaison officer to
run OEM (initially McReynolds, then Wayne Coy) and gave that officer
direct control over administrative and PR services that OEM provided its
component agencies (Lee 2018a, 34–38). For Smith, FDR's desire to create

a home-guard agency in OEM was even more drawn out than the OPM experience. Smith and Coy envisioned an agency responsible for tangible and concrete civil defense duties, while FDR was hazier, particularly thinking about having it serve as a domestic morale-building agency. In that role, it would engage in public relations to promote public support for the national mobilization. In addition, Mrs. Roosevelt, Vice President Wallace, and New York mayor La Guardia (the eventual appointee[23]) all kibitzed about the constantly changing draft (Lee 2018a, 62–64, 78–79). It was the executive order from hell. FDR finally signed the order creating the Office of Civilian Defense (OCD) in May.[24] It, too, was within Coy's OEM.

Capitol Hill: FY 1942 Budget and Lend-Lease, Spring

As was now becoming routine, Smith was actively involved in preparing the president's budget message to Congress. As usual, FDR read BOB's draft carefully and made some suggestions. Smith brought him the second draft of the message on January 2, then page proofs on January 3 and 4.[25] On Tuesday, January 7, FDR, Smith, and Blandford held the embargoed annual budget seminar for the press. Smith and Blandford actively participated in it more than Smith had the previous year (Roosevelt 1972, 17: 10–48). The president sent his budget to Congress the next day. Indicating how much of a public figure Smith was becoming, a political cartoon on the front page of the *Star* showed him and FDR driving a tank titled "$17,000,000,000 Budget" and Smith saying to Roosevelt, "Say, Chief, I've got it started. But do *you* know how to stop it?"[26]

Getting a head start, the subcommittee of the House Appropriations Committee responsible for the Independent Offices bill held a public hearing on the president's request for BOB's budget on December 20, 1940. It was a detailed and extensive hearing, covering sixty-two transcript pages, with committee members grilling Smith about BOB's activities and the justification for FDR's recommendation to increase BOB's budget again for FY 1942 (US House 1940c, 724–86). The subcommittee was persuaded. In its report, it supported another expansion of BOB's budget by $200,000 for its regular duties and $200,000 for its (temporary) defense duties. These increases were necessary so that the bureau would become "a modern, up-to-date organization with personnel adequate in number and ability to meet the ever-increasing demand for careful and intelligent consideration" of departmental budget requests. This increase would fund fifty additional budget staffers, mostly in the new Fiscal Division and in the Administrative

Management Division. New funding for defense budgeting "will consist primarily of engineers trained for field inspection work. It is believed these inspectors will save many times their cost to the Government" (US House 1941a, 3). This recommendation was approved as the bill worked its way through the House floor debate, Senate Appropriations Committee, and Senate floor. Roosevelt signed it into law in April.[27]

Unlike the previous year, when he had testified on the Hill only about his own agency's budget (chap. 3), Smith was sometimes before Congress as a spokesperson for the entirety of the federal budget and, especially, funding for defense. This was a role he sought and welcomed. On January 8, he attended a closed executive session of the House subcommittee to discuss the allocations the president had made from his discretionary defense fund. Smith said he would be glad to submit reports on expended allocations at the end of each fiscal year, but not the current or projected ones. For the latter, "there were some items of a secret nature which should not be revealed at this time as a matter of public policy."[28] The subcommittee called him back on January 17 for a public session about the president's allocations of discretionary defense-related funds to the agencies funded in the annual independent offices bill up through January 1941 (US House 1940c, 843–50). Smith emphasized that the predictable defense-related spending for those agencies was included in the president's regular FY 1942 budget plan and therefore appropriators would have full foreknowledge of them and could make decisions about them. However, he stressed, "there must be some flexibility to meet unusual conditions. What emergency situations will arise during the next year no one can foretell. . . . It is my belief that the President should have a fund through which he can take steps to meet these emergencies as they arise" (US House 1940c, 844). This subject and Smith's role came up during the (quite partisan) floor debate on the Independent Offices bill. Subcommittee chair Clifton Woodrum (D-VA) referred to the closed executive session. He said Smith had explained well that most of the expenditures were "emergent," that is, were urgent and could not wait for a supplemental appropriation bill to pass Congress. Furthermore, the details of the president's allocations were "a matter about which there should have been no public debate and no public consideration whatsoever."[29]

After a two-month fight, Congress passed the Lend-Lease law and Roosevelt signed it on March 11, 1941. However, that law was an authorization to spend money, not an appropriation. He immediately asked Congress to approve $7 billion. Things were happening so fast that policy was being made on the run, if at all. Two days after signing the authorizing bill, Smith was part of a group of senior administration and military officials testifying at closed House hearings to explain the plans for spending the money. Over three days, committee members asked him very, *very* detailed questions about how the money would be spent, what the contractual provisions would include, where the contracts would physically be filed, if any funds would be spent to buy munitions in foreign countries, what the management of the program would be, and if lumber prices were indeed going up or down (!). In response, Smith often had to give general answers, such as what he presumed would happen, what a standard operating procedure would likely be, if the president had not yet given direction on the matter, and so on (US House 1941b, 9–14, 25–74). Smith was tight-lipped publicly. When a reporter from the *Times* called to ask him about it, he declined to say much.[30] In the subsequent story the next day, the reporter wrote that "so far as could be learned," Smith's testimony focused on general lend-lease policy.[31] When the bill reached the Senate, Smith again testified at a closed hearing, much of it off the record (US Senate 1941a, 38). Again indicating his rising public profile, AP moved on its national wire a photo of Smith and Knudsen in the Senate hearing room and reviewing papers before the beginning of the closed hearing.[32] The funding passed. Then, to bring some order and organization to the quickly launched Lend-Lease, Smith prepared an executive order creating the Division of Defense Aid Reports.[33]

Figure 3. Smith and William Knudsen, Director General of the Office of Production Management, preparing to testify at Senate hearing on funding Lend-Lease, March 21, 1941. Credit: Bettman Archive via Getty Images. Used under license.

General Manager of the Executive Branch

Beside budgeting, BOB was already responsible for many government-wide duties, including drafting executive orders, preparing reorganizations, statistics, mapping, legislative clearance, and administrative management reforms.[34] Important issues were nonetheless falling between the cracks and Smith proactively intervened to manage them.

Office Space

With the sharp expansion of the defense emergency in 1941, office space in DC for federal agencies was becoming increasingly tight. The Federal Works Agency (created by Reorganization Plan I in 1939) constructed and managed buildings, but it was not doing the kind of planning and coordinating that was needed now. To Smith, the Works agency seemed reactive, receiving requests for space and then either renting or building to fulfill those individual requests. What was needed, he felt, was long-term and strategic planning: build, rent, or buy? In the district, Maryland, or Virginia? Temporary structures or permanent? Moving entire departments and agencies to the heartland for the duration or keeping them in the capital? Smith stepped into this vacuum. On February 25, he convened a meeting of senior BOB officials and two from the Federal Works Agency.[35] They tried to get a big picture of what was being planned.

A few weeks later, he updated FDR on what he was learning. A freeze on civilian construction by federal agencies was in effect, as a way to make room for the costs of military and defense construction. Yet, even in those circumstances, BOB had felt it necessary to permit sixty (!) exceptions, including six to proceed to immediate construction. FDR said he had heard about a plan for eight new federal buildings in nearby Maryland. He told Smith he had not approved such a plan and wanted to be sure Smith blocked it until Smith could fully brief the president and give him a chance to make a decision about *each* one separately.[36] (This was a good example of FDR's interest in—and knowledge of—the smallest details of federal decision-making.) About a month later, Smith updated FDR, recommending approval of constructing a federal campus of permanent office buildings in Suitland (MD).[37] Separately, the Senate Appropriations Committee was considering funding six temporary buildings in Arlington (VA).[38] As happened in WWI, the idea was to build less expensive structures, colloquially called tempos, which would be razed after the defense emergency.

Knowing how valid the needs for office space were, Smith approved the funding.[39] For the next round, Smith met with FDR to talk it over. BOB proposed four more tempos with 750,000 square feet to be built within the district. Without even looking at BOB's proposed sites, FDR snatched the list and said, " 'Let me set up my priorities.' . . . The President seemed to be familiar in detail with every spot in the District that we suggested. He marked on the map his own suggestions."[40] Smith was relieved that FDR's list was (unknowingly) quite close to his own recommendations. It was a small indication they were on the same wavelength.

In mid-November, he updated the president on the latest plan for additional tempos. Earlier, Roosevelt had objected to using concrete as construction material for these structures because those buildings after the war might then be treated as relatively permanent structures. He did not want that to happen. Smith informed FDR that all tempos funded in the latest release of money would be made of wood. "I cannot guarantee that these temporary buildings will fall down in six or seven years. . . . However, I can guarantee that they will be of wood construction similar to other temporary buildings and therefore can be readily removed."[41] Roosevelt also approved sending a request to Congress to appropriate $6.5 million for building offices in the suburbs.[42] In the retrospect of history, these early conversations about the need for office space and likely sites in Arlington were the seminal moment of the eventual idea for the Pentagon. In April, the *Post* published a sketch of the War Department's "dream building"— a five-sided structure in Arlington costing $35 million.[43] As if he had nothing better to do, Smith's role meant that he was pulled into the long drawn-out fight over the precise location and size of the building.[44] These included meetings,[45] phone calls from the White House,[46] memos to the president,[47] and a memorable car ride with FDR and several other senior officials to look over the proposed Pentagon site.[48] At one point, during a meeting in the Oval Office, FDR told two top army officers, the chair of the National Capital Park and Planning Commission (his uncle, Frederic Delano), and Smith "to go into the adjoining Cabinet room and work it out among themselves."[49] His message was not to come out until they had a deal. They did.[50] Smith's extensive involvement in building the Pentagon was a good example of how he was inevitably in the middle of just about any important federal management matter.

Another way to create urgently needed office space in the capital was to decentralize the executive branch, by moving civilian agencies that were less directly involved in the emergency to other cities for the duration. Smith confirmed that BOB was considering the idea but denied the rumor that the first would be moving the Interstate Commerce Commission to Chicago.[51] Two reporters from Smith's home state of Kansas called to find out if Topeka was a potential destination for civilian agencies.[52] There was enormous resistance from civil servants who would have to move and from agency heads who felt they might then be tarred with the image of being second-class members of the federal universe. On the other hand, the costs of living and the costs of office space were usually lower than in DC and the recipient cities were delighted at the prospect. One of the few agencies that (somewhat) voluntarily agreed in midyear to the decentralization effort was the Home Owners Loan Corporation, which moved to New York City.[53] During the first week in December, a House subcommittee held hearings to give agencies a sympathetic forum to oppose being moved out of the capital.[54] BOB was called to testify at the hearings. Perhaps *it* should be moved out of Washington, jabbed unfriendly members. Smith's AA, Frederick Lawton, testified that BOB's duties "could not possibly be carried out if the offices were moved out of the District."[55] That would mean during its budget season representatives of all federal agencies would all have to travel to another city to present their budget requests. Asked point-blank by a committee member if there was "any pressure" on BOB (by whom?) to pursue decentralization, he answered, "No."[56] His appearance, probably insisted upon by the subcommittee, was partly an expression of congressional humor, of putting the shoe on the other foot and enjoying watching the powerful BOB squirm at least briefly.

One of the unintended consequences from the increases in federal agencies, buildings, and employees in the district was rush-hour traffic congestion. Smith was in charge of that, too. He and BOB staff developed a plan of staggered office hours for federal workers in DC. Smith's attention to detail included making sure there was a substantial publicity campaign on the new schedule to reach as many people as possible.[57] By the end of the year, even after the Pentagon's size and site was finalized, office space was a never-ending problem. Again, in late November, Smith felt the need to reconvene another summit meeting to plan and coordinate the next stage of a government-wide program. Conveying a sense of the complex organizational machinery involved, he invited all suppliers (the Public Buildings Administration and its parent, the Public Works Agency) and their customers from the Navy, War Department, OPM, and OEM. A dozen people in all.[58]

Civil Service

One of the government-wide issues Smith and BOB worked on was a uniform policy in the federal civil service for salaries and salary advancement. In

September 1940, Smith had submitted to the House Appropriations Committee a suggested comprehensive policy and its financial implications (US House 1940i). In 1941, the House Civil Service Committee held hearings on a bill to enact into law the policy Smith recommended. He testified that BOB's research "confirmed the impression that there had been widespread differences in the opportunities for salary advancements and inconsistencies" in departments and agencies (US House 1941c, 12). He was recommending salary policies that would be consistent horizontally (between agencies) and vertically (career paths within each agency and among people holding identical jobs). Smith addressed the obvious conflict between two competing principles of public administration. "Discretion in granting salary advancement is considered by many administrators as an essential prerequisite to the full utilization of the incentive value of promotions. Freedom of administrative discretion is the antithesis of formula; yet freedom of discretion may result in inequities in administration" (13). In this case, he favored a general formula over none at all. Once implemented, the plan would not entail permanent new costs. It might even save money with less turnover and more job satisfaction. In particular, "the emergency situation calls for the highest degree of employee morale. . . . The Government is currently losing a number of highly competent persons because of the absence of any salary advancement plan" (16).

The next day, the head of a federal employees union endorsed the bill. Usually an adversary of management and penny-pinching BOB directors, he instead "paid high tribute" to Smith's work.[59] The eventual House committee report consisted mainly of a full reproduction of Smith's testimony, which "to the committee is a fair and concise description of the bill and its purposes" (US House 1941d, 2). That was very unusual. The bill passed unanimously. Then, astonishingly, the Senate committee report recommending the bill also reproduced Smith's *House* testimony in toto "for the information of the Senate" (US Senate 1941b, 3–6). The Senate similarly passed it unanimously. The *Post's* columnist for federal employees wrote that "credit for getting the bill through so easily belongs to Budget Director Harold Smith" and the chairs of the House and Senate committees.[60] For Smith, the long and successful effort indicated that fact-based research and recommendations based on professional public administration made for good government and good politics. As usual, the passage of a law did not end a budget director's role. In this case, he met with staff to finalize a BOB circular to all agencies for implementing the salary advancement plan.[61] In November, Smith estimated that sixty thousand employees in the capital would get pay raises during the remaining months of FY 1942.[62]

Policy Coordination

Smith may have claimed he did not make policy, but whatever it was called, it nonetheless had to be coordinated whenever the situation arose. During 1941, he convened several summit meetings to hash out coordinated federal activities. Creating a comprehensive and nonduplicative approach to training for defense-related employment necessitated two meetings.[63] In May, he convened a conference to agree upon a unified list of the administration's priority legislative requests to Congress. He invited senior officials from nine defense-related agencies to attend, indicating how extensive the array of agencies involved in the topic was.[64] Even after the creation of OPM, production-related problems seemed to be a permanent topic, whether conflicts between OEM agencies, between civilian agencies and the military, or between the administration and Congress. These often spilled out into the press, sometimes with strategic leaks by the losers of a production fight, seeking to overturn the decision through negative publicity. In mid-May, Smith decided to intervene. He organized an all-day conference with the principals to hash out a consensus and stop the infighting.[65] The list of invitees indicates how many senior people were involved in the subject and Smith's unique standing to convene it and lead it. Attendees included Vice President Wallace, presidential AA Currie, an assistant secretary of state, two from NRPB, five from OPM, five from the Office of Price Administration (OPA), three from Treasury, three from USDA, three from Commerce, two from Labor, five from the Fed, and assorted others.[66] It was a big meeting if only because production was such a big topic. Even though the problems of production and priorities were ongoing ones throughout the mobilization and the war, Smith was trying to get everyone on the same page, or, at least, reading from the same book. At the very least, he wanted to keep honest disagreements about policy in-house. Keeping the subject out of the media and Congress was, in part, a political orientation. Smith wanted to prevent and protect FDR from political attacks.

Another major policy issue Smith was concerned about was inflation. The sharp increases in spending on materiel and the military were increasing employment and spendable income by the workforce. In addition, the priorities for defense production were gradually crowding out the supply of consumer goods. This was the classic formulation of inflation: too much money chasing too few goods. Working with his (relatively) new Fiscal Division, Smith understood the need for a federal fiscal policy of taxing and spending that would prevent inflation from getting out of hand. One solution was to soak up income by increasing taxes for Social Security. Another was price controls, as missioned to OPA (Lee 2018a, 104–08). Yet, effective anti-inflation policies could inevitably affect large groups with political influence, such as farmers wanting to benefit from (finally) increasing prices and unions wanting their members' wages to get ahead of inflation and catch up from the Great Depression. In July, Smith sent a comprehensive memo to FDR calling for "an integrated program of anti-inflationary measures."[67] Smith continued being concerned about the problem during the rest of the year. For example, he met with Fiscal Division staff again in August to assess the state of the economy.[68] In late September, FDR met with his senior economic advisors (including Smith) and agreed to send a modestly comprehensive anti-inflation bill to Congress. FDR was willing to support the low-hanging policy fruit that would not generate serious political opposition, but he was reluctant to take on major constituencies. FDR preternaturally did not want to fight if he could at all avoid it. He preferred to wait and see how these economic problems—or any policy problem for that matter—might unfold. The media acknowledged Smith as one of the administration's leaders most concerned about inflation. One story was headlined, "Budget Chief Urges Inflation Check."[69] That no one questioned why a *budget* director was involved in fiscal and monetary policy was an indication of how well Smith had established his broader role compared to his predecessors.

Reorganizing for an Unlimited State of Emergency, May–November

In the spring of 1941, Hitler seemed invincible and unstoppable. Taking over a botched Italian offensive in North Africa, Rommel quickly went on the offensive against the British army and succeeded in moving east toward Egypt. At the same time, Hitler took over another botched Italian invasion of Albania and Greece. Despite active resistance by Commonwealth troops in Greece, the Germans succeeded in conquering all of Greece. When Churchill ordered a last stand on Crete, they were again being defeated by an airborne attack. Supply convoys (with Lend-Lease equipment) through the north Atlantic to Britain were being sunk by German submarines almost as fast as new ships could be built. In this context, Roosevelt decided to act. He announced a fireside chat for May 27, 1941. The sense of its importance was reflected by how it was treated at public venues: major league baseball games were interrupted to let the spectators hear the speech over the public address system, streets seemed deserted, and phone traffic dropped in half.[70] The president described how Hitler's successes were coming closer and closer to threatening the US and the western hemisphere. If Germany moved south from (Spanish) Morocco, it could capture Dakar, the Azores, and the Canary Islands. From there, a bomber could reach Brazil in seven hours. Across the north Atlantic from Norway and Denmark, a conquest of Iceland and Greenland would put eastern Canada in bombing range. He could not allow any of these possibilities to happen. Therefore, Roosevelt proclaimed an unlimited state of emergency to mobilize the country to an even more activist defensive posture and preparedness.[71] (Hitler's invasion of the USSR started three and a half weeks later.)

It fell to FDR's "great reorganizer" to adapt the structure of the executive branch to handle the new near-war conditions. The day after the proclamation, FDR signed a memo that Smith had drafted appointing Ickes as Petroleum Coordinator for National Defense (Roosevelt 1969, 1941: 196–99). In rapid succession, Smith drafted executive orders creating the Committee on Fair Employment Practice,[72] Office of Scientific Research and Development,[73] Coordinator of Information (later the OSS),[74] Economic Defense Board (chaired by Vice President Wallace),[75] Coordinator of Inter-American Affairs (Nelson Rockefeller),[76] Supply Priorities and Allocations Board,[77] Office of Defense Health and Welfare Services,[78] Office of Facts and Figures,[79] Office of Lend-Lease Administration,[80] and an executive order expanding Ickes's energy role to Solid Fuel Coordinator for National Defense (Roosevelt 1969, 1941: 470–72). Other reorganization ideas were under consideration in October and November. FDR suggested merging the CCC and the National Youth Administration (NYA).[81] Smith was quickly summoned to Capitol Hill to meet with a House Appropriations Subcommittee on the budgetary implications of the merger on CCC's current operations. Some members, even conservatives, may have favored cutting government spending, but *not* for CCC camps and projects in their districts.[82] Smith was also working on a possible executive order to strengthen the consumer division of OPA and another to reorganize the defense transportation office.[83] With BOB's duty to handle all executive orders, there were also non-reorganization ones as well, including a federal takeover of an aviation plant,[84] freezing assets of several European countries,[85] and freezing Japanese and Chinese assets.[86] As usual, BOB also was in charge of reviewing bills Congress sent to the president and recommending either signing or vetoing them. For example, Roosevelt vetoed a bill on wheat marketing quotas (Roosevelt 1969, 1941: 341–43).

In 1941, Smith did not prepare any formal reorganization plans. In part, one difficulty was that Congress would have to renew the Reorganization Act of 1939 beyond its expiration in January 1941.[87] Roosevelt was in favor of that in principle but left it to Smith to lobby congressional leaders. It was a signal where it was on his priority list. The Democratic leaders Smith talked to did not have much enthusiasm to push it, either, even though they, too, were for it in principle.[88] Evidently, they preferred to let sleeping dogs lie. (Congress did not renew a president's reorganization authority subject to a legislative veto until after Truman became president.) Another likely reason for the lack of urgency was that the five plans Smith and FDR had submitted in 1939 and 1940 largely emptied the cupboard. In addition, as far as FDR was concerned, the expiration of his formal reorganization power was all right. It meant an even lesser role for Congress vis-à-vis what he wanted to do organizationally during the defense mobilization. Fewer handcuffs, more flexibility. He knew he was able to accomplish just about all structural changes with executive orders, letters (such as appointing Ickes as petroleum coordinator and William Donovan as coordinator of information), and through the emergency powers a president held when a proclamation of emergency was in effect, limited or otherwise. (After Pearl Harbor, the First War Powers Act gave Roosevelt broad reorganization powers without the requirement of a sixty-day waiting period or the possibility of a legislative veto [Emmerich 1971, 247–49].)

As in 1940, Smith continued encouraging BOB staff to get out of Washington and into the field to inspect and assess the projects that, during the budget process, they were limited to judging on paper based on agency submissions and requests. Setting an example, in June he was gone for three and a half weeks.[89] He had agreed to give an address at the University of Kansas commencement ceremonies. Smith decided to drive there and back in his car (alone) so that he could stop and inspect industrial production facilities, army camps, and navy installations. He wanted to get a tangible and in-person sense of how the organization of the arms mobilization was going. Smith drove about three thousand miles.[90] The trip was beneficial not only for personal and tangible observations, but also gave him added credibility when he spoke about the defense mobilization during the second half of the year, whether to the media, Congress, public audiences, or inside the administration. For example, at a July press conference, he referred to his trip: "I have just spent three and a half weeks visiting defense plants and I got the definite impression that we are going to have a pretty sharp step-up in production pretty soon."[91] In private, what he saw during the trip made him pessimistic about the organization of the production effort. Smith had lunch with Ickes on July 1. According to Ickes:

> He reported sentiment to be very doubtful. He said . . . that citizens do not understand the attitude of the President. They are at a loss to account for the inactivity that persists, in spite of

glowing speeches made. He is inclined to think that we have let the time go by when we could effectively move in the direction of real aid to Britain. He felt as I have been feeling about the lack of leadership by the President.

Smith usually talks frankly to me, but I have never known him to be as frank as he was on this occasion. He was critical of the defense set-up and critical of Harry Hopkins [head of Lend-Lease]. He thinks that the President is doing a very bad job of administration to some extent because he tries to do too much himself. . . . He complained that the President would issue contrary and self-contradictory memoranda on the same subject. This results in confusion and, as Smith remarked, it won't look well when the history of this Administration comes to be written.[92]

Even discounting for exaggeration by Ickes (who at the time was mad at FDR for undercutting his powers as petroleum coordinator), the account conveys Smith's professional frustration with FDR's freewheeling and ad hoc operating style. Smith preferred a more buttoned-down and well-organized policy, management, and paperwork machinery. Ickes's version also conveys Smith's view—shared by New Deal hawks in the administration, including Ickes—that FDR needed to be bolder in leading public opinion to support an even more vigorous American role in the European war. However, even if Ickes's telling is roughly accurate, it is important to see Smith's personal commitment to serving the president in whatever role the president wished. Smith felt free to provide Roosevelt with his own perspectives and advice. After that, Smith's professionalism was to implement diligently whatever the president directed him to do, even when he disagreed or was dissatisfied with the decision and direction that FDR chose at that moment. That Smith stayed on until the end of WWII is an indication that, notwithstanding his unhappiness in mid-1941, he was loyal to Roosevelt and agreed more often than not with the administration's policies and direction. After all, Smith had the option of exiting and criticizing from the outside, but never came close to choosing that possible action.

Return of the Conservative Coalition: The Byrd Committee, August–December

Throughout his presidency, Roosevelt faced a conservative coalition in Congress consisting of conservative (usually southern) Democrats and minority

Republicans. When they were unified monolithically, they often had a voting majority in both houses of Congress. Their critique of the New Deal was ideological, opposing the expansion of the role of the federal government, deficit spending, regulation of business, and the centrality of the White House over the legislative branch. One prominent example was its successful opposition in 1937–1938 to enacting recommendations of the Brownlow Committee report, such as giving a president the same powers over the CSC as he had over BOB (Lee 2016a, chap. 2). FDR's successes notwithstanding such reflexive opposition led to the coalition being somewhat muted after he won election to a third term in 1940. It was hard to stop such a powerful political steamroller that reflected such deep public and voter support.

However, the gradual rise of the importance of national defense beginning in 1939 gave the conservative coalition on Capitol Hill (and its external allies) an opportunity to rebrand itself. Now, its leaders were able to depict their earlier positions in a new light. Reframing their critique of Big Government, they now based it on the need to divert federal spending and effort to national defense. They asserted that nonessential funding for purely civilian activities were detrimental to the defense mobilization. This shrewd strategy gave new life to their now-clichéd tropes. The new context gave their arguments some political traction on Capitol Hill and with the public. The press called them "the economy bloc," a neutral term that hid their underlying political and ideological agenda.[93] One of the leaders of the conservative coalition was Senator Harry Byrd (D-VA). During the 1940 presidential campaign, he had attacked Roosevelt as bungling the defense mobilization because few *combat* planes had been delivered. In this effective political framing, Byrd was simply a concerned patriot wanting the national defense effort to be successful, rather than being seen as attacking Roosevelt for partisan or ideological reasons. FDR successfully muffled the attack (Lee 2012, 35–40). A year later, in the summer of 1941, Byrd renewed that attack line, now claiming production statistics from the administration were false and exaggerated (Lee 2018a, 111–12). Again, his point was to convince the public that the production effort was a mess and the president was to blame.

In August 1941, the Senate Finance Committee (of which Byrd was a member) was crafting a bill to increase taxes to help cover some of the increased federal defense costs. Byrd moved that the committee exercise its powers under the 1921 Budget Act to require BOB to submit a report with proposed spending cuts to achieve savings of $1 billion, $1.5 billion, or $2 billion. The motion was adopted and the chair of the committee sent the requisite letter to Smith, requesting a reply by mid-October (US Senate 1941c, 13). Then Byrd moved to amend the tax bill to create a joint House-Senate committee to recommend reductions in nonessential federal spending. The motion also required the BOB director and secretary of treasury to serve on the committee. It passed (US Senate 1941d, 22–23). The House concurred and Roosevelt signed the tax bill into law.[94] This now meant the new Joint Committee on Reduction of Nonessential Federal Expenditures was a permanent and statutory committee of Congress. Furthermore, it would not automatically expire at the end of that session of Congress as was routine for temporary and select committees. Byrd knew what he was doing. Smith talked it over with Roosevelt. Byrd's motion "had been so carefully drawn in connection with the Budget and Accounting Act that [it] requires the Budget Director to supply information upon request to the Appropriations and Finance Committees of Congress [and] that there was no way of dodging the issue." FDR said Smith should frame his report as presenting merely hypotheticals, not as recommendations by the bureau, let alone by the president. As for the level of cuts required by the committee, "the President thought such proposals ridiculous and he talked at some length about what this would mean." They both agreed "there has been very much confusion about non-defense expenditures and perhaps the submission of information to show what such cuts would mean would be a blessing in disguise in that it might afford an opportunity to educate the people . . . and put at rest some of the misinformation about the Budget." Being careful, Smith was not sure if he should even run a draft past the president before releasing it. If he did, then, if asked, he could not deny that the president had had a role in its preparation and, at least implicitly, had endorsed it. Being equally careful, Smith reported, "the President only said that he would look at the report if I wished him to do so."[95]

Even though the burden of putting together the draft of the report fell on BOB staff, Smith dedicated large amounts of his time going over it personally. It was due on October 15. He met with senior staff for one and a half hours on October 7, convened another meeting on Sunday the 12th, worked on it until 11:15 p.m. on the 13th, and until 1:00 a.m. on the 14th (technically, by now the 15th).[96] When it was almost done, he decided to brief FDR, but carefully did not show him any text, only lists of where such hypothetical cuts would have to come from. Roosevelt "discussed briefly the absurdity of such heavy cuts, pointing out the fixed charges, such as, for example, veterans' pensions" that had to be excluded from consideration.[97] In his report, Smith went to great lengths to negate any realistic consideration of the three required scenarios. He had *many* qualifications

(US Senate 1941c, 1–12). First, he was not recommending them, merely complying with a legal obligation to report to the committee. Second, the concept of "nondefense expenditures" had no precise meaning and was not used in federal budgeting as an operating concept or as a line-item category. In addition, beyond military spending or even OPM-related spending, many civilian agencies engaged in activities that supported the defense mobilization. In some cases, they straddled both categories. For example, the Coast Guard engaged in routine shore patrols (a nondefense activity), but also was operating Atlantic patrols due to the European war. TVA's power generation (a nondefense activity) was now being shifted to supply electricity to defense plants. How was he supposed to divide each baby? Third, across-the-board cuts could not be implemented, even if solely applied to those that were substantially civilian. Many were legal obligations of the government, such as pensions, construction contracts, and debt service. These would have to be precluded from any calculation. Other commitments might not be legal obligations, such as assistance to farmers or grants-in-aid. Theoretically and legally they could be cut, but realistically these were quasi-obligations as well. (Not to mention, politically untouchable.) As a result, any seemingly small percentage cut of the entire federal budget would be magnified enormously for the few spending categories that were, relatively clearly, nondefense. In particular, the cuts would disproportionately affect "social and economic programs" (precisely what the conservative coalition wanted to do). Fourth, as of October 1941, the president and BOB were putting the finishing touches on the president's FY 1943 budget plan, to be submitted to Congress two and a half months hence. This was a thousand-page report that took about four months to prepare. It was simply too late to insert these kinds of cuts into the FY 1943 budget plan, even if they wanted to. In addition, the rising importance of defense expenditures and the need to cut back on what could be deferred (such as public works and park maintenance) were already baked into the president's budget proposal. Fifth, even in a defense emergency, the normal functioning of the government, such as law enforcement, must continue. It would "be an utter waste to wreck the machinery for law enforcement now only to rebuild it later." Finally, BOB always was looking for ways to make the federal government more efficient, such as the work of the Division of Administrative Management. Whether they were defense or nondefense functions, BOB was already implementing spending cuts wherever it could identify them.

With FDR's support, Smith wanted to utilize the report to educate the public about how and where the federal government spent nonmilitary money. To achieve that, he wanted to release it with a splash and maximize press coverage.[98] Being careful about congressional etiquette, he called the chair of the Senate Finance Committee, Walter George (D-GA), to consult with him about releasing it to the press. Perhaps do it jointly?[99] Apparently, George wanted the publicity and insisted the release of the report should come from the committee.[100] However, he consented to release it on Saturday to maximize coverage in the Sunday papers. Smith then assiduously promoted coverage of the report by, for example, briefing AP's Perlmeter about it on an embargoed basis. Perlmeter wrote his story in advance and AP moved immediately upon the release at noon on Saturday.[101] This gave afternoon papers a chance to publish it that day and beat out the Sunday issue of their local competitors.[102] The subsequent coverage was extensive. Besides many papers running the AP story,[103] some had stories written by their capital reporters including a front-page story in the *Post*, an extensive story and chart in the *Times*, and the *Baltimore Sun*.[104] On Monday, the *Herald Tribune* editorialized in favor of using Smith's report as a basis for cutting spending.[105] In addition, the next issue of *Time* magazine covered it with a decidedly sympathetic slant to Smith's viewpoint, noting the impracticality of what the economy bloc wanted to do. It stated, "Most of the saving would have to come from subsidies to farmers, youth and relief. Congressmen would as soon vote against these projects as they would vote against home and mother, the Stars & Stripes, or the Ten Commandments."[106]

A few weeks after submitting his report to the Finance Committee, the joint committee created by the tax law convened for the first time. Members elected Byrd as chair. He promptly said that the BOB report was too general.[107] However, Smith was boxed in because he was a member of the committee *by law*. He could not even resign from it. Skipping meetings was not much of an option, because Byrd did not convene the committee for any public hearings. Those would be easy to miss because no committee action would occur. Rather, all the meetings in these early months were executive sessions, when decisions might be made and votes held. Smith told FDR he wanted the president's advice about how to handle this uncomfortable position.[108] Smith reluctantly attended many of these long sessions, a waste of time for him. For example, he attended two half-day meetings in November and several more in December.[109] At the request of the chair, for the November 28 hearing, he brought with him the two BOB examiners who specialized in budget estimates for the CCC and NYA (two popular targets for conservative criticism). They were there to answer highly detailed factual questions from committee members, but not make any recommendations (US Congress 1941a). There was another problem Smith had with the committee: Morgenthau, the other statutory member, supported cutting nonessential spending as a way to minimize the amount needed for tax increases. This put Smith, again, at odds with Morgenthau, a fiscal conservative who liked balanced budgets and disagreed with the premise of Keynesian economics. FDR was comfortable with conflict and would not order Morgenthau to toe the line. The treasury secretary, always loyal to FDR, felt that to have credibility on the Hill when he pushed for a tax increase, he had to be proactive in calling for cuts in nonessential spending, too. He was just doing his job. That meant the two statutory members of the joint committee from the executive branch, ostensibly from the same team, were working at cross-purposes. As they often were, Morgenthau and Smith were adversaries and each disliked the activities, views, and behaviors of the other.

When the committee filed its first report in December (a few weeks after Pearl Harbor), Morgenthau happily endorsed most of its recommendations, declining to support only a few of them. Smith disagreed with the whole report. He said he could not support any recommendation that contradicted the president's upcoming FY 1943 budget, scheduled for submittal to Congress in a few weeks. "I obviously cannot join in a report which may contain recommendations at variance therewith," he said (US Congress 1941b, 9).[110] For him, serving on the committee was a conflict of interest as well as contravening the constitutional separation of powers between the legislative and executive branches. Based on this critique, Smith gradually distanced himself from the committee and then routinely absented himself from its hearings and executive sessions. (Later, during the war, the committee's work became increasingly and pointedly anti-FDR [chaps. 5–6; Lee 2005, 123–28; 2018a, 173–74].)

Spokesperson for the Administration

Smith had had a very modest public profile in 1940, limiting himself to three speeches on budgetary matters and only occasionally agreeing to be quoted in press coverage (chap. 3). He significantly changed his behavior in 1941. In July, he quietly hired Howard R. Marsh, a writer/editor, to be BOB's de facto PR officer.[111] At the hearing on BOB's FY 1942 budget, he opaquely mentioned that the new Fiscal Division sought to find a way to report on government finances "in a manner which can be understood by the layman as well as the accountant" (US House 1940c, 730).[112] His list of staffing of the division included an "associate editor" at $2,900 a year (734). This was evidently a reference to Marsh.[113] Hiring Marsh meant Smith gradually recognized the importance of public relations as an element of governance. Given the media hothouse in the capital, Smith was intuiting that doing good works was not enough; they needed to be *known*. Furthermore, given the political amnesia that was so common on the Hill and enabled by the media,[114] it was not enough to say something once; Smith would need to find a way to reiterate the same message regularly. If the conservative coalition was repeatedly criticizing FDR's federal spending (and getting ongoing media coverage for those claims), then Smith and BOB needed to reciprocate by making the case publicly in favor of Roosevelt's budgets just as frequently. Once was not enough. Smith understood that PR in public administration comprised more than just required and mandatory activities, such as public reporting, annual reports, and the like. Rather, publicity was a powerful tool in the political marketplace, particularly if he could frame an issue before the conservative coalition did. For example, proactively announcing savings in nondefense spending was advantageous tactically compared to replying to (yet another) generic attack on wasteful spending.

The differences in Smith's public communications between 1940 and 1941 were stark in volume as well as subject matter. Perhaps he was simply more comfortable in his job and his relationship with FDR. However, it is also likely that, apart from his evolving activist PR strategy, he was alarmed about world developments and wanted to help mobilize public opinion to support the defense mobilization. Implicitly, this orientation would also have the indirect effect of promoting political support for FDR. During the year, Smith gave three major speeches (one that was broadcast nationally), participated in an educational roundtable on national radio, published several articles, held a few press conferences, released multiple statements to the media, and sometimes agreed to be quoted in newspaper stories when reporters called him. These are presented here chronologically, to convey a sense of how unfolding international developments likely contributed to his increasing public communications role.

His first major address was in late January to a public administration conference at the University of Alabama. Convened by Professor Roscoe Martin of the university's Bureau of Public Administration, its theme was to help southern budget directors and their staffs assess financial trends and potential impacts on their work due to the defense mobilization. It was, in the retrospect of the new profession of public administration, an all-star cast, including Rowland Egger, Albert Lepawsky, and James Martin. One of the reasons Smith accepted was that he was eager to reach his state counterparts in the South.[115] In part this was because he wanted to amplify a general message to state and local governments urging them to defer capital projects during the emergency and, counterintuitively, not pay off their debts with their surpluses (because that would put more money into circulation and be inflationary). He also felt that, due to history, southern governments routinely held the federal government at arm's length and therefore might need more convincing to engage in such voluntary cooperation. He began with the parochial topic of federal budgeting and confessed that the spending for defense was at levels "which stagger the mind" (Smith 1941b, 91). From there he segued to his message to state and local governments that "it is essential to postpone all those government expenditures which might compete directly with defense production for labor, material, or productive facilities" (92). But, mostly, he wanted to advocate for the broader issue of federal spending. Responding to conservative criticism, he said that Roosevelt was determined "not to impair the efficiency of the general administration by excessive cuts. He also insists on the continuation of social services which he regards as essential for a workable democracy" (93). He defended deficit spending by arguing against the facile criticism of FDR's increase in the national debt. Smith emphasized that government deficits are "comparable neither to the family budgets nor to corporate accounts" (96). He said, "Those who speak of our fiscal policy as leading to national bankruptcy are talking sheer nonsense" (100). The speech attracted little public attention.[116] Senator Lister Hill (D-AL) had it reprinted in the *Congressional Record*.[117] That hinted some degree of agreement with it, but, carefully, he did not say why he wanted to insert it for publication. Syndicated columnist and *Newsweek* reporter Lindley wrote that Smith's speech was "the most sensible discussion of Federal finances I have read recently." He regretted it was "a little-published speech" because it deserved more attention from the capital press corps and opinion leaders.[118]

In response to a request from the Municipal Finance Officers Association, Smith wrote an article for the February issue of its monthly on "A day in the federal Bureau of the Budget" (1941c). He had asked all BOB staff to submit reports on what they did on September 19, 1940. He summarized that they were involved in 870 different topics, ranging from budget preparation and execution to legislation, assistance to administrators, coordination of statistics, and information services. He emphasized that budgeting was a year-round activity and that BOB was involved in all manner of nonfinancial matters. (Also, early that year, *PAR* published his 1940 ASPA/APSA conference paper, discussed in chap. 3 [Smith 1941a].) In spring 1941, reporters seemed to be paying more attention to Smith. *Time* magazine noted his work on setting up a home defense agency.[119] A few months later, it identified him as one of two officials who recently "have risen to power in Washington" (the other was Wayne Coy). The article described him as "an unusually able administrator. Pallid, with a pale mustache, short and chunky in build, he is talkative, friendly, and regards himself as a policy-carrier-out, rather than a policy maker."[120] The *Wall Street Journal* flagged for its readers the rise of BOB. "Almost unnoticed, both in and out of Washington, the bureau of the budget has suddenly blossomed forth as one of the most powerful agencies of the federal government." Director Smith "sees the Chief Executive probably more than anyone outside of his immediate family." Though a New Dealer and "a quiet, soft-spoken man of even temperament, he is no wild-eyed reformer and has [a] background of practical experience in government."[121] Similarly, Blair Moody, the Washington reporter for the *Detroit News*, wrote a profile of Smith as representing a new era in FDR's presidency, a professional interested in efficiency and management, rather than a politician interested in patronage. He said Smith sat at "the nerve center of the New Deal" and focused on "a scientific study of how to give the taxpayers their money's worth."[122]

In midyear, Smith was more proactive about media relations. He wanted to convey messages about financial policy that reported on administration activities and promoted civic support for its economic mobilization. In May, he released a statement to AP on the need for intergovernmental financial cooperation during the defense emergency. Elaborating on some of the themes from his Alabama speech, he called on state and local governments to reduce borrowing, cut public works projects, finance any necessary construction projects with cash, and expend budgetary surpluses by buying federal securities.[123] Demonstrating his commitment to the concept of public reporting in public administration, as well as explaining FDR's fiscal policies, in late May Smith released an updated report on changes in the FY 1942 budget since the president's budget plan had been submitted in January. (The beginning of the fiscal year was still a month away.) He estimated a $4.6 billion increase in spending, bringing it to $22 billion in total, and a new estimate of the deficit for the year of $12.7 billion. Smith released the report on a Saturday, guaranteeing some coverage in the big Sunday papers. Notwithstanding the eye-glazing nature of budget numbers, the story got relatively widespread coverage, sometimes even on the front page, indicating its importance.[124] About a month later, Smith held a press conference, again on a Saturday for the Sunday papers, and permitted direct quotes. He announced that federal spending on military and materiel would soon be at a billion dollars a month, a truly startling level.[125] His purpose may have been defensive, to preempt attacks on the administration. He conceded that industry's ability to accept and perform production contracts was currently less than what the government had available to spend. However, he expected that by fall, production capacity would have increased to match spending. He also sought to knock down the political attack that the federal government was still spending too much on nonessential civilian projects, as charged by Byrd and others in the conservative coalition. Smith said that nearly all civilian agencies were now tilting toward assisting the defense program in one way or another. He also said that based on budget classification categories it was not possible to identify supposedly large amounts of inessential spending. Furthermore, he emphasized, modern warfare now consisted of more than just military and armaments. Rather, it was a broad array of economic, industrial, agricultural, and financial activities, all contributing to a national mobilization. His press conference garnered extensive play.[126]

The University of Kansas, Smith's alma mater, invited him to speak at its commencement ceremonies in early June in Lawrence. It was the university's seventy-fifth anniversary, and it wanted the event to be a major celebration of its jubilee. His speech was set to be broadcast live on a national radio network on Sunday, June 8.[127] Smith titled it "Democracy on Trial," indicating that he was not planning to talk about dry budgeting minutia to an audience of professionals and specialists. Rather, he wanted to put his federal work in the context of international developments and for the message to be readily understandable to a national lay audience. Smith's theme was that isolationism was a threat to America's national fate. He surveyed the military and economic policies of totalitarianism and said that they posed a threat to the US—not in the abstract, but now. For example, Nazi economics focused on self-sufficiency and was antithetical to free trade. (The economic term for this was *autarky*.) That meant so many traditional markets for American exporters were already closed off to them because of German conquest and control. This, in turn, degraded the health of the national economy. He also said that totalitarian economics was *already* harming the US and the western hemisphere. Smith claimed that the free market could not compete with "ruinous competition in this hemisphere—where the Nazis are already underbidding us, through the use of enslaved European labor" (Smith 1941d, 6). He also described how Nazis used propaganda as "part of the machinery of deception." In Europe, Germany had repeatedly claimed it wanted peace, until it launched invasions. In a thinly veiled reference to American isolationists, he said the US should not fall for that. Furthermore, the traditional American sense of physical safety with oceans separating it from Europe and Asia was no longer a guarantee of peace. He reminded the audience that the freedom of the high seas, especially the Atlantic, was hanging by a thin thread. It was only Britain's continued resistance to Germany that prevented the Atlantic Ocean from being controlled by totalitarian navies. If the UK were to lose the "Battle of the Atlantic,"[128] then the US Navy would face "a hostile naval building capacity exceeding our own by six or eight times" (4).

Smith then pivoted to discuss how America could handle these threats. "One of the fallacies of isolationism is the proposition that by defending democracy we shall lose it" (9) due to the needs of total war. But "democracy is not that feeble." Furthermore, some of America's strengths were "our organizing ability, and our administrative capacity" (8). That was as close as he got to reference his budget role and his belief in professional public administration. In his peroration, Smith said, "We must awaken to a full appreciation of the meaning of democracy to us. Only then shall we magnify its strength. We must be alert to the danger of the moment. We must support those nations which are fighting for democracy. We must reinforce our economic defense. We must be ready to make sacrifices. We must see that Hitler's inside job makes no headway" (9–10). Several of the Sunday newspapers highlighted the upcoming speech in their listings of radio programs.[129] That probably increased his national audience. There was minor post-speech press coverage outside of Kansas.[130] The day after the speech, Kansas's governor held a luncheon in Smith's honor in the state house in Topeka and invited about twenty-five state leaders in business and the professions to attend. To that audience, Smith spoke more concretely about fiscal policy. He emphasized that fears of the implications of deficit spending on armaments was, so far, not coming true. Interest rates and inflation were relatively low, making him optimistic about the near future. In addition, compared to WWI, government statistics and financial accounting were much improved, giving the federal government credible and comprehensive information for its policymaking.[131] (After the luncheon, he drove to see the farm where he was born and grew up.[132] He had not been there since moving to Michigan in late 1927.)

Smith continued advocating publicly for the administration's interconnected economic and defense policies. He flew to Chicago to participate in a live national radio broadcast on Sunday, August 3, from the radio studio of the University of Chicago. Its educational radio director, Sherman Dryer, organized a weekly round table discussion on important subjects in public affairs.[133] The goal was to promote nonpartisan conversations to enlighten public opinion. It advertised itself as the "oldest educational program continually on the air, [and] is broadcast entirely without a script" (Smith 1941e, 1). The subject was "Defense: Who'll Pay the Piper?" The other two participants were affiliated with the university: Albert Lepawsky, a lecturer in political science (and executive director of the Federation of Tax Administrators) and Henri-Simon Bloch, a German émigré and economics lecturer. Both seemed to lean to more traditional business economics and were skeptical of the fiscal policies of the administration. That put the burden on Smith to explain and defend FDR's taxing and spending policies. Lepawsky led off by quoting the statistic that the federal government was spending $19,375 *a minute* on defense. Smith swatted away that kind of alarming headline number: "I am not certain that it is very important to know how much we are spending every minute" (3). Rather, he wanted to focus on macro-economic principles. At every turn in the conversation, he tried to bring the discussion back from scary scenarios to firm policy approaches. When the two cited the huge size of current spending authorizations and appropriations, he turned to a more tangible number, actual expenditures (4–5). Similarly, when they talked about unmanageable spending and debt, he talked about what proportion of the national income (a standard economic concept) the US was spending or planning to spend, compared to the UK (6). He also emphasized how much the US national income had risen since the depression, making comparisons about federal deficit spending then and now as largely out of context and immaterial. He pointed out the most recent increases in national income, from about $76 trillion in 1940 to about $90 trillion in 1941. That brought perspective to claims the US was going broke. In general, he sounded like a self-assured and professional macro-economist, more comfortable with Keynesian economic policy than the two PhDs he was debating.

When discussing tamping down inflation and consumption by increasing taxes, Lepawsky tried to bait him by repeating the mantra that the federal policy was "to impoverish the taxpayer so he cannot spend the money." Smith retorted, "Certainly not! I wouldn't put it in that light" (16). As for the current rate of inflation, he said it had increased 5.5 percent since the beginning of the large defense spending. "Now, in and of itself, that is not a very dangerous situation. As a matter of fact, speaking quite broadly, the whole situation, as of the moment, is about what it was in 1937" (19). At the end of the program, looking to the future after the end of the defense emergency, he tried to deflate the exaggerated concerns coming from business economists (who were largely conservative politically) about a postwar depression and high unemployment. Smith sought to focus on fundamental and modern federal macroeconomic policymaking:

> I don't want to bring it down to what *we* are concerned about but rather I think to the great many things the government is doing to institute controls at this time that will level off some of our fiscal problems. After all, we don't want to dip into another depression. I think sometimes you economists have been so interested and so in love with business-cycle studies that you might be disturbed if somehow or other a combination of governmental activity and business enterprise tended to smooth out some of these fiscal difficulties so that we'll scoot into a post-defense period without the fears and without the dislocations. (20, emphasis in original)

(Smith stayed an extra day in Chicago to meet with Brownlow and work with PACH staffers on ASPA business.[134])

In anticipation of the beginning of BOB's high season in the fall to prepare the FY 1943 budget, Smith engaged in publicity about the outlines of the likely budget. He had routinely done this for the FY 1941 and 1942 budgets, but now seemed to feel that greater public attention needed to occur. This might help soften the impact of what inevitably would be another even-more staggering budget in terms of spending and deficits. Perhaps he wanted to prepare public opinion so that the eventual plan released in January would not be such a shock. He spoke to AP's Perlmeter in mid-September, who quickly moved a story that "Harold D. Smith, budget director, today began the preparation of a record-breaking budget for the next fiscal year and it may cost the Treasury $32,000,000,000."[135] A few weeks later, just after the end of the first quarter of the fiscal year, Smith held another news conference—again on a Saturday—to release revised estimates for defense spending during FY 1942.[136] He now estimated that defense spending would be $18 billion for the year and that the rate of spending would reach $2 billion a month by spring. It was a gasp-inducing number. Justifiably, it was front-page news around the country in the Sunday papers.[137] Smith last major public address in 1941 was to the American Municipal Association's annual conference in Chicago in late October. Here he felt at home, having first attended its meetings in 1924 as a staffer at the League of Kentucky Municipalities and then as head of the Michigan Municipal League. Also, he had been AMA's president in 1934–1935. Smith called for cities to adopt financial policies that would be in harmony with the defense mobilization. As he had suggested in his January talk to state budget officials, Smith called on municipal governments to minimize capital spending, tax to create surpluses, and invest them in Treasury instruments. Those actions, he said, would greatly help in maximizing defense construction and production, reduce inflationary pressures, and help finance the defense effort. He also talked about the need to plan for the post-defense era to minimize economic dislocation, create jobs, and catch up on construction and other capital projects (Smith 1941f). The media paid little attention to it, with a bylined story in the *Christian Science Monitor*, brief coverage in the *Wall Street Journal*, and a story that AP moved on its national wire.[138]

A few weeks before Pearl Harbor, Smith experienced some media coverage that provided a lesson in public relations. AP's Perlmeter was always on the hunt for stories, but not necessarily the kind of eye-glazing budget reports Smith liked to issue. Rather, Perlmeter welcomed tips about smaller matters that might pique the interest of the public at large. Human-interest stories often garnered more coverage and, likely, more readership than the typical Washington fare. In mid-November, Smith told AP that to protect limited supplies of metal, he had directed the War Department to cease using bronze markers on graves. Bronze needed to be hoarded for military production purposes. This small change in policy would divert six and a half additional tons of bronze to armament factories. AP moved the story and it was a big hit, in the sense that so many newspapers ran it.[139] For Smith, this minor budgetary story successfully conveyed the seriousness of metal supplies for production. It also conveyed how conscientiously BOB was scouring federal agency budgets for savings and defense needs. For readers, it was about a tangible subject that was understandable in their context and not as abstract as reports on billions of dollars. This minor event contributed to Smith's steep learning curve about media relations. Smaller bite-sized subjects got more coverage and could serve as a synecdoche for larger and more important matters. In all, during 1941, Smith had moved a long way from his earlier professional standards. When he started at BOB, he depicted budgeting as a nonpartisan profession, that public administration could and did separate itself from politics and policy, and that he was not part of policymaking in the White House. Now, he most definitely was *not* modeling that ethos. Quite the opposite. Despite being president of the American Society for Public Administration and a strong advocate for its professional standards, he became an all-out public advocate for the policies of the *political* administration he was a member of.

A Political Celebrity, Like It or Not

When Smith gave public talks, spoke on the radio, issued press releases, and held news conferences, he was proactively seeking positive news coverage for the administration's policies or reacting to negative coverage. During 1941, he also began receiving a different kind of coverage. This reflected his emergence as a public figure who was of interest to journalists and was unrelated to any specific news. This could be called passive media relations. It came in the form of softer features, profiles, and assessments of his importance. He was becoming a celebrity, whether he wanted to or not. The first coverage of that sort, and which set off a long set of echoes, was a feature profile written by AP. Most of it was relatively routine, describing Smith's quiet importance, his discretion, and professional background. It also had a few personal details about him, such as his hobby of building wood furniture in his basement and helping his eleven-year-old son Lawrence build a boat. The startling disclosure was that this man who was in charge of spending $17 billion was not the family's budgeteer. Mrs. Smith was. She managed the family budget, paid bills, and wrote checks. He claimed "he couldn't remember signing one for years." Now *that* was irresistible as a human-interest story. Too cute! The headline said it all: "Smith's Boss of U.S. Budget, but Wife Is Banker at Home."[140] This seemingly fascinating tidbit was repeated many times thereafter. It became a long-running trope and staple of media coverage of Smith. Even if unintended, it was brilliant PR because it humanized him and made his relatively inside-baseball job more tangible and interesting to readers. Reporters could not resist using it. It was practically like journalistic catnip. It was an anecdote that wouldn't die.[141] The downside of this meme was that it reinforced the analogy Smith strongly disliked and conservatives loved: that government budgeting was like family budgeting. Families could only spend what they had. They could not engage in deficit spending. Therefore, the federal government should tighten its belt, cut spending, and balance its budget just like a typical American family.

More soft profiles followed during the year. Inga Arvad wrote a daily profile in the *Washington Times-Herald* titled "Did You Happen to See?"

Smith agreed to a thirty-minute interview.[142] Her September profile said he was "quiet, amiable," and "leans back leisurely in his armchair and puffs one of his eternal big, fat, cigars." An interesting observation from him was that "he knows how to give the right answers to the wrong questions. 'I sit here and hold people's hands,' smiles Harold Smith. 'Sometimes I wish somebody would hold mine. Not that this isn't an interesting job, but anyone gets discouraged now and then.' "[143] It was a mild hint of the difficult job of being FDR's budgeteer. *Woman's Home Companion* included Smith as one of the most important men in Washington. He was "the least known and possibly the most influential" figure in the administration, particularly because he "was a scientist rather than a politician."[144] Some of the syndicated political columnists highlighted Smith, too. Alsop and Kintner wrote that Smith's "opinions are more and more weighty in White House councils."[145] Lindley said Smith "has gradually become one of the most powerful men in the Administration."[146] A columnist for *Barron's*, a pro-business weekly that routinely criticized the New Deal, identified Smith as a refreshing break from those ideologues and big-government types. Smith was "a professional 'good government' man" who "became the President's 'business manager.' " In particular, the piece praised Smith on economic policymaking because of his "aggressive leadership in pulling Administration economists together, giving their work cohesion and direction."[147] There was another problem with this kind of media coverage: photographs of Smith. It was relatively routine for feature writers to arrange for a photographer to take pictures. The problem was that budgeting did not lend itself to an action-style photo. Inevitably, the pictures were little more than portraits of Smith at his desk. In one case, the solution was for Smith to walk over to the White House and show him meeting with the president's appointments secretary, Pa Watson.[148] At least that was better than Smith at his desk. Another time, the photographer wanted an "action picture." The best that they could come up with was of Smith "pouring over the Budget."[149] Perhaps the marker that confirmed Smith's rising status as a celebrity occurred in midyear. The *Key West (FL) Citizen* regularly printed on its editorial page a syndicated feature called "Today's Birthdays." On June 6, the first listing for that day was "Harold D. Smith, Director of the Federal Budget, born at Haven, Kansas, 43 years ago."[150]

Fighting with Morgenthau, March–November

In the skirmishing around the Byrd Committee, Smith and Morgenthau had clashed publicly. Morgenthau considered himself a kind of super-secretary, more than just a routine chief financial officer (CFO) of the federal government. He viewed his portfolio as covering *anything* dealing with money, which was just about everything the executive branch did. In addition, as a fiscal conservative, he preternaturally disliked deficit spending. When large additional increases in defense expenditures kept occurring in 1941 (including Lend-Lease), he proactively urged Congress to cut nonessential spending. Smith quietly fumed. So did Morgenthau, who was still unhappy about Roosevelt's 1939 decision to remove BOB from Treasury and place it in the new EOP. It will be recalled that near the end of the preparation of the FY 1942 budget in December 1939, Morgenthau repeatedly refused to increase Treasury's projection of revenues for the year, which would have reduced the estimated deficit (chap. 2).

The rivalry and personal dislike for each other increased in 1941. But it was much more than that. They were fighting for primacy over fiscal policy, such as taxing versus deficit spending, and influence with the president. In March, Smith lightly complained to FDR about Morgenthau's self-definition of his empire. Morgenthau had told Smith that the president wanted Morgenthau to attend all Oval Office meetings dealing with preparing requests for supplemental and deficiency appropriations. If that were accurate, it would significantly reduce Smith's sense of his exclusive responsibilities and give Morgenthau much more power and influence. Roosevelt smoothly replied "that there had probably been some misunderstanding." Rather, that FDR had "merely suggested" that BOB make sure to have an "exchange of information" with Treasury regarding fiscal matters. Smith tartly replied that he routinely sought "methods of informing" Morgenthau about such issues, mostly about any impacts on federal expenditures.[151] Smith was expressing himself carefully. Informing someone is one-way communication after the fact. That was the opposite of consulting, conferring, or other methods of joint decision-making. Their mutual antagonism came to a head over the next few weeks. At a meeting of senior departmental staff, Morgenthau let loose about Smith. Referring to his own initiative to cut nondefense spending:

> Morgenthau: I am so licked on this thing. I asked you for this over a month ago, and the Budget didn't give it to me. . . . I am going to say, "The Bureau of the Budget wouldn't give me the information which I have been asking for for over a month." . . .
>
> . . . I have to go to the enemy. . . . I am ready to say publicly that the Bureau of the Budget, I just can't get anything out of them, and you can tell that to Harold Smith, too. If you think I am going to sit here and let Harold Smith give me a

sit-down strike—and I have been begging for this information. And when you give it to the President, he grabs it. He is tickled to death to get it. He is tickled to death. Harold Smith is so busy building up his personal machine that he hasn't got time to do what he is hired for. He is all the time trying to grab new power. . . . He is constantly trying to build up his own personal machine.[152]

At the same time, Smith was drafting a memo to FDR complaining about Morgenthau:

I cannot let the statement of the Secretary of the Treasury, that a billion dollars can be cut from the Budget, pass without some comment. . . . Nothing but harm and confusion can result from the statement, in my judgment. If the pronouncement had come from the United States Chamber of Commerce or the National Economy League, it would have been in character, but to come from a Cabinet member of this Administration, particularly when he is not familiar with the detailed subject matter, arouses my concern, to say the least. The implication, it seems to me, is clear—the President and his Budget Director did a very poor job of budget-making, if the Budget could have been cut by one billion dollars.[153]

He never sent it.[154]

They had a showdown in Morgenthau's office on May 13. Bell was the only other person in the room and afterward wrote a summary of the conversation. Each said their piece to the other, essentially repeating their earlier positions. Neither would yield. Their only consensus was to blame the heads of other agencies being targeted for cuts, especially WPA's commissioner, for making things worse with their public statements.[155] They then moved on to Morgenthau's complaint to Smith that a proposed executive order Morgenthau had submitted. It would create a Capital Funds Control Committee (not incidentally giving Treasury new leverage over other departments). Why hadn't it been signed yet? Smith replied that the subject might be related to another executive order he was working on: economic warfare. Morgenthau and Bell said they were unrelated. Smith did not see it that way. Another stalemate. At the end of the meeting, Morgenthau said he appreciated the frank talk and suggested they meet once a week to keep talking about Treasury-BOB matters. Bell did not record any reply from Smith.[156]

They met again the next week. Morgenthau asked to be updated on the executive order he had requested. Smith said he had not yet had a chance to talk it over with the president because he was busy drafting the OCD executive order. Now, he "might be able to give some thought to that whole subject." He mentioned that Commerce Secretary Jesse Jones was also interested in some controls over imports and Smith "thought the two might have to be studied together." This could hardly have pleased Morgenthau who thought everything financial was his exclusive domain. Again, no yielding by either side, though Smith held the upper hand with his control over all executive orders. In the meantime, there had been conflicting public statements by the two if the Lend-Lease funds would cover British contracts for arms that had been signed before the Lend-Lease law. Smith had testified to Congress that they would and Morgenthau said they would not. Their only agreement was to let Bell try to figure out a way out of the problem. Smith then raised another issue, relating to Treasury's too conservative estimates of revenues for the president's FY 1943 budget plan versus BOB's. Bell suggested finessing the problems by placing the difference into some pending supplemental appropriations bills that technically were not part of the FY 1943 budget, but rather were late additions to the FY 1942 budget. "The Secretary said that might be a way out." Again, Bell was directed to implement the solution. It was hardly a compromise.[157]

These two summit meetings resolved nothing, especially the mutual antipathy that each felt for the other. At a staff meeting in October, Morgenthau again criticized Smith. "One of these days I am going to come out publicly and say something about Harold Smith. I would love to say something about his report to Congress [Byrd Committee] on economy. Of all the weak-kneed dishwater I ever read in my life, his report on that thing was the most supine, intellectually dishonest thing I have read in a long time. . . . My God, it turned my stomach. . . . I am just sick and tired of having that man shoot at us all the time, and you know every time you call him he apologizes or blames somebody else."[158] Smith felt the same, complaining over lunch with Ickes. "Smith doesn't get along any too well with Morgenthau. . . . Smith complained that Morgenthau by indiscreet statements and interviews on occasion balled up the fiscal policies of the administration pretty completely. He doesn't think that Morgenthau particularly qualifies for the job."[159] But they had to somehow get along.

Each could not avoid working with the other. For example, in the midst of all these arguments, Smith, as ASPA president (along with Luther Gulick, ASPA's vice president), came to Morgenthau's office to invite him to address the annual ASPA conference in December. Morgenthau accepted, with the condition that it would be broadcast live on the radio.[160]

Preparing the FY 1943 Budget, October–December 6

In late 1941, Smith followed the pattern he had set the previous year. He was gradually reducing his direct participation in preparing BOB's recommendations for the president's budget plan. His first major interaction was on October 6, when he attended BOB's hearing on the Post Office Department budget, including with Postmaster General Frank Walker.[161] A month later, Smith attended the Navy Department's hearing, including a presentation by Secretary Knox.[162] Apparently, he did not attend any others. The next stage in the process was for in-house boards of review to examine tentative budget recommendations from the staff of the Estimates Division. In November, Smith participated in several boards of review, including USDA and FSA, but evidently not all of them.[163]

Then it was time to bring BOB's recommendations to Roosevelt for his final decisions (except the Post Office, which FDR delegated completely to BOB, as he had done the previous year). Beginning in mid-November, FDR approved without change the estimates for the civil functions of the War Department and the Panama Canal government. He rejected any increases in the Smithsonian Institution's budget and directed Smith to cut the budget of the American Battle Monuments Commission "to a minimum in light of conditions abroad."[164] At later meetings, FDR approved without change the bureau's estimates for Justice, Commerce, and Federal Power Commission while making changes in the estimates for USDA, State, Labor, VA, and the Federal Works Agency.[165] On Saturday, December 6, the president's only meeting of the day was with Smith and Blandford.[166] In the hindsight of history, it displayed his composure and focus on work notwithstanding the tense international situation. Earlier that day he had sent a personal appeal to the Japanese emperor to urge peaceful resolution of the problems between the two countries. During the meeting, he accepted a phone call from Navy Secretary Knox. Knox told him "of large Japanese convoys and ship movements of their Navy." When he hung up, he shared the news with Smith and Blandford and then said, "we might be at war with Japan, although no one knew."[167] Nonetheless, without any pause, he then turned back to the business at hand and concentrated on it.

Roosevelt approved without change the FY 1943 estimates for Interior and the Home Loan agency and made one modification to the Navy estimate. He reduced the size of the Marine Corps by six thousand men because the Navy was in the midst of changing guard duties at naval installations from Marines to a new civilian guard service. The rest of the meeting was about routine business. Regarding the future of CCC and NYA, he said he liked Congressman Lyndon Johnson's proposal to merge them through an authorization bill (hence giving the merged agency statutory status). He asked that Smith follow up with Johnson and report back on Monday (December 8). Based on Smith's recommendations and the documents he brought to the meeting, Roosevelt signed the paperwork for the Navy to buy Floyd Bennett Field, expanded the authority of the National Advisory Committee on Aeronautics to construct facilities on a cost-plus basis, and released $4 million from his discretionary defense fund for construction of tempos near the War College. He also raised a few topics on his own initiative, asking about the status of buying some more land in Arlington and suggesting that Smith examine if the public golf course at the municipal park on Haines Point Island (in the Potomac) would be a good site for additional tempos.[168] He also signed an executive order recommended by Smith and Coy relating to the composition of the Defense Communications Board.[169] In the context of what was going on, it was a remarkable meeting for its routineness.

The rest of Smith's work that day was similarly routine. He made and received several phone calls, including the governor of Iowa and Congressman Jerry Voorhis (D-CA).[170] He cohosted (with Coy) a summit meeting on housing construction, conferred with BOB staff, and gave a luncheon talk at a nearby hotel. It was a conference of state finance officials sponsored by the Municipal Finance Officers Association. The title of his talk was "Planning Finances for Defense."[171] He left work late in the afternoon and was not planning to come in on Sunday.

≈

In general, it had been a pretty good year for Smith. Notwithstanding his difficulties with Morgenthau, he had the president's trust and full access to him, had maintained good relations with Congress and the media, and was gradually reshaping BOB into the institution he wanted it to be. That Smith was spending less of his time on preparing the FY 1943 budget (compared to the previous two budgets) was an indication that after two and a half years as BOB director, his intense focus and priority on strengthening the organization was finally paying off. He had bulked it up with a substantial number of new hires—each of which he had personally interviewed and approved.[172] He appointed directors to all the bureau's divisions that he had confidence in, including the new divisions on administrative management and fiscal policy. Altogether, Smith had created an efficient, smooth-running, and powerful machine in his image. His timing (and luck) could not have been better. With the onset of the war, he needed to focus on the new matters that confronted federal budgeting and management. To a large extent, he already had been gradually pivoting away from in-house leadership to being the outward-facing CEO, dealing mostly with external matters. He had confidence that his handpicked leadership team and cadre of elite analysts could run the business and meet his exacting standards. He was ready.

In a book about Washington that was published in November, the author (a reporter) summarized how much Smith had accomplished within FDR's messy operating style:

> Harold D. Smith is a professional administrator and student of government. . . . After Smith became Federal budget director things began to happen. He expanded his agency and absorbed many of the jobs that used to be done by personal emissaries without White House title, ending the 'palace janissary' system. He became the President's 'business manager,' and one of the fountainheads of the move to give unity and force to the proposals of sound economists. . . .
>
> If some hard-headed professional administrators, such as Budget Director Harold D. Smith, were given authority to reorganize New Deal bureaus on a business basis, throw out the crackpots, and streamline administration toward the real objectives of the President, the effect on the country would be electric. (Moody 1941, 91–92, 285)

For Smith it must have felt like a gratifying way to end the year, a public acknowledgment of his hard work and professionalism in difficult times.

Chapter 5

The First Year of the War, 1942

Pearl Harbor and First Month of the War, December 1941

Wartime public management, it turned out, was more than merely hurry-up public administration. The pace of work changed because the work itself changed. Smith would be overseeing management of the war effort from multiple perspectives: budgeting, fiscal policy, reorganizing, expanding, decentralizing, and explaining all this to the public at large and media. He did all that in the teeth of insidious undermining of FDR's war policies by the congressional conservative coalition. This was an enormous and stressful undertaking. Inevitably, perhaps, it led to some problems with his health and energy levels. As soon as he heard the news on Sunday afternoon, Smith hurried to work. He was there from 4:00 to 11:00 p.m. In particular, he focused on the nearly finished draft of the presidential message to accompany the FY 1943 budget proposal that would be sent to Congress in the first week of January.[1] Clearly, it needed to be revised substantially. There was much to do. Those first few weeks were incredibly hectic, with scores of details that needed to be attended to. Judging from his call list, he seemed to be on the phone more often than not, whether making them, getting them, or returning them. Already a workaholic, he now was at the office even longer hours. On December 10, he worked until 11:15 p.m., until 10:30 p.m. on the 17th, and on the 22nd his last meeting started at 8:00 p.m.[2] To shoehorn in the ASPA/APSA conference in New York from Saturday, December 27, to Monday the 29th, he worked a regular day on Friday and then took the train at 1:00 a.m. Saturday. (It was the railroad version of a red-eye.) His return train left New York at midnight between Monday and Tuesday so that he could be at work for a full day on Tuesday.[3]

Smith saw the president frequently in those weeks. On December 9, the day after war was declared, he attended a White House summit meeting with Vice President Wallace and the Supply Priorities and Allocations Board (US Civilian Production Administration 1946, 40). He then had individual appointments with FDR on December 15, 18, and 19, usually accompanied by Assistant Director Blandford or OEM head Coy.[4] The meeting on the 18th was a relatively leisurely hour over lunch, indicating Roosevelt's recognition of the important role for BOB in the war as well as his measured and deliberate approach to his wartime leadership, this merely ten days after the war declaration. Much of the conversation, of course, focused on the big issues, such as revising the budget message, war appropriations, and tax policy. However, Roosevelt was still the same person who was interested in the smaller issues as well. They talked about how to deal with the future of the CCC and NYA. After all, there might be some demographic groups still in need of the services of those agencies, such as those below the draft age, "veterans, territorials, and Indians." He asked Smith to re-review the pending FY 1943 estimates for the two agencies and report back. Roosevelt "seemed to feel quite sure that large reductions in CCC must take place." At Smith's request, FDR agreed to issue a statement endorsing Smith's fiscal recommendations to states, such as reducing capital projects, reducing borrowing, and investing budget surpluses in federal notes. Smith also asked for, and received, guidance on his statutory membership on the Byrd Committee, wartime reorganization powers, and a draft executive order on transportation.[5]

Smith also moved quickly to work on other impacts of the war. He immediately began planning the outlines of a military and arms procurement budget for the war, estimating it to be in the range of $150 billion, yet another jaw-dropping amount.[6] However, he advised FDR to begin with conservative figures that reflected realistic assessments of actual production capacity. "I am inclined to believe that it is better to have a money figure for public consumption which we are reasonably sure of attaining rather than a higher and more doubtful figure, which, if not attained, would be a basis for public disappointment and criticism."[7] Ostensibly, it was fiscally conservative advice, but it was also political. In particular, Smith quickly concluded that the budget message needed a big picture discussion of wartime fiscal policy even if not directly related to the actual budget document that was limited to one fiscal year. He wanted to present an overview of the administration's integrated economic program, ranging from new taxes, deficits, price controls, production priorities, consumer shortages, and, especially, the president's anti-inflation policy. He told the president, "I believe that it will give the country a feeling of confidence that such a program is being formulated for adoption."[8] More political advice. FDR was amenable to that approach.

Morgenthau and Tax Policy

However, there was one catch. For the taxation side of the message, Smith would yet again have to tangle with Morgenthau for Treasury's revenue estimates. Morgenthau would not only insist on his central role in fiscal policy but would repeatedly try to reverse FDR's and Smith's priorities by urging more conservative approaches, such as greater tax increases (vs. bonding) and greater cuts to non-war spending. This time Smith tried to get around all that by assuring FDR that he already intended that the revised draft would "include what we believe to be the general outline of the Treasury tax program" and that he would "try to iron out the text with the Treasury"—tellingly not saying who in the department he would iron it out with.[9] He probably meant Bell. Roosevelt, knowing the tension between the two, overlooked the hint and instead said he wanted Smith to coordinate with Morgenthau.[10] FDR then dictated a note to Morgenthau asking him to "cooperate" with Smith on "a general outline of a tax policy" for the war to be included in the budget message.[11] Morgenthau made the most of it. When Smith called him on December 19, Morgenthau insisted that the president's instructions were for Smith to deal with *him*, not Bell, and in person, not through exchanges of written drafts.[12] He also strategized with his staff, who recommended sending a preliminary document to BOB soonest, even before any meeting, so that Smith would not be able to claim to FDR that he never received any written Treasury memorandum by the deadline for the message.[13] Morgenthau kept complicating it up. What about input from Price Administrator Leon Henderson? Let's coordinate with Currie and the Fed.[14] He was trying to maximize his leverage before meeting by implying those agencies were *endorsing* his tax plan. It seemed like he wanted to take full control over that section of the budget message. Besides still emphasizing the need to cut nondefense spending, he also insisted that the funding formula for the war be two-thirds through taxes and only one-third from bonding. Even the enormity of the early predictions of costs of the war would not get him to budge off that principle.[15]

Smith and Morgenthau finally met on December 30. It was at the White House with the president soothingly there to conciliate and to coerce the two to agree on the wording of that section of the budget message. It took nearly two hours.[16] Even then, they were not totally done, with Morgenthau trying to lure Smith to his office for lunch on Friday, January 2.[17] In the midst of all this back-and-forth, Smith vented to Ickes, saying how great was "his dislike of" Morgenthau, partly because of the opposing roles they were playing on the Byrd Committee. Being discrete, Smith also referred obliquely to how much he "also objects to some of Morgenthau's activities in other directions," but did not share the details with Ickes.[18]

La Guardia's Mismanagement of the Office of Civilian Defense

The beginning of the declared war was also an opportunity for Smith and Coy to ask FDR to reconsider Mayor La Guardia's tenure as head of the Office of Civilian Defense. They had both worked to draft the OCD executive order and then, because of their respective responsibilities, were actively aware of La Guardia's management (or lack of) of the new agency. He had a hyperkinetic style and, as part-time CEO, was not interested in eye-glazing management that required sitting in his office. He was a public guy (Lee 2012, 106–07; 2018a, 182–83). One incident particularly bothered Smith. When Smith initially became concerned about La Guardia's management of OCD, he suggested to La Guardia that BOB's Administrative Management Division could do a study of the agency's management and recommend organizational improvements. La Guardia, distractedly, agreed to the management audit.[19] Meanwhile one of Smith's new hires was James Sundquist, a newly minted MPA from Syracuse University. Based on his graduate and PACH work, Sundquist was considered something of an expert on civilian defense and local government.[20] He was promptly assigned to work on assessing OCD.[21] A few months later, OCD hired Sundquist, in part because he already had some expert knowledge about the agency's operations and budget.[22] Then the BOB management audit of OCD hit in November.[23] La Guardia was furious that the study implicitly criticized his management style. He would not acknowledge it having any credibility. When he found out that Sundquist had worked on the BOB report, he fired him.[24] Smith was infuriated by this petulant political behavior, at such discrepancy with the nonpolitical and professional style of BOB's culture, particularly the Administrative Management Division's reports on organizational improvements. Smith made a point to tell Roosevelt that La Guardia "was not able to secure and retain competent staff because of his rather careless habit of firing people without much concern."[25] Smith rehired Sundquist.[26]

After La Guardia won reelection as mayor in November, Smith and Coy had hinted to Roosevelt that perhaps this was a good time to ease La Guardia out of OCD (Lee 2018a, 182–83). FDR did not take the hint. Now, six days after Pearl Harbor (and a week after Sundquist's firing), they sent a short memo to Roosevelt saying they were "despondent and despairing" of La Guardia's performance. "We think it is terribly important that we have a very frank discussion with you about this matter."[27] Roosevelt agreed that La Guardia should probably go, but he hated firing people, especially doing so in person. He tried to do it in a roundabout way. On December 15, he asked Smith to prepare a report on improving administration of OCD. Perhaps Smith's document should suggest "that La Guardia would be relieved of all administrative duties and would perhaps be appointed as the Chairman of a board for OCD."[28] Smith's report suggested merging the OCD and the defense welfare agency into an Office of Home Security and giving the new organization a clear and unified mission.[29] FDR then asked La Guardia to meet with him. With Smith in the room, Roosevelt told La Guardia "that he felt the Mayor could not handle both jobs . . . and that the Mayor ought to get an assistant, at least to handle the administrative work." La Guardia launched on a long tirade that all criticisms of him were political and that the press was unfairly criticizing him. During this meandering harangue, "the President was fairly firm in his conversation with the Mayor, [but] it was quite evident that the Mayor was not giving the President any help in finding a solution to the situation. . . . The President did say [again] that the Mayor should get some good administrative person who could stay on the job on a day-to-day basis." La Guardia would not concede anything. Seeing that the conversation was not going in the direction he had hoped, FDR told the mayor that he wanted him to meet further with Smith about a possible reorganization of OCD to improve its performance. He suggested the two of them sit down right away to talk about it. They stepped outside the Oval Office to talk. "It was fairly clear that the Mayor felt I was causing trouble for him." Smith tried to deescalate by saying simply that they "should explore the organization problem."[30] La Guardia said nothing further and walked away.

Later that day, Smith had lunch with Ickes. As he had about Morgenthau, Smith vented to Ickes:

Smith has also been charged by the President with an effort to do something about LaGuardia, whom the President finds very much on his hands. The fact is that the President would like to have LaGuardia resign as head of Civilian Defense, but he hasn't the gumption to force the issue. Smith has had a talk with Fiorello, making certain suggestions about the Civilian Defense work. I do not understand that Smith suggested that Fiorello resign, but Fiorello volunteered that if the office of Civilian Defense were raised to cabinet rank then he would resign. Smith is inclined to doubt whether the resignation would be forthcoming even in such an event and I agree with him because Fiorello for a long time has desperately wanted to be a member of the cabinet. . . . But, according to Smith, the affairs of Fiorello's office are in a maze. No one can make heads or tails of it and to Fiorello it means an opportunity to go shooting about the country by airplane making speeches.[31]

Finally, in mid-January, the president was compelled to act because Congress was about to pass a bill shifting OCD to the War Department. That would go against several of FDR's management doctrines: it would freeze the status and mission of OCD into law and could only be changed by another law, it would shift home defense from a civilian activity to a military one (and hence less subject to critical questioning), and it would place the agency farther from FDR's direct control. Roosevelt quickly preempted Congress by announcing the appointment of Harvard Law dean James Landis as the "executive" of OCD. Supposedly, Roosevelt had consulted with La Guardia in advance and that La Guardia supported doing that. It wasn't quite that cooperative nor voluntary. On January 2, Roosevelt told La Guardia what he planned to do, impliedly with or without La Guardia's approval.[32] The White House public announcement said nothing about any change in La Guardia's status. Finally, after an awkward two weeks, La Guardia (and Mrs. Roosevelt, OCD's assistant director) resigned (Lee 2018a, 183). The bill never passed because La Guardia's mismanagement was a major reason for its momentum. Roosevelt's (belated) maneuver had worked.

Initial Wartime Organizational Needs

The declaration of war gave Smith a freer hand to exercise his power to force civilian agencies to move out of Washington. He was using the president's new powers under the First War Powers Act (sometimes called the Overman Act for its WWI version). There still was the usual opposition, but it was hard to argue that the basic idea was wrong. The District of Columbia was bulging with new, war-related workers and the need for available office space was critical.[33] (The federal government was also buying, leasing, and constructing buildings there [chap. 4; Lee 2018a, 135–36, 189].) On December 19, Smith held a press conference announcing the move of twelve agencies and ten thousand employees out of the Washington area.[34] They were moving to Chicago, Philadelphia, New York, St. Louis, and Pittsburgh. Other cities quickly wanted to get in on the action.[35] Later recipients included Cleveland and Richmond (VA). Smith kept emphasizing that the transfers were not about the importance of any agency to the war effort, rather if it was *essential* that its entire workforce be in DC.[36] He also said that "this was just the beginning" and many more agencies would move.[37]

Smith also continued engaging in refashioning the executive branch through executive orders. Roosevelt signed executive orders creating the Office of Defense Transportation and Office of Censorship.[38] Other urgent executive orders that were not organization-related were also processed by BOB, such as streamlining wartime procurement.[39] On December 18, Smith reminded Roosevelt that the Overman Act limited him to reorganizations that were directly related to the war effort. That excluded other potential restructurings. Smith wanted the president to apply to Congress to renew his reorganization powers under the 1939 act because it gave him a broader latitude, though subjecting any plan to legislative veto. FDR did not indicate any enthusiasm for such an initiative and Smith had to drop it.[40]

Promoting Professional Public Administration: ASPA Conference, December 27–29

Throughout 1941, Smith had taken seriously his obligations as president of ASPA. He routinely met with association staff and lay leaders on the matters that he needed to give guidance on, such as policies for *PAR*, developing the program for the 1941 conference, coordinating with APSA, and appointing a nominating committee for the next year's slate of officers.[41] Only its second president, he was in a position to help develop and frame the association's work, culture, routines, and ethos. The capstone of his ASPA service was a presidential address at the annual conference in New York City held jointly with APSA. He titled his speech "The Management of Government in a Democracy" (1941g). In it, he argued that there was a fundamental misunderstanding of the role of public administration in a democracy. Its purpose was to implement the will of the people, not to impose anything on the citizenry. Only after the political process had established goals for government would public managers step in to implement that policy. Public administration "is only a tool—[to] be sharpened and adjusted to the task. It must be used thoughtfully and skillfully, for without such conscious application all other resources become less useful" (1). Government management was a process to achieve goals, little different from how an individual citizen lived. "He plans, he directs, he uses the opportunities at hand, he aims at his goal" (3). Public administration was merely the same thing writ large.

Smith flagged the contradictory criticisms of American public administration. On one hand, bureaucracy was criticized "as paralyzed by inertia, bound by unnecessary procedural restrictions, and lacking in imagination" (2). On the other hand, American bureaucracy was also critiqued as putting the US on an inevitable path to dictatorship and that it was antithetical to democracy. This was also not true, Smith said, because "in the one case, the state uses the people; in the other, the state is of use to the people." Furthermore, "the implication here is that to gain efficiency in democratic government, management must obliterate individual liberties. This implication is fallacious" (8). Smith focused on the need for coordination in large organizations. It was no longer true that "almost any person could successfully administer the public's business" (5). Rather, there was an authentic need for trained experts in "scientific management" (2). However, unfortunately, the new profession had "built up a jargon of their own. Around the field of public administration there has been erected a barbed-wire fence of terminology." That "tends to obstruct public understanding of the role of the administrator" (4). Referring to Pearl Harbor, Smith observed, "In recent weeks we have seen democracy make up its mind, and our enemies shall discover how effective management in that democracy can be." He concluded by stating that "public administrators can help achieve a public acceptance of that [democratic] role by demonstrating that they conceive it in their duty to strive to attain the ends set for them by the citizenry, and their duty to employ those means most consistent with the high purposes of democracy" (10). It was a fitting description of what his job would be for the next five years. Smith's speech received minor media coverage, such as the last paragraph in a *Times* story about the conference.[42] Later in 1942, the National Municipal League published an abridged version in its monthly journal.[43]

Fiscal Year 1943 Budget and Capitol Hill, January–May

Come the New Year, the FY 1943 budget message was still not done—specifically the discussion of fiscal policy. Smith and Morgenthau were still fighting. Morgenthau had invited Smith to come to lunch at his office on Friday, January 2. Smith declined, insisting it be on neutral ground. They met at a downtown restaurant.[44] Smith and Jones, head of BOB's Fiscal Division, continued drafting the budget message after the luncheon and into the night. Smith headed home at 10:30 p.m. On Saturday, FDR reviewed the revised draft and made some changes. Smith told him that he would continue working with "representatives" of Treasury (rather than the secretary) on the taxation and revenue sections of the message.[45] On Sunday, January 4, Smith and Blandford met for most of the afternoon with Under Secretary Bell and Assistant Secretary John L. Sullivan to wrangle further on that section of the budget.[46] At 5:00 p.m., Smith presented to the president what he thought was the wording Treasury had signed off on. Roosevelt reviewed it for forty-five minutes and then approved it.[47] Off to GPO. They both thought they were done. As usual, FDR held an embargoed press briefing on the budget on Tuesday, January 6. Smith and Blandford were there and actively participated, answering questions from the media as well as elaborating on presidential comments (Roosevelt 1972, 19: 8–50).[48] The budget was officially sent to Congress the next day. Incredibly, *that day*, Morgenthau called Smith to complain about the budget message and said there were sections he still "objected to." It sounded like he was not planning to keep those objections to himself. A round-robin of conference calls and meetings ensued all day.[49] Smith, probably sputtering, badly wanted to keep any disagreements in-house. But his public disagreements with Morgenthau over the Byrd Committee report in December signaled how hard that would be. A tip-off came from the coverage in the *Wall Street Journal* about the budget message. It focused, almost oddly given the catholicity of a budget, on likely opposition to the president's taxation requests.[50] There were no Treasury fingerprints in the article, but he probably guessed Morgenthau and his team worked behind the scenes and off the record to help shape the reporter's framing of the issues.

Later that week, Smith headed to the Hill for the annual hearing on BOB's budget by the House Appropriations Subcommittee for agencies funded by the annual Independent Offices bill. He presented a summary of the agency's record for the preceding year and its request in the president's new budget proposal. At the time, BOB had 361 staffers (US House 1942a,

1087–88). He was requesting an additional 104 to deal with the increases caused by the war, in particular to be able to send BOB's defense engineers and other staff into the field for inspections and interviews with local officials (1102). He also mentioned his long-term goal for a field service, but said that, given the circumstances, he was not asking to establish and fund it in this annual cycle (1099–1100). The members took him through their paces of a routine review of an agency, asking about staffing, expenditures, and other sundry matters. However, in general, subcommittee members were complimentary about his record. Chair Clifton Woodrum (D-VA) said, "I think the Budget are doing a grand job and a very effective job" (1101) and middle-ranking majority member Joe Starnes (D-AL) agreed. He said what appropriators rarely ever said to an agency facing them: "I do not think this committee should be any too squeamish about letting them have additional money, because I think it is a very good investment if they need it for additional personnel" (1102). The hearing then veered into directions that indicated Smith was successfully reframing for them his role as the source for authoritative information and explanations about the entire executive branch. BOB was more than just a standard issue agency, one of dozens of miscellaneous federal entities collected into the Independent Offices bill. Members were beginning to view BOB as a prism for seeing and overseeing the entirety of the federal government. Members asked about monitoring if states fulfilled their match obligations for federal grants (1100–01), executive-branch-wide data on reserves of appropriated money that BOB was holding back (1106), its central role in clearing *all* executive orders (1107), placed in the hearing record a BOB report on HR specialists at departments and agencies (1108–12), and requested a detailed listing of allocations from the president's discretionary emergency fund (1124). Smith also reported that BOB was engaging in additional studies and investigations based on congressional requests, including PR,[51] movie production, and employees detailed to congressional committees (1092).

A few months later, Smith had an opportunity to emphasize this strengthened role for BOB. In May, the Senate Military Affairs Committee held a session on the need for rubber conservation. (It was an informal hearing as part of an executive session.) Smith was one of the testifiers (US Senate 1942a, 86–89). He highlighted how much this kind of subject overlapped with the bureau's role. For example, relating to legislative clearance, he said that legislation was needed to clarify the president's power in this regard, notwithstanding the more general scope of the War Powers Act. Another relevant role was that BOB had drafted executive orders, such as the mission of the OEM's Office of Defense Transportation. Reflecting BOB's role in making recommendations regarding bills sent to the president, he reminded the members of a related piece of legislation on federal acquisition of cars and tires from dealers. His most unusual comment was that stronger policies were needed, including the possibility of confiscating vehicles and imposing national speed limits because "no amount of talk quite impresses upon the people of the country the seriousness of the situation" (88). That none of the senators argued with him about that comment was an indication of the growing recognition that BOB's role extended beyond budgeting. (Neither did any reporters, including those from the *Chicago Tribune*.[52]) In June, he issued a circular to all federal agencies detailing the items they must turn in, including rubber floor mats.[53] Smith also had personal credibility on the issue of cutting rubber consumption. Earlier that year, Kluttz reported that Smith practiced what he preached. When the original tires on the federal car assigned for BOB's use were worn out, he insisted on replacing them with retreads even though, under federal policies at the time, it qualified for new tires. They were "probably the first on any official car. The guardian of the Nation's pocketbook saved about $25 on the deal."[54]

Organizing for Victory

Reorganizing

The organizational story of 1942 was of executive orders: creating, merging, transferring, reorganizing, amending, fine-tuning, and undoing. Even though the presidential reorganization powers of the 1939 act had expired in January 1941, the First War Powers Act, passed by Congress in December 1941, delegated broad powers to the president to reorganize the executive branch in the interests of winning the war. That's all Smith really needed. He pushed vigorously. To some, Smith's insistence on rational organization was "doctrinaire," but FDR more often than not agreed with him (Kotlowski 2015, 344). Sometimes Roosevelt sat on drafts of reorganization executive orders until he felt the timing was propitious or because he hadn't yet firmly made up his mind. For example, a reorganization of PR agencies sat on his desk for about a month (Lee 2005, 151–56). Sometimes Smith was impatient with the delays because he felt that meant managerial problems festered organizationally (and, also, politically). At one meeting with Roosevelt, Smith told him to expect several executive orders and he hoped FDR "could get them signed as soon as they were completed," because he "felt that Washington would settle down to work and much of the friction would be eliminated." With appointments secretary Watson standing there, Smith told the president he "wanted to extract a firm agreement from him and Watson that as soon as these Orders were finished," he could "come pounding on the door to discuss them with the President so that these matters could be closed." According to Smith, FDR lightheartedly "told Watson to let me in when I hollered."[55] A week later, speaking to the president about another executive order, FDR was mildly and uncharacteristically irritated and said "that he felt he was being pushed around" by some other people about the draft order—some for and some against what Smith had prepared. "I put on my most genial smile and reminded the President that he was not easy to push around, for which I was duly grateful. He made some remark

Figure 4. Smith at his desk in the Executive Office Building, March 21, 1942. Credit: Associated Press Images. Used under license.

about his stubborn Dutch ancestry and then launched into an exposition of what happened."[56] In the end, of course, Smith was glad to handle any loose ends necessary to revise the order and Roosevelt was ready to sign it.

The org chart of the war effort was in constant flux. To outsiders and to FDR's permanent critics, this was proof that Roosevelt was mismanaging the war effort, of bungling, of the "mess in Washington," political compromises, and indecision. To Smith, each executive order had an underlying justification based on the circumstances at the time, the successes or failures of individual agency heads, and necessary compromises. In a sense, it was a reality check of the maxim about government organization: everything related to everything else. No matter how rationally he tried to slice the pie, there were always turf wars, disagreements, accusations, and justifiable deals. At times the problem was people, appointees who may have been indecisive, or too persuadable by the last person they talked to, or unable to prevail in a bureaucratic knife fight. The first major conflict was over the organization of the production effort. OPM just was not working the way it was supposed to, namely, to coordinate production, priorities, and prices. Nor was the new coordinating and policy body over it, the Supply Priorities and Allocations Board (SPAB). FDR also lost faith in OPM's Knudsen for these larger issues. Smith told the president "the defense organization was badly in need of attention."[57] At the same time, Associate Supreme Court justice James Byrnes had kept in touch with Roosevelt and Hopkins and was aware of the problems. At Hopkins's suggestion, Byrnes wrote a four-page memo to the president suggesting the need for revising the structure. He suggested converting SPAB and OPM into one board, but with a chief executive who could make, without board approval or votes, authoritative and binding decisions. He also suggested that FDR name Donald Nelson as its boss (Byrnes 1947, 15–17). Smith liked both Byrnes's proposed structure and the person to head it. Somewhat tepidly, he acknowledged that Nelson "was the best man *available* in the organization for the job. It was probably preferable to take him with his *known* limitations than to take a new man whose positive or negative qualities were unknown."[58] That wasn't much of an endorsement, but along with everyone else, Smith was being pragmatic. The need for action was now.

At the time, the ill Hopkins (head of Lend-Lease) was living in the White House and largely confined to his bedroom. Also, Winston Churchill was visiting, in part to talk about Lend-Lease and the need to increase production of materiel. He, too, was a guest at the White House. The final decision came in a meeting in Hopkins's bedroom in his pajamas and

Churchill in his onesie. Only Smith and Byrnes were in business attire, lending the scene, he humorously observed, "the only touch of dignity."[59] It was so urgent they quickly drafted a press release for Roosevelt to announce that night: He would be signing an executive order to re-create SPAB and OPM as the War Production Board (WPB) and would designate Nelson as its chair and as the chief executive over all the production-related agencies.[60] It was a brutal firing of Knudsen, but he was later commissioned as a senior officer in the army air force to assist with production bottlenecks. Moving quickly, Smith prepared an executive order that FDR signed three days later.[61] It was prepared in such haste that a week later, FDR had to sign another, to clarify the functions and duties of the board.[62] In April, he further assigned "additional" duties to WPB and OPA.[63]

That major decision was in the midst of a dizzying array of the creation of other, narrower, wartime agencies: the National War Labor Board,[64] War Shipping Administration (WSA),[65] National Housing Agency,[66] Office of Alien Property Custodian,[67] War Relocation Authority,[68] War Manpower Commission (WMC),[69] Women's Army Auxiliary Corps,[70] Office of War Information,[71] Office of Strategic Services,[72] War Relief Control Board,[73] Rubber Director,[74] Office of Economic Stabilization,[75] Petroleum Administration for War,[76] Food Administrator,[77] and US Typhus Commission.[78] In some cases, his executive orders reorganized existing agencies, such as major restructurings of the army and the War Department and of the navy and the Navy Department.[79] Another category of structure-related executive orders mostly dealt with intra-federal transfers without creating new entities. They included transferring some functions and offices from Justice to the Alien Property Custodian,[80] a "retransfer" of merchant marine training from the Coast Guard to WSA,[81] transferring the US High Commissioner for the Philippines to Interior,[82] transferring some of the functions of the US Employment Service to WMC,[83] and transferring the entirety of the Selective Service System (the draft) also to WMC.[84] On at least one occasion, he abolished an agency. In 1933, FDR had used an executive order to create the Electric Home and Farm Authority. It encouraged and financed consumer acquisition of electrical appliances. Given the shortage of electricity during the war, FDR did not want a federal agency working at cross-purposes with that goal. He abolished it, also by executive order.[85] On another occasion, he abolished the Board on Survey and Maps and transferred its role to BOB.[86] This gave Smith the power to oversee and coordinate federal mapping, similar to his extant power to coordinate federal statistical collection. Roosevelt also used executive orders to change the names of nonstatutory agencies.[87]

At the beginning of the war, BOB was so busy creating new agencies and giving advice to existing ones about creating new sub-units that it issued a memorandum on "Organization Nomenclature in the Federal Government." The circular confessed that many terms were used interchangeably, such as agency, authority, board, administration, and commission. Notwithstanding BOB's efforts at uniformity, "there is really no sharp line of difference between the use of some of these terms, and their current use is apt to be determined somewhat by happenstance rather than any underlying design." On the other hand, it was trying to hold the line on the traditional hierarchy of units within a cabinet department from the secretary downward: bureau, division, section, and unit.[88] While executive orders were the most common venue for creating and revising war units, many related to issues of existing organizations, such as policies, powers, and limitations. Roosevelt strengthened the powers of the Board of Economic Warfare,[89] revised the power of the Petroleum Coordinator,[90] clarified the respective roles of the State Department and Board of Economic Warfare,[91] and issued an "amendatory executive order" about the role of Treasury regarding alien property.[92] There were also scores of executive orders that did not relate to organizational matters, rather to war management more generally, such as prompt handling of war contracts[93] and federal inspecting and auditing of production factories.[94] With BOB's hegemony in drafting and submitting executive orders relating to organization, budgets, management, and legislative clearance, Smith was involved in all of them. None reached the president's desk without Smith deciding to submit it.

Half a year into the war, Smith optimistically told Ickes that he thought FDR and the bureau "have almost come to the end of their reorganization of war agencies."[95] He was anticipating that he would soon return to more mundane organizational and structural matters unrelated to the war, such as Ickes dream project: moving the US Forest Service to Interior. (That never happened.) Despite Smith's optimism, organizational changes were a permanent and ongoing feature of the war and, of course, the postwar era of disestablishing the infrastructure. This plethora of wartime governance through executive orders led to conservative challenges. Influential (and conservative) *Times* columnist Arthur Krock highlighted Smith's largely unknown yet central role in all executive orders. That made him "a human battleground between the power-seeking groups."[96] *United States News*, a conservative weekly newsmagazine, raised concerns about what it called the "Kitchen Congress" (a play on kitchen cabinet). It asserted that the president's power through executive orders was greater than Congress's power to pass laws. According to its calculations, in the first year of the war, Congress had passed about one law per day, while FDR signed about two and a half executive orders a day—all controlled by Smith. "Cabinet officers who drop a proposed executive order into the hands of Mr. Roosevelt in private almost invariably find it winds up in the offices of Harold D. Smith, the Budget Director." This was out of balance and a danger to democracy, the article argued. In fact, Congress "now is debating whether it has given too many" powers to the president. It quoted the conservative Democratic chair of the House Judiciary Committee as alarmed by this trend because it threatened the principles of "a government of the people and a government of laws."[97] One of Smith's assistants urged him to consider some counter-publicity to knock down the assertions of the article.[98] He evidently decided not to take it head on, focusing instead on the theme of how much money BOB had saved the taxpayers by reducing nonessential spending. This conservative critique of executive-order-based agencies gradually gained steam during the war. Congress passed a bill in 1944 to limit funding to executive branch agencies established by statute and prohibit funding to agencies created by executive orders. FDR signed it because he knew another bill about to reach him a few weeks later narrowed the prohibition by permitting using funds from the president's discretionary war account for executive-order-based agencies (Lee 2016a, 99–101).[99]

Decentralizing

It will be recalled that in 1941, Smith began pressing for moving some federal agencies out of the capital as one way of providing office space for defense-related agencies. As a rule, agency heads, employees, and their allies on Capitol Hill fiercely resisted these changes. Pearl Harbor and the declaration of war did not change this political dynamic. Based on the First War Powers Act that Congress approved in December, Roosevelt delegated to Smith the authoritative power to move agencies out of DC, whether they liked it or not. Mostly, they didn't. His directives in December 1941 were as opposed as bitterly as those before Pearl Harbor (see first section in this chapter). The underlying message was how unfair it was that the war would inconvenience *me*! Another argument was that there already were housing shortages in the cities they were being moved to, so what was being accomplished?[100]

In January, Smith became more insistent on issuing and implementing such orders and the counterpart pushback from Capitol Hill and agencies rose, too. On January 2, he began another round of announcements. The Immigration and Naturalization Service, a unit of Justice, would move to Philadelphia.[101] A month later, he said he was doubling the number of USDA employees who had to move, with the Farm Credit Administration going to Kansas City and the Farm Security Agency to Cincinnati.[102] The drumbeat of his removal orders continued all year: some of the staff of the Custodian of Alien Property to Chicago;[103] FDIC to Chicago;[104] some units of the VA to New York;[105] part of the Social Security Board to Baltimore and others to existing regional offices;[106] Treasury's Bureau of Public Debt to Chicago;[107] some CSC staffers to Winston-Salem, North Carolina;[108] the Navy's Bureau of Supplies and Accounts to Cleveland;[109] and more than three thousand Treasury and War Department staff to Chicago.[110] In a front-page political cartoon, the *Star* poked fun at Smith by depicting him as writing a letter to the president stating: "How about moving Congress out of Washington? It would relieve us of a lot of things."[111] When self-serving lobbying by employees of Interior's Fish and Wildlife Service got particularly intense and personal, Smith let his guard down a bit and wisecracked to the *Post*'s Kluttz: "I have begun to feel that fish flourished only in Washington and—as for wildlife—I can imagine nothing wilder than life right here since the decentralization plan was announced."[112] Federal employees who lived in Virginia and Maryland were constituents of House and Senate members and Smith quickly heard from them opposing the move. For example, on January 2, Congressman A. W. Robertson (D-VA) called Smith to voice the concerns of his voters.[113]

Civil servants living in DC did not have elected representation, but members of the House and Senate District of Columbia committees tended to view them as quasi-constituents who needed their protection. They, too, strenuously opposed Smith's efforts. In particular, Senator Pat McCarran (D-NV), chair of the Senate DC committee, went on the warpath. (A reminder that in 1940 he had fiercely fought FDR and Smith on the CAA reorganization [chap. 3].) McCarran denounced the decentralization plan and quickly convened the committee to hear from Smith and several other BOB staff about it. McCarran demanded that Smith bring with him BOB files on the plans justifying these particular decentralization decisions.[114] Smith said he could not attend because he was already committed to another hearing but, more importantly, declined to submit any BOB files. In a letter to McCarran he said, "I would have some hesitancy about complying with the request, in view of the fact that I have acted in this matter at the direction of the President, and the papers in question are records of the executive office and to some extent confidential in character."[115] This was another early assertion of what decades later came to be called executive privilege. Roosevelt met with McCarran, but insisted that the decentralization was necessary to make room for wartime employees who had to be in DC.[116] McCarran took the fight to the floor of the Senate with a resolution declaring that decentralization was "without authority of law and contrary to the will of the Congress," that no moves could occur "without the consent of the Congress," and that BOB submit a report with "a full and complete disclosure of all facts in connection with each and every agency of office directed to move."[117] It was debated for four hours on the floor of the Senate on January 14, only five and a half weeks after Pearl Harbor.[118] It was a test of wills between supporting the president in wartime versus parochial vested interests along with the conservative coalition seeking to undermine FDR politically—war or no war. For them, ideology trumped national unity. After a long, acrimonious, and bitter debate (of twenty-three densely printed pages of the *Congressional Record*), McCarran's resolution was defeated 26–33.[119] Roosevelt and Smith had prevailed, but the vote indicated how tenuous their support was. If four of the senators who were present (thirty-seven were not) had changed their votes, the resolution would have passed.

This fight was one of the first of a long series of relatively artificial political controversies stirred up during the war. The argument over decentralization was an early synecdoche of what Washington politics would be for the entire war: the conservative coalition and interest groups loudly opposing an administration policy and trying to undermine FDR politically—all with the claim of supporting the war, merely calling out Roosevelt's supposed managerial bungling. Their ongoing meme was of "a mess in Washington" that was entirely the president's fault. One of the lessons that Smith learned from this decentralization controversy was that merit-based decisions were not enough. Political criticisms that the media picked up needed to be rebutted quickly and forcefully. Charges needed to be answered. He gradually incorporated PR into his decision-making, to frame issues before conservatives could or to provide a factual counter-narrative to whatever they were claiming. For example, in late January, in advance of another round of required moves, he worked on a press release to provide the details but, more importantly, to make the case that these were justified and necessary.[120] There was also a political flip side to the decentralization controversy. There were plenty of cities who welcomed hosting decentralized agencies. The same week that

McCarran was pulling out all the political and rhetorical stops against it, the bitterly anti-Roosevelt *Chicago Tribune* applauded it, noting that Midwestern congressional delegations "joined today in reaffirming their determination to support the plan."[121] Senator Richard Russell (D-GA) and one of that state's congressmen called Smith to ask that some agencies be moved to Atlanta,[122] a member of the House Democratic leadership called to see about moving agencies to his hometown of Boston as did the mayor,[123] and a Maryland senator came to Smith's office to discuss moves to Baltimore.[124] In Detroit, to demonstrate the municipal government's cooperative and welcoming approach, it vacated the offices of its traffic court to make room for federal agencies.[125] A few months later, Detroit's municipal legal counsel called to inquire about more moves to the city.[126] A touchier phone call was from Edward Flynn, chair of the Democratic National Committee, urging that more agencies be sent to Cleveland because that would "help out."[127]

Expanding

The bitterness of the decentralization effort was not occurring in a vacuum. Smith tried to balance out these criticisms by publicly making the case that there was a valid and concrete need for the office space and housing. On January 17, he issued a press release estimating that 85,000 new federal employees would be hired for the war effort and that they had to be in the capital. Along with new nonfederal workers and their families, the population of the metropolitan area would probably increase by 250,000 people.[128] Office space and housing for these new civil servants were interrelated. To meet the crunch in office space, the federal government was renting half a million square feet of apartments and residences. Building more offices, whether as tempos or more permanent structures, and then moving employees out of rented apartments was another way to open up living quarters for incoming workers.[129] FDR approved the erection of more tempos, even in the Ellipse (if the Secret Service would approve).[130] Smith quickly convened another summit meeting of all relevant federal agencies to coordinate the additional construction.[131] Another method for obtaining the staffing needed by war agencies was to facilitate the transfer of current civil servants from low-priority agencies to high-priority ones. Smith prepared, and FDR signed, an executive order to that effect.[132] Smith then issued a categorization of all executive branch units from highest to lowest priority.[133] As with the pushback about decentralization, agencies and their staff complained when they disagreed with Smith's priority classifications. Smith had to emphasize that his list of priorities was not subject to challenge.[134] This effort can also be seen as a public demonstration of the administration's commitment to shift its workforce from nonessential agencies and tasks to war-related ones. (See section on the Byrd Committee.) A parallel complaint from Capitol Hill conservatives was that the wartime expansion of the federal government was occurring in such a pell-mell fashion that machinery and equipment already owned by federal agencies was being wasted, forgotten, even abandoned, on a large scale. Smith again acted to blunt such attacks through his own counter-PR and public actions. He announced that he authorized the Army to take control of any equipment it needed from CCC camps (that were being closed, also pell-mell); WPB said it was doing the same from NYA machine tool training shops; and Smith drafted for FDR an executive order transferring CCC motor repair shops, personnel, and property to the War Department.[135]

Fiscal Policy: Taking the Initiative for an Anti-Inflation Program, March–October

It will be recalled that Smith had created the Fiscal Division in 1940 because he felt BOB had a central role in federal fiscal policy and macroeconomics (chap. 3). Budgeting, he felt, was merely part of a whole, a coordinated program to assure economic growth and full employment. The next year, as 1941 unfolded from the perspective of the economy, he became increasingly worried about the possibility of major inflation due to the increase in federal defense spending (chap. 4). Roosevelt, always the ad hoc decision-maker, knew the validity of the concern but was not yet willing to take major action. Now, in mid-March 1942, Smith sent a memo to FDR saying, "The nation drifts swiftly and surely toward inflation. . . . What is needed is a unified and far-reaching fiscal, monetary, wage and price control policy." Roosevelt, again, acknowledged the problem and replied with a brief but vague endorsement, "OK—Work fast."[136] That was good enough for Smith to try to get the federal policy leviathan lumbering forward toward that goal. After huddling with the economists in the Fiscal Division, ten days later he submitted to FDR the outline of a comprehensive and integrated economic program that addressed wages, prices, and tax policy. He suggested that its enactment, including a message to Congress and a fireside chat, would be "a master stroke" by FDR.[137] (That sounded like political as well as policy advice.)

With an eye on public opinion (and Congress's fingertip feel for it), Smith quickly arranged to write a Sunday column for national distribution by the World Wide news service. Published across the country in the Sunday papers on March 29, Smith argued that the "financial joy ride on the deficit spending of the Federal Government" was over. Yes, the surge in defense-related spending and the concomitant increase in employment and incomes had been necessary and—economically speaking—relatively successful. But with the country now at war, it was *already* at full employment. New war-related economic problems included manpower shortages, the diversion of manufacturing from consumer goods to armaments, and sharp controls over scarce resources such as rubber and petroleum. That was a formula for major inflation and disruption. He argued that the only solution was a federal policy that increased taxation and forced savings, along with controls over wages and prices. Victory would come only with sacrifice and civic support (Smith 1942a). Some newspapers promoted the column in ads in their Saturday editions. The *Star* said it was "an article all should read."[138] The *Detroit Free Press* advertised it as "a special article" that would be in Sunday's editorial magazine.[139] When Smith met with FDR on April 1, Roosevelt said he was enthusiastic about the program. He said he might even address Congress personally and have the speech broadcast on the radio. In particular, it "would give him a chance to answer critics" who were attacking him about inflation. He asked Smith to work with Sam Rosenman on drafting a message to Congress and a fireside chat. Smith promised to coordinate the tax aspects of it with Morgenthau.[140] The president's enthusiasm was short-lived. The reality of implementing Smith's program was sinking in. It would impact labor, farmers, and business, as well as the likely congressional opposition to tax increases. Furthermore, Morgenthau had called Roosevelt to complain that he had not been consulted on the program (evidently focusing on Smith's initial memo to Roosevelt, rather than regarding meetings after April 1). Reflecting afterward, Smith said,

> It seemed to me that when the President was confronted with the specific things that would have to be done to accomplish this program, he showed signs of worrying about some of the details, all of which added up to a pretty stiffly regimented economy for the period of the war. While I did not have the

feeling that he was reneging upon the program in any way, I did feel that it worried him. He had begun to think of the practical problems which would be faced in Congress in getting the program implemented.[141]

What followed was intense bureaucratic warfare between agencies with different agendas and personalities with different foci. A two-hour-plus meeting of all the principals in the Cabinet Room of the White House on April 10 was of arguing and bickering, rather than seeking consensus. Rosenman said, "While I tried my best to get agreement . . . , it was impossible" (1952, 334). Trying to avoid the press, Smith entered and left the White House through a side door. The press caught wind of the summit meeting and waylaid some of the attendees for comment. Smith was asked for "the bad news on taxes" and he cryptically replied, "It will be bad enough."[142] Eventually, "a queer division" of all the major players except Morgenthau agreed on a program and submitted it to FDR.[143] That included Fed chair Eccles, Vice President Wallace (head of the Board of Economic Warfare), OPA head Henderson, USDA Secretary Wickard, and Smith.[144] After that, Rosenman remembered "countless other conferences" and consultations to get agreement on the program, to draft the message to Congress, and draft the fireside chat (Roosevelt 1969, 1942: 225). Finally, Roosevelt sent a message to Congress on April 27 and had a fireside chat the next day. Generally, he called for sacrifices and unity and, specifically, listed a policy agenda of seven elements. However, the eventual details were not as stringent as Smith had originally hoped.

Nonetheless, Smith went on something of a PR offensive to sell the anti-inflation program. On April 29, he addressed a convocation of the PR officers of all major federal agencies in a BOB conference room. He urged them to speak in one voice in support of the president's program and the need for them to engage in a proactive and unified PR effort to sell the program to the public. For example, he suggested that they arrange for senior officials of their agencies to give a series of speeches on the aspects of the program that related to their agencies.[145] A few months later, he gave a talk on a national radio network.[146] Titled "A Call for Action," Smith's talk summarized the president's seven-point program and explained the rationale for each. In general, he criticized the you-go-first mentality of labor, farmers, and business. Sure, each claimed they would eventually support something that affected them, but first the other guy needs to be clamped down on. He was urging rising above narrow and short-term self-interest of advocating and protecting special advantages. He said that in the long run, all constituencies would benefit from stabilizing inflation. He admitted that it was "a tough program," but that the overall circumstances required it. His speech was considered so important that it was reprinted in *Vital Speeches of the Day* (Smith 1942e). The media also considered Smith's speech news, reporting on it in their daily coverage.[147] The *Wall Street Journal* reported that Smith's critical comments about congressional resistance to tax increases "obviously rankled" those on the Hill, even if his point was relatively accurate.[148] A few weeks later, a business columnist wrote that Smith had "intimated that the difficulties are partly the product of politics." For example, labor opposed wage controls while supporting limits on farm prices, while famers were arguing the opposite.[149] The *Post* and *Herald Tribune* both editorialized with sympathetic comments on the overall rightness of Smith's arguments.[150]

Indeed, as Smith had feared, inflation got worse over the summer. Congress refused to enact tax increases and to limit farm prices. Morgenthau's adamant advocacy of voluntary savings programs to encourage bond buying (instead of compulsory ones) was also a failure. According to Ickes, Smith "blames Morgenthau for the middle [*sic*, muddle?] we are in with respect to inflation."[151] Finally, in October (a month before the election), Congress passed a (relatively weak) price stabilization bill, in part simply delegating to the president more power to take control of the economy. Roosevelt promptly signed it, created an Office of Economic Stabilization (OES) in the White House,[152] and in a coup, announced that (former senator) James Byrnes would resign from the Supreme Court to head the new office. He would be a kind of czar of economic policy, even something of an assistant president. Smith was pleased by the decisive action, finally, though quietly unhappy that Byrnes's portfolio might impinge on Smith's assertions of BOB's leadership role in all matters relating to fiscal policy. To give Byrnes a running start, he and senior members of the Fiscal Division met with Byrnes and his team in Byrnes's new office to talk about what they had done up to this point. They also submitted a folder with further information on economic stabilization matters.[153] In the meantime, thoroughly exasperated with Morgenthau (despising is probably the more accurate term), he decided to try to marginalize him, at least for ongoing and routine business. Smith created a back channel to promote cooperation and coordination without personally interacting with Morgenthau. Smith, GAO comptroller general

Warren, and Under Secretary Bell agreed to meet at least monthly to discuss and work out any overlapping issues or conflicts.[154]

Manager-in-Chief of the Executive Branch

In April, Smith celebrated his third anniversary as BOB director. On the occasion, FDR sent him a letter of congratulations with a lighthearted compliment. He wrote, "Your three years of service as Director of the Budget may not have added to your life expectancy, but I can assure you that your faithful work has increased mine."[155] It was a strong signal of confidence, trust, and appreciation. For example, when Vice President Wallace complained directly to FDR about another agency impinging on the jurisdiction of Board of Economic Warfare he chaired, FDR declined to get involved. He told Wallace to bring it up with Smith because "all disputes of a technical nature were to be left to Harold Smith" (Wallace 1973, 68). Another time, Roosevelt scribbled on a Smith memo about yet another interagency squabble: "H.D.S. Unscramble. F.D.R."[156] The frequency of Smith's meetings with FDR seemed to subside significantly after the initial rush of the war. They were on the same wavelength and did not need to meet as frequently. By the fall, before the beginning of their conferences about the FY 1944 budget, Smith would sometimes go nearly a month without meeting with Roosevelt.

By now, BOB had established its primacy in the executive branch. A public brochure it issued about its work stated that BOB "has become one of the principal management arms of the President and it has been organized and expanded to perform duties appropriate to that role. This includes . . . developing improved plans of administrative management and advising Government agencies with respect to improved organization and administrative practice; bringing about more efficient and economical conduct of Government service, . . . and keeping the President informed of the progress of Government agencies in carrying out work programs" (US BOB 1942, 2). A business publication, not inclined to cover FDR favorably, described Smith as "making a big reputation as a competent administrator."[157] Another reporter described him as "the President's incorruptible right-hand man for purposes of internal administrative coordination" (Kiplinger 1942, 335). Sometimes there were glitches in the controls he tried to foster over the executive branch. When that happened, he vehemently defended the bureau's primacy and worked to prevent it from happening again. For example, Landis, the new OCD director, submitted directly to the president a suggested policy and press release on blacking out federal buildings. When Smith found out, he was furious. He wrote to Press Secretary Early that "this letter should have come through the Budget office in the first place." He was particularly annoyed because "two or three things have happened recently that are extremely awkward and embarrassing to the Administration." He asked Early to assist him "in seeing that these matters that are poked in at the White House get our consideration."[158]

The war also led to a change in the leadership of the agency. One of the reorganizations that Smith worked on in the spring was to unify all housing-related agencies.[159] When Rosenman, Smith, Blandford, and Coy presented their draft executive order to FDR, the conversation naturally turned to who should head it. Rosenman suggested Blandford. "The President said to Rosenman that he would have to make his peace with Harold Smith, the President, and himself" for doing that. Smith lightly protested that it had taken him six months to pry Blandford from TVA "and now they proposed to take him away in seven minutes."[160] Without saying so aloud, Smith knew it was a good idea. In early March, Blandford was sworn in at a farewell ceremony at BOB.[161] Smith quickly asked Coy, OEM's liaison officer, about taking the job. Smith and Coy frequently worked together on common issues, often talking on the phone, meeting, or having a working meal. Coy agreed, if the president would okay it. A week after Blandford's departure, Smith met with FDR. "I reminded the President that he had stolen a man from me and that stealing one from him was only fair play, at which he indicated that he enjoyed my point."[162] Smith pivoted quickly to lobby Congress to increase the salary of the assistant director to $10,000, parallel to a separate pending proposal that his own salary would increase to $12,000, the same as the comptroller general. Congress accepted the former and rejected the latter.[163] That meant Smith and Coy had the same salary. Smith tried to be philosophical about it, knowing the vagaries of congressional politics. As it turned out, in power-conscious Washington (and to reporters), this outcome became a badge of honor. The impression was that Smith thought so highly of Coy's skills that he could accept with equanimity the two having the same salary. A routine criticism of bureaucrats was that they were status conscious and insisted on the perks appropriate to their station, including a higher salary than those at the next level down the hierarchy. The oddity of their identical salaries added to Smith's image of uprightness, diligence, commitment to public service, and that his values and priorities were admirable. Coy took office in April and served as assistant director until January 1944 (Lee 2018a).

Smith continued convening summit meetings to coordinate federal policy and to unjam bureaucratic logjams. These included conflicts between the vice president's Board of Economic Warfare and Ickes's role as petroleum coordinator,[164] allocation of manpower,[165] overtime policies,[166] and the Civil Air Patrol (CAP vs. Army).[167] Oddly, Alaska was a recurring problem all year. Subjects that he had to get involved with included the idea for the Alaska Highway,[168] lack of coordination between the Navy and Army about locating installations there,[169] assessing the record of the appointed governor,[170] jurisdiction of the Interior Department versus the Army over the territory,[171] conflicting reports and lack of authoritative information about developments there,[172] and whether to invest federal money to explore for oil there.[173] Sometimes he had to clean up after FDR and, softly, admonish him for going against an organized and systematic management approach. At a November press conference, FDR unexpectedly announced that federal employees would not be eligible for draft deferments. He was evidently responding to yet another charge by Senator Byrd and fellow critics, this time that federal civil service employment was a way to dodge the draft.[174] Smith scrambled to undo the damage.[175] He sent a very strongly worded protest to FDR for announcing a policy without giving BOB a chance to clear it with relevant federal agencies. In fact, for months he had been struggling to develop a coherent policy on the subject. He wrote:

> I dislike to write you a note in this vein, but I know no other way of getting the issue immediately before you. After reading your release on deferment yesterday, I confess that I went home last night literally mumbling, I was so dumbfounded. . . . On the face of it, the release seems to deny—which I know you did not intend—the whole basis of occupational deferment. It seems to deny, too, the importance of civilian government. I do not wish this memorandum to be a matter of record. If you will tear it up, I will destroy the carbon. Nevertheless, it comes from the bottom of my heart.[176]

FDR was unrepentant. He dictated a reply, saying that he would be glad to talk it over with Smith. However, in the meantime, he wanted to convey exactly why he did it:

> The simple fact is that sometimes a large dose of castor oil is necessary for a very slight cold. We have in the Government

an enormous number of men who ought to be with the fighting forces. . . . I will make you a good sized bet that in the hundreds of Government office people, young men without a lot of children are running mimeograph machines or blueprinting machines where the work could be done just as well by women or older men. That is just one example of dozens of cases which must be disclosed. The fact remains that it is being said by thousands throughout the country that the best refuge during this war is a Government job.[177]

Eventually, Smith succeeded in backfilling by establishing a policy that assumed no deferments and creating a three-person committee to hear appeals from agency heads on retaining individual employees on a case-by-case basis. Smith recruited Ordway Tead, a well-known management theorist, author, and professor in New York, to serve on it.[178] All requests would first be screened by William McReynolds, head of EOP's Liaison Office for Personnel Management (Lee 2018a, 226–27).[179] Difficult cases could even potentially go to the president for final decision.[180]

On other occasions, Smith weighed in on management principles and leadership weaknesses. For example, he felt strongly about retaining civilian control of nonmilitary activities, rather than subsuming everything under the military in time of war. In one case, in late 1942, when the issue of occupation policy was becoming relevant (after the Allied invasion of North Africa), Smith argued to the vice president that occupying authorities set up in conquered or liberated territories should be civilian dominated and independent of the Army, rather than administered by the Army (Wallace 1973, 136n1). Around the same time, he had also lost confidence in McNutt's management of WMC. In some cases, Smith recognized that problems were structural because WMC had mostly advisory rather than executive powers. However, he also advised FDR that McNutt was not a strong enough administrator or leader to take on the workforce problems of the war.[181] BOB's government-wide oversight and management policies were often closely linked to the conversion to war. They included conservation of electricity by federal agencies,[182] blacking out federal buildings (Roosevelt 1972, 19: 194–95),[183] saving paper (253–54),[184] combing federal installations to salvage rubber,[185] reducing oil changes in federal cars to twice a year,[186] ordering non-war agencies to transfer office supplies to the military,[187] an executive order giving BOB control over surplus supplies and equipment held by all agencies,[188] banning buying new typewriters,[189] and canceling

Christmas Eve as a vacation day for federal workers (Roosevelt 1972, 20: 278). War or no war, Smith and BOB also had duties regarding the more prosaic elements of overseeing public administration throughout the executive branch. They included issuing revised standardized government travel regulations,[190] uniform financial reporting,[191] standard working hours,[192] financial apportionment (Seckler-Hudson 1944, 6: 94–95), and position control for agency staffing (165–80).

At a meeting with staff in the Administrative Management Division, Smith tried to articulate his management principles for the agency. First, nearly every topic handled by one division also overlapped with another. Therefore, the need for continuous "clearance," that is, that internal cooperation was essential for BOB to perform well. He did not want to see any centrifugal or autonomist tendencies. All for one and one for all. Second, he urged patience. Government moved slowly, even in war. Third, staff should seek voluntary cooperation with executive-branch agencies when promoting reform. Diktats tended not to work or last. Finally, he said they "should be willing to take a kick or two without giving up."[193] Obstacles and setbacks were inherent in accomplishing management reforms and efficiency. It was a concise summary of his own operating style as well as the professional culture he was trying to institutionalize in BOB.

Spokesperson for the Administration through Intensified PR

The first year of the war became a pivotal time in a cresting of the conservative coalition's criticism of FDR and the New Deal (Caro 2019, 74). The declaration of war turned out to be a lever that opened the door for attacks that were more pointed because now there appeared to be a brighter line distinguishing essential and nonessential spending. Ditto for essential versus nonessential agencies and programs (especially New Deal ones). The war was an opportunity to pour old wine in new bottles. Instead of the obvious ideological and partisan motivations for opposing FDR before, now the framing was that the criticizer was a patriot who supported the national war effort and was, sadly, concerned that the administration was bungling it. Their criticisms were presented as seeking to help bring victory by identifying the president's many mistakes. A political scientist aptly depicted the endless criticism of FDR's management of the war effort as "damning him for not being perfect" (Hart 1943, 31). Writing nearly sixty years later, Fleming emphasized that "lost to memory was the ferocious antagonism between Roosevelt and Congress" during the war (2001, 558).

In their memoirs shortly after the war, WPB's Nelson and Bruce Catton (his PR officer) tried to convey this atmosphere. Nelson was astonished that the media "always blew up each of our intramural arguments into a show a little larger than life-size. . . . Many rumors of disagreement were planted or inspired by some who wanted to injure WPB" (1973, xii–xiii). Catton was less restrained in describing the atmosphere:

> The we-hate-Roosevelt people were successful beyond their dreams during the war, and 1942 was the year of their first big triumph. . . . Any action which the administration might take (other than those actions directly concerned with military matters) was sure to be unsound and ill-advised and was more than likely to be revolutionary; thus they always had something to criticize, and the criticism never had to be documented since it was based on an axiom rather than on facts and reasoning. Better yet, this created a game in which both ends could be played against the middle; for the very fact that this criticism was being made could then be used as a basis for further criticism, the idea being that there must be something terribly wrong or the administration wouldn't be under so much attack. (1969, 180)[194]

Based on his behavior in 1942, Smith evidently concluded he needed to contribute to reversing this media depiction of the war effort and the success of the conservative coalition's role in amping it. Up to now, Smith had a media image of an official who "is little known to the public" (Kiplinger 1942, 334–35) and who "shies from publicity."[195] Another reporter concurred saying "he shuns personal publicity" (Childs 1942, 85).[196] This image of modesty was helpful because it gave Smith's public statements added credibility and gravitas in contrast to Washington's more prevalent publicity hounds and credit-takers. In general, Smith's actual behavior vis-à-vis media relations had been evolving toward a more proactive strategy of public communication. As he had in the previous years, he continued giving speeches to specialized audiences and, sometimes, to lay people, but now more frequently and more widely. He also wrote more. He grafted on to the enhancement of his now-routine activities much more of a mass media communications effort, including press releases and press conferences. He focused mostly on updates about the wartime mobilization. In all these enhanced and newer PR efforts, he was trying his best to convey what the federal government was *accomplishing*.[197]

On Friday, April 24, he issued a press release summarizing a report that the House Ways and Means Committee (which handled taxation) had requested of him. It provided an updated picture of his estimates of spending and revenues for the current year (FY 1942) and for FY 1943, the budget Congress was in the midst of considering. His key message was a positive one, of the administration's strong ramp-up of its defense and then wartime spending. Responding to events, spending had quadrupled since the previous fiscal year. "The pace of our war effort is even faster than these annual figures would indicate. Thus, weekly expenditures have increased rapidly, and are up 70 percent since Pearl Harbor." He also made a point of emphasizing that even "with such all-out war effort, about $50 billion of national income will remain for civilian use. This sum will provide more of the necessities of life than during the depression but less than during the past year."[198] As he intended, the release dominated weekend news coverage. On Saturday, the focus was on the hard news aspects of his release.[199] By Sunday, his release was getting more analytic coverage[200] and even editorial commentary. The *Star* observed that Smith's report "should make some very unpleasant week-end reading for Adolf Hitler and his Axis associates."[201] The *Baltimore Sun* opined that Smith's "figures tell an amazing story of the way in which American industry is responding to the demands for more tools to win the war."[202] On Monday, Ernest Lindley, one of Smith's favorite columnists, analyzed of the implications of Smith's report.[203]

Smith followed up with three speeches to specialized audiences in May and June. On May 8, he was the main speaker at a regional conference of the Council of State Governments in New York City. He called for a unified and cooperative fiscal policy that harmonized the federal government's wartime needs with budgeting by states (1942b). His speech received substantial media coverage.[204] A week later, he spoke in Chicago to a similar conference for Midwestern officials (1942c). His message was largely the same and it, too, was covered in the media.[205] Finally, in early June he spoke to a regional conference for municipal officials in Syracuse (NY). While targeting his remarks more specifically for mayors and urban officials, his message was consistent about fiscal policy (1942d). He acknowledged the difficulties that cities faced due to the war, but urged them to cut spending while not cutting taxes either.[206] A large audience of five hundred heard his message.[207] Also to a specialized audience, Smith wrote an article about the impact of the war on federal budgeting and the implications for municipal finance. To these budget professionals he emphasized, "Far from being a casualty of war, the Federal budget system is proving its vitality and strength. . . . The principle and the practice of official accountability to the people are being preserved" (1942f, 5). Besides his national radio address on the administration's anti-inflation program (1942e, discussed earlier) Smith gave another talk to a lay audience in an October speech titled "Progress Toward Victory." Speaking to the Muskegon (MI) Chamber of Commerce, it was an effort to communicate to the citizenry-at-large a positive message about the war effort. He was determined to knock down the persistent and nit-picking criticisms by the conservative coalition. Sure, there were some mistakes and there could be improvements in winning the war.

> None of us should be satisfied until that job is finished. But I think it is important that our dissatisfaction with this or that element of the program should not obscure the over-all accomplishment. The war effort has too often been discussed in terms of negatives. The things that are not going well receive a disproportionate amount of attention. . . . I am anxious that the argument over our relatively minor and recoverable failures does not lead us into confusion and dissension. More than ever it is important that we keep our facts straight, that we maintain a sense of proportion and a clear perspective. (1942g, A4046)

The speech got modest media coverage, but the AP filing got his message and theme right.[208]

Most different from preceding communications patterns was Smith's push for more frequent BOB press releases to report repeatedly on budgetary matters and to highlight the record of the administration. With Marsh on the staff as a PR specialist, Smith could generate more releases and reports. And he wanted to. Smith had also figured out that media coverage was, in part, drawn to entertaining and interesting stories, even humorous ones. That insight also contributed to his successful higher media profile in 1942. In particular, his relationship with AP's Perlmeter continued to deepen and he often gave Perlmeter exclusive stories. Besides the relationship of trust they had developed, AP was the dominant American news service. That meant a story by Perlmeter and other AP reporters would reach practically every daily newspaper in the country. Smith apparently tipped off Perlmeter the exact day FDR had signed off on the budget message for FY 1943 and sent it to the printer.[209] A few days later, Perlmeter wrote a feature column for the Sunday papers summarizing Smith's recent speeches to state and municipal government officials. He framed Smith's fiscal policy recommendations as a way to have jobs for veterans after the war. They could be employed for the large backlog of public works that governments were postponing because of the war and with the funds those governments were salting away. He approvingly quoted Smith saying that "it is this consistent action by all governments—Federal, State and local—which I hope will successfully counteract the forces of unemployment and deflation in the post-defense period."[210] Perlmeter later told BOB's Marsh that the version published in the *Star* had been edited down and that "the story was carried in more detail in some out-town newspapers."[211]

Trying for some humor in a relatively prosaic story about increased funding for the navy, Smith released a statement for another Sunday news cycle that "the Navy is in for a tremendous run of good luck . . . [that] sees 7s and 11s written all over the Navy's future work." The release then explained about how these two numbers appeared uncommonly frequently in BOB's consideration of the budget request.[212] In another lighthearted release, Smith ruled that the federal government would uphold its treaty obligation to the Choctaw tribe in Oklahoma of an annual gift of $320 worth of iron and steel, notwithstanding wartime scarcity of metal supplies.[213] Several short stories followed during the year, including how many people were now working for the government and the record pace of spending was reaching $1 billion a week.[214] In August, Smith gave AP an exclusive release for a Monday story (when news was relatively scarce for morning papers) on what BOB was doing to relieve the president of unnecessary and routine paperwork.[215] The other reporters he trusted were the *Post*'s Kluttz and syndicated columnist and *Newsweek* reporter Lindley. Kluttz, who wrote a daily column aimed at a readership of civil servants, frequently cited Smith, usually in a positive or neutral context. Indicating the relationship, a column in July referred to Smith as the "hard-working Budget Director."[216] These things did not just happen. Smith understood the need for the care and feeding of the press. For example, in August, Kluttz organized a monthly contest of ideas from federal employees for improving federal operations and saving money. He wanted an outside jury to give weight and gravitas to the awards (a $100 war bond) as well as increasing the chances their ideas could be enacted. Kluttz asked Smith to serve and he agreed.[217] (The other two were McReynolds and Congressman Robert Ramspeck [D-GA], chair of the House Civil Service Committee.) Marsh promised Smith that he would not have to spend much time on it because Marsh could handle the preliminary screening of submissions. And, besides, doing a favor for a daily columnist who watched BOB like a hawk?! It was a no brainer. For Smith, serving as jury member for the contest was like a publicity gift that never stopped giving.[218]

Lindley had a higher that average interest in public administration and economics. For example, when Coy had been appointed LOEM in April 1941, Lindley wrote, "Coy knows public administration as few men do who have not given their lives to it—and in the process lost all their imagination. Like Budget Director Smith and a handful of other first-rate public administrators, Coy is able also to understand public policies and to devise means of furthering them."[219] Lindley had written a column in April analyzing the significance of Smith's report on wartime spending and revenues. He occasionally called Smith to get his off-the-record take on news developments. For example, he called on January 16, April 17, June 6, and December 31.[220] Indicating a very high level of trust and desire to influence coverage, on February 4, Smith called Lindley to *suggest* a column. At the time, in the second-guessing and finger-pointing after Pearl Harbor, there was media criticism of Congress for lack of adequate funding for the fortifications on Guam (which fell relatively easily to the Japanese).[221] Trying to shift the blame, the chair of the Senate Naval Affairs Committee quickly blamed BOB because it had never *specifically* recommended line-item funding to strengthen the defenses of Guam.[222] Smith wanted to share with Lindley his version of the story.[223] Lindley wrote a column alluding to Guam in passing, but he did not discuss BOB's role.[224]

In October, BOB tried to stimulate more positive coverage of the administration.[225] It released a quarterly summary updating figures on spending and taxing for the fiscal year. It received substantial coverage.[226] When sharing a copy with FDR, Smith noted that the data "supports your press conference statement that the production program is coming along in good style."[227] With relatively obvious political implications a month before the midterm elections, Smith was trying to break through the noise with some positive and pro-administration news. On the other hand, in one of its last issues before the election, *Life* magazine (part of the *Time* corporation) ran a photo spread titled "The Roosevelt Party." The article pointedly mentioned that all Americans supported winning the war. Therefore, "the one nationwide issue on Nov. 3 boils down to this: Are Franklin Roosevelt and the men in power with him doing a good enough job of running America and fighting the war? And if they are not, would it be better to put more of their political opponents in office? On the following pages LIFE prints photographs of 42 high-ranking members of the Roosevelt Party. . . . These are the individuals who are running the U.S. today. They are the 'Ins' in the great political campaign of 1942."[228] The feature was a heavy-handed hint of the Republican preferences of its publisher, Henry Luce. Smith was the fourth person listed, after Hopkins, Byrnes, and AA David Niles, and before Rosenman, Lubin, and Coy. He was probably startled and unhappy to be one of the forty-two members of the Roosevelt *party*. It went against his posture of being an apolitical and nonpartisan budgeting specialist. Slightly mitigating the magazine's identification of him as political, the caption for his picture stated, "He is a college-trained expert on public administration who stays out of political limelight. He gives the President more specific advice than anyone and is an expert on planning big Government reorganizations."[229]

The Tydings and Byrd Committees and Smith's PR Counteroffensive, October–December

Some press coverage during the summer demonstrated what Smith was facing from Byrd and his allies. A profile of Byrd in the *Herald Tribune*'s *Sunday Magazine* sanitized his anti–New Deal ideological motivations and instead praised him for "waging a crusade to save taxpayers' money."[230] An editorial in the *Post* similarly praised Byrd's "axe."[231] Along with consistent negative depictions of FDR's management of the war by the Byrd Committee that continued in 1942, another front for the conservative coalition that year was a separate committee chaired by Senator Millard Tydings (D-MD).[232] In February, the Senate approved a resolution submitted by Tydings for the appropriations committee to create a special subcommittee to investigate expediting the war effort, such as by transferring more civilian employees from non-war to war agencies and, generally, "reducing governmental expenses."[233] The three-person subcommittee, chaired by Tydings, quickly began bombarding the administration with questionnaires, sometimes in apparent coordination with Byrd (Lee 2018a, 173–74). In July, the Tydings subcommittee released its report. It bared its teeth regarding how conservatives felt about Smith's reconceptualization of BOB's mission and activities. The report was especially scalding about Smith's support for the Keynesian theory underlying the work of the Fiscal Division. Using as a baseline the 1921 Budget Act that assigned BOB the duty to pursue economy and efficiency, the committee sought to explain the cause of the failure to perform the mandate of the law under which it operates. Patently, the ineffectiveness can be attributed to one or more of three factors, viz.:

(a) Inadequate staff.

(b) Inexperienced or unqualified staff.

(c) Intentional or inadvertent failure to execute responsibility.

. . . The committee, however, is of the considered opinion that the ideologies and the adherence to certain theories in regard to governmental fiscal policies impair, and to an extent nullify, what might otherwise be obtained by the technical expertness it undoubtedly possesses. Certain officials of the Bureau of the Budget and the National Resources Planning Board have been and are yet carrying on a very discreet, but nonetheless pernicious, propaganda to the effect that there must continue after the war even greater mounting deficit spending. . . . Surely the lack of development of advance plans of coordinating the programs undertaken by nonwar agencies can be attributed primarily to a lack of proper functioning on the part of the Bureau of the Budget. (US Senate 1942b, 28–29)

The report "urgently" recommended "a thorough investigation of the Bureau of the Budget, covering in such investigation the fitness of the personnel, methods of operation, failure to take prompt action looking forward to placing the Federal Government upon a streamlined all-out war basis, and whether the Bureau should be made independent of the Executive and responsible only to the Congress" (34). It was a full-throated conservative attack. It concisely and openly depicted what Smith and FDR were up against. That's why Smith felt he needed to be more proactive in publicly presenting a counternarrative to the voters. Indicating one of the underlying purposes of the Tydings report, a few weeks after releasing it, the senator sought and obtained Senate permission to print *twelve thousand* more copies of it for public distribution.[234] His report, along with those from the Byrd Committee, served as a kind of ideological reference book for use by candidates, party organizations, and business publications seeking in the run-up to the election to attack FDR's record of (mis)managing the war effort. Like the piece in *Life*, the Tydings report was a call to action to elect more conservative candidates in November (Lee 2011, 160).

Smith understood what was happening and what the (political) stakes were. He was determined to counterbalance the conservative publicity with his own. In addition to his speeches and public statements, he also focused even more on a media-based PR counteroffensive in coordination with the White House. For example, at a June 12 press conference, Roosevelt praised the Navy's effort to reduce paperwork (in contradistinction to the separate effort to conserve *paper*).[235] Hours later, Smith issued a press release stating that a BOB initiative had already reduced red tape for a savings of over $1 million. The government could save even more, he pointedly noted, if only (ahem) *Congress* would reduce some required reports. Smith briefed Perlmeter on the upcoming release.[236] It was widely covered, perhaps because it was a tangible example.[237] Indicating the trench warfare between pro- and anti-administration voices, conservative reporter (and syndicated columnist) Frank Kent accurately summarized the BOB release, but then noted it was printed on two sheets of paper, using only one side of each. He archly insinuated that BOB was not practicing what it preached because it did not print the statement on both sides of paper.[238] A few weeks later, Smith followed up with a report on reducing freight-shipping costs. Understanding the importance of building alliances on the Hill and letting pols take credit, he released the report through a friendly committee chair in the House who had suggested the subject of the study.[239] Kluttz wrote a column on the BOB report based on a wire service story.[240]

A few weeks before the election, Smith took his biggest shot. It was a comprehensive rejoinder to the claims from Byrd, Tydings, and colleagues. BOB prepared a fifty-eight-page report with data on current non-war federal expenditures. Roosevelt transmitted it to Congress as a presidential report (US House 1942b). FDR also used the report as the central news peg at his October 16 press conference. He quoted liberally from it and Coy was on hand to answer any highly detailed questions from reporters (Roosevelt 1972, 20: 147–52). The report showed major reductions in non-war-related spending, with the eye-popping top line statistic that 92¢ of every dollar that the federal government was now spending related to the war effort.[241] Columnist Louis Lyons later wrote a complimentary analysis of the report. He said it was "full of surprises," such as that legacy cabinet departments were now spending 30 percent less than in 1933 and that other traditional spending categories, such as (routine) construction programs "have been

greatly reduced." He lightly criticized Smith for his "unemotional" summary of CCC spending, given how much it had contributed to a healthy
male citizenry ready for war service. According to Lyons's calculation, 95¢
of every dollar was spent on the war.[242] It was one of the few opinion
columns to praise the report. And, inevitably, it was a somewhat boring
read. Smith must have been disappointed that Lyons's column came out
after the election. Otherwise it could have been used by Democratic speak-
ers and surrogates in the way that conservatives used the Tydings report.
It could not have been coincidence that Senator McKellar two weeks later
(and just before the election) tried to blunt the impact of the BOB report.
He announced the pressing need for a new effort by Congress to "slash"
non-war expenses. In his view, there was so much more that could be cut.
Countering his claim, as far as the restrictions that objective wire service
reporting permitted, the (unnamed) AP reporter noted that "it may be
found difficult to make any savings unless some departmental activities
generally looked upon as contributing to the war effort are curtailed."[243]
The caveat, buried in the story, was a constructive, if low-key, point from a
well-informed and politically neutral observer who was contrasting fact-lite
political rhetoric with budgeting reality.

The political stakes of that long year came to a head on Election Day,
November 3, 1942. All year, conservatives had attacked Roosevelt for his
wartime leadership. Mostly, the year was full of bad news from all fronts,
such as the fall of Corregidor and lack of any major American offensives.[244]
To conservatives, these negative headlines were objective confirmation of
their critique of the president.[245] Their framing of the war succeeded. The
Democrats lost forty-five seats in the House and eight in the Senate. While
the party retained its majorityship in both houses, the margins were narrower.
That meant the leverage of Democratic conservatives increased, because when
joining with Republicans they now had a decisive voting majority. The next
shoe Byrd dropped was a hearing in early December amplifying the ongoing
complaint by business that they were flooded with excessive and intrusive
federal questionnaires. Some duplicative, some seemingly silly bureaucratic
fishing expeditions, all a burden. This was red tape at its worst, they said,
because it was costly and time-consuming for corporations. A particular
ominous example that the committee focused on was the scary looking code
on one questionnaire: 1-1071-PLOF-5-NOBU-COS-WP. Surely, this was an
example of the bureaucracy gone amok.[246] Within a day, Smith knocked
it down. It was merely an innocent combination of printer's symbols, he
said. For example, PLOF-5 merely meant it was the first of a five-page

publication. NOBU meant no backup, a printing instruction. COS was the code for collating and stapling. WP was the directive to wrap it. Smith tried to take advantage of the embarrassing opening this false accusation provided. He pointed out that the antigovernment scare-mongering by the committee based merely on an odd code on a questionnaire was yet "another example of the tendency to leap at conclusions when Government agencies are under attack."[247]

However, to everyone's surprise, on the substantive issue of federal questionnaires sent to businesses, Smith largely agreed. After all, the Division of Statistical Standards had become part of BOB in the 1939 reorganization. One of its goals was better coordination of federal statistical collection. In his role as a statutory member of the Byrd committee, he attended the hearing and made the point that coordination and cooperation were worthy goals (US Congress 1942, 12–15). For once, the Chamber of Commerce and Smith were allies. Within a few weeks, Smith announced new BOB controls over federal questionnaires.[248] With the help of the conservative coalition, he had obtained another lever for more centralized managerial oversight of the executive branch. The embarrassment of the false accusation notwithstanding, for the larger issues, Byrd was still dominating the headlines. Smith decided that he needed to give FDR on a regular basis some ideas, facts, and other information the president could use in his twice-a-week press conferences to try to neutralize the conservative onslaught. At his press conference on December 8, Roosevelt took on another Byrd accusation that at least one-third of federal employees were not essential and should be let go. FDR said that, contrary to impressions and rumors, only 12 percent of federal employees were in the capital and that 60 percent of federal civil servants were engaged in direct wartime activities (Roosevelt 1972, 20: 282–86). It was headline and front-page news.[249] The headline of sympathetic coverage in the liberal New York newspaper *PM* said, "FDR Debunks Byrd Figures." The article included a knock at Byrd's operating style: "As usual, Byrd voiced his conclusions before beginning his investigation."[250] However, Byrd was not intimidated by the implicit presidential attack on him and the joint committee. He knew how to have the last word. He told a reporter he would press on in his battle to cut the size of government and that the president's claims were simply wrong or misleading.[251] To another reporter, he made a thinly veiled attack on Smith. Byrd said, "I can only reach the conclusion that his subordinates, who should know better, have not given him the true facts."[252] Conveying the righteousness that the economy bloc felt as well as overlooking its ideological bent, a conservative columnist depicted the fight between the Byrd Committee and the administration in Manichean terms:

> It is too bad that instead of combating the facts and refusing to recognize the situation, he [FDR] cannot bring himself to admit the existence of an undeniable evil and join with those who, with no motive save a patriotic one, are trying to correct it. If he would do that he would not only increase competency and shorten the war but save himself considerable future bitterness.[253]

Besides submitting information more frequently for FDR's use at his press conferences, Smith also decided he needed to step up the number of BOB releases to "fill in" between press conferences or when FDR was on vacation. He felt that "the public seems to get the impression that we are doing nothing" and he was determined to reverse that, or at least counter it.[254] For example, on December 10, he announced that through simplification in bookkeeping recommended by the Administrative Management Division, the federal government was saving $3 million and the equivalent of two thousand employees.[255] Later that month, in another press release, he said that BOB's drive to identify surplus office equipment and move it to war-related uses had already reclaimed $250,000 worth of supplies, 10 rail cars of nails, and a locomotive. In addition, he had reclaimed 4,500 typewriters and expected eventually to retrieve 30,000.[256] At a Christmas Eve press conference, FDR announced that Smith had sent a questionnaire to all agencies requiring them to identify additional staffing and activities that could be reduced in the near future. BOB would then submit quarterly reports to him with results of this ongoing effort.[257]

Promoting Professional Public Administration

As ASPA's past president, Smith continued being involved in the activities of the association and in promoting the profession. Brownlow (the current president) and Smith spoke frequently, sometimes about ASPA business, sometimes about improving federal management.[258] For example, Smith and Brownlow met with the National Resources Planning Board to discuss its efforts at postwar planning, talked about finding an appropriate person to run the National Capital Park and Planning Commission, and brainstormed about finding the right candidate to become WMC executive director. Would a successful city manager have the right qualifications? No, they decided, such experiences would be too narrow for a large federal agency.[259] Smith also spoke frequently with Luther Gulick, head of the Institute of Public Administration.[260] In the second half of the year, Gulick was involved in management improvements at WPB and frequently conferred with Smith and Coy.[261] Other leaders in the field Smith interacted with included Don Price and Lyle Belsley.[262]

He supported several initiatives to advance the profession, including the Committee on Comparative Administration to discuss "the experience of other countries in matters of over-all national administration."[263] He routinely talked to Professor Pendleton Herring for updates on Smith's initiative of recording a history of the war's administration *during* the war.[264] Smith met with Robert Crane, head of the Social Science Research Council. They discussed the "failure of management in this country" and ideas for organizing a project to investigate it.[265] He also met with a senior British public administrator visiting the US to compare notes on the profession.[266] Smith was particularly interested in advancing training in public administration and related topics. He talked to Albert Lepawsky at the University of Chicago regarding the "possibility of making funds available for defense training in public administration" and Barbara Terrett of the American Society of Planning Officials about a "practical training course in planning."[267] He also met with the president of American University in DC about the institution developing and offering a new course "on budgetary control."[268] It was tentatively titled "Budgeting: An Instrument of Planning and Management." Smith promised that BOB would be as supportive as possible, including providing senior staffers as guest lecturers.[269]

Roosevelt continued relying on Smith to promote improved management in the executive branch. In November, the comptroller general (a former Democratic member of Congress and FDR appointee) informed the president that he was thinking about appointing an in-house professional as assistant comptroller general, instead of the past practice of political appointments to that position (Lee 2018b). FDR asked Smith for his advice. Smith eventually told the president that he concurred in the idea because the person "is undoubtedly the best career man in the General Accounting Office for the job."[270] Setting the precedent of shifting the position from a political appointee to a professional would help strengthen a neutral and apolitical culture at GAO. On another occasion, when dealing with the failings of WMC, FDR asked Smith to help McNutt "find a good Executive Director

and overhaul his administrative organization. I told the President I would
be glad to do that."[271] In June, Smith received public recognition for his
contributions to public administration. American University announced that
it was awarding him an honorary Doctor of Laws degree as "the individual
who has made the most significant contribution to sound governmental
administration" based on a national poll of leaders in political science, public
administration, and government service.[272] The university provided a more
detailed rationale for the award in a profile it published a year later. In the
first issue of a booklet series titled "Governmental Portrait," it said that
Smith recognized "the need for skilled and imaginative management in the
public service comparable to that required in modern industry. . . . Smith
has devoted his life to the yoeman [sic] work of bringing an awareness of
this need to communities throughout the country and to developing in
pragmatic fashion the skilled management essential to the conduct of large
government enterprises" (American University 1943, 3). He "has helped to
change the prevailing belief of many years that any person can successfully
administer the public's business. His career is a living testimonial to the fact
that disinterested and skilled administrators make unique and vital contributions to the functioning of democratic government in the modern age"
(9–10). In particular, "without personal or political ambition, Mr. Smith
has devoted his energy to stimulating good management in Government,
his imagination and foresight tempered by practicality and patience" (11).
Smith was very proud of the honorary doctorate and routinely listed it on
his resumes and biographical sketches.

Preparing the FY 1944 Budget, October–December

As he had the previous year, Smith was not as personally involved in the early
stages of the preparation of the annual budget and rarely attended in-house
hearings or boards of review. He occasionally met with senior federal officials
when they came to BOB for their reviews.[273] His first in-house working
meeting was on October 12, 1942, when he met with Coy and two senior
officials of the Estimates Division to map out some general guidelines for
preparing the budget.[274] In early November, he told FDR that he and Coy
"hoped to make the Budget grind as short and agreeable as possible, having in mind your other burdens." He suggested scheduling them on a few
Saturday afternoons over the next month, when the president usually had
lighter appointment schedules and could converse in a more leisurely way.

If they could arrange that, Smith noted, "I think we can cover the subject rather rapidly."[275] They had their first meeting on November 10 (a Tuesday). Roosevelt went through their recommendations on the independent agencies and generally "took a vigorous stand against small increases in any of the independent establishments," except those with authentic wartime roles such as the Civil Service Commission. He mentioned that he eventually wanted to merge the American Battle Monuments Commission into the War Department, which ran the national cemeteries. He also gave them specific guidelines for the budgets of several USDA bureaus.[276] They had additional short meetings on November 25 and 30, and December 8 to cover more departments and agencies.[277] As usual, one of the last budget items to be finalized was BOB's own budget. Roosevelt approved Smith's draft, including shifting positions that had previously been funded from the president's emergency discretionary funds to the regular budget, as well as a new $200,000 appropriation to establish a BOB field service with four offices. When Smith said that the bureau's list of upcoming management studies included use of cars by federal agencies, Roosevelt asked that they examine if "various camps of the Army are over-supplied with staff automobiles," which he thought was the case.[278]

Smith was determined to get out ahead of the PR framing of the budget. Notwithstanding the general secrecy around the budget until introduced by the president, he did not want to *react* to predictable stories from Capitol Hill about how the economy bloc (now strengthened by the election results) was sharpening its knives for the inevitable waste they knew would be in the FY 1944 presidential budget. On December 1, AP moved a story from Perlmeter on the upcoming budget. Without revealing too many details, its source, or any not-for-attribution quotes, the story summarized what it called the president's upcoming Victory budget. It would be over $100 billion for the fiscal year, a truly staggering amount. The only reference to Smith was about how Roosevelt, Smith, and Coy were "sifting and resifting the figures" as they finalized the budget. Perlmeter made a point of telling readers that the annual budgeting ritual "is one task that Mr. Roosevelt always has performed personally, though this year he may not have time to red-pencil the budget in such minute detail as before."[279] There can be no doubt that Smith or Coy leaked the story to him.

When they were done with the budget itself, they quickly segued to discussing the budget message. Smith said a preliminary draft was ready for Roosevelt to review. Roosevelt said he would like to get it right away because he was leaving for the weekend and wanted to be able to review it then.

Smith also reminded FDR of the problems Smith had had in previous years prying revenue estimates and tax plans out of Morgenthau. Nonetheless, Smith "felt it most important to include in the Budget Message specific references to the revenue program of the Government and perhaps specific references as to the tax program to raise the revenue."[280] In fact, a week before, FDR had sent Morgenthau a note (evidently prepared by Smith) saying that BOB was "responsible for the drafting of the Budget Message." This was a mild effort to disabuse the secretary of his routine assertions that the revenue section of the message was exclusively his responsibility. FDR also said he was unhappy that in the last few years there had been publicity leaks about the budget message ahead of the president sending it to Congress. He told Morgenthau he did not want that to happen this year and directed Morgenthau not to share drafts with his staffers. Then, in addition to this typed message, Roosevelt handwrote a message on the memo to make clear how strongly he felt about this: "I want all leaks stopped."[281] A few days later, as a way of emphasizing his territorial claim, Morgenthau hosted a summit meeting of all senior administration officials involved in economic policy. It was promptly leaked, probably by one of his staffers. The story said "Morgenthau had no comment" on the meeting. Nonetheless, the anonymous leak served the purpose of highlighting the centrality of his role.[282]

After Three Years at BOB: Health Problems

The pace of work was beginning to take a toll on Smith. His health collapsed in mid-1942. He felt so unwell he could not make it to the office on Saturday, June 20. He did not feel any better after resting all weekend. On Monday, he went to the naval hospital in Bethesda for a physical exam.[283] (As a WWI navy veteran, he qualified for medical services there.) He delayed telling FDR for nearly a month. Finally, in mid-July he told the president that he had a "slight heart disability."[284] Elaborating a bit, he told Ickes he had "some trouble with his carotid artery."[285] Kluttz opaquely reported, "Smith is taking it easy for a change. Doctor's orders . . ."[286] Dr. Masters at Bethesda warned Smith of the potential serious consequences of trying to continue with the status quo. He told Smith that he must slow down his daily schedule, take more time off, get exercise, lose weight, and generally try to relax. Smith tried to be lighthearted when he told FDR, "This is really the first vacation I have had since I have been out of college."

He assured the president that Assistant Director Coy "was handling things nicely" and would be able to deal with any matters FDR directed to BOB in Smith's absence.[287]

For the better part of the summer and early fall, Smith usually worked shorter hours or did not come in at all. Some afternoons, he left early to play golf with colleagues or his wife.[288] (When they had moved to Washington in 1939, they bought a house in an Arlington [Virginia] neighborhood called Country Club Hills. One of its attractions was being adjacent to a course. Mrs. Smith also loved playing golf and he said she was a better golfer than he was.[289]) By September, he had gradually increased his working hours and came into the office every day. Later in the month, Smith told Ickes "he is in pretty good shape now but he is still keeping easier office hours."[290] He was feeling so much better that he disregarded the doctor's instructions after the June exam to schedule a follow-up appointment. Masters called in late September to insist.[291] On October 7, Smith met again with Dr. Masters and was apparently better. Smith had scheduled that check-up for early in the morning because he was in a hurry to make it to a 10:00 a.m. meeting on Capitol Hill with two senators.[292] Occasionally, in the fall and early winter, Smith stayed home all day or left work in midafternoon to play golf.[293]

≈

In all, 1942 had been both an exhilarating and crushing year for Smith. From the day after Pearl Harbor, he focused on rebudgeting the federal government for war, along with managerial priorities of reorganizing, expanding, and decentralizing. He fought for a reasonable fiscal policy that balanced spending, taxing, and deficits along with the need for a forceful anti-inflation policy to tamp down on price increases caused by war spending. Amid that, he had to fend off aggressive efforts by the congressional conservative coalition to undermine FDR politically, including a more vigorous PR effort to counter the coalition's incessant complaints about how Roosevelt was bungling the war effort.

Chapter 6

The Second Year of the War, 1943

By 1943, the war was becoming routine and normal. That did not mean it was getting any easier. In fact, it seemed like the longer the war went on, the more problems arose. Sometimes that was because FDR's short-term and ad hoc decisions simply could not last as long-term solutions (such as stabilizing prices and wages), sometimes because new issues arose (such as the governance of the occupied territories in North Africa), and sometimes because considerations of postwar planning became more concrete (such as disposing of surplus property). Also, the year was a major turning point in the war. Military news from Europe included the surrender of the German army in Tunisia in May, the invasion of Sicily in July, and the invasion of Italy in September. Diplomatically, the year included the Casablanca conference in January (FDR's declaration that only unconditional surrender would end the war) and the Teheran conference with Stalin in November.

The greatest difference between 1942 and 1943 was Congress. For the next two years, Smith and the rest of the administration had to face the 78th Congress. The results of the November 1942 elections meant that the conservative coalition of conservative Democrats and minority Republicans had a voting majority that could control outcomes on the floors of the House and Senate. Milton succinctly summarized the implications of the election results: "Democrats managed to retain control of both Houses; but the President distinctly did not" (1944, 308–09). Roosevelt agreed. At about the midpoint of the 78th Congress, he told Smith that "for all practical purposes we have a Republican Congress now."[1] From the beginning, the conservative coalition was eager to flex its muscles both policy-wise and politically. Compared to Smith's decent working relations with Congress previously, even given dealing with the pre-election attacks from the conservative coalition in 1942 (chap. 5), 1943 would be much, *much* more difficult.

Above and beyond dealing with Congress, for Smith 1943 was a tough year all around. For example, looking outward, he told FDR he was "greatly concerned about the effect of over-optimism concerning the progress of the war upon the public attitude toward the various Government control programs," such as rationing.[2] When letting his hair down over lunch with Ickes at the beginning of the year, he confessed losing confidence in several of the key leaders of the civilian mobilization, including WPB's Nelson and WMC's McNutt.[3] Midyear, Smith said to Ickes he was "thoroughly unhappy about certain situations in Washington and apparently has thrown up his hands."[4] A few weeks later, Ickes said that Smith "looked and acted unhappy."[5] After FDR declared in December he was no longer "Dr. New Deal" and instead was "Dr. Win-the-War," Smith was so discouraged "he wondered whether he ought not to get out of the administration. He had talked with Wayne Coy, who felt as he did."[6] Nonetheless, Smith soldiered on, loyal to Roosevelt, a patriot when the nation was at war, committed to professionalizing public administration at such a time, and believing in what he was doing.

Finalizing the FY 1944 Budget Message, including Fighting with Morgenthau, January

The calendar year began, as usual, with a last-minute fight between Smith and Morgenthau over the revenue section of the president's annual budget message. This time, it was the worst of Smith's four budgets. Perhaps the mutual dislike and rivalry between the two simply kept escalating over time, with neither willing to let the other prevail. It was probably a near-toxic mix of bureaucratic territoriality, primacy with FDR, and economic policy differences. Morgenthau and Treasury continued insisting on the conservative doctrine of consistently balanced budgets—whether through spending cuts and/or tax increases—while Smith and BOB's economists supported deficit spending as permitted by the new Keynesian economics (chaps. 3–4). Their mutual loathing played a part, as well. Their fight ended up delaying the introduction of the budget past the legal deadline. On New Year's Day, Smith was still drafting the budget message.[7] That day and the next he shared limited parts of it with Treasury Under Secretary Bell. According to Bell, Smith said that the president had already largely signed off on the revenue section of the message. Smith also claimed that while meeting with FDR, the White House doctor had come in and told them that Morgenthau was very ill and that FDR then turned to him (Smith) and said not to bother Morgenthau with the budget message (Blum 1967, 56–57). The draft included some tax policies Treasury opposed, such as mandatory savings programs for taxpayers (to reduce consumption) versus Treasury's preference for voluntary savings programs, such as bond drives. Bell and Morgenthau of course hit the roof, both for process reasons of a fait accompli and for substantive policy reasons.[8] Morgenthau complained directly to the president, who soothingly told Bell that the message was not in final form and he welcomed Treasury's input. At a White House summit meeting with FDR refereeing between the two camps, the president revised some language in the revenue section of the budget message to finesse over the differences. Smith would have to go back to Roosevelt with the new final version for approval. On Wednesday afternoon, January 6, Smith had his last meeting for FDR to sign off on it. "I told the President that I felt rather unhappy over the fact that I was not able to get substantial agreement about the tax aspects of the Budget Message, and I expressed regret that this had caused him so much trouble. . . . I said that I felt beaten but unbowed. He said, 'I feel the same way,' and laughed."[9]

By now, it was clear that the budget was late, in apparent violation of the statutory requirement when it should be transmitted to Congress. At a press conference on January 5, Roosevelt said the delay of a few days in the literal submission of the budget to Congress was largely a mechanical one due to the printing process for such a large document. He revealed that the budget would be about a thousand pages, the longest ever.[10] Missing the traditional deadline along with its unprecedented length made the budget an irresistible target for the media. The next day, Smith was featured in a front-page political cartoon in the *Star*. He was pictured sitting next to Gus Giegengack, Public Printer (head of GPO), who was busy at a typesetting machine. Behind Smith was a pile of paper nearly reaching the ceiling, titled "Biggest budget in history." Smith sighed to Giegengack, "About printing it, Gus. The longer I can postpone sending it over there [Congress], the better I like it."[11] Roosevelt held his annual briefing (which he liked to call a seminar) for the White House press corps on the budget on Saturday June 9. Smith and Coy were there. Smith greeted him saying, "Good morning, teacher," and handed him some last-minute notes as the reporters were filing in. It was a long session, about two hours (Roosevelt 1972, 21: 28–85). As usual, Roosevelt did most of the talking, though Smith and Coy actively participated. As they were adjourning, FDR said to the reporters, "Have a good time! I'm glad I don't have to write a piece on this!" One reporter replied, "You're lucky," and another said, "You're fortunate." The formal budget was released two days later on Monday, June 11.

Elections Have Consequences:
A More Conservative and Assertive Congress

FY 1944 Appropriation for BOB, January–April

The year started off pretty well for Smith, with his annual appearance before the friendly Independent Offices Subcommittee of the House Appropriations Committee. This panel had consistently—even before Smith's appointment—supported expanding BOB to increase its ability to monitor and control federal spending and activities. Chair Woodrum began the hearing by saying that BOB's growth had contributed to an "impressive" record of accomplishment. The increased funding from the subcommittee "can legitimately be used and expended in the initial considerations of these appropriations [and it] is where you will stand a chance of doing something about it. It is too late after the money is spent and you are looking over the dead carcass of the situation" (US House 1943a, 1157). Smith's budget proposal was to increase funding for BOB by about half a million dollars, from $2.2 million to $2.7 million (1166). About half of that would be to establish a field service and the other half to cover personnel costs for people hired during the preceding fiscal year and temporarily funded from discretionary and emergency accounts. Some of the questioning by members focused on government-wide activities, an acknowledgment that Smith was largely an overseer of the executive branch and could be a source of information about larger issues than just the appropriation for one relatively small agency. That was precisely the role Smith was seeking to establish for BOB. When he concluded his testimony, he said, "If at any time, aside from these formal appearances, you would like any additional information, we shall be glad to give it" (1211). Starnes (D-AL) concluded the session by reiterating the compliment he had expressed a year earlier, "I think you are doing a swell job, Mr. Smith" (1211). The subcommittee and committee recommended full funding of BOB's request.

For Smith, the year began going down (Capitol) Hill from that point on. During the House floor debate, members adopted an amendment to cut BOB's budget by $180,000. Overturning the committee's recommendation meant that conservatives were in control, that they felt the penny-pinching appropriators were not tough enough or tight enough. Smith then asked the Senate to restore that amount (US Senate 1943a, 351–53). Led by the combative McKellar, it instead cut the amount further. When the bill finally reached the president, the increase in BOB from the previous year was only about $100,000.[12] Smith decided to apply any net increases to establishing the nucleus of a field service, though not at the level he had planned.

Byrd Committee, February–June

All year the Byrd Committee issued a stream of reports that were critical of the size of government. As a member of the committee and supplier of government-wide data in response to requests from Byrd, Smith knew the committee was working on a report about automobile use in the federal government. And he knew that it, of course, would be critical. Trying to deflate the headline impact of the report, he took action just before it came out. On February 6, he released a statement about a new BOB directive reducing the number of tires non-war agencies held in their inventories. He said he was retrieving about a hundred thousand tires from individual agencies for war-related use and was centralizing control of such supplies into the Treasury's Procurement Division. He said, "This may be a normal supply of tires in normal times, but it is hoarding in times like these. I dislike to spank Government agencies publicly, but conditions like these will not be tolerated."[13] It was a slick move. A week later, when the Byrd Committee issued a report on federal vehicle use, it was compelled to quote Smith's press statement as a confirmation of the thrust of the report (US Congress 1943a, 3). In March, Byrd gave a statement to the *New York World-Telegram* that White House staffing was "swollen" in comparison to WWI. He said that when Wilson was president, the number of people working in the White House was 48, while now it was 906.[14] Smith had his staff check the accuracy of the statistics. It turned out that Byrd had inflated his count by including not only the White House Office category (47), but also BOB (500), NRPB (292), and employees maintaining the building and grounds (60).[15] However, Smith apparently decided not to rebut the charge publicly.

In May, Smith again knew that the committee was about to release another report, this one on federal travel and communications. Again, he tried to beat Byrd to the punch. On May 25, he issued an order to all federal departments and agencies to stop buying twenty-eight types of office equipment from the commercial market. He said his cease-buying order was necessary because some federal agencies—mostly their field offices—were ignoring WPB priority regulations and were paying "exorbitant prices" and drawing down the availability of scarce supplies and materials.[16] The next day, Byrd released a report on excessive federal spending on agency travel expenses and costs for phones, telegrams, teletype, and postage. He declared that the amounts "can be drastically cut" (US Congress 1943b, 1). A month later, the committee released another report, this one on personnel. It was a litany of complaints and charges, including a 55 percent increase in staffing "not in war production" (a very carefully worded category, different from war-*related*), an "alarming rise in personnel," that the effect of federal hiring was to "drain the personnel market" for other employers, "top-heavy pay rolls," and general "waste and ineptitude" (US Congress 1943c, v). At the end of the year, Byrd released a summary of the committee's work in 1943. Smith pointedly refused to sign it.[17] He said, "While the progress report of the committee includes much that I endorse," it also made some claims that had "no basis." For example, the report stated, "hundreds of thousands of unnecessary Federal employees are still kept from more valuable war work by reason of their needless and duplicating activities." It also implied that the number of nonessential employees was "400,000 or more" (US Congress 1943d, 8).

House Civil Service Investigation, April–October

Early in 1943, the House passed a resolution calling on its Civil Service Committee to conduct a special investigation of federal civilian employment, particularly to "investigate the effect of such policies and practices upon the conduct of the war, with the view of determining whether such policies and practices are efficient and economical" (US House 1943b, 239). In less diplomatic terms, this sounded like the premise of the investigation already had a conclusion: there were too many non-war-related civilian employees. The committee was being tasked to implement this assumption by identifying how many should be fired and where. The committee's investigation included extensive hearings into BOB, sometimes focusing on it as possibly yet another standard-issue federal agency that was overstaffed, sometimes on its government-wide scope of oversight and control. Besides Smith, BOB witnesses included L. C. Martin, head of estimates; F. J. Bailey, head of legislative clearance; and Donald Stone, head of administrative management. Smith's testimony was extensive, covering three committee sessions (US House 1943b, April 14: 240–71; May 11: 273–92; May 12: 293–316). The members were deeply familiar with civil service laws but had little knowledge of BOB. In part, the testimony was to educate them about BOB's missions, how it was structured, what it did (and could not do), and why.

In the end, that aspect of the committee's investigation yielded little relating to BOB. According to an interim report in October:

> Some students of the civil-service structure are of the opinion the Bureau of the Budget has wide, discretionary powers over Federal management. . . . Evidence before your committee shows conclusively that the Bureau of the Budget has extremely limited authority over the various agencies and departments. It can, and does, study proposed budgets of the departments. It can, and does, slash cost estimates. But the Bureau of the Budget has absolutely no authority over management. It could not, for example, demand adoption of control systems in overstaffed agencies, even where such systems have proved of enormous help in other departments. Even in its determination of the numerical strength of an agency, the Bureau of the Budget frequently overshoots the fiscal mark and a year or more lapses before the proper adjustment is made." (US House 1943c, 12–13)

Little more could be done to improve the situation until *Congress* acted:

> The bald fact is the uncoordinated departments of the executive branch of the Federal Government lack an over-all, centralized authority with powers of management control. Therein lies one of the basic troubles of personnel duplication, overlapping of functions, and overstaffing. The time has arrived when the Congress should give serious consideration to this fundamental ill. Until this situation is corrected the taxpayers can expect a continuance of needless hiring and duplication of effort. (12)

Given this statutory context, "improper management, therefore, cannot be laid at the door-step of the Chief Executive" (13). In other words, FDR was not to blame, nor was BOB. It was an unusual conclusion considering the direction of the winds on the Hill. Credit should probably go to chair Robert Ramspeck (D-GA), a conservative yet something of a fact-based policy wonk when it came to the intricacies of federal civil service laws.

The committee's final report at the end of the 78th Congress, in December 1944, reinforced the interim report. It recommended that "the power to require the adoption of better management practices should rest with some agency or official with definite responsibility to deal with this subject. Some feel the power should be lodged with the Budget Bureau. . . . The committee urges that legislation be considered dealing with this problem; that power be placed with some official or agency by which the departments and agencies in the executive branch can be coordinated and controlled as to their housekeeping and management problems. We believe that if this is done millions of dollars can be saved each year" (US House 1944a, 17). The report's conclusions on these macro-policy issues were discordant with the set ideological views of the conservative coalition: FDR was mismanaging the war effort, FDR had too much power, staffing of non-war agencies was bloated, and extensive duplication existed in federal operations. Smith was lucky, he had dodged a bullet. The report focused on micro-recommendations regarding overstaffing in, for example, the West Point laundry, the State Department's hiring of veterans, the Navy's *Bellevue* magazine, and the Army's mail and files unit (US House 1944a, v).

House Investigation of the Federal Communications Commission, June–July

Besides the investigation of civilian employment, the new conservative House also approved a resolution to create a select committee to investigate the Federal Communications Commission (FCC). It was led by conservative Eugene Cox (D-GA). From the beginning of the New Deal, a long-running conservative trope had been that federal regulation of radio licenses (and, crucially, *renewals*) implicitly leaned on stations to air materials provided by federal agencies (Lee 2012, 40–41). Now, conservatives claimed that the FDR-nominated majority under chair James Fry was mismanaging the agency and enumerated fifty charges, including incendiary accusations such as interference in the war effort and endangering national security.[18] To New Dealers, this was largely a political attack, rather than a normal fact-seeking investigation. Before the beginning of its public hearings, the ranking Republican on the committee, Richard Wigglesworth (R-MA), asked Smith to permit a committee investigator to examine BOB files relating to the proposed transfer of

FCC's radio intelligence office to the military.[19] Smith, by now experienced with congressional efforts to impinge on his in-house interactions (chaps. 3 and 5), knew that based on the administration's precedents he should decline and he so notified FDR.[20] When he replied to Wigglesworth, he stated that the records were "confidential papers, and disclosure of them would not comport with the public interest." Therefore, "I have been directed by the President not to make the Bureau files available to the committee or to testify as to their contents if called as a witness" (US House 1943d, 34). The committee then subpoenaed him to appear at a public hearing in July. Before Smith began his testimony, the committee chair swore him in, thus making him eligible for perjury and contempt of Congress charges. Smith again declined to produce the documents, describe them, or even confirm where they were physically located (34–39). It was a tense meeting, with Smith being as vague as possible and exceedingly careful about what he said while the committee kept asking him the same questions repeatedly. As far as he was concerned these were presidential documents and he opaquely alluded to someone from the White House collecting relevant BOB files when the issue first came up. For the media, this was high drama.[21] Finally, when asked if he was declining because it was a public hearing and if his answer would be different regarding a closed executive session, he said he would have to confer with counsel before answering. The eventual answer was the same. Months later, a radio industry publication reported that the committee would not be bringing contempt charges against Smith "in the light of war conditions."[22]

1943 Revenue Bill, October–November

During the war, every year the administration routinely asked Congress to pass a tax bill to help cover some of the costs of the war. Generally, Congress did. But not in 1943. With the more conservative Congress, the tax bill instead was reframed as a synecdoche for the endangered free enterprise system, under threat from the over-taxation of the New Deal. In one effort to reduce the amount of revenue necessary to cover part of the war's costs, in October, the House Ways and Means Committee called Smith to testify on the spending side of the budget. With victory coming in sight, then should not the costs of the war begin going down? If that were the case, then less new revenue would be necessary than predicted when the president submitted his FY 1944 proposed budget in January. At a closed executive session (as opposed to a public hearing), Smith testified for three hours. According to a syndicated column, it was "a scathing off-the-record session," including one member who "put the screws on" Smith for Army spending.[23] However, no matter how much committee members pressed, he said he expected no significant reductions in spending, whether due to war developments or based on supposed exposés about wasteful spending.[24]

Next came the Senate Finance Committee. The committee's focus was on a claim by a congressman that the Army had not spent $13 billion allocated it and therefore, the need for revenue could be lowered by that amount. Smith said that the assertion was "very misleading" and largely a "bookkeeping savings" because, in part, the money was held in the Army's financial reserves and the Army could reallocate unexpended funds for other purposes. Smith also told the committee that any potential temporary dip in Army spending would be offset by a substantial increase in Navy spending that was just around the corner. In all, he said, total war expenditures were increasing rapidly.[25] This was not what the committee wanted to hear. A few days later, a front-page cartoon in the *Star* made fun of the confusing story. War Secretary Stimson says to Smith, "Well, Congress said I had 13 billion and I'm returning it back unspent." Smith, sitting at his desk covered with papers and books, replies, "You didn't have 13 billion dollars, so how could you turn it back?"[26] It was not his best hour, particularly given his ambition for BOB to be the lead federal agency on all matters of fiscal policy, taxation included. The final version of the annual tax bill raised very little new revenue and was sprinkled with giveaways and tax breaks for various businesses and other special interest groups. FDR vetoed it. Stunningly, both Houses of Congress overrode his veto.[27] It was a low point in FDR's wartime leadership and a high point in the conservative counterrevolution.

Congressional Oversight of Individual Projects, November

In 1942, FDR had endorsed Ickes's suggestion of spending $1 million to explore for oil in Alaska. It was, relative to the scope of the war effort, a minor idea. However, it turned out that, separately, the Army was considering a much more extensive project, including drilling there for oil, building a very long pipeline, and financing an oil refinery. Its initial paperwork estimated spending about $25 million. However, using other discretionary War Department and army funds, the project ballooned to about $119 million. In addition, the Army agreed it would give up the refinery at the end of the war. Senator Harry Truman (D-MO) was chair of a special committee to investigate wartime spending waste. The Canada oil project (known by the shorthand of Canol) was one of the projects he investigated.[28] Smith testified on BOB's role in the project. Its record put BOB in a good light: monitoring major defense projects, hiring experts needed to assess specialized subjects, and sending investigators to the field (US Senate 1943b, 9551–62). The blame fell on the Army. Press coverage stated that Smith "served notice" that the War Department was on its own to try to justify the project.[29] In this case, Smith escaped not only unscathed, but also looking good. An editorial declared that his role and record on the project was "wholly sound."[30] In a sense, BOB performed precisely as Smith had shaped it to be: careful and detailed oversight, expertise, second opinions, but not micromanaging.

Separately, Representative Jennings Randolph (D-WV), chair of the House District of Columbia Committee, criticized the operations of the central garage in Washington for federal vehicles. He said that the garage was underused and was more expensive for storing cars than private operations. Smith replied in a nondefensive tone. Yes, BOB was involved in the plan and that idea was "sound in principle and should be encouraged. . . . Like all new enterprises, the costs of this operation are higher as it gets underway and can be expected to reduce progressively as the facilities reach maximum utilization."[31] Smith also argued, "The useful life of vehicles could be prolonged and ultimately operating costs could be lowered as the result of the improvement and standardization of maintenance practices."[32] It was classic public administration: centralization, standardization, and economies of efficiency. Randolph harrumphed that, nonetheless, if it was not successful soon, it should be closed.

First Supplemental National Defense Appropriation Bill, October–December

After the first quarter of FY 1944, and based on FDR's requests, Congress considered an omnibus bill covering additional defense appropriations for the rest of the fiscal year. One item requested by the president was to increase BOB by $355,300 (US House 1943e). This was partly to recapture the requested funding that had been rejected in the Independent Offices bill and partly to cover other additional costs. Smith wanted to hire eighty-one new staff and transfer ninety-one positions currently funded by temporary and emergency funding to permanent funding. It was an ambitious request, particularly because the bill was not being heard by the friendly Independent Offices Subcommittee of the House Appropriations Committee, but rather by its Subcommittee on Deficiencies. Clarence Cannon (D-MO), chair of

the committee and subcommittee, described the political context of the bill
when Smith testified in October:

> The greatest complaint that we are having today from the laity,
> so to speak, is that every bureau and department of the govern-
> ment is overstaffed. You hear it in radio broadcasts; you see it
> in the magazines; you read it in the columns . . . that every
> office in the Government is full of people who have nothing to
> do, who are falling all over each other. And you hear a great
> many circumstantial stories, many of which are apocryphal, but
> widely circulated to the effect that there is much overstaffing.
> (US House 1943f, 844)

In other words, the conservatives had conquered the media and public
opinion. Their political claims trumped facts. Smith tried his best to deal
with this political storm surge. He emphasized the facts coming from the
statistics BOB routinely released on federal employment levels, gave examples
of agencies with diminished staffing, described the overall personnel cuts BOB
had pushed for, and—closer to (his) home—said that BOB's efforts to reduce
overstaffing or duplication could be improved by expanding BOB's staff.
That would give it greater ability to monitor personnel levels. For example,
BOB management studies often led to reductions in personnel because they
recommended such things as cutting red tape, streamlining procedures, and
eliminating unneeded questionnaires. These were not glamourous and none
led to headline results, but they were fact-based and consistent. At the time,
one of the politically popular ideas on the Hill was to order a 15 percent
across-the-board cut in personnel in all agencies and departments. Smith
gently argued against it because it was not merit-based and not targeted. He
also made the point that, for example, firing federal employees working in
government arsenals might reduce the head count, but someone (presumably in the private sector) would have to provide staffing to manufacture
munitions. Smith doubted that, by definition, federal employees at arsenals
were less efficient than if they worked for business doing the same thing.
"I suspect that in many cases they are more efficient than people working
elsewhere, or certainly just as efficient" (868).

The most withering and sarcastic interrogation was conducted by John
Taber (R-NY), the ranking minority member on the committee and the
subcommittee. When Smith talked about his new initiative to coordinate
and examine public works projects (which would be staffed by engineers

hired based on funding in this request), Taber wanted to know where the new staff would come from. "I am getting reports that the derelicts on the Resources Planning Board [which had just been defunded] have been drifting into your office in almost a deluge." No, said Smith, the "report that you get is just obviously wrong." He could recall hiring only two professionals and two secretarial. When Taber insisted on a hard count, Smith later submitted a list of seven former NRPB staffers he hired, four professionals and three secretarial (880). It was hardly a deluge. Taber was working his way through a kind of hit list compiled by the conservative coalition. What about staff Smith hired from the just abolished National Youth Administration (NYA)? "How many of that crowd have gravitated into your office?" None, said Smith (881). Taber wanted to know how closely BOB monitored the overseas activities of the Office of War Information (OWI). He said that OWI was "having thousands of campaign buttons struck off and distributed overseas to the armed forces." He was implying that OWI was propagandizing members of the armed forces to vote for Roosevelt in 1944, should he run again. Smith said he had never heard of that, but would be glad to double-check. The eventual submission from BOB stated that OWI had not done that. Perhaps the congressman was referring to "50,000 lapel clips that have been distributed abroad as token gifts to less literate native populations, principally in the Middle East and Egypt. The inscription on these clips is in Arabic or in English and Arabic" (881).

Taber claimed he knew about movies OWI was producing for overseas use. (Conservatives condemned early New Deal movies as political propaganda masquerading as mere documentaries, such as *The Plow That Broke the Plains*.) None that he knew of, answered Smith. Taber asked about another OWI activity: "I am advised that they have revived the W.P.A. theater project to take it overseas. What can you tell me about that?" Smith did not know anything about it, but promised to check. He later reported to the subcommittee that OWI "has not reestablished any phase of the Work Projects Administration writers and artists section" (882). Next up, OCD. What had Smith done about "curtailing its activities with the manifest reduction in need for its activities?" Smith said that OCD's personnel was down 335 people from the preceding quarterly report. Taber scoffed, saying that this number of people "would be a minor item" for an agency with a $13 million annual budget, would it not? Smith coolly replied that the reduction totaled a quarter of all OCD employees (882). What about OPA and all the complaints about "their ridiculous activities"? Smith answered that based on the information he had, OPA needed more staff to deal with the problem. Taber countered, "They say so, but when you come to examine their activities, you find they have got too much help." Smith refused to back down. Taber then homed in on OPA's regulation of rents, "They are doing things that are perfectly ridiculous. . . . They have got too much help." Smith declined to argue, but in his post-hearing submission for the committee record, he contradicted Taber with statistics that OPA rent control staffing was already down in the preceding year by about 900 people, from about 3,300 to 2,400. In salaries, that was a reduction of $1.9 million (882). Taber shifted to complaining about some of the budget requests the president had submitted to Congress based on Smith's recommendations. Referring to the message from the president about USDA and the Reconstruction Finance Corporation (RFC), he said, "I would like to know who it was that worked on that estimate." Smith drew the line and refused to name any staffer (883). All recommendations from BOB to the president were his own responsibility, not that of his staff. Furthermore, all recommendations to Congress came from the president. Taber retreated to requesting a listing of the staffing (not names) of personnel in each subsection of the Estimates Division. Smith did so (885–90). Taber later accused BOB's Legislative Reference Division of "requiring requests for information from Members of Congress [to agencies] to be submitted to the Budget." Smith politely, but unequivocally, answered, "We never had any such policy" (895).[33]

Toward the end of the hearing, Smith tried to refocus the attention of the subcommittee members to the bigger picture. First, BOB was a staff agency, not an operating agency. Therefore, it did not exercise the kind of direct micro-control over the executive branch that he was being asked about. Second, the only spending BOB recommended was for programs and activities that had been approved by Congress. BOB's mission was the budgetary implementation of legislative policy. Third, BOB staff are "civil-service employees who carry out the policies of the administration, and it does not make any difference what administration is in power or what the policies are. It is their job." Fourth, while he was conscious of the public mood to cut government, "in terms of public opinion, it gives us no answer to specific problems." Finally, the rapid wartime expansion of the federal government was an unprecedented management effort. Under such condition, BOB (and the administration) could not be expected to be perfect. In such a large organization, having some missteps "is inevitable" (893).

Smith must have been shocked when the committee recommended a version of the bill that cut the administration's request by 82 percent. In relative terms, the committee was less tough on BOB, cutting the request for $355,000 in about half, to $175,000. In the context of the rest of the bill, that was a general expression of support for BOB. That was still not acceptable to Taber and his fellow Republicans. They filed a minority report saying that any signal of support for BOB by the committee was "gratuitous" and "unwarranted." The estimates it submitted to Congress were not tough enough and not focused enough on cutting spending—as had been the traditional role of BOB before Smith. Instead, "bigger and bigger budgets appears to be its motto," Taber said.[34] When the bill reached the Senate in November, it was referred to an appropriations subcommittee chaired by McKellar. Smith gamely hoped that the unpredictable McKellar might at least be attuned to his agency's efforts to oversee spending, staffing, and management. That was not what happened. McKellar was on the warpath. One of his first questions was, "Is it the purpose of the Bureau of the Budget to get all American citizens on the pay roll of the Government in some way or another?" (US Senate 1943, 328). He said that BOB should set an example in cutting its own spending, rather than appearing with dozens of other agencies requesting more money.[35] In particular, McKellar wanted to argue about BOB's policies of apportioning, reserving, and impounding funds appropriated to agencies. He claimed that these BOB activities exceeded its legal powers and that only Congress could make such decisions. McKellar quoted from federal law and challenged Smith to prove that he had not violated those legal limitations. They argued back and forth, with McKellar calling it "a very fair and frank conversation, and we have all been perfectly candid with you" (342). To wrap up that part of the hearing, he asked Smith to submit a legal brief justifying BOB's powers to limit appropriated spending. Smith did (738–41).

The version of the bill approved by the full committee was a full-fledged political declaration of war by McKellar. The bill recommended no supplemental funding for BOB.[36] It also banned any reallocations, reserves, or impounding by BOB. Such modifications could only be made by Congress. On December 1, Senator Hayden (D-AZ) called Smith to give him the bad news right away. He said that McKellar was "very bitter" about BOB allegedly assuming powers that McKellar thought belonged to Congress, notwithstanding BOB's legal brief identifying the legal basis of its activities. Hayden also said he believed "McKellar's ill health was responsible for his illogical attitude."[37] That was little consolation. In the floor debate, Truman, fresh from his investigations of defense spending, opposed McKellar's amendment. He said, "Good business practice requires a constant review of financial programs in the light of changing conditions. . . . I could name instance after instance of tremendous sums which would have been wasted had not the project been stopped before it got a good start."[38] McKellar responded as forcefully as he could. After debating the amendment over several days, the Senate approved a slightly watered-down version of it.[39]

Smith was stunned. If the amendment became law, it would be "a threat to central budgetary administration."[40] Reeling from the extent of hostility on the Hill to the competence of BOB, he concluded, "As Director of the Budget I have probably made a serious mistake. I should have been getting around talking to Congressmen for the last five years."[41] He quickly mounted a charm offensive to persuade House members to reject the Senate version. He even had an hour-long meeting with Taber! (A good lesson never to lose one's temper no matter how much a legislator baits you or tries to provoke you at a hearing. Today's adversary might be tomorrow's ally.) Taber understood the principle at hand and was vaguely sympathetic. Smith conceded to himself after their meeting, "I do not know to what extent he was really interested, but I thought possibly I had made some impression."[42] Cannon was adamant. He was against the McKellar amendment and, in two consecutive conference committees, refused to let the House accede either to the amendment or any compromise version of it. The showdown took place on the floor of the House on December 16. He moved that the House "insist" to the Senate that it opposed the McKellar amendment and that it would not recede from its position. This language was not "an economy" effort, as McKellar tried to frame it. Rather, "it would lead to extravagance" because agencies would quickly spend appropriated funds on projects, even if the circumstances and needs changed. "We should not be relaxing the restraints and controls which are in the interest of economy and the conservation of funds." When he finished, Taber spoke. He *agreed*. Given fast-changing war developments, "it is going to be absolutely necessary for the Budget [bureau] to impound funds on all sorts of projects or we are going to face financial ruin." The House stood by its opposition to the McKellar amendment by an astonishingly lopsided 283–18.[43] McKellar, facing the obvious, folded. The final version of the bill gave BOB an increase of $55,000, a pittance (about 15%) compared to what Smith had asked for, but an increase nonetheless.[44] Given the political mood—conservative, anti-spending, anti-big-government, anti-FDR—the end result for BOB was a near-miracle. In part, it was probably a tribute to Smith's consistency of performance since 1939: fact-based, unemotional, nonpartisan, encyclopedic in his knowledge of federal operations, accepting all phone calls from the

Hill, and being a low-key persona in his many congressional appearances. His BOB had established a record of delving in detail into government operations and making informed decisions, sometimes for more spending, sometimes less.

Reorganizing for Victory

Executive Orders

Organizationally, 1943 was a roller coaster. Roosevelt's ad hoc and unortho-dox view of good organization was largely a reactive one. Habitually and instinctively, FDR was "loath to act until the blaze was out in the open" (Milton 1944, 308). When a problem arose that absolutely needed fixing, he preferred signing another executive order to change the organization chart of the war effort. Those problems needing resolution sometimes reflected real-world and on-the-ground problems that cropped up, sometimes intra-mural fighting within the administration over turf, sometimes so-called crises trumpeted by the conservative coalition and the media. In each case, it was up to Smith to discuss the issue with FDR to get his general guid-ance, consult with the stakeholders within the executive branch, and then draft the executive order. Generally, Smith recommended solutions to such problems based on his views of what sound public administration was in terms of powers, responsibility, and harmonization with other entities. In particular, was his "insistence upon the development of fields of *function* to replace institutional overlaps" (308, emphasis added). Organizing by function meant clarity of power and elimination of loose ends, such as other agencies claiming some vestigial jurisdiction. But this principle was not possible on all occasions, particularly when the president was factoring in more than theoretical management principles.

In January, Smith submitted an executive order that strengthened the powers and scope of the Office of Defense Transportation (ODT), an increasingly important agency within OEM due to the importance of logistics and priorities.[45] This became apparent a few months later in a labor dispute and union strike that shut down the American Railroad Company of Puerto Rico. Roosevelt signed another executive order directing ODT to take control of the railroad and directly run it as long as necessary to keep it in operation until the company and union came to an agreement.[46] (When another strike by three railroad unions threatened to shut down the entire system, he signed an order giving the secretary of the army, rather than ODT, the power to seize and operate all major and regional railroads.[47]) Due to conservative political claims that many "subversives" worked in the federal government and were undermining the war effort, FDR used an executive order to create an Interdepartmental Committee to consider such accusations.[48] The actual results were relatively anticlimactic considering the rhetoric, with the committee itself ordering 24 firings and precipitating 143 voluntary resignations (Roosevelt 1969, 1943: 66–67).[49] Many executive orders aimed to resolve turf battles between federal agencies. In March, Smith prepared an order that sought to clarify the overseas propaganda operations of the federal government. There had been constant friction between OWI, Coordinator of Information/OSS, and the Rockefeller office for Latin America. The executive order largely gave the primary role for above-board communications to OWI (which, meanwhile, had been stripped of domestic PR by Congress).[50] Other reorganizations included creating the Solid Fuels Administration to handle coal supplies[51] (largely as a parallel organization to the Petroleum Coordinator) and reestablishment of the Committee on Fair Employment Practice as an independent OEM agency for matters of racial discrimination in defense industry hiring.[52] There were seemingly never-ending organizational details that could only be cleared up with further executive orders drafted by BOB, approved by Smith, and submitted to the president. In one case, the contraction of the PWA, which had been a major civilian construction and jobs agency in the New Deal, led to Roosevelt terminating it and transferring its small number of remaining projects to the Federal Works Agency.[53] Others included expanding the powers of the War Shipping Administration[54] and reshuffling roles for courts-martial between the War Department and the army's judge advocate general.[55]

One of the long-running interagency fights related to international economic policies. It sometimes involved the State Department (and its Office of Foreign Relief and Rehabilitation Operations), Lend-Lease, and Treasury. However, the public controversy was mostly between Vice President Wallace, chair of the Board of Economic Warfare (BEW), and Commerce Secretary Jesse Jones, who also headed the Reconstruction Finance Corporation (RFC). Giving formal and operational responsibilities to a vice president had been an unprecedented action by Roosevelt. Wallace had served adequately as USDA Secretary before becoming VP in 1941, but in part at USDA he had been more an idealist than a day-to-day detail-oriented bureaucrat. It turned out that he was also politically tone deaf. Rigid to the point of ignoring potential compromise, the riveting public fight between Wallace and Jones played out as an ideological boxing match: Wallace as one of the most liberal members of the administration and Jones as one of its most conservative. Smith tried, repeatedly, to work out the problems behind the scenes.[56] White House politics were also at play. Press reports claimed that Byrnes and Hopkins were out to get Wallace and kill BEW, while Smith and Coy disagreed.[57] They asserted that Wallace and BEW executive director Milo Perkins "had done an excellent administrative job."[58] Unable to resolve the fighting, FDR finally decided to intervene hastily, including publicly castigating both men (Roosevelt 1969, 1943: 298–99). Without warning Wallace, Roosevelt signed an executive order abolishing BEW, replacing it with an Office of Economic Warfare and transferring to it some of the RFC's subsidiary corporations.[59] While that resolved the public controversy between Wallace and Jones, it did not fix the inherent organizational and coordination problems involved. The quick reorganization had left untouched other relevant agencies, such as Lend-Lease and the Office of Foreign Relief and Rehabilitation Operations. Barely two months later Smith had to prepare another executive order, this one creating the Foreign Economic Administration and placing within it almost all these other federal entities.[60] Not all proposals for reorganization went forward. For example, Admiral King, the chief of naval operations, contacted BOB to ask for a reorganization of the Navy. At first blush, it was the kind of assignment Smith and Stone liked to do. However, cautiously, Smith talked to the under secretary of the navy about the request. Did the department support the request? It turned out that this was something of a power struggle between the uniformed service and the civilian department, as well as between King and Secretary Knox. Smith immediately understood the politics and agenda behind of the request for the reorganization. BOB declined to pursue the study.[61]

Office of War Mobilization

The most important reorganization of the year was the creation of the Office of War Mobilization (OWM). Congressional criticisms of FDR's war leadership usually called for creating a single official with full powers over the civilian side of the mobilization. Bernard Baruch, who held a vaguely similar position in WWI, thought he would be perfect for it and worked behind the scenes to create the impression that the public was demanding it (Lee 2018a, 106–07). At the same time, James Byrnes was already getting restless at the OES and scouting for a new portfolio. Finally, Congress was on the verge of passing legislation to create a super-agency with power over all nonmilitary agencies. It was something of a trifecta for Roosevelt to finesse all three of these factors by signing an executive order creating an Office of War Mobilization (OWM) and appointing Byrnes to head it.[62] Reporters quickly described Byrnes's new role as more than a czar, perhaps he even was now the *assistant president*. Coy, Smith's deputy, viewed the new office as a kind of chief-of-staff role for the domestic front, albeit without formal and legal line powers to order people around (Somers 1969, 48–49). Smith, who had final responsibility for drafting the order and submitting it to Roosevelt to sign, was, privately, quite against it. According to Coy, Smith's conception of BOB was that *it* was the super-coordinating agency for the executive branch. OWM would, by definition, lessen BOB's powers, centrality, and role. After the war, Smith told Somers in an interview that OWM was an "abortion" (67).[63] Coy experienced Smith's distaste on a daily basis. In his own interview with Somers, Coy said that Smith "refused to take official recognition of Byrnes as a Presidential spokesman. He dealt with Byrnes on an austere formal basis. He stubbornly resisted visiting Byrnes. He tried to follow the practice of simply writing memos to Mr. Byrnes."[64]

Three months after FDR signed the OWM executive order, Smith told Ickes "he wondered what Byrnes was really accomplishing." He had "doubts as to whether he [Byrnes] is really delivering the goods."[65] A few months later, Smith was upset that the responsibility for handling contract termination and disposal of surplus property was up in the air. Was BOB the lead agency or OWM or an operating agency? At one point, he threatened to issue a formal budget circular informing agencies that BOB had no role in surplus property and to direct all inquiries to OWM.[66] He then sent a sharply worded memo to Byrnes on the subject,[67] who promptly replied in kind. In a vague apology, Smith followed up ("Dear Byrnes") and said he realized that he had been "singularly inarticulate" in his original memo. The conflict "has absolutely nothing to do with personalities," rather "the growing number of jurisdictional problems."[68] The next day, the two met. Smith characterized the meeting as his "effort to overcome any misunderstanding which might have resulted" from his memo.[69]

However, there was one initiative by Byrnes that Smith must have been delighted by. In June, when the administration was struggling with how to raise additional revenue to cover some of the war costs, Byrnes intervened.[70] In his first press conference as war mobilization director, he announced that his new status gave him primacy in policy matters regarding taxes and revenue.[71] This must have chagrined Morgenthau because Byrnes suddenly outranked him in a much more explicit way than Smith had been asserting in the past. Byrnes was viewed as the assistant president and FDR did nothing to undermine Byrnes's claim of control over that policy area. This was further good news for Smith because Byrnes also recognized BOB's role in fiscal policy. He invited Smith to participate in a summit he was quickly convening along with Morgenthau and Fred Vinson, Byrnes's successor at OES. An article in the *Times* confirmed this standing, saying that "Mr. Byrnes is reported to regard the tax program as a matter for the Bureau of the Budget and the economic stabilizer as well as the Treasury."[72] In this new world, Smith was suddenly Morgenthau's equal. Better than a supplicant and beggar every year when preparing the budget message.

Decentralization, January–May

During the first half of the year, Smith continued decentralizing the executive branch, in part to create office space and in part to create housing. In January, he ordered 360 employees of the War Department to move to Philadelphia.[73] The next day, he said that the decentralization effort had led to the vacating of five thousand houses and eight hundred apartments around the capital for incoming war workers.[74] In early May, he ordered three hundred staffers of the VA's insurance bureau to move to New York.[75] That was his last decentralization order. In the middle of the month, Kluttz revealed that "plans to transfer several large bureaus out of Washington have been dropped. The acute office space problem here has been whipped."[76] For the first time since Pearl Harbor, there was now even a very small amount of vacant office space in the capital. Civil servants who dreaded having to move could finally stop worrying.

"Mr. Fix-it": General Manager of the Executive Branch and Presidential Coordinator

During the war, Smith came to see his role vis-à-vis the president more clearly. He had evolved to become FDR's "Mr. Fix-it." Roosevelt was increasingly turning to Smith to deal with complicated policies, problems, or personalities to resolve. Some of these assignments were directly or indirectly related to BOB's relatively catholic mission, whether budgetary or managerial. Others did not. As the president's confidence in Smith kept rising—and with the president increasingly preoccupied by the war—he knew he could turn to Smith to look into something and seek to fix it in a fair and rational manner. The term "Mr. Fix-it" appeared in a profile of Smith in the *Saturday Evening Post* in March.[77] The reporter apparently heard Smith use it to describe his handyman role in the administration. It effectively conveyed Smith's centrality and omnibus role in the running of the executive branch. Smith used the term in conversations with others, as well. Roger Jones, a longtime staffer in BOB (during and after Smith) said that on several occasions Smith described himself to Jones as having become the President's Mr. Fix-it. According to Jones, Smith was ambivalent about this role because it meant he sometimes had presidential assignments that went beyond BOB's formal and statutory duties.[78] Other descriptors were used to explain what he did. In another profile he was described as "President Roosevelt's 'trouble-shooter' and finder-of-men-for-tough-spots."[79]

Even though Smith was very unhappy about the super-coordinating powers assigned to Byrnes, it turned out to be less of a threat to his role than initially apparent. Byrnes was a *policy* guy, along with a heavy overlay of the politics of policy. He traveled light (with only a few staffers) and only intervened when policy and political matters necessitated a czar-type or his assistant presidential role to work out major problems. Management bored him, as did paperwork. He had no interest in administering anything (Lee 2018a, 236–39, 256). While the distinction between policy and administration can, at times, be quite thin, Byrnes's interests and use of his powers left a large scope of other matters to Smith. Smith was still the de facto general manager of the executive branch as well as a presidential policy coordinator for anything that Byrnes took a pass on. For example, Smith continued convening summit meetings to deal with bottlenecks in implementation of war programs. In July, he brought together the two managers who were fighting over responsibility for community facilities and forced them to work out an accord.[80] A few months later, he convened a summit meeting to coordinate programming and budgeting for farm labor. Participants included USDA, WMC, and the War Food Administrator.[81] Similarly, many of the executive orders that Smith prepared related to the less glamorous scut work and mundane details of management and administration. From the declaration of war, there were long arguments in the administration and on Capitol Hill about how many hours comprised "full time" work: forty, forty-four, or forty-eight? Roosevelt finally tried to settle part of it by signing an executive order requiring a forty-eight-hour workweek for civil servants and munitions workers.[82] Smith had tried to include the Post Office in it, but failed. (It remained at forty-four.) Smith also prepared executive orders relating to such diverse matters as agency reports to BOB to facilitate budgeting,[83] powers of the Panama Canal Zone government,[84] and uniform rates for dependents at some military hospitals.[85] During 1943, Smith also decided that the bureau needed to recodify the many budget circulars it issued and sent to executive branch departments and agencies. Based on a long-running numbering system going back to its founding in 1921, BOB had promulgated 424 policies that it imposed on departments and agencies. This was confusing and out of control, particularly because some were obsolete and others had superseded preceding ones. Therefore, on August 1 he announced that BOB was beginning a new series (dubbed with the prefix "A-"). He had whittled the number of active and important circulars down to thirty-two, a major simplification for agencies struggling to comply with BOB policies (US BOB 1943).

Early in the year, Smith convened an unusual all-staff meeting. His comments were revealingly frank and conveyed the impact of the war. Commenting generally about the federal government, he recognized that the rapid expansion of the executive branch had caused problems (and consequent public and congressional complaints), that federal employees had low morale, and that federal agencies were not functioning effectively. Homing in on management issues, one of the problems was that "we probably have not enough supervisory talent, or we do not have it properly placed, to deal with a problem such as this." The impact of an ineffective utilization of the workforce was another major management problem. The country had gone from a crisis of unemployment in 1933 to labor shortages in 1943. In fact, the mandate for a forty-eight-hour workweek for civil servants had been needed not only to neutralize political complaints, but also due to the authentic need to stretch the productivity of the limited number of civil servants. Adding to the problem, Smith acknowledged that some "industrial plants are hoarding manpower" and that some federal agencies were likely doing the same. The key, he said, was not to get discouraged and not to lose focus on problem solving. Smith tried to be philosophical about the turn of events, saying, "Sometimes I feel that I have lived a lifetime in that single decade." He acknowledged that changing circumstances called for new adaptations by BOB, including accepting the basic validity of the negative public opinion of how the federal government was conducting the civilian war effort. No matter what the agency had already tried or done, he urged a fresh look at longstanding or seemingly intractable problems. He suggested that if staffers adopt an attitude of " 'Well, let's see what we can do with them now,' we will get a lot farther." He also appeared to be concerned about some siloing occurring in BOB divisions. He urged employees to work "horizontally" and with relevant staff in other divisions. He concluded with an exhortation:

> We are going to have a lot of tough nuts to crack. We may not be a big enough nut cracker to crack them, but I think we need to tackle the whole job in a forthright manner. I know that you will. I think we have to satisfy ourselves about the issues before we can satisfy the President of the United States and the Congress of the country. I think that by using our talents we can help restore to the Federal service and to the Government generally a faith in it that perhaps has been lacking. I think that is a job worth undertaking from the standpoint of the war effort and the postwar effort. . . . I am asking you to put your shoulders to the wheel to see if, as a unit, we in the Bureau of the Budget can really do something to restore confidence in personnel and Governmental policy.[86]

BOB Field Service, 1943–1946

Less than a month after starting as BOB director, Smith identified the need for the bureau to have a field service.[87] Yes, he could send DC-based staff on inspection trips around the country, but that was not the same as having men (as they all were in those days) *already* stationed around the country and with the sole mission of looking over federal activities. He kept seeking the opportunity to bring the idea into fruition. In the spring of 1942, during congressional consideration of the FY 1943 budget, Smith mentioned to the House Appropriations Subcommittee his desire for a field service, but that he had not included it in that year's budget request given the overwhelming focus on the first wartime budget (US House 1942a, 1099–1100). In late 1942, Smith decided that the war picture had stabilized enough to include funding for the field service in the president's FY 1944 budget. Notwithstanding the much tougher scrutiny on Capitol Hill in the spring of 1943 to BOB's budget (discussed earlier in this chapter), Smith had managed to eke out an increase of $100,000. He treated it as a congressional down payment for a field service.

On July 24, 1943, Smith issued BOB Office Memorandum No. 100, establishing the field service. To signal that the service was intended to serve the needs of *all* BOB divisions, it would be a new silo within BOB, rather than a unit within an existing division. This conveyed that any division could request the field staff to look into an existing or proposed federal installation, whether for purposes of improving, for example, the work of the estimates division, the administrative management division, or the war projects division. Smith also indicated that the routine of sending Washington-based staff in the field could continue, but only after advising the field service of that intention. That hinted the field service could suggest that the cost of the trip might be unnecessary because it could perform that particular mission more efficiently and less expensively. Finally, Smith announced that the first office would be in Houston, to be followed quickly by opening two more offices, in Chicago and San Francisco (Seckler-Hudson 1945, 4: 158–59). A month later, Smith issued Office Memorandum 107 that *required* divisions to coordinate travel by their staff with the appropriate regional office, if only to help set up meetings in advance and make other arrangements to increase the productivity of their visits (155). By October, when Smith testified before the House Appropriations Subcommittee on the supplemental funding bill for the remainder of FY 1944, he said that the just-opened Houston office had already conducted a study of duplicating and printing at federal offices in Kansas City. He reported that "less than half of the potential capacity of the equipment is being utilized." Another project focused on identifying surplus property that Treasury's Procurement Division could take over and then offer to other agencies. The Texas office was also looking into questionnaires that local and regional federal offices sent out (as opposed to national surveys issued from Washington). Such a new source of information would give BOB's Statistical Standards Division a broader reach in its effort to coordinate questionnaires and eliminate unnecessary ones (US House 1943f, 839–40). The next month, when testifying before the counterpart Senate subcommittee, Smith said the field service was now conducting "additional surveys" at other metropolitan areas with multiple federal offices (US Senate 1943, 324). To both subcommittees, Smith said that these very preliminary results confirmed the need for the field service. He said that with the supplemental appropriation he was requesting, he intended to open three more field offices in cities with large clusters of federal offices, each to be staffed by two to three professionals and one to two secretarial staff. His ultimate goal was to open a field service office in each of the twelve Federal Reserve districts around the country.[88]

In early 1944, Smith was back on the Hill, now testifying on the FY 1945 budget. He said the San Francisco office had opened in November 1943 and the Chicago office in early 1944. His request for the coming fiscal year included about $250,000 to expand the field service. That amount would permit hiring sixty-six more staffers. Some would be placed to fully staff the current offices and most to staff up to six more offices. He said that the brief record of the Houston office was fulfilling his expectations. New projects included reviewing war-training programs, daycare facilities, and agency field offices (US House 1944b, 927, 933, 953, 975). But the mood of the committee, which had supported expansion of the bureau up to now, had changed. It cut his request by $236,000, barely enough for a handful of new field staff. Smith appealed to the Senate Appropriations Subcommittee to restore the cut. He again described the purpose of the field service and what had been accomplished so far. He said that the next office would be in Denver, followed, probably, by Atlanta. McKellar, again, was on the warpath. He was wholly unsympathetic to the project, saying, "I think your scheme is wrong." He kept referring to the offices as "regional" ones, suggesting line authority, delivery of services, and uniform district boundaries. Smith kept correcting him, but McKellar paid him no mind. McKellar even challenged BOB's legal right to have any offices outside the capital, even though the statute specifically mentioned funding BOB's "personnel services in the District of Columbia and elsewhere" (US Senate 1944a, 227–45, 316–59). The bad news was finalized in June 1944 when the president signed the Independent Offices Appropriation Act for FY 1945. It prohibited BOB from using any funds for "the maintenance or establishment of more than four regional, field, or any other offices outside the District of Columbia."[89] This meant Smith was left with a partial field service of Dallas (the office had moved from Houston), Chicago, San Francisco, and Denver. That was only about a third of what he had been planning. As would be expected, the results of this diminished project would remain modest and limited. The limitation also crippled the concept, practically assuring that it could not be a *national* success story.

Nonetheless, Smith and BOB soldiered on. The offices were accomplishing some concrete results. For example, the field service released a publication on *Management Techniques* that it had taught at its Training Institute. The twenty-page report summarized some tools of what it called "management engineering," including process charts, efficiency of motion, office methods, human engineering, and conference leader techniques (US BOB 1945). In early 1945, the assistant chief of the service wrote an article about it in *PAR*. He listed some of its accomplishments so far as eliminating duplicative surveys from regional offices of federal agencies, coordination of space control, and intergovernmental coordination. It also played a role as a convener of local federal officials to try to coordinate their field activities in that location (Latham 1945).

The field service limped along for several years, despite Smith's repeated efforts to reenergize it. In early 1945, his congressional testimony requested funding to expand the service in FY 1946 (US Senate 1945a, 311–13). McKellar, of course, denied it and the prohibition on opening more offices was retained in the law.[90] For FY 1947, he testified about the accomplishments of the existing offices, including saving about $1 million in OPA spending in Chicago and eliminating six thousand ineligible people from war housing waiting lists in California (US House 1946a, 17–19). However, again, the annual funding bill retained the statutory limit to four offices.[91] Congressional consideration in the spring of 1946 of the president's budget request for FY 1947 was Smith's last. After he left BOB in mid-1946, the service limped along into the early 1950s, when it was quietly abolished. In the 1960s, BOB twice asked Congress to fund a reestablishment of the field service, but "the Congress has refused to go along" (Carey 1969, 456). A 1979 history of BOB/OMB did not mention the existence of a field service (Berman 1979). A later historical review of BOB noted that the existence of the field service is "little remembered" (Dickinson and Rudalevige 2004–2005, 642). In retrospect, Smith's conception was meritorious; he just had bad luck in terms of political timing.

Committee for Congested Production Areas, 1943–1944

One of the straws in the wind of a positive role a field service could play was as a convener of forums for all federal agencies with offices in that locality. At the same time he was trying to get the field service up and running, Smith also pursued a parallel effort to coordinate the production activities of federal programs that were clustered in the same metropolitan area.[92] In the winter of 1942–1943, there were reports about serious problems arising in urban areas with major concentrations of war and production plants and facilities. They included rapid labor turnover, absenteeism, and low worker morale—all affecting productivity. In part, these problems were caused by a lack of adequate urban infrastructure to cope with the large growth in industrial production, such as housing, transportation, schools, recreation, public health, and health care. This led to the Army and Navy Munitions Board asking Robert Moses, a high-profile professional public administrator and construction czar in New York, to study the problems in San Diego and make recommendations to resolve them.[93] Moses reported on the need for some kind of central and relatively powerful position to coordinate and oversee planning, operations, and services that were being provided in San Diego by multiple federal agencies. Smith reviewed Moses's report with BOB staff and consulted with federal and external stakeholders.[94]

Smith submitted an executive order to Roosevelt on April 6. In his cover memo, he apologized for not talking it over in advance with Roosevelt to get his input. However, Smith noted, "there is so much heat on me to get something done immediately, as a result of the situation in Portland, Maine and in various parts of California, that I am sending it over, hoping that you will be able to deal with it quickly." He said that the idea for a high-level coordinating committee was somewhat experimental, but that "no one has been able to suggest anything better."[95] The order created a Committee for Congested Production Areas (CCPA) and Smith would chair it because he was not from any of the operating agencies involved and therefore would be viewed as neutral and disinterested. CCPA would hire a director and, besides that person, there would be little staff hired because most of the work would be done by officials detailed from the affected agencies. Finally, Smith told FDR that if the idea did not work, CCPA could be easily rescinded. FDR promptly signed it. The order delegated to CCPA the power to designate a city as a congested area and then to appoint an "area director" who, in turn, would convene an Area Advisory Committee. Significantly, based on recommendations from the area director, decisions by CCPA "shall be *controlling* on all federal agencies to which they apply." Agencies were required to issue orders and instructions to comply with directives from CCPA "to *insure compliance* with the policies and decisions of the Committee."[96] These were, indeed, major powers compared to voluntary cooperation and coordination by autonomous and rival agencies.

When released to the press, the vagueness of what specifically these problems actually were led to some puzzlement. The *Post* summarized the order but avoided speculating on the issues that needed to be addressed. Instead, it simply said that the situation was so serious that the only other alterative seemed to be "modified martial law" in those areas.[97] AP's coverage hinted that the problem was "commercialized vice and . . . other social problems."[98] The real estate column in the *Los Angeles Times* quoted the endorsement of CCPA by the president of the National Association of Home Builders. He said that CCPA, "under the chairmanship of Harold Smith," would go a long way to resolving the problem of building homes when there was a lack of "necessary community facilities." Workers needed more than a place to live; they also needed schools, stores, recreation centers, and hospitals.[99] On the other hand, a conservative columnist quickly attacked CCPA. The committee was a "mystery" and there was "quite a lot of confusion as to its necessity." He speculated that the new agency might be a WPA-type agency and hire thousands of people outside the civil service based on political patronage. He even suggested that its employees were likely to be "faithful fourth termers."[100] Politically, this was a clear signal to the conservative coalition to keep a close eye on CCPA, perhaps even terminate it like NRPB.

Smith quickly convened the first meeting of the committee on April 13.[101] A few weeks later, he hired Corrington Gill, as CCPA's director.[102] Gill, then at the War Department, had previously served under Harry Hopkins as deputy director of WPA.[103] In May, Smith updated Roosevelt that CCPA was up and running. The members were assistant secretaries of war and navy, and heads of WMC, WPB, Housing (Blandford, his former deputy), and Federal Works Agency.[104] To make sure that it would be a powerful committee, he limited its membership to senior agency officials only. No subordinate alternates could be named without Smith's permission—contrary to the common practice of principals routinely assigning less powerful aides in their places. At its initial meetings, the committee promptly focused on five areas that needed urgent attention: Norfolk (VA), Portland (ME), Newport (RI), and two in California: San Francisco and San Diego. The next month, Gill tried to reduce the conservative coalition's concerns. He said that CCPA's interventions were intended to be as brief as possible, it was coordinating with twenty-five federal agencies, it focused mostly on concrete goals such as sewer extensions, and it would be modestly staffed, with about fifteen in DC and perhaps up to five in each congested area.[105] Even after hiring Gill, Smith was actively involved in CCPA's operations, whether conferring with Gill, handholding legislators from congested areas, and talking with local officials.[106] In October, to get a better sense of what CCPA was facing in Detroit, he went to inspect federal operations there, particularly the problems at the Ford plant in Willow Run.[107] Detroit's director of public welfare told him that even though the Ford Company had consistently combative relations with the United Auto Workers, an underlying issue was the hostility of white workers there and elsewhere to working alongside Blacks.[108] The head of the federal public housing authority in Detroit made similar comments.[109] At the end of the year, the *Times* reported that CCPA's work included racial issues in Los Angeles and venereal disease in Norfolk.[110] By spring 1944, Gill reported CCPA had constructively worked on fire protection, bus service, housing supply, recreation programs, and school construction.[111] But the conservative coalition, still running Congress as a result of the November 1942 elections, did not let its guard down. In June 1944, it passed legislation defunding CCPA effective December 31, 1944.[112] In a postmortem published in *PAR*, Gill credited whatever success the committee had had to the organizational culture that Smith had insisted on; namely, that "it was a neutral agency with no ax to grind, no narrow interests to push" (Gill 1945, 32). In the final report that Smith submitted to the president, he emphasized that— unlike so many wartime squabbles—CCPA "acted in complete harmony in deciding questions of policy" and successful implementation was—again, unusually—confirmed by positive letters from members of Congress, local officials, and the private sector (US CCPA 1945, iv).[113]

Toward the end of 1943, a minor in-house personnel issue came up that signaled an important landmark in the pace of BOB's war work. A senior official in the temporary War Projects Unit told Smith that he was leaving BOB "because of certain falling of[f] of work in that unit and consequently no need for all the staff."[114] In other words, the high tide of budgeting and planning for the war had peaked and there was now going to be a gradual but consistent contraction of the unit's workload.

Promoting Professional Public Administration

The problems that emerged in 1943 regarding managing the war effort confirmed to Smith that he needed to keep pushing for strengthening public administration as a field of practice. He wanted BOB in general, and Stone's Division of Administrative Management in particular, to play a leadership role in promoting professional reforms and improvements. For example, the division released to the executive branch a model program for personnel management in federal agencies covering staffing, structure, and responsibilities.[115] It also sought to increase the use of standardized manuals for financial activities (Stone and Tiller 1943). Externally, Stone promoted advancing the profession, including articles (Stone 1943) and speeches to specialized audiences.[116] Smith encouraged all staffers, not just Stone, to be active professionally, including outward-facing and public activities. During the war, all writings and speeches had to be cleared by OWI. However, when BOB shared the clearance policy with all staffers, it emphasized, "It is not the intent of this notice to discourage staff members from making speeches or writing articles . . . [They] not only promote a better understanding of the Government and its problems, but also tend to increase the usefulness of the author."[117] For example, the chief budget examiner wrote about wartime budgeting in an accounting journal (Moe 1943). Understandably, as past president of ASPA, Smith particularly urged his staff to write for *PAR*. In 1943, they wrote (or cowrote) articles about improving administrative reporting (Latham 1943), the management of the copper recovery program (Graves and Carey 1943), and the role of an assistant to an agency administrator (McGee and Burton 1943). Another staffer wrote a book review (Graham 1943). These writings also enhanced the standing of BOB under Smith's leadership, spreading the word about the agency's elite cadre of presidential management experts.

Smith also continued being personally active in ASPA. He attended several dinner meetings of the Washington chapter, including presentations by Gulick, Joseph Harris, and Senator Robert Taft.[118] He served on ASPA's nominating committee and helped plan the program for the next (truncated) wartime annual conference.[119] He maintained close contact with Brownlow and Gulick, sometimes about ASPA, sometimes about wartime management.[120] Smith was also supportive of the yearlong preservice internship program run by the National Institute of Public Affairs and financed by the Rockefellers (Lee 2019a). In the summer, the cohort came to his office and he gave them a short talk on the state of public administration. Smith was frank about managing the war effort:

> He discussed the importance of good personnel and commented on the waste of personnel, in both government and business, through improper utilization of all talents. He also reviewed his thinking about budgeting. He pointed out that, as in the case of many reform movements, once a law was passed, the reformers packed up and went home, leaving things to the administrators. So, for a while, after 1921 budgeting deteriorated, but the process is recovering now. He commented that budgeting involves planning.[121]

His observations were somewhat downbeat, but accurately captured the flow of events and his experiences that year. Nonetheless, they also confirmed his full commitment to developing the profession and its continuing important role in good government.

Spokesperson for the Administration

Speeches

Smith traveled little in 1943, giving two speeches out of town and submitting one paper to an international conference (which he did not attend). Grinnell College in Iowa awarded him an honorary doctorate in May and Smith gave the commencement address. He endorsed liberal arts education, saying it was a necessity for democratic citizenship. At the same time, he criticized the American higher education system for not producing the managerial talent that the country needed, especially when at war and then for the postwar period. Universities were graduating men and women trained in the natural sciences and skilled with technical knowledge. However, the need for administrative leadership was not being fulfilled. He defined management as "the selection, the appraisal and the proper direction of many techniques; it requires a broad knowledge which can direct the efficient use of varied instruments, each in proper relation to the other. These necessary managerial qualities represent both art and science." Implicitly criticizing some campus-based public administration training programs, he said, "Broad-gauge training for management is not primarily a vocational exercise despite what some educational leaders would have us think. According to my view, such training should be based on that wide education which develops the ability to direct and aid social progress" (Smith 1943a, 5).

Going against the orthodoxy of the emerging profession of public administration, he urged a merging of training programs in business and public administration:

> How great a contribution the colleges could make if they taught public administration and business administration not as separate subjects but in conjunction. Surely we are learning that public administration is becoming more and more business administration, and business administration more and more involves the public weal. A composite approach in the teaching of these subjects would go far to bridging a dangerous gap in the thinking and actions of our administrators in government and in business. It would break down futile antagonism. By demonstrating the similarity of the problems of business and government, by indicating the mutuality of interest, such teaching would produce

an understanding which is sorely needed today. More than that, it would build a unified front which will be required during the complicated days of reconstruction ahead of us. (8)[122]

The speech received no attention from the media, although Mrs. Roosevelt quoted from it in her syndicated "My Day" column.[123]

In the fall, Smith traveled to Ann Arbor, his former hometown, to give a talk at the University of Michigan's annual Press Club conference. He spoke about the need for postwar planning to cope with the returning veterans, industrial reconversion, and the tidal wave of consumer spending that had been constrained during the war. There was a backlog of demand for housing, cars, and consumer goods and, with the ending of war bond sales, the money to buy them. However, he concluded on a different theme, criticizing the press for the ongoing negative tone of coverage of the federal war effort, exaggerating mistakes, and the seemingly permanent meme that Washington was ignoring the public-at-large and did not know what it was doing. "I am convinced that too frequently the tendency is to separate Washington from the grass roots of the Nation. This tendency is erroneous in concept and consequently harmful to democracy." Because so much of postwar activities will occur at the local level, such as catching up on deferred public works, "most of the issues which are likely to arouse your criticism of Washington, lie largely within your own control," rather than the federal government (Smith 1943b, 94). The speech mostly received coverage in Michigan newspapers, although a national wire story ran in the *Star*.[124] Smith also received an invitation to submit a paper to be read at the 10th Chilean Scientific Congress. Marsh urged him to accept it, because "it becomes a gesture to the worth of the scientific congress and perhaps indirectly a compliment to our South American neighbor."[125] Smith submitted a paper on the importance of fiscal policy and its integration in budget making. He also discussed the impact of the war and planning for the postwar period through budgeting and fiscal policy (Smith 1943c).

Media Relations

Smith and Marsh developed a relatively active press release program for the year. When BOB was required to provide summary reports on federal spending and federal employment, they frequently released them as state-

ments to the press, partly to counteract with facts the accusations and
misinformation coming from the Hill. One highlight of their efforts was
when the president released an update on the FY 1944 budget based on
final congressional appropriations. FDR began his semiweekly press conference on July 27 by summarizing the report and highlighting its significance.
According to the transcript, he admitted it was "rather dry" and lightheartedly said, "it contains ten pages of words and *(to himself, counting)* one,
two, three, four—five pages of very interesting figures—*(laughter)* in very
small type. *(More laughter)*" (Roosevelt 1969, 1943: 321–22). He proceeded
to give a short verbal summary of the information and what it meant
about the war effort. (As soon as he finished, the first question from the
press was on something else.) Nonetheless, the major metropolitan papers
gave it significant spot news coverage in their Sunday editions.[126] Besides
covering it as news, the *Times* and the *Post* printed the entire statement.[127]
(Indicating the importance of the document in the eyes of the administration, the full report was included in Roosevelt's published papers [310–
21].)

Other BOB press releases received a modicum of coverage, including
an April announcement on plans for hospital care for returning veterans,[128]
a November update on the budget,[129] and a December report on federal
employment.[130] He also gave a relatively rare on-the-record interview in the
spring about the urgent need for more tax revenue.[131] Finally, in November, Smith and BOB received a mixed review from *Fortune* magazine, the
pro-business publication of the influential *Time-Life* publishing colossus. In
an essay on reforming the federal government after the war, it praised the
current BOB and urged strengthening it further:

> The Bureau of the Budget has for several years been among the
> least publicized but most useful of government agencies. No
> other executive agency's request for funds may be submitted
> to Congress without its approval. Armed with this authority, it
> has performed invaluable service in streamlining administrative
> organizations and procedures, eliminating waste and duplication,
> coordinating legislative proposals from the various executive
> departments, gathering and supplying information, engaging in
> long-range planning, and inspecting government projects in the
> field. We would suggest no change in its organization or opera-
> tion except to enlarge its field inspection staff and to extend its
> jurisdiction over government personnel.[132]

The proposal to expand BOB's scope to include HR consisted of abolishing the Civil Service Commission, replacing it with a single civil service administrator,[133] and making him (as most were in those days) responsible to the BOB director. That would make BOB a de facto overall management control agency, in charge of both budgeting and personnel, the two major components of public administration staff services. However, for Smith, these welcome recommendations were counterbalanced by the recommendation to shift BOB back to Treasury so that the department could function as a comprehensive central fiscal bureau, a move he opposed.[134]

A News Figure

Media attention to Smith as a news figure—rather than source of spot news—seemed to crescendo in 1943 with a quartet of major and positive media events: a front-page profile in the *Wall Street Journal*, a feature article in the *Saturday Evening Post*, on the cover of *Time* magazine, and a visit from Walter Lippmann. The news peg for much of the coverage was the paradox of Smith and his work, namely, that he was a very important person in the capital but that, unlike the typical Washington type, was not a press hound seeking attention and was not well known to the public-at-large. The front-page profile in the *Wall Street Journal* in January said that while he was "a supporter of the New Deal, Mr. Smith is in no sense an extremist. His engineering background gives him a scientific and nonpolitical outlook on government. And it is in a detached, scientific manner that he tackles problems." In fact, given all the in-fighting going on in Washington at the time, the reporter suggested that if Roosevelt expanded Smith's power "many believe a lot of Washington confusion might be cleared away."[135] Two months later, Smith was featured in a glowing profile in one of the foremost weeklies of the time, the *Saturday Evening Post*. Written by Blair Moody, Washington correspondent (and columnist) for the *Detroit News*, it was a very positive depiction of "probably the least-known man of power in Washington."

> He never hurries. With a large, scholarly head that thrusts forward almost abnormally between heavy shoulders, he walks, talks and grins slowly, the last man on earth you'd take for a political ball of fire. And yet in less than four short, swift years he has risen from nowhere to become advisor and personal agent, the business manager and efficiency expert, the messenger boy and, when necessary, the muscleman of Franklin D. Roosevelt.[136]

The profile also tried to present the private person, including photos of Smith with his family and dog reading the Sunday paper, cutting his son's hair, singing while accompanied by his daughter on the piano, and building furniture.[137] But, in general, it focused on Smith's quiet behind-the-scenes work to coordinate the war agencies, assure that spending requests were substantiated by facts, and rationally deal with conflicts between agencies.[138] The article ended with this self-deprecating quote by Smith: "I've never thought I was very smart, but I do think I can make a contribution. We are trying to implement good government and stifle bad. This is my contribution."[139]

In June, Smith was on the cover of *Time* magazine. Being the subject of a cover story meant the person had achieved a kind of journalistic gold medal of being important. The cover's caption stated, "Czars may come and czars may go, but he goes on forever." (A reproduction of the cover faces the title page at the beginning of this book.) The article explained why Smith was so important and so powerful: "The secret of Smith's freedom from enemies is that he is not a politician. Other officials . . . know and respect him for what he is: a professional administrator, with no political ambitions, no special interests to serve, no social reforms to promote."[140] It described him as follows: "In a crowd, Mr. Smith is the fellow in the brown suit. Middle-sized and homely, he had pale blue-grey eyes behind rimless glasses. . . . His friends joke that 'Harold has only one speed: low gear.' He works hard at his job, including most evenings, and has very little time for fun." Like the *Saturday Evening Post* story, this one included some information about his personal life and had a picture of his family celebrating his forty-fifth birthday. The profile ended in typical *Time* style: high praise of Smith while subtly inserting the magazine's ongoing editorial positions of internationalism (support for Roosevelt's role as war leader) and moderate Republicanism (criticism of Roosevelt as Democrat):

> In a sense, he is any and every Mr. Smith of the U.S.A. In his high Government post he is a solid, reassuring symbol of the average American's patience, common sense and optimism. He does not let his knowledge of Mr. Roosevelt's administrative failings blind him to the President's great qualities of leadership. He knows that America has survived plenty of mistakes in the past, and is sure it can survive plenty more.

The fourth signal of Smith's importance in the eyes of the media's cognoscenti, Walter Lippmann came to talk with him. On July 16, Lippmann, probably the country's most influential columnist, visited Smith in his office and they had an off-the-record conversation that lasted an hour.[141] It is likely that Smith was a main—but unnamed—source for Lippmann's column the next day. Lippmann tried to draw a larger lesson from FDR's intervention in the public bickering between Vice President Wallace, head of the Board of Economic Warfare, and Jesse Jones, secretary of commerce. Lippmann praised the executive order that finessed the fighting by merging all their programs into a new Office of Economic Warfare (a few months later renamed the Foreign Economic Administration). It was an "indispensable reform" and that reflected a "philosophy of administration." The implicit principle behind the reorganization was "that the lines of authority run clearly to the right places." Other aspects of the management of the war effort could similarly benefit from such reforms in order to increase "administrative efficiency." All these phrases and the characterizations of public administration must have come from Smith because they reflected his ongoing principles and management values. Lippmann concluded by urging FDR to strengthen the powers of the cabinet to hear disagreements, work out preferred solutions, and then be able to impose them on the principals involved.[142]

Smith continued getting good press and soft news coverage all year. In January, a syndicated columnist praised him, calling Smith "a happy combination of the poker-faced accountant and the old-shoe corner-store crony."[143] The next month, a profile distributed by International News Service described him as "deliberate, unsensational, and boundlessly conscientious." It repeated the story of how his wife handled the family budget because, he said, "she's better at it." He was "of old pioneer stock" from Kansas, and "bears more resemblance to a small-town Middle-Westerner than to the popular conception of American's No. 1 public servant."[144] An article in the May issue of *Cosmopolitan* focused on FDR's team. It described Smith as "a quiet, well set-up, friendly man" who handled the war budget "with ease, calm and distinction."[145] A column in September began with the arresting news, "The United States government is saving money. No, your glasses don't need changing, and it's no mistake of the printer's." It went to explain and praise how significantly Smith and BOB were holding down costs and saving money.[146] Another flattering profile in November described him as a "blond genial gent of 45 . . . mild enough normally, but he can be as hard as a doorknob."[147] Reflecting this kind of soft news media coverage, Smith continued to be treated as a minor news celebrity. A syndicated illustrated entertainment feature called "Private Lives" gave readers amusing and unknown details about important people. (It was a kind of believe-it-or-not for people in the news.) In May, it described him as the "Washington Warbler," explaining the "suppressed desire of Budget Director

Harold D. Smith: a career in grand opera." It showed a sketch of Smith in a business suit (evidently from a stock news photo), but now holding music sheets and singing.[148] The next month, a weekly news quiz asked, "Who is the director of the United States bureau of the budget?" The options for the answer were Harold D. Smith, James M. Landis, and Wayne Coy.[149] Smith also occasionally appeared in lightly humorous front-page political cartoons in the *Star* (mentioned earlier in this chapter). He was also depicted in a much more hard-hitting cartoon in the conservative *Chicago Tribune*. It depicted him as one of six "White House 'Master Minds'" who were very liberal and had excessive influence on policy. It showed them viewing American taxpayers as the "world's prize human guinea pig" and wondering "what experiment shall we try on him today!"[150]

In general, Smith's higher profile in the media in 1943 is likely in part attributable to his increasing trust in Marsh's news judgment and comfort with the drafts that Marsh prepared for speeches and press releases. Marsh was frequently in Smith's office, such as for drafting the annual budget message,[151] to help Smith as juror for Kluttz's contest of best suggestions from civil servants,[152] a statement on the need for more revenue,[153] a statement on excess federal personnel,[154] a press release on federal hospitals,[155] Smith's commencement speech at Grinnell College,[156] a press release on BOB policy to reduce federal paper consumption,[157] and a press statement on federal employment totals.[158] Marsh also routinely attended FDR's press conferences and then returned to the office to fill Smith in on any potentially relevant comments.[159] For example, after attending Roosevelt's press conference on September 14, Marsh hurried back to fill Smith in on FDR's comments regarding taxes.[160] Smith clearly enjoyed Marsh's company. They frequently shared meals, probably a mix of business and relaxation.[161] Smith occasionally invited Marsh to join him out of the office, such as a half-day trip to inspect USDA's experimental farm in Beltsville (MD) and for his testimony before the House Civil Service Committee.[162] They also occasionally played golf together.[163] For a person as discrete and careful as Smith, Marsh was one of the few people he could let his hair down with, along with Ickes at their lunches, and always with Coy.

Health: Smith and Coy's Partnership

Smith's health continued to be shaky throughout the year. In mid-March, he had a checkup at the Bethesda Naval Hospital and a few weeks later, he conferred with a Dr. Schuh on what Smith's secretary delicately referred to as a "personal matter."[164] The next month, he returned to Bethesda for another appointment.[165] When he had lunch with Ickes during the summer, Ickes wrote, "I have never seen him so depressed." In part, the comment likely related to governmental events and presidential decisions Smith was unhappy about. However, the observation appeared to cover Smith's mental and physical health as well. According to Ickes, Smith said "very frankly that he was in a passive state of mind."[166] Passivity suggests possibly depression, exhaustion, and feeling overwhelmed. Hinting at this, the next month he called one of his doctors at Bethesda and asked for a prescription for sleeping pills. He also asked for a supply of B_1 vitamin pills.[167] His navy doctor eventually referred him to Bethesda's heart specialist. In September, Smith had an appointment with Dr. Howard Bruenn, the new (and young) chief of cardiology. It was an extensive examination, taking up most of the morning.[168] In the fall, based on advice from General George Marshall, he also tried to stop smoking. When he ran into the army chief of staff at a White House ceremony, Smith told him that he was having "personal difficulties when I stopped smoking."[169] In late November, another doctor at Bethesda called Smith to talk about his general health status.[170] Two weeks later, Bruenn also called to talk about the same thing.[171] Both were concerned about Smith's status and prognosis.

Running BOB in 1943 ended up being a partnership of two relatively unhealthy, but conscientious, managers. Like Smith, Assistant Director Wayne Coy's health was fragile (Lee 2018a, 51, 239–40). He, too, was sometimes away from work because of that. Lunching with Ickes in late August, Smith said, "Coy is really not at all well. He has a serious kidney complaint as a result of which at intervals he gets a lot of poison in his blood. Apparently, the trouble is incurable. An operation might take care of it but an operation is dangerous and the result might be doubtful which would only make matters worse."[172] Healthy or otherwise, they got along swimmingly. Smith's daily calendars document how frequently they were in touch. Their offices were in the same suite, separated by a shared reception and secretarial area. Often Smith would start and end his day by touching base with Coy. They often had lunch together, too.[173] During the day, Smith routinely made a point for Coy to sit in on major meetings and decisions. Not only would that facilitate Coy participating in any particular decision, but also it meant that Coy would be so up-to-date with what was going on in-house that he could easily pick up wherever Smith left off when Smith was gone (whether traveling or recuperating). They were something of a tag team, even trying to coordinate their respective absences so that one of them would always be at work to keep things going smoothly. After Coy was out for a few days in May, on his first day back Smith briefed him so he would be up to date.[174] In mid-August, Coy's status became semipublic knowledge with Kluttz hinting obliquely at it by reporting that Coy "is taking an extended vacation."[175] Smith sometimes talked to Mrs. Coy on the phone to get a sense of how Coy was doing and when he might be back.[176] In late December (when the budget was largely done), Smith took two days off for a long weekend. Coy covered for him. On Monday morning, the first thing Smith did when he came in was to confer with Coy "for about an hour, catching up on activities of the past two days."[177] Similarly, when Smith was out, the routine meetings with FDR would continue without interruption. Coy would go alone and then dictate a summary of the conversation, the same as what Smith always did.[178] It was as though two ill and exhausted workaholics who worked closely as a team were tantamount to a single healthy one. A book by a *Times* reporter about the wartime bureaucracy hinted at this, noting that "Smith suffered a serious breakdown a couple of years ago and Coy . . . had been a very sick man" (Crider 1944, 34). Despite their overlapping health problems, the efficient machine Smith had built up since 1939 kept humming along without any major bumps or gaps.

Private Life: Farmer Smith

As he began doing in 1942, Smith continued his conscious and deliberate effort to take breaks from work. He and Mrs. Smith were both avid golfers and that hobby gave him an outlet for mild exercise away from work. However, in 1943 his absences from the office were not usually vacations for health-related rest and leisurely recreation. Instead, they were about his decision to try to increase his income by farming. It was not intended to be a hobby farm nor was he planning to be a gentleman farmer. Instead, his short-term goal was to add to his income and, eventually, perhaps be able to retire there.[179] Farming was hardly a stress-free activity nor one of mild physical activity. Perhaps it appealed to a workaholic like Smith as a way to keep his mind off work and be preoccupied with other things. Nonetheless, farming was hardly an activity that his cardiologist, Dr. Bruenn, would have recommended to someone with heart problems.

In the spring of 1943, he bought a relatively run-down 385-acre farm in Raccoon Ford, Virginia, near Culpepper. It was about seventy miles from

Washington. The farmhouse was dilapidated and needed major renovations before the family could move in.[180] He persuaded his Iowa brother-in-law, Ernest E. Hosfelt (and spouse, Mrs. Smith's sister), to move to the farm and be its full-time resident manager. Smith's brother, Lloyd, was a Yale graduate with expertise in forestry who was working at WPB in Washington. Lloyd agreed to advise him on managing the timbered sections of the farm. Smith began spending time there in late April and was away from the office for a week (April 25–May 2).[181] He had lunch with Ickes a few days after he got back and said he thought it was "good farming land" and was planning to start raising hogs.[182] He also told FDR, who promptly volunteered his advice about farm products Smith should focus on, such as deer meat.[183] By July, it was an open secret in Washington, with a reporter lightheartedly commenting on the parallels between Smith's public role in dealing with the shortage of wartime manpower and those shortages impacting his private life, too. He would have to do most of the farm's manual labor by himself.[184]

Smith spent increasingly long stretches at the farm and away from work, such as June 16–21, June 28–July 5, July 28–August 7, October 21–24, November 13–15, and November 26–29.[185] He brought the same methodical approach to farming that he did to public administration. His diligent secretary occasionally noted the progress of his farm projects as he collected facts, examined, considered, and then acted. For example, when he had a Morgan horse at the farm, whom he named Gypsy King, he carefully thought about what mare would be a good match.[186] In early September, he called the owner of a Morgan mare to make an appointment to examine her,[187] but did not finalize the purchase with registration certificate until two months later.[188] At the end of the month, he traveled to another farm to examine the mother of his Morgan and consider keeping it at his farm (while the farmer was in the army) in exchange for her next colt.[189] As would be expected in farming, he had routine problems that needed attending, such as his pigs having eye infections.[190] Compounding these kinds of usual farming problems, he also faced the shortage of products and supplies caused by the war, particularly the high priorities assigned to military and arms production needs. His truck broke down and he attended an auction to bid for a secondhand pick-up.[191] He hurried to a Sears & Roebuck where Marsh had noticed a rare saw and mandrel set.[192] He called around looking for a concrete mixer.[193]

These activities were normal. Given his diligent attention to work beginning in 1939, one can even cut him some slack for doing some of these activities while on office time. However, a more severe criticism that seems justified is that he used his network of senior administration officials to ask for help. He called the secretary of agriculture to talk about the eye infections his pigs had.[194] He called senior officials at the Farm Credit Administration to facilitate a federally backed mortgage.[195] He called the executive director of the Council on Intergovernmental Relations for data about farms and for help locating architectural drawings for standardized small houses.[196] He called a USDA official to obtain the form farmers needed during the war for selling products and he called another for information about hog wire and farm machinery.[197] He bought his pigs at a public auction at USDA's experimental farm in Beltsville (MD). He was tipped off about a defense housing site that had surplus materials and equipment for sale and hurried there to buy them.[198] He asked one of his employees about WPB's priorities list because he wanted to buy an electric saw.[199] Some of these activities seem to have crossed an ethical line by using his access to benefit his farm, access that regular farmers would not have. Presumably, the people he called were on friendly relations with him, but that closeness would have been in a professional and work context. He was asking them to help him in his private capacity. He seemed oblivious to the apparent ethical lapses his behavior posed. Perhaps he was misusing his public office; perhaps—given his loyal public service and fragile health—he should be somewhat forgiven for doing this. Either way, he was not modeling ethical behavior or principles of public office for other professional public administrators.

Preparing the FY 1945 Budget

In the fall of 1943, Smith had only modest interactions with the Estimates Division when it was preparing a rough draft of the FY 1945 budget. In June, he approved the circular that the division was about to send to departments with guidelines for their budget requests.[200] In the fall, he participated in some budget planning sessions for specific agencies, but not on any consistent or comprehensive basis. They included the State Department's Office of Foreign Relief and Rehabilitation Operations, OWI's Domestic Branch, the Coordinator of Inter-American Affairs (the Rockefeller office), and the Rural Electrification Administration.[201] The only Board of Review he participated in was for USDA.[202] His first meeting with the president to go over some agency budget recommendations was in early November. It went quite fast, with Smith briefing him on each agency, FDR asking a few questions about major items, but then approving all without any major revisions.[203] A few days later, Roosevelt was about to leave for his first summit meeting with Stalin and Churchill in Teheran. He called Smith and "delegated [Smith] his budget-making powers until he returns."[204] This was a significant expression of trust, given that FDR would be gone from the White House until December 17, the high season for BOB finalizing the president's annual budget request. Even after he was back, Smith had no further meetings with him or other contacts about the budget.[205] Smith, so accustomed to Roosevelt's close guidance on budgeting matters, was a bit at sea. For example, in late December (after FDR was back), for a final important USDA policy issue, he had referred it to the president for a decision. But it quickly "was returned to the Director for solution" on his own.[206]

Similarly, when Smith shifted to drafting the budget message, he admitted he "had almost no guidance this year" from FDR compared to previous years.[207] In a different conversation, he said "the situation was very confused concerning what the strategy of the administration ought to be" in the budget message. He confessed to a senior administration official he trusted "that perhaps we have lost a few tricks."[208] The main thing for Smith was that he did not want to have any last-minute fights with Morgenthau, who always seemed eager to bother FDR with his complaints. On December 27, he called Under Secretary Bell and said he was "not disposed to be fighting with the Treasury over any of the Message."[209] He wanted to share the appropriate sections of the draft for input on a timely manner. Bell agreed. On New Year's Eve, Smith was still hard at work at his office trying to wrap up both the budget and the message.

∼

For Smith, 1943 had been a difficult year, given the conservative coalition's control of Congress, the developments in the war and related domestic policies, festering problems in management and organization, and the beginning of FDR's gradual drift away from frequent contact. In one respect, Roosevelt had shown enormous trust in Smith by letting him prepare the FY 1944 budget with little input (and while away for the Teheran summit). Nonetheless, Smith consistently preferred ongoing interaction with the president to be sure that BOB was in touch with FDR's latest thinking and his changes in priorities. The deterioration in Smith's health and his increasing dependence on Assistant Director Coy in 1943 demonstrated the toll the stress of work was having on him.

Chapter 7

The Third Year of the War and Fourth-Term Campaign, 1944

Noticing FDR's Gradual Decline

Roosevelt was gone for about a month in late 1943 for a summit meeting in Teheran with Stalin and Churchill. He was back in mid-December but was tired from his trip. Upon his return, he dedicated most of his time and energy to report to Congress and the public on the results of the summit. Then, his physician said that FDR had the grippe (or the flu) and had ordered him to bed to rest. The president conducted very little business in the second half of December and early January, talking to few people on the phone and seeing fewer in person. Smith had last seen him on November 4, 1943.[1] The next time Smith met with him was two months later, on January 7, 1944. According to Smith, Roosevelt "seemed worried and worn out." He had "never seen him so listless. He was not his usual acute self." Smith had occasionally met with the president in his bedroom and did not consider this unusual. But "never so groggy." As he did every January, Smith came with his draft of the annual budget message. In the past, FDR would read it aloud and, as he went along, make suggestions for revisions. This time, seeing how weak Roosevelt was, Smith offered to read it to him, to save his voice and energy. FDR declined, quietly reading it to himself. In the middle of reading the draft, it looked like he had nodded off. "I could not see his eyes, but it seemed as though they were completely shut." Either he was just exhausted from the long trip and the flu, "or else that Admiral McIntire had doped him heavily in order to keep him quiet."

Smith was so taken aback by the experience, noting, "It has been difficult to shake the impression from my mind."[2]

To avoid bothering Roosevelt, Smith was intent on finalizing the FY 1945 budget message without in-house controversy. He readily yielded to suggestions for changes from senior administration officials to muffle disagreements. He even sought to mollify Morgenthau. Despite Smith's efforts at clearing the draft well in advance through Bell, Morgenthau *still* found a reason to complain directly to the president. FDR told Smith that he had received only one complaint about the budget message—from Morgenthau. Smith explained to Roosevelt: "The Secretary of the Treasury had taken a preliminary copy—despite my efforts to reach an understanding as to our procedure—and had commented to the President prematurely on a tentative provision about compulsory savings."[3] The next day, Smith and Morgenthau talked on the phone. Smith, without argument, yielded and agreed to take a sentence out of the message even though it was merely repeating a statement of policy in the previous year's message.[4] Morgenthau, the sore winner, promptly called a subordinate to crow about getting his way.[5] There were further indications of the president's condition. For the first time in his presidency, he did not deliver his State of the Union address in person. Instead, he submitted his message to Congress in writing and, that evening, read a shortened and popularized version of it as a kind of fireside chat. Nor did the president participate in his annual budget seminar with the White House press corps. This year, Smith and Coy conducted it.[6] It was such a break with Roosevelt's custom that the media made a point of reporting it.[7] Two newspapers included this detail on their front pages.[8] In early spring (March 19–April 8), he spent three weeks convalescing at the White House and Hyde Park, seeing few people, some days no appointments at all and in bed. Then, he was gone for another month (April 8–May 7), resting at Bernard Baruch's plantation in South Carolina. He did very little work during that time, mostly signing mail and documents for about half an hour each day (Hamilton 2019, 246). There were other indications inhouse. Smith had seen Roosevelt sixteen times in 1943, but only eight in 1944 (along with a five-minute phone conversation on December 21). He went long stretches without any direct contact with FDR: March 14–May 8, May 10–July 12, July 14–August 30, and September 1–October 29.

His July 13 meeting with the president included a discussion of the annual budget summation that BOB routinely prepared based on the completed appropriations bills passed by Congress for the just-begun fiscal year. In 1943, FDR had released it at his July 27 press conference and had talked about its importance at great length (chap. 6). Smith now asked FDR how he wanted to handle releasing it this year? Roosevelt was about to leave for a (supposedly nonpolitical) one-month voyage to inspect military facilities in the Pacific. The president told Smith to release it in Smith's name.[9] The gap in their meetings between August 31 to October 30 is largely due to FDR's campaign for reelection (including husbanding his energies for campaign appearances and travels). It was roughly comparable to the infrequency of their meetings in 1940 when Roosevelt was also running for reelection. Having only one meeting in November and none in December during the height of BOB's budget season was another indication of FDR's fading strength and focus. At the end of their November 27 meeting, Smith said there were still many budget-related decisions to come and that he hoped to see Roosevelt regularly from that point on. "The President said that since he was going away, he doubted that we could get together for at least several weeks. I pointed out that the schedule is moving so rapidly that I would have to decide these matters on his behalf. He said that was just what he wanted me to do. Then I indicated that I would expect some howling about my decisions and that I would want him to back me up. He said very cordially and emphatically that he would do so one hundred per cent."[10] As when preparing the FY 1945 budget in late 1943 on his own while Roosevelt was in Teheran, the *president's* FY 1946 budget was really, again, Smith's, not Roosevelt's. In his dictations after their meetings in 1944, Smith sometimes commented on FDR's status:

> January 21: "I was quite happy at his general appearance of good health and his jovial mood."

> February 16: The meeting was the first after the president's awakening from a nap and Roosevelt indicated that he was still groggy. He "said he had only one eye open."

> March 13: "The President yawned and said that unfortunately he was sleepy this early in the day" (it was 12:30 p.m.). He said the reason was that he watched a "harrowing film the night before." Later in the meeting, Smith complained to FDR about a memo the president had dictated in January at the behest of the War Department. In it, FDR told Smith not to send any BOB examiners to the European theater of operations. When Smith complained about it to FDR (who quickly backed down), Smith noted to himself, "[the memo] was dictated while the President was ill. I never really considered that it represented a point of view to which he had given any thought."

May 9: "Hereafter no one will have more than 15 minutes—whereas we had been allotted half an hour—because Admiral McIntire will not let the President work more than three hours and will not let him have lunch with anyone to talk business."

July 13: "The President seemed fit and jovial."

August 31: "Throughout the conference the President seemed to have the attitude of one who was relaxing and who, therefore, was not very decisive about anything. I should say that this conference compares with only one other in the last five years in the extent of its indecision."

October 30: "He seemed jovial and vigorous."

November 16: "He looked fine."[11]

Smith had a second source of information about Roosevelt's health. As Marsh had done in 1943, he continued attending the president's twice-weekly press conferences. This was a way to keep Smith informed of any unexpected policy pronouncements that he should know about.[12] However, in 1944, Marsh's attendance seemed to have another purpose: an independent observer of the president's condition. His written reports to Smith now routinely included observations about FDR, as well as summarizing what he said.

March 7: "The President seemed extremely alert and in good spirits."

March 10: "President in good form."

March 24: The session was "devoted almost entirely to announcements by the President, several of which he read. He was in rather poor voice."

March 28: "The President coughed much and obviously it was painful, did not inhale any cigarette smoke; naturally, he did not look at all well."

April 7: "The President, although still showing the effects of his recent illness, appeared in much better health and voice."

May 16: "The President looked even better than last week and seemed in better spirits."

June 23: "The President seemed in excellent fettle."

August 25: "The President coughed considerably and spoke in such a low voice that he was very difficult to follow."

August 29: "The President seemed in very fine fettle, good color and voice."

September 8: "The President seemed in good form."[13]

Clearly, while the secular trend (and hindsight) demonstrates his gradual decline, Roosevelt was able occasionally to rally and display his skills, particularly when in public or for political purposes, such as his reelection campaign. Nonetheless, FDR's apparent lassitude regarding sound management and dealing with problems on a timely basis was beginning to bother Smith much more than it had in the past. He began talking openly to Ickes about leaving after the election. In August, Smith was particularly discouraged and unhappy because there were "certain matters in connection with reconversion that the President does not appreciate *or even realize.*"[14] A month later, Smith told Ickes that he planned to resign after the election. "He doesn't care much about staying on, considering the mess that we are in administratively."[15] The next month, Ickes noted, "He is all ready to turn in his resignation and said frankly that he would not want to continue with the Administration unless it had a better organizational setup."[16]

An Ill Wind from Capitol Hill: BOB's FY 1945 Appropriations

In previous years, the House Appropriations Subcommittee for Independent Offices had been a supportive ally of Smith's goal to expand BOB to fulfill its mission. The subcommittee readily recommended increasing his budget and staffing and repeatedly complimented him during public hearings. No longer. Perhaps Smith was simply overreaching. He was seeking a funding increase of nearly $1 million and a staffing increase of 120. In part, the increases would provide for a fully functioning field service with national presence as well as several new activities, such as an engineering staff to coordinate and examine public works projects, postwar economic planning, and staffing for the Federal Board of Hospitalization in an effort to standardize federal hospital services and planning. Smith was grilled on a wide range of subjects and asked for highly detailed information, especially by Republican members. They asked how many of his staff had draft deferments; why BOB was paying $900 a year for a teletype news machine; if in-house budget hearings by the Estimates Division on agency budgets were available in writing; its FCC budget recommendations; OWI's contract with Short-Wave Research, Inc.; Post Office penalty mail; training courses; cost of printing payroll checks; overtime payments for per-diem employees; elimination of a particular questionnaire; and mileage reimbursements for use of private cars by staff of the Federal Housing Administration. It was an extensive hearing, lasting the better part of a day and covering sixty-one pages in the published hearing record (US House 1944b, 925–86). In the end, the committee was still modestly supportive. It recommended about half of the increase Smith asked for, with total funding of about $2.3 million for the year.

Demonstrating a severe lack of political astuteness and a tin ear, Smith decided to appeal the House decision to the Senate—the subcommittee chaired by Senator McKellar. Given Smith's previous tangles with McKellar, what could have made him think McKellar would give him even more money than the House? It was a stormy hearing, of McKellar arguing with Smith and repeatedly interrupting him. McKellar accused Smith of illegality, even contempt for Congress. Smith did not yield any substantive ground on his and BOB's actions but made a point to verbalize a semi-apology: "Mr. Chairman, I would hesitate very much to have this record show, without any response from me, that I treated the Congress with contempt or that I am violating the law" (US Senate 1944, 277). A few minutes later:

McKellar: You do not even give the chairman of this committee an opportunity to ask you a question.

Smith: Pardon me.

McKELLAR: You go on talking; and I do not think you mean to be disrespectful, but that is very disrespectful. (279)

After two and a quarter hours, McKellar still was not done with him. He had Smith come back a few days later for two more hours. In all, the hearing on BOB's budget (including attachments and submissions) covered 110 pages. McKellar challenged the legality of the Federal Board of Hospitalization and BOB's staffing of it. He claimed that board had no statutory status and that BOB was substituting its judgment for exclusively congressional powers. He accused BOB of usurping legislative power by promulgating its own legislation. Looking over Smith's explanation of the origins of the board, he said, "If that is not legislation, gentlemen, I never saw legislation, and, of course, it is without force and effect. So far as I am concerned, I would vote against it, because, Mr. Smith, as hard as the proposition seems to you, you have to come to Congress for your authority. We are not going to give you authority to legislate or permit you to legislate for the people of this country" (325).

McKellar's committee recommended to the Senate funding for FY 1945 at $1.8 million, about its FY 1944 level.[17] He also prohibited any field offices, prohibited hiring expert consultants, cut funding for newspaper subscriptions, and banned leasing a teletype news machine. Smith was nearly apoplectic and appealed to Roosevelt to lobby the congressional leadership to restore the cuts. He said that the entire concept of the EOP was under attack from the Hill, given the defunding of NRPB and the disappearance of OGR into OWI. Now, BOB "is being threatened for the first time, partly because of its strength in the Executive Office."[18] In the end, the House and Senate split the difference, giving BOB funding of $2 million for the fiscal year, permitting it to keep its current four field offices but banning opening any more, and permitted it to retain the teletype machine.[19] Considering the political winds, the modest increase in his budget over McKellar's implacable opposition was a win, even if it did not feel that way to Smith.

Reorganizing for War and Postwar

In the beginning of the year, Smith and FDR maintained their practice of using executive orders to facilitate federal operations and to stay ahead of any statutory handcuffs imposed by Congress. In January, Roosevelt signed an executive order creating a War Refugee Board within EOP, hence finessing the usual bureaucratic turf battles, especially between State, War, and Treasury.[20] The next month he signed two executive orders to deal with some of the political issues raised on Capitol Hill, as well as the policy and organizational issues consistently raised by Smith. One created a Surplus War Property Administration and the other a Retraining and Reemployment Administration, both within OWM.[21] Discernably, the president's previous consistent desire to stay one step ahead of Congress nearly disappeared in the second half of 1944. This may have reflected his dissipating energy and medical condition and/or a desire for political peace with the outgoing conservative 78th Congress as he prepared to run for a fourth term. In June, Congress sent him a bill creating an Office of Contract Settlement. Based on an analysis by political scientist V. O. Key, then working in the Division of Administrative Management, Smith strongly recommended a veto.[22] Separately, Smith told Rosenman that the modulated tone he used when he made the case to Roosevelt deserved "much more vigorous and violent language." He said the bill and similar ones to follow were making the organization of the war and postwar effort "more acute and dangerous."[23] Nonetheless, Roosevelt decided to sign the bill, creating the Office of Contract Settlement as an independent agency.[24] It was a sign of how much had changed politically.

In October, FDR signed a bill creating a Surplus Property Administration that superseded his February executive order. He said he was signing it reluctantly, in part because the many restrictions that Congress inserted into the law reflected special interest lobbying. In fact, the head of the executive-order-based agency promptly resigned, saying the law would be administratively unworkable (Roosevelt 1969, 1944–1945: 300–02). The president similarly signed a bill converting Byrnes's Office of War Mobilization from an executive-order-based one to a statutory one. It also renamed the agency Office of War Mobilization and Reconversion (OWMR) (302–07). Further reflecting this changed orientation on matters of organization, the primary role of FDR's Great Reorganizer now shifted to being the presidential voice in congressional deliberations on the subject. In the five years that Smith had served as BOB director, his presence on Capitol Hill was mostly limited to testifying before the two appropriations committees (and mostly on BOB's budget). In mid-1944, Smith shifted to testifying on behalf of the administration when Congress was considering organizational bills. Smith was becoming a public advocate rather than a behind-the-scenes reorganizer. Nonetheless, it was an extension of his sense of the broad role of BOB as a central management agency as well as the willingness of some congressional leaders to accept the validity of that role, even if only as a suggestion-maker.

The organizational problems in the military's conduct of the war had created an inevitable political perspective on whether the armed forces should be merged after the war into a single military department. The House created a Select Committee on Post-War Military Policy and appointed Woodrum as chair. Based on his role as chair of the appropriations subcommittee for BOB, he was more familiar than most members were with the organizational and managerial activities of BOB. He asked Smith to submit a report to the committee with his views about a postwar merger. At the beginning of the committee's hearing on May 19, Woodrum introduced Smith's report, shared copies with the members, and inserted it in the committee's published record (US Congress 1944c, 295). Smith called for better coordination and indicated that some of his suggestions did not need to wait for the war to end. In general, "we must pay more attention to the management phases of warfare." Similarly the national economic and production mobilization needed to focus on "even minor deficiencies in the management of these resources" (304). For example, he suggested "that a corps of trained administrators, the product of civilian rather than service schools, may need to be developed within the armed forces" (303). Smith's ten-page statement attracted some press attention even though he had not appeared in person to read it or answer questions.[25] As soon as the hearing recessed, Woodrum called Smith to ask if the statement represented the president's recommendations. Smith demurred, saying that while he had discussed the topic with the president in the past, "he would hesitate to say that this particular statement now had the President's approval."[26]

A few weeks later, the House Special Committee on Post-War Economic Policy and Planning held a hearing on the "economic problems of the transition period." Smith came to the hearing with a prepared statement. In it, he not only addressed the general economic issues that would face the country after the war, but also commented on the fragmented planning now going on in individual executive agencies and congressional standing committees with narrow policy foci. He called for an overall coordinating role in the Executive Office of the President to prepare integrated plans for congressional consideration. Given the conservative opposition to planning and the defunding of NRPB, he addressed the subject head on:

> I wish to comment on the fear, sometimes expressed, that the development of planning machinery in the Executive Office

may encroach on the field of Congress in the determination of basic governmental policy. Such fears are not well founded. They indicate a failure to distinguish between planning and legislative decision. In making law, Congress always has drawn heavily upon the executive branch for data, analyses, and plans. . . . One of the obvious difficulties of the Congress is the maze of fragmentary, partially considered, and often inconsistent and conflicting opinion and analysis with which it is confronted on major issues and the limited time at its disposal for resolving the many issues before it. The more thoroughly problems can be explored by the planning machinery of the executive branch, the more quickly and accurately congressional committees can appraise them, discover and weigh the alternatives, and reach conclusions. (US House 1944d, 410–11)[27]

Something odd happened that morning at the hearing. Smith came with his prepared statement, apparently expecting to be called to testify. He was not. The conservative chair, William Colmer (D-MS), adjourned the hearing at 11:45 a.m. and simply inserted Smith's statement into the record (407). It is possible that the hearing ran long and Smith could not stay for a later session. However, it is also possible that Colmer deliberately wanted to muffle appearances calling for concerted federal planning and action. Rosenman told Smith he agreed with the statement and the *Post* editorialized in favor of it, but it largely sank from view, perhaps exactly what Colmer wanted.[28]

General Manager of the Executive Branch

Smith's ongoing roles as the manager-in-chief of the federal government and branch-wide coordinator of public policy continued in 1944 as in the previous years. Some activities were mundane and routine and do not need to be recounted in detail here. However, there were several relatively newer developments that represented his central managerial efforts.

Management Improvement and Work Simplification Campaign

In the past, BOB's approach to improving management in the executive branch seemed to have been either authoritarian or retail. The former included such actions as letters or memos to all agency heads, budget circulars, and rulings on personnel ceilings. The latter were one-agency-at-a-time efficiency studies by the Administrative Management Division. In 1944, Smith and Stone seem to have decided on a different approach. They shifted to a softer and friendlier approach that was largely educational and encouraging. A popularized step-by-step approach might be more effective at penetrating deeper into the bureaucracy and being noticed. They were pivoting to a more wholesale approach. In this metamorphosis, the division was encouraging management reform throughout the executive branch with brochures, training programs, and other forms of (relatively) mass communication. In part, this reflected a growing awareness by Smith and Stone of the limits of the initial strategy of treating the division as a management consulting firm for the executive branch. The vastness of the federal government necessitated more of a shotgun approach. In January, they released their first *Management Bulletin*. It was a fifteen-page mimeograph booklet that presented a management improvement worksheet. The form was intended to "assist in appraising agency operations and in formulating a positive, continuous program of action" (Smith 1944f). As a carrot, Smith said that further decisions about cutting an agency's personnel ceiling would depend in part on the quarterly reports of their management improvement efforts. The implication was that reports demonstrating management reform and more effective utilization of personnel would improve chances of not being subject to further cuts.[29]

In March, the next *Management Bulletin* was an eleven-page typeset brochure with a how-to orientation. Titled "An Agency Management Program," it consisted of a series of fifty-five questions for managers to ask themselves and then provided next to each question a column for writing answers and possible implementation actions. Smith gave a copy to the president and said he liked the checklist approach because it is "similar to that used by a filling station in greasing a car. In short, we hope to grease the bureaucracy."[30] In his introduction to the checklist, Smith wrote he hoped that each manager "will find in it at least one idea he can use in improving management of his agency" (Smith 1944g). As with the January *Bulletin*, he tried to incent them by saying that future decisions about personnel ceilings would reflect how effectively BOB judged an agency at implementing the management improvements suggested by the questions. Trying to draw more attention to the effort, in early April, Marsh proclaimed to an OWI PR man that "the response of these agency officials has been encouraging; most of them are referring the bulletin to key subordinates and asking for realistic appraisals."[31] The daily column for civil servants in the *Washington Daily News* claimed that "as a follow-up, it [BOB] is sending its agents to each agency in turn to discuss the list in detail."[32] However, that seems to have been an exaggeration.

Smith continued to be interested in ways to make the new approach to government-wide management improvements more effective and successful. In July, he hosted a meeting for all division heads to see a "demonstration of the Peter Rabbit sales technique" developed by two staffers. It was a way to "put over management improvement in an attractive way."[33] The focus was on a visual presentation that easily conveyed the steps for simplifying work processes.[34] Sketches and cartoon-style depictions could be more successful at communicating ideas than text. This orientation reflected Smith's clear understanding that a popular approach to communication and persuasion would increase the chances of successful implementation.[35] Smith even lobbied the secretary of the navy to release a Lt. McPhail, apparently a graphic artist, to work full-time on the project at BOB.[36] The Navy refused.[37] At the end of the year, BOB asked Congress for a deficiency appropriation relating to publishing materials for continuing and enhancing its management improvement campaign.[38] Congress approved an additional $25,000 for printing expenses (although not exclusively for this project).[39]

Planning Public Works for the Missouri River

Some bureaucratic problems were intractable. In the Missouri River basin, the upstream population wanted public works to increase the supply of water for irrigation while the downstream population wanted flood control. To make matters worse, irrigation was the domain of Interior's Reclamation Bureau, but flood control was the mission of the Army Corps of Engineers. Still, it seemed like a compromise would be relatively easy. Smith and FDR called for integrated and unified planning for all public works on the river. Bizarrely, some of the advocates on each side criticized this approach because they claimed it was a stalking horse for the administration's support for the other agency. Smith and FDR talked about it several times but did not seem to be able to persuade the two sides that they were taking a neutral position and merely urging comprehensive planning.[40] Eventually, FDR sent a message to Congress proposing creation of a Missouri River counterpart to the TVA as a way to bring both sides together (Roosevelt 1969, 1944–1945: 274–76). It flopped. Reviewing the record after Roosevelt's death, Rosenman was as stupefied as Smith had been. He concluded that "many special interests and pressure groups" were able to sink it. Their two main arguments were that such a river authority "would injure their own interests; and valley Authorities were 'unsound in theory'" (278). Perhaps it was a commentary on Roosevelt's fading power, the increasing influence of the conservative coalition's antigovernment and pro-business themes, and unabashed open pursuit of economic self-interest—the public be damned. In a side incident to the Missouri River fight, in February, Ickes brought a pro-reclamation bureau draft letter when he met with the president. He asked FDR to sign it on the spot and Roosevelt did. (Perhaps another indication of his fading concentration.) The letter, of course, screwed up the administration's position on congressional consideration of a rivers and harbors bill. It took Smith much effort to undo the damage. He promptly (mildly) criticized FDR for doing it and read the riot act to Ickes.[41] He drafted a letter for Roosevelt to send to the committee chair, confessing "sometimes matters get pulled out of their proper channels," but requesting that the letter not be deemed an official communication, rather "a personal note to you."[42] Correctly, Smith's position was that any statement of policy or communications with Congress about legislation had to be coordinated and cleared by BOB. It was also a good reminder of Smith's ongoing efforts to impose discipline on a White House that was used to operating in Roosevelt's improvisational style before Smith arrived.

Overseeing the Management of the War Effort

Another odd fight occurred between the War Department and BOB. During the buildup of US forces in the UK, Smith and Stone assigned Eric Biddle, a member of the Administrative Management Division, to a permanent posting in London. His job was to examine US government operations there and recommend ways to improve the efficiency and coordination of the war effort. In midyear he returned to DC (coincidently the week of D-Day) for consultations and planning, then headed back.[43] Smith felt that Biddle's work had constructively improved field operations by federal agencies in Great Britain. He then decided to send a pair of examiners beyond the UK into the larger European theater of operations. The War Department objected and persuaded Roosevelt to dictate a memo to Smith prohibiting the assignment. Smith raised the subject when meeting with Roosevelt in March. "The President made a few placating comments, then took out his pencil and wrote on the bottom of the memorandum, 'Go ahead—it would help.'"[44] Even after that written presidential authorization, the secretary of war again wrote to Smith that the trip would not be approved.[45] Yet again, Smith had to appeal to FDR.[46] Nonetheless, the Army prevailed. It would not back down and the trip never happened.[47]

In July, Smith had a brief meeting with Roosevelt. He knew, given that the president had announced in June he would run for a fourth term, that this would be one of his infrequent meetings until after the election. He was also conscious of FDR's fading concentration and health. Nonetheless, Smith told FDR that there were problems in the organization and management of the war effort. These were "developing situations which made me very unhappy personally because I felt ineffective in dealing with them on his behalf, but I did not want to sit around just watching these situations continue. They only caused him trouble, to say nothing of getting the Government service in bad" with Congress, the media, and the public. Smith was expecting that FDR would wave those issues off and shift full attention to politics. He didn't. "He seemed quite interested. He asked me how I thought the Army and Navy were doing. I told him that on the whole they were doing very well, but I then used the WPB as an example of a house divided against itself, about which something ought to be done." Smith briefly gave his take on the leadership problems at the top of the agency. Changing the chair (Nelson) and vice chair (Wilson) might go a long way to improving the agency's operations. Somewhat to Smith's surprise, the president, he noted, "indicated that he would like to talk to me about the subject and he made me feel that in a way he was saying that he was not just dismissing the subject."[48]

Spokesperson for the Administration

Compared to the previous year, Smith had a significantly higher public profile in 1944. Between January and the election, he give seven speeches, five in person (four out of town), and two on national radio networks. He made only one speech after the election. While it is unreasonable to conclude definitively that his increased public profile was directly intended to support FDR's reelection, the oddity of the timing of his appearances and the fact that most were out of town calls for at least a tentative observation. After all, the administration was being pummeled by the conservative coalition and some often false impressions of the president's policies were affecting public opinion. In his own small way, Smith wanted to do his part to balance what the public was hearing. He was defending the administration's record and, by implication, making the case for a fourth term for FDR (or, if he ended up not running, for a like successor).

Speeches

A few days after FDR sent his FY 1945 budget proposal to Congress, Ernest Lindley called and asked if Smith would appear on a public affairs program hosted by Lindley on a national radio network.[49] Lindley, a reporter for *Newsweek* and a syndicated columnist, was one of Smith's favorite journalists due to his interest and understanding of public administration and economics. Smith gladly accepted, if only to reflect his respect for Lindley as well as to have a chance to talk about the budget with someone who had above-average expertise on the subject. The format was relatively formal, with a script worked out in advance, even if delivered in a conversational manner. Smith met with Marsh several times to finalize a script he was comfortable with.[50] Besides talking in general about the FY 1945 budget, Smith particularly pointed to the small proportion spent on non-war activities, the already declining spending on military construction, and a leveling off of spending on munitions (Smith 1944a). These "good news" trends were often ignored by the conservative coalition and the media. For Smith it was an opportunity to get the word out. Indicating Smith's public standing, the *Chicago Tribune* flagged his appearance to readers as one of the "special events" on the radio that day.[51] Given the context of wartime rationing and cuts in nonessential foods, the radio program was, incongruously and hilariously, underwritten by the "Council on Candy as Food in the War Effort," a subsidiary of the National Confectioners' Association.[52] It hinted at the kind of special interest lobbying occurring around wartime priorities and controls. Afterward, Lindley sent a thank-you note to Smith, commenting on his "excellent radio voice."[53]

The American Road Builders' Association invited Smith to address its annual conference in February in Chicago. Smith asked a staffer who was familiar with the organization if he should accept. Was this group "a good one to speak before"? The staffer replied that his view of the association "was not too favorable."[54] That was probably because in American politics the highway lobby, well funded by contractors, exerted continuous pressure for spending more, *more*, MORE—no matter how much was already being spent on road construction. (As Michigan's budget director, Smith had battled the state's highway commissioner on effectuating spending cuts and usually lost.) Smith was therefore planning to decline. Then he got a call from the chief clerk of the House Appropriations Committee, Marc Shield. Smith had had many interactions with Shield over the years and

Shield had been helpful to him behind the scenes. Shield knew one of the association leaders and asked Smith to accept.[55] Given his past good working relationship with Shield and the committee's crucial role vis-à-vis BOB's mission, Smith had little choice but to accept.[56] However, it was more than a political favor. Smith was impressed with Shield's skills and at the end of the year, when it looked like Assistant Director Appleby would be leaving, Smith offered the job to Shield, who declined. Smith noted, "[Shield explained] there is so much pressure to get him to remain on with the Appropriations Committee that he could not accept a job with any other governmental group."[57] Smith's speech focused on the audience's interest, although not always giving them the news they were hoping for. Looking back at public works and road building as a public policy to reverse the economic effects of the Great Depression, he said that it was surprisingly modest. Yes, it contributed to the recovery, "but it was not decisive" (Smith 1944b, 121). In part, that was because federal spending on public works did not fully offset the contraction in public works spending by state and local governments. Pivoting to the postwar situation, he said that BOB was enhancing its oversight of comprehensive planning for federal public works and that its evaluation of proposals would be judged by a more rigorous cost-benefit analysis. However, he pointed out that not all projects could or should be decided on that basis. Reflecting his lifelong commitment to the purposes of government, he said, "We have frequently lost sight of the simple fact that we should build public works primarily because we need the public services such works will provide after completion" (123). He also drew the attention of this self-interested audience by stating that he expected most public works in the immediate postwar era to be conducted by state and local governments, which had often deferred them during the war and meanwhile had deliberately accumulated financial reserves (to reduce consumer spending) to fund postwar projects. The speech got decent press coverage, including the *Times*, the front page of the *Wall Street Journal*, and a national wire service story.[58] In general, Smith was trying to convey publicly that the lobby's turn was coming after the war, but to reduce expectations of huge federal spending increases on highways and to convey that cost-benefit analyses would be increasingly rigorous when examining proposed projects.

A few weeks later, Smith gave a talk to the DC chapter of the Society for the Advancement of Management. He focused on planning as an integral element of good management. He acknowledged the political criticism of planning by the conservative coalition as a "radical" activity associated with "long-haired professors or wild-eyed thinkers." But, in reality, effective public administration was inherently a planning process. In the same way that corporations necessarily engaged in planning, so, too, the federal government could not operate in a comprehensive and integrated fashion without planning (Smith 1944c). The *Herald Tribune* covered Smith's promotion of more federal planning as news.[59] In context, the speech was an effort to rally support for rational planning as an element of management to counter the success of the conservative coalition in defunding NRPB and generally denouncing all government planning as antibusiness, collectivist, even communistic. In March, Smith spoke at a luncheon of the Pittsburgh Chamber of Commerce on the subject of business-government relations. He called for improved relations between business and government. From his perspective, the preternatural hostility between the two during the New Deal had been largely and successfully bridged during the war. The two sectors were working as harmoniously as possible to maximize wartime production. Why could that not be continued in the postwar reconversion period? Smith also discussed management as a generic and similar activity whether occurring in governmental or for-profit organizations. One of the major problems of the war mobilization "that has confronted government and business alike is the shortage of managerial skills" (Smith 1945a, 147). At the beginning of the war, Smith observed, "there simply were not enough trained men. We lacked a stockpile of managerial skills, just as we lacked reserves of many other strategic resources. As a result, errors were made and blunders occurred. . . . We often accomplished results mainly by sheer awkwardness and brute force." To Smith "the management skills required by government and business are basically the same." Furthermore, he noted, "in the future we ought to see a stronger, two-way flow of managers, from government into business, as well as from business into government" (148). Smith was offering a policy and political olive branch to business as well as conveying his opinion that business and public administration were quite alike.

In June, Smith gave a talk at a conference of the Municipal Finance Officers Association in Cleveland. He compared the principles underlying the tradition of legislative control of budgeting versus the newer doctrine pushed by Roosevelt of using budgeting as a tool of managerial control and oversight. He conceded that some of the aims of legislative and executive control were at odds, but argued that they could be meshed. "Legislative budget control can become *most* effective when it operates through a fully developed system of executive budget management" (Smith 1944d, 187, emphasis in original). He concluded by stating, "We must learn to think of the budget not as an incomprehensible book but as a living process of democratic policy formation and policy executive. Then, and then only, will the budget serve equally well the purposes of legislative control and executive management" (188). Seeking to improve his somewhat rocky relations with Congress during the FY 1945 funding fights earlier that year, Smith sent copies of the speech to all the members of the House Appropriations Committee.[60] In addition, within months, ASPA's *PAR* published it.[61] In this speech, Smith was offering an olive branch to Congress. His next out-of-town speech was on education. In 1943, Smith had given the commencement address at Grinnell College in Iowa and shared some of his thoughts about trends in higher education (chap. 6). This year, he was invited to share his observations at the summer Institute for Superintendents and Principals at the University of Wisconsin (Madison). He accepted because of "his unhappiness over the reactionary feeling and thinking at the college level."[62] In part, he wanted to reflect on the seemingly eternal fights over the role of the federal government in education and its organizational structure to do that. "I have little sympathy with the comparatively small group of educators who become overly concerned regarding government control, and who consequently stimulate fear of governmental aid of any kind. . . . When educators reconcile their own thinking and direct their combined influence toward common goals, they will have taken a decisive step to end the conditions to which they object" (Smith 1944e). Smith also cautioned against "inflexibilities" in the educational field, including "a factory-like educational organization." He predicted that in the postwar period the needs of students would be far different from what they had been before the war and therefore educators should prepare for this new cadre of students.

Smith also spoke on a national radio network in early August.[63] It was a fifteen-minute speech, "The War Budget Is Everyone's Problem," for the series called "World Statesmen" and hosted by Richard Eaton.[64] His theme was about "the budget's impact on the economy, as indicated by war expenditures."[65] Again, while it was a nonpolitical and nonpartisan address, it nonetheless put FDR's war management record in a positive light. At the end of the year, Smith gave a talk on "Blind Spots of Management" to the Philadelphia chapter of the Society for the Advancement of Management.[66] His main point was that management training focused too much on methods and techniques and was dominated by specialized training, such as personnel and planning. This led to organizational rigidity and stifling creativity of employees. Instead, he urged a focus on objectives, whether by business administrators or public administrators. This kind of reorientation was now needed in management training schools as well as by practitioners.

Furthermore, Smith insisted that broad-gauged managers "with high social intelligence" were needed at the top of business and government organizations. Their jobs were similar because both have "a great responsibility for the nation's social and economic advancement. The long-term goal of both business and government must be a sound and prosperous nation" (Smith 1945a, chap. 3). Harvard professor Pendleton Herring liked the speech so much he wanted to get Chester Barnard (author of the landmark 1938 *Functions of the Executive*) together with Smith to pursue the idea further.[67]

Media Relations

Marsh was active in the spring and summer with ideas for press releases, articles, and speeches. Some of the subjects were on non-war spending, Lend-Lease, OCD, reductions in budget estimates, and the work of the United Nations Relief and Rehabilitation Administration (UNRRA). While some of Marsh's ideas did not come to fruition, Smith and Marsh were clearly seeking to raise the profile of BOB, correct misimpressions about federal spending, and generally flag the good works of the administration that were otherwise being ignored.[68] One of Smith's few press conferences occurred on August 1. In coordination with the White House, he convened the media to announce the revised estimates of the FY 1945 budget with updated estimates of receipts and expenditures, as well as the final appropriations bills signed in time for the beginning of the fiscal year on July 1.[69] About twenty reporters attended.[70] It was a "good news" story of BOB forecasting a reduction of federal spending by $3 billion in FY 1945 based on wartime developments. It received extensive coverage in the daily press, which did not treat it as election-related or politically motivated.[71]

Three editorials captured the political zeitgeist of the time. The *Herald Tribune* damned with faint praise Smith's report because "the over-all budget situation is at least slightly less dismaying than it appeared originally."[72] The *Hartford Courant* said that the savings were largely "a paper transaction" and it looked forward to Senator Byrd's recommendations to cut spending.[73] The *Chicago Tribune* blasted Smith and BOB. In a particularly vicious smear, it noted that Smith "has placed in responsible positions two of the most notorious of the pre-war spending bund." It cited a claim by Congressman Martin Dies (D-TX), head of the Un-American Activities Committee, that many senior officials in the administration "had been in communication with the Communist-CIO political action committee," including former USDA officials Appleby and Louis Bean, both of whom were now at BOB. (Smith had hired Appleby as Coy's successor.) "They had played an important part in discovering ways to spend money so that the department became the third biggest spending department in the government." Worse, they were "close advisers of Henry Wallace" when he was USDA secretary.[74]

In September, Herbert Corey, a writer for the *Nation's Business*, the monthly of the US Chamber of Commerce, interviewed Smith.[75] His profile was published in the November issue. It was extremely complimentary, focusing on his quiet ways of dealing with conflicts between administration pooh-bahs and how he built up BOB to cut unnecessary spending and have the in-house expertise to examine agency projects and proposals independently. "Some office-holders do not love him, as he has remarked. But they do not stamp on his toes. Persons wearing dancing pumps rarely stamp on toes in steel shod boots—and Mr. Smith's boots are steel up to the kneecaps." The profile even included a dig from him at the double standards of business. Most complaints about intrusive and unnecessary federal questionnaires came from business. But, Corey noted, "Smith finds that the business men who get into the Government are great lovers of questionnaires. 'You wouldn't think so. But they write longer and more detailed questionnaires than the regulars, and defend them more positively.' "[76] It was a remarkable PR accomplishment by Smith: an image of financial probity and honesty, apolitical, a record of cutting spending, and his openness to business. It was quite a feat, coming from the national Chamber of Commerce. Smith also continued to be viewed as a minor political celebrity. In a syndicated illustrated feature called "Private Lives" he was depicted as a frugal spender. Titled "A Bargain Hunter," it showed a sketch of him looking over shoes on sale at a department store: "In private as well as public life, U.S. Budget Director Harold D. Smith once, in pre-ration days, bought four pairs of shoes that had been marked down to $1.95."[77] As with the profile in the Chamber of Commerce monthly, Smith's image as being parsimonious with money had established itself deeply.

Running BOB While Roosevelt
Was Running for a Fourth Term

Smith may have claimed that he was an apolitical budget director, but he certainly was aware that 1944 was an election year and that, if FDR decided to run for a fourth term, Smith would support him as much as possible. As early as April, Smith had presidential politics on his mind. When lunching with Ickes, he asked Ickes to hold off on pushing for more control over petroleum. If the subject were to become public by leaks from departments opposing Ickes's idea, that "may open the President to attack."[78] Smith wanted to prevent that. In other words, he cared less about the merits of the idea than the politics of it. Then, Navy Secretary Frank Knox died in late April. Smith promptly suggested that Roosevelt replicate what he did in the previous presidential election year, when he had appointed Republicans Knox and Stimson to head the Navy and War Departments, respectively. Smith mentioned Wendell Willkie and Harold Stassen as appropriate Republicans to be the next navy secretary.[79]

By early May, Smith was positive that FDR would run. After a meeting, he dictated, "If there were any question in my mind about the President's intention to run for a fourth term, it was put aside by the President's general remark that if he cut the Army budget it would be in directions that would have political significance."[80] Two days after Roosevelt announced he would run again, Smith had another conference with him. FDR greeted him jovially. "I responded to his greeting by saying that I was glad he was again going to be a candidate." Later in the meeting, when talking about dealing with the national debt after the war, Smith said his fiscal experts "were much concerned that during the President's campaign he might advocate retirement after the war of any specific annual amount of the national debt. He said that there was no danger of his doing that, that the retirement of the debt was dependent upon a great many circumstances."[81]

Just before the Democratic convention in Chicago, the economists of the Fiscal Division suggested to Smith that they could draft the section on employment for the party's plank and policy platform. Smith said it was already too late, implying that he would have supported doing it if the suggestion had come earlier.[82] The housing specialists at BOB were also paying attention to the party's plank. They told Marsh that the version adopted at the convention was a victory for the private housing industry over the supporters of public housing.[83] Smith and Ickes often talked politics when they had lunch that summer. In July, they talked about the rumors of who would replace Vice President Wallace on the ticket. They had heard political gossip that Commerce Secretary Jesse Jones was on the short list. Both hoped it would not happen, with Smith saying, "Jones was the slickest man in these parts."[84] The next month, after FDR had picked Truman, Smith told Ickes that he "was of the opinion that the President had lost ground since Chicago." Smith also did "not think that Truman will add any strength to the ticket."[85] At lunch in late September, Smith reported that his some of his friends in Detroit told him that "Truman had made a very poor impression when he spoke" at a campaign event there.[86] Shortly after FDR dumped him, Wallace talked to Smith. He said he nonetheless intended to campaign for the ticket. He asked Smith for some economic data on postwar employment and reconversion because he wanted to speak about how Democrats would handle the economy and federal budget after V-E and V-J Days. Smith promised to get him the information. Smith and Wallace also talked about the convention. Smith said "how deeply pained all his people were. He said he thought Jimmie Byrnes was the one originally responsible for getting the President in the frame of mind that he ought to have someone else than me to run with him" (Wallace 1973, 373).

Between the convention and the election, Smith was quietly active to help the campaign. For example, he helped FDR make news that would depict him as forward looking and with plans for the future, to contradict the Republican meme that FDR and the Democrats were tired, out of steam, and had nothing to offer for the future. Smith drafted a letter for FDR to sign and release at a press conference in late August.[87] It directed BOB "to speed up preparations for the eventual reconversion of the nation's productive energies to peaceful pursuits" (Roosevelt 1972, 24: 73–80). It led the news coverage of the press conference, even making the front page of the Republican *Herald Tribune*.[88] Smith repeated the same PR trick a few weeks later, when FDR signed and released a letter to Smith directing him to prepare a study on liquidating war agencies and reorganizing the federal government once the war was over (Roosevelt 1969, 1944–1945: 271–72). Full press coverage ensued, including a front-page story in the *Times*.[89] Byrd tried to negate any positive political effects of these actions on public opinion by promptly complaining that Roosevelt was neither cutting enough nor doing it quickly enough.[90] When they had a relatively extensive meeting in late August, one of the topics Smith raised was the idea of merging the military after the war. What were FDR's views? The president said he supported BOB conducting a thorough examination of the possibility. "However, he feels that there should be considerable caution about publicity. He does not want to get the subject into political discussion."[91] In October, the National Education Association sent both candidates a questionnaire for their views on federal policy vis-à-vis K–12 education. Due to his role in legislative clearance and familiarity with the president's policy positions, Smith could have drafted a response. Instead, he flagged it for Rosenman to handle as soon as possible because "it falls into the realm of political strategy" particularly because the association was planning to publish the responses of the two candidates before the election.[92] A few weeks later, Smith submitted to Rosenman a draft statement on postwar employment for use in the campaign.[93]

In late October, New York governor Thomas Dewey, the Republican presidential nominee, gave a speech on foreign policy in Minneapolis. It was a slashing attack on FDR's military and foreign policy record. One of his charges was that FDR underfunded the military when preparing his FY 1941 budget request in the fall of 1939, even though the European war had already started.[94] Rosenman quickly asked BOB to check the allegation for accuracy. BOB's reply stated, "Mr. Dewey is in the position of emphasizing a seven per cent cut and ignoring the 800 per cent increase in spite of the cut." Furthermore, he ignored contract authorizations (different from appropriations). "Thus the total recommended appropriations and contract authorizations for the War Department for [FY] 1941 was more than 13 times those of the previous year." In his cover memo to Rosenman, Assistant Director Appleby said that BOB's attached documentation "shows rather clearly a serious misrepresentation on Dewey's part."[95] Marsh had drafted the one-page critique of Dewey's claim.[96] Based on his journalistic experience, Marsh tried to write it in newspaper style to make it as simple as possible. However, Appleby conceded, the subject was "a very involved procedure" and therefore some details about budgeting categories were necessary. Rushing to knock down Dewey's claim, hours later the White House press office released the entire BOB statement late in the day, just in time to make the morning papers. Several newspapers quoted from it extensively, notwithstanding its disemboweled nature: a statement attributed to an agency, rather than the convention of government statements coming from a specific named person.[97]

Smith's last meeting with FDR before the election was on October 30. Roosevelt was in good spirits and talked about his recent appearance in Chicago. He said "it was probably the biggest crowd in history."[98] Smith replied, "I did not think he needed to be too much concerned about the outcome of the election. He said that he thinks the situation is better now than it was a month ago. . . . The President then commented that it is certainly an aggravation and a nuisance to have the election come up at this time. He seemed to feel rather keenly about the fact that his attention has to be distracted from the more immediate international problems."[99] In all, Smith was distinctly, but quietly, involved in the reelection campaign behind the scenes, a behavior quite at odds with his public representations about budgeting as an apolitical activity as well as his media image of nonpartisanship.

Two days after the election, Smith submitted a pro-forma resignation. He said, "I feel strongly that the people of the country are to be congratulated on their decision. All along I believed that the decision was of tremendous importance not only to this country but to the whole world, and its importance increased in my mind as the campaign went on. . . . I want to reaffirm my sincere loyalty to you and my great confidence in your leadership." Nonetheless, authentically reflecting his comments to Ickes during the year of his unhappiness about the disorganization of the administration, Smith also made strong recommendation to reorganize the president's Executive Office. He said, "The conflicting delegations and assumptions of authority are compounding trouble for you. . . . The agencies complain increasingly and sometimes use Executive Office fumbling as an excuse for going their own way, thus in part creating the atmosphere of disunity about which there is complaint." The letter concluded with "my resignation to be accepted at your pleasure."[100] (For Roosevelt's response, see end of the chapter.) The next day, Smith went to Union Station to welcome FDR back from Hyde Park. He "rode in the official procession to the White House, where the President shook hands with the White House staff."[101]

Promoting Professional Public Administration

Smith continued to be active in shaping the new profession. He was frequently in touch with prominent leaders including Brownlow, Gulick, Mosher, Emmerich, and Harris. On his way back from a speech at the University of Wisconsin, Smith stopped in Chicago to spend a day at the 1313 building of PACH and talked with several people based there.[102] He was also in touch with the head of Public Administration Service, one of PACH's arms.[103] As the past president of ASPA, he continued to be active in the leadership of the five-year-old organization. After three years as president, Brownlow was ready to step down. When ASPA had been founded, the consensus of the leadership was that the presidency would alternate between academics and practitioners. Hence the sequence of Mosher to Smith to Brownlow. Now, was the turn for a practitioner. In January, Brownlow called Smith to talk about this expectation. He argued for the "desirability of selecting for next year's president of the Society an academician rather than an administrator because this is a political year."[104] It was an odd argument, given that every even-numbered year was an election year. Smith acquiesced. However, by agreeing, he was participating in a major precedent about ASPA's culture and leadership. The expectation of consistently alternating presidencies between faculty and administrators had been broken. ASPA gradually but inexorably moved toward academic dominance in its membership. Even though Smith agreed that the man succeeding Brownlow would be an academic, there was disagreement about who it should be. Smith wanted William Anderson of the University of Minnesota, whom he knew well from the Committee on Public Administration of the Social Science Research Council in the 1930s.[105] However, Gulick was the eventual choice. He ended up serving for two years, in part because of the cancellation of the annual 1945 conference due to additional wartime restrictions on nonessential travel.[106]

Smith continued to encourage BOB staff to participate in professional activities, including writing for ASPA's *PAR*. Three of its four issues that year included a contribution by a BOB staffer. A member of the Administrative Management Division coauthored an article about investigating the operations of government agencies (Seidman and Yavner 1944) and another about WPB's coordination of its headquarters with field offices (Carey 1944). They were also active reviewing books, including on Australian public administration (Morstein Marx 1944) and bureaucracy (Vieg 1944). In addition, Smith encouraged the creation of a professional association of budget officers. Several departmental budget directors were interested in creating a counterpart to the Society for Personnel Administration.[107] They wanted a similar professional organization for public budgeting specialists, initially for those working in the federal government in the capital. Smith met with the organizing group and gave them his blessing.[108] This promptly led to the founding of the federal Budget Officers Conference.[109] Over the next few years, it issued several reports and helped organize training programs for budgeteers.[110] However, it never quite jelled into a major organization like the personnel society.[111] Also, several of Smith's speeches (discussed earlier) related to the profession of public administration and his view of its role in democracy. They included "Administration and Planning" and "Blind Spots of Management," "Teamwork: Government and Business," and "The Budget as an Instrument of Legislative Control and Executive Management."

Private Life: Health, Farm

All year, Smith's health continued to be fragile. In January and twice in April, he went to Bethesda Naval Hospital for extensive examinations and checkups, each lasting about half a day.[112] In November, after hurting his leg in an accident on his tractor, he returned for treatment of the injury and an X-ray (it was not broken).[113] The next week, he missed work for two days due to illness.[114] Indicating how much his health was an ongoing matter of concern to colleagues, Ickes, his frequent lunch partner, made a point of commenting whenever Smith looked better than usual. In April, Ickes said Smith "had a good healthy color" and in May that "he was looking fine, with fine color."[115] Such sporadic observations silently emphasize the opposite, how Smith routinely looked: without color, without vigor, without energy.

Smith's farm took on a greater proportion of his attention in 1944. The farm was not a health-oriented activity to give him rest away from the office (chap. 6). Rather, he intended it as a moneymaking venture to add to his income. For example, he had borrowed money to cover some of its expenses and, when his corn crop was failing, was enormously worried about how, without produce to sell, he could cover the debt.[116] Farming was also a dangerous activity. In February, he suffered flash burns when doing electric melding and missed a day of work.[117] As mentioned earlier, in November he injured a leg during an accident on his tractor and rushed to Bethesda for treatment. The farm was most certainly not a pleasant (or doctor ordered) distraction from work in order to relax. It was a major endeavor consuming increasing amounts of his time and attention. He often took long weekends to work there, such as Friday to Tuesday.[118] (A reminder that the standard workweek for federal civilian employees was forty-eight hours. Saturday was a normal eight-hour workday.) He also took more extensive vacations to work on the farm, such as the week of July 3–7, August 8–13, week of September 4–8, December 9–13, and December 26–28. As an appointee of the president, he was not under any formal guidelines or policies about time off. His absences likely exceeded the vacation time granted to classified civil servants, thus not being a model for subordinates. Nonetheless, they knew how hard he worked as well as his fragile health and likely did not begrudge him the time away from the office.

His farming was a common topic with friends in high places and the media. He told FDR that he had spent the weekend "doing a night-shift job with the tractor on the farm."[119] He and Ickes (who was somewhat closer to being a gentleman farmer) commiserated about the lack of rain and their fears that a drought might ruin their corn crop.[120] Smith called the secretary of agriculture to help locate a lime spreader and, a few months later, the secretary offered to come to the farm to look over his hogs.[121] When a columnist interviewed him for a profile, he shared the story of buying a used tractor that frequently broke down. He recounted that, based on USDA recommendations, he had planted a field of "wong," which he said was an Asian barley that was better than the common type used in the US. He was also trying out a new Russian wheat, which supposedly did not need replanting for twenty-five to thirty years. In all, he depicted himself as a happy farmer, seeking to use the latest science to be better at it than when he was growing up on the family farm in Kansas.[122] However, Smith's preoccupation with his farm while at work and his use of federal employees for information and help became even more pronounced in 1944 than in 1943. In-house, he asked an Estimates Division staffer for catalogs on electric welders[123] and two staffers for help getting a priority certificate for steel.[124] He asked a staffer at the Estimates Division to obtain federal aerial photos of the lands adjacent to his farm,[125] talked to another at the Administrative Management Division about some of his farm problems,[126] called the head of the BOB field service and asked if a staffer at the Chicago office could help him locate a corn elevator chain,[127] and asked a staffer in BOB's Estimates Division how a farmer could qualify to locate and buy a chain hoist through the federal surplus war material network.[128] He sent Marsh to a federal surplus yard to look for a motor for the farm.[129] One of BOB's secretaries connected him to her friend who owned a Morgan stallion.[130] Farther out into the executive branch, Smith called a specialist (with a PhD) at the USDA model farm to help find an ear-notcher for pigs,[131] the chair of the federal Council on Personnel Administration to help find a Morgan stallion,[132] another USDA specialist at the Bureau of Animal Industry about a virus his pigs had,[133] and the head of the Pathology Section of USDA's Bureau of Animal Industry about a sick bull.[134] He called a senior USDA official about buying cattle from the department's model farm in Beltsville.[135] The head of USDA's Section on Farm Equipment and Machinery gave him advice on using a lime spreader.[136] One must conclude—in hindsight, based on twenty-first-century guidelines for professional ethics in public administration—that Smith abused his position of public trust for personal benefit.

Preparing the FY 1946 Budget

In the last few years, Smith had largely withdrawn from personal participation in the early stages of BOB's consideration the of the annual budget, relying on assistant directors Blandford and Coy who were experienced with the

BOB budget-building process. However, the FY 1946 budget was Appleby's first. Smith decided to be more involved this year, probably because of that. In September, Smith conferred with him to arrange a schedule for Boards of Review that both could attend.[137] Suddenly, in late October, Appleby told Smith he had accepted another job.[138] That meant Smith *had* to participate actively in all the Boards of Review in October and November.[139] This was an extraordinary commitment of time on his part, but he really had no choice. Also, perhaps he wanted to demonstrate that his health and farm were not reducing his attention to routine business. It is also possible that he already could tell that FDR would not have much personal involvement in reviewing budget recommendations and therefore Smith could counterbalance the president's absence with his own deep dive into the document. His first budget meeting with FDR was on November 27. He told Roosevelt that he would like to confer with him in depth about the major policy items in the budget as they had done in Smith's early BOB years. The president waved him off, saying that as "he was going away," he doubted that they "could get together for at least several weeks." That would be too late. Instead, he gave Smith blanket authorization to make all the decisions and promised to back him up "one hundred percent."[140] For Smith that would be more than satisfactory, even if a few (predictable) emergency personal appeals from cabinet members might force FDR to intervene a bit. The next day Roosevelt left for Warm Springs (GA) and did not return until December 19. Between Warm Springs and Hyde Park, of the ten weeks between the election and inauguration, Roosevelt was away for five of them (Lelyveld 2016, 245). Smith was on his own to finish the budget, notify departments, deal with appeals,[141] and begin drafting the annual budget message.

The White House press corps was none the wiser. On November 21, they asked Roosevelt how the budget was coming along and he blandly claimed, "I have done just about what I have done at this time of the year. I have still got quite a number of conferences scheduled with Harold Smith. Getting along all right" (Roosevelt 1972, 24: 248). After returning from Warm Springs in mid-December, they asked again. He, again, deflected them saying, "I haven't had a chance to see Harold today. I am going to see him tomorrow" (263). Three days later, on December 22, they re-raised the subject, asking, "Have you had a chance to talk to Budget Director Smith?" He answered that he "talked to him on the phone yesterday" (274). His answer obscured who had called whom. He knew that reporters would assume that the president called people, not the other way around. By now, the Battle of the Bulge was Topic A. The German surprise attack began on December 16 and was initially very successful. All of a sudden, confidence that the war would be over soon, or at least by mid-1945 evaporated. Smith's secretary added an unusual note to his December 22 calendar. After listing a two-hour meeting Smith had with the senior staff of the Estimates Division to talk about the implications of the attack, she included an observation on the war news: "(The Germans are still counter-attacking and apparently progressing on the Western European front)."[142] In fact, the phone conversation with Smith that Roosevelt mentioned at his press conference on December 22 had been about the military situation. Smith, very concerned about losing touch with FDR, called the president requesting some urgent guidance. This was a very unusual thing for him to do and indicated his heightened sense of being at sea budget-wise and fear of being out of sync with the president's latest thinking. Smith asked how FDR wanted either to revise the budget or, at least, reframe it in the budget message. Roosevelt and Smith agreed that all mention of the war being over and preparations for reconversion should be deleted from the message. Instead, its theme should be of the US continuing an "all-out war until our enemies are defeated." They had only talked for five minutes.[143]

~

It will be recalled that in some of his lunches with Ickes in 1944, Smith had groused about the management failures of the administration, FDR's lack of intense personal involvement, and Smith's preference to resign after the election. Indeed, after Roosevelt was reelected, he had promptly submitted a letter of resignation, in the context of fulsome praise for Roosevelt as well as calling for reorganizing the Executive Office. About a month later, he got a response.

December 9, 1944

Dear Harold:

It is only now that I have got down (or rather I should say up) to your letter of November nineteenth. Every once in a while it is good to realize that I am Commander-in-Chief. Your case is an example.

I would no more accept your resignation than fly by jumping off a roof. You are essentially persona grata and doing a grand job. If you talk any more about resigning I will act. A Marine Guard from Quantico will be stationed at your side during every minute of every twenty-four hours. Enough said!

I will have a little more time after January first and I do want to talk with you some more about the organization of the Executive Office. That is really a good idea on your part—though the other one is bum.

Always sincerely,

F.D.R.[144]

Smith was smitten. He stayed, of course.[145]

Chapter 8

FDR's Fourth Term, 1945

The first three weeks of January 1945 should have been crammed with FDR's usual to-do list. Based on the routine pattern of behavior he had established in his previous three terms (and five years with Smith), he would receive last-minute appeals from some cabinet members about Smith's draft of the budget message (inevitably Morgenthau), lead a two-hour budget seminar with Smith for the White House press corps (embargoed until he sent it to Congress), go to Capitol Hill to read his annual State of the Union Address, send the budget to Congress, and then take the oath of office on the 20th. But this was not a routine year. The president had not participated at all in drafting the budget or the budget message, did not attend (let alone lead) the budget seminar, submitted his State of the Union Address in writing (reading a shorter version on the radio that night from the White House), and had a perfunctory inauguration (in front of the White House, not on Capitol Hill). Two days later, he left for the Yalta summit and was gone until the last day in February. After about three weeks at the White House, he was in Hyde Park March 24–28 (without any meetings), returned on the 29th, spent about seven hours at the White House and had a few meetings, then left later that day for Warm Springs. He had no meetings there from March 30 to his death two weeks later.

Interacting with FDR

Smith's first meeting in 1945 with Roosevelt was on New Year's Day. (His last one had been on November 27.) The president "looked very well," he observed. Smith spent most of the short meeting getting guidance on resolving the nearly permanent bureaucratic turf battles between the State Department and other agencies operating overseas. He presented a draft policy proposing a firm principle for future controversies. FDR read it word for word, commenting out loud as he went along. When he finished, he said he liked it and did not suggest any revisions. Being careful, Smith asked for some written confirmation that this indeed would be the fixed policy of the administration for the fourth term—otherwise the usual fights would occur, the principals appealing to the president. Roosevelt agreed to Smith's request, writing on the memo, "Go ahead with this idea." Smith had hoped to spend the rest of the meeting going over the budget message draft, but he had run out of time. Smith told the president that he had been careful—based on the experience of previous years—so "there was no question of a controversial nature in the Message." The only comment FDR made was that he wanted a section about his plan to pay off the war debt as promptly as possible. Smith handed the draft to FDR, who promised to read it that evening.[1] (He did not.) After the meeting, and for the next few days, Smith worked with Rosenman on the draft.[2] Morgenthau mean-while—of course—protested in writing to the president, this time about a tax-related policy that Byrnes asked for (such as mandatory salary deductions for bond-buying instead of Morgenthau's insistence on voluntary campaigns to buy war bonds). As he had in the past, Morgenthau fought for full control over every detail in the revenue section in the budget message. He called Smith, ostensibly to thank him for making sure the draft was acceptable to Treasury, but really to confirm that Smith had no role in Byrnes's action.[3] That permitted Morgenthau to state in his letter to FDR, "I am advised by Mr. Harold Smith that he likewise was not consulted" by Byrnes.[4]

Smith's next meeting with FDR to finalize the message was on January 4. It was like meeting a different person:

> He seemed a little more stooped than usual. His face was a bit more tired and the cigarette holder did not seem to have its usual jaunty tilt. With all, he appeared as a man who, while in possession of his very great faculties, seemed tired in using them. Somehow as I sat beside his desk, I was struck by the picture of the President stooped over the desk.[5]

Because the president had not read the draft Smith gave him on January 1, he read through the entire message, but not out loud as had been his custom. With Rosenman in the room, he wanted to be sure that the message and

State of the Union draft were in harmony. Rosenman promptly mentioned that Morgenthau had called him and vehemently protested Byrnes's actions. "The President looked up and asked him if Morgenthau had been as mean to him as to the President." Clearly, FDR's famous first-class temperament and ability to shrug things off was frayed nearly to the bone. The frankness of the comment also hinted at how FDR really had long felt about Morgenthau (including Morgenthau's near constant complaints to him about Smith). It turned out Morgenthau was not the only one to appeal budget decisions. In mid-December, Commerce Secretary Jones appealed BOB's recommendations for the department's FY 1946 budget in a letter to the president. It sat in FDR's in-box untouched until January 5 when Smith was asked to draft a reply. Smith tartly recommended sending a letter to Jones reminding Jones that the department would be getting more than in the previous year and that an appeal based on not getting everything a department had asked for was hardly meritorious.[6] After their January 4 meeting, Smith returned to his office shell-shocked from what he had just observed. Loyal to the end, Smith observed, "I left the conference resolved that I would do my best not to trouble the President with anything ordinary or petty and that I would do everything possible to relieve him of every burden of administration that the Bureau of the Budget could conceivably handle. I will choke off staff memorandums to the President prepared for my signature and I will in other ways do my best to relieve him of any burden that I can."[7]

Roosevelt still sometimes had his good days, too (Lelyveld 2016, 104). Four days after this discouraging meeting, the old Roosevelt was back. He referred to Smith a letter from the head of the VA asking for more office space in the postwar era, including for storage of the expected large increase in personnel files of veterans. Roosevelt asked Smith to draft a reply to the letter and then dictated a cover memo to Smith with suggestions for what to include in the draft. The dictated memo in its entirety read:

> It has been my thought that after the war is ended all the personnel records of the Armed Services should be placed in the Pentagon Building. As they will have to be kept for many years and the administration of these records can be kept at a minimum, because the people who wish to see them are constant in number, while not very great.
>
> At the same time, it is my thought, as one of the public works, we should continue the plans for the War Department building. A part of it is already up. And at the same time, we

should build the Navy Building on the north side of Hospital Hill. The plans are ready to go ahead with.

The War Department will doubtless object to giving up the Pentagon Building, but it is much too large for them if we get a decent peace.

In the building of the Pentagon Building, I directed General Somerville that the space be given enough weight carrying capacity to carry records safely. You might check on this.

F.D.R.[8]

The memo conveyed Roosevelt at his best, including a strong memory, attention to detail, and well-developed views on federal operations. Smith had another meeting with the president on January 19. One item was federal funding for the Red Cross's overseas programs. This was a complicated subject because several federal entities provided aid in the freed and occupied territories. At the beginning of the discussion, Smith handed Roosevelt a chart on the subject. Five rows displayed the agencies delivering or funding relief: the army, Lend-Lease, UNRRA, foreign government purchase, and the Red Cross. There were six columns for countries where those services were delivered: France, China, Russia, Italy, the Balkans, and Poland. Almost every cell in the table had a different configuration. It is possible, of course, that Smith brought the chart simply to enable clarity about the confusing situation in order to obtain precise presidential guidance. However, handing Roosevelt a chart at the beginning of a discussion was unusual for Smith to do. He had rarely done that in the past. Therefore, it likely that Smith was so alert to FDR's fading memory and span of attention that he knew such a visual aid would be essential to reduce confusion and keep the conversation tightly focused.[9]

On March 12, Smith had his first meeting with Roosevelt since the Yalta summit and his address to Congress on March 1. He began by saying to FDR "that he looked well but that he seemed to have lost some weight. The President said, 'Do you think so,' as if he might be a bit sensitive about the subject. He indicated that he has not gotten much sleep recently" and was eager to go to Warm Springs to rest. Smith wanted to stick to the business at hand, but Roosevelt began talking about "his conversations with the kings of Egypt, Saudi Arabia and Ethiopia about planning and the use of resources. . . . The President reviewed briefly the accomplishments of the five-year plan in Russia and that he believed we should do some real planning in this country—perhaps we should have a five-year plan." Finally, Smith noted, "our conversation *drifted* back" to the subject Smith was trying to talk about. Later, when Smith moved on to another subject, "this conversation then *drifted* into a discussion that went back to planning."[10] Smith must have walked away from the meeting very discouraged about FDR's ability to lead and focus.

Marsh continued attending FDR's press conferences and reporting on them to Smith. The roller coaster of Roosevelt's good and bad days seem apparent. During his March 2 press conference, Roosevelt "was in good humor and seemed in good health, and somewhat tanned. He spoke in unusually low voice, however." On March 13, "the President seemed in extremely good form." The March 20 press conference "was short and quite perfunctory without great news value in subject matter. The President was slightly impatient and unwilling to talk."[11] (That was his last in DC, with only one more in Warm Springs on April 5.)

The last meeting Smith had with FDR was March 23. In part, Roosevelt seemed to be his usual self. He signed an executive order Smith brought, asked Smith to draft a letter accepting Nelson Rockefeller's resignation, and agreed to consider signing an executive order to move the Rural Electrification Administration from USDA to Interior.[12] On the other hand, parts of the meeting were disheartening. Regarding a letter to Congress on appropriations for FY 1946, the president asked Smith to draft a letter for him. Smith suggested, when he provided the draft, that he hoped FDR would then make it more personal, if he would "add his own language. The president said he would." (He did not. He signed it without any changes.) When Smith moved on to talk about another subject, FDR apparently did not recall their earlier conversation about it before he left for Yalta. Smith tried to move the topic forward to potential actions, but was not successful at getting any presidential guidance. On another topic, Smith recalled, "I reminded the President that I had talked with him once before about this." FDR responded. "He recalled our previous conversation," but then gave Smith no explicit direction for dealing with it. Roosevelt was not being helpful on those subjects and did not give forward-facing guidance the way he usually did.[13]

A few days later, Smith and Ickes had lunch. According to Ickes, Smith recounted that during his recent meeting at the White House, "the President, apparently in the middle of the conversation, forgot what had already been said. Harold thinks that he [FDR] is becoming forgetful and inattentive."[14] A week later, Ickes reported that Smith was "even more strongly than at our former meeting of the opinion that the President was not standing up to his job. He feels that his [FDR's] health is not what it should be and that the President has a disposition to shove things aside that he should tackle and dispose of."[15] Regardless of how precise Ickes was in his summaries of these two conversations with Smith, clearly Smith was *extremely* alarmed about the president's ability to do his job. On April 10, Smith received a memo from FDR. Presumably dictated by FDR in Warm Springs, it read in its entirety:

Confidential

April 9, 1945

Memorandum for the Director of the Budget

Please treat from Mr. Byrnes as secret. I wish you would have a talk with him as quickly as possible and I will take it up when I get back. He and you know more about it than other people in Washington.

F.D.R.[16]

The note referenced an attached memo that Byrnes had sent FDR raising major concern about an unnamed pending policy. Given that Byrnes and Smith rarely had personal contact and did not get along, the president's request conveyed that if these two not only agreed, but *strongly* agreed about its importance and urgency, then Roosevelt would treat the matter very seriously.[17] It was Smith's last interaction with Roosevelt.

Inauguration

Smith's last meeting with FDR before he left for Yalta was on January 19, the day before his fourth inauguration and three days before sailing off. Smith needed guidance on several important issues that were likely to be prominent in the fourth term. For example, he told Roosevelt he thought he should obtain legal power to issue subpoenas. He said that he suspected "possible crookedness on the part of some Government officials" in the surplus property program. He worried that "if adequate safeguards are not provided, his Administration, which has been very free of scandal, might run into a lot of trouble." Roosevelt generally concurred and said that Smith should start by touching base with congressional leaders for their reactions to the idea. Another item was on finding a new commissioner of education. Roosevelt had long wanted to get rid of Studebaker but needed a qualified and politically acceptable replacement before doing so, as well as giving Studebaker some other place to land (Lee 2005, 96). The president wondered if this might not be a good position to appoint a woman. Mrs. Roosevelt had been pushing him for this and already had sent her preferred nominee to meet with Smith. Smith concluded that because of that person's affiliation with one of the main political combatants in that policy area—the National Education Association—her nomination would likely be subject to intense criticism from key stakeholders on the other side of the issue. They likely would try to torpedo it politically. Smith thought that a state commissioner of education might have the right qualifications for a nominee: knowledgeable about the subject matter, experience in running a public agency, and some demonstrated political dexterity in the minefield of proposals for federal aid to education. Roosevelt directed Smith to continue examining potential nominees.[18] This was not particularly helpful for Smith. (Their next meeting was almost two months away, March 12.)

On the morning of the inauguration, the *Times* speculated that Smith's meeting with Roosevelt the day before was because "the budget director is often consulted on departmental changes" and that the reason for the meeting was likely to finalize Wallace's still unconfirmed fate.[19] It was not. Smith amusingly recounted the media scrum upon leaving the White House on the 19th with still-VP Wallace to have lunch:

> The Vice President suggested that we go out the side door in order to avoid the newspapermen. But when we got to the basement side door John Crider, of the *New York Times*, seemed to be blocking the way. Crider was persistent in asking questions of the Vice President, but Wallace insisted that he had absolutely nothing to say. As we got outside, a flock of newspapermen came racing down the steps from the side door. Wallace told them flatly that we had nothing to say, and we both quickened our steps to his car.[20]

The actual purpose for the lunch was relatively prosaic, to plan some policy initiatives Wallace had in mind for his still-secret appointment to Commerce.

That evening, Smith attended a preinaugural ball. The next day, he walked over to witness the swearing in and speech on the White House grounds and then went to a reception at the White House that evening. (Mrs. Smith accompanied him to both social events.) The day after the inauguration, Mrs. Roosevelt invited Smith to join her for lunch with all the members of the Roosevelt family who were in town (except the president, who did not attend).[21] After lunch, she and Smith met to discuss education, including, probably, her preference for education commissioner.[22] On the first full day of his fourth term, Roosevelt finally announced what had long been rumored, that now–former vice president Wallace had asked to be appointed secretary of commerce. But Secretary Jones, a conservative and combative Democrat, refused to resign or go quietly, even after meeting with FDR earlier that day. FDR, who disliked firing people, had no choice but to remove Jones from his secretaryship through a public letter. Jones had one more card to play. He wore two "hats," the second as head of the RFC and other government-owned corporations that lent money to businesses. Jones insisted that his firing only affected his secretaryship, while Wallace claimed it covered both. (By now, Roosevelt was on his way to Yalta.) The fight over confirming Wallace was a donnybrook between the conservative coalition and the left wing of the New Deal. Indicating the alignment of forces and FDR's fading influence, the Senate Commerce Committee voted to recommend rejecting the Wallace nomination. Separately, a parallel conservative initiative was to delink a secretary's automatic control of the credit agencies. That would weaken Wallace's nomination and possibly keep Jones in power, if only at these public corporations. Congress quickly passed it. Roosevelt, by now en route back from Yalta, had little choice but to sign it into law.[23] Otherwise, he would risk the Senate rejecting Wallace's nomination in part because some senators feared how a non-businessman (contra Jones) would run the lending corporations. Unintentionally, the new law backfired politically on conservatives. Now, if confirmed, Wallace would not control the lending agencies. That made his nomination less threatening. It opened the way for moderate senators to swing to support him, however tepidly. Six weeks after FDR nominated him, the Senate approved the appointment 56–32. Smith, a Wallace supporter, was delighted. He attended Wallace's swearing in on March 2 and then had lunch with him (again) to plan what Wallace hoped to do in office.[24]

Two postscripts to Wallace's confirmation demonstrated the intensity of the ideological wars between the conservative coalition and FDR. On the first weekday after Wallace was sworn in (Monday, March 5), Roosevelt nominated OES director Fred Vinson to head the lending agencies. Conservatives on the Hill praised the nomination. The Senate confirmed Vinson the *next day*, compared to six weeks for Wallace.[25] The same day that FDR named Vinson, a news story in the *Baltimore Sun* said BOB was drafting an executive order to move four independent regulatory commissions to Commerce: the Federal Trade Commission, Federal Power Commission, Securities and Exchange Commission, and the Interstate Commerce Commission. The story claimed, "Technicians in the Budget Bureau, it was learned today, have been working intensively for approximately a month" on the executive order. The story even pinned down the BOB divisions that were working on it: "the fiscal and administrative management sections of the Budget Bureau."[26] It was the kind of accusation that would inflame the conservative coalition. The very liberal Wallace (abetted, impliedly, by Smith) was plotting to get his grubby hands on business regulation that was supposed to be independent and quasi-judicial. Byrd quickly denounced the scheme on the floor of the Senate.[27] Smith was startled because he *knew* BOB was not preparing such an executive order.[28] The story was a pure invention, likely from a conservative politician wanting to keep stirring the pot by saying to a sympathetic reporter something along the lines of, "Hey, I've heard that when Wallace had lunch with Smith right after the swearing in last Friday, they talked about . . ." Even in wartime, when it came to the fight between business and the federal government that had begun in 1933, pure rumor without any independent confirmation was enough to justify publication in an ostensibly respectable newspaper.

Problems on Capitol Hill: FY 1946 Budget

On January 8, Smith led the annual budget seminar sans the president. Instead of occurring in the White House, he hosted it in the State Department Building. He brought along the heads of the Estimates and Fiscal Divisions who might be better versed on highly specific questions.[29] It lasted almost two hours.[30] As usual, the briefing was embargoed for a day until the president formally sent the budget to Congress.[31] Most press coverage summarized the president's message rather than the briefing.[32] For its spot news coverage, the *Times* cautiously quoted "Budget Bureau officials" without naming them.[33] In a more analytical piece in the Sunday paper, it noted that Smith drew grins from reporters when he characterized the budget as "a rather conspicuous document."[34] The AP quoted Smith that the merchant marine was "largely paid for" already and also that this reflected a larger theme of the entire budget: shifting from "building up" the war effort to a "maintenance" of effort approach.[35] United Press cited Smith as believing that any future revisions to this budget based on war developments "would be down rather than up," in contrast to what had been the case earlier in the war.[36] Lindley wrote a perceptive column that must have come from Smith.[37] He noted that up to now, criticisms of the size of the budget "were rooted in the old-fashioned and erroneous idea that the Federal budget is something to be considered more or less apart" from the economy. (This was especially true for the conservative coalition, being routinely appalled at the size of every budget and insisting it should be less.) This year, the president's message presented the budget in the context of the macro-economy, comparing its size in proportion to *something* (such as GNP or other economic metrics). "Budget Director Harold Smith is responsible for the innovation," he wrote. The innovation "puts the Federal budget in a larger framework, where it belongs."[38]

While Roosevelt was away, Smith had to face congressional appro-priators regarding BOB's budget for FY 1946. For his own budget, Smith included a request to increase his funding by a net of $325,000. He planned to increase the funding by about $670,000, but anticipated cutting the temporary war unit by about $344,000. In terms of staffing, he was seeking funding for eighty-five additional full-time employees, with about thirty-five for expanding the field service (US House 1945, 1270). Chair Woodrum, a southerner, asked about the politically controversial subject of planning. Was BOB spending any appropriated money on planning? No, said Smith (1279, 1311). Splitting hairs, economic projections by the Fiscal Division were not, by his definition, planning. Minority members pressed Smith for specifics and details on his claims of saving the federal government money and general administrative controls over the executive branch. The subcom-mittee continued being supportive of bulking up BOB. It approved an increase in funding of $107,000, about a third of what he had asked for. It would translate to about twenty-two new employees (US Senate 1945, 292). Nonetheless, with postwar cutbacks looming, it was a net increase, not something all agencies received. Learning from his mistake the previous year, Smith did not appeal to the Senate to fully fund the increase he had requested. Better to let sleeping dogs lie. But McKellar would have none of it. He requested that Smith testify, even though there was no appeal pending. Smith replied that, given that he had no appeals pending before the Senate committee, perhaps his attendance would not be a necessary? That led to this McKellar explosion:

McKELLAR: Mr. Smith, you sent word to the committee that if the Senate was willing to let this appropriation go through as it was, you did not care to come down, did you not?

SMITH: Yes. I took this point of view, that I had presented the case in the record, and I felt that I would be glad to come down if you wanted me to come down here, but I did not want to be in the position of trying to push the committee to do something. That is, I think the control of finances is as much a problem of Congress as it is on the side of the Executive.

McKELLAR: You will find it is a great deal more the problem of Congress than anyone else. (US Senate 1945, 321)

McKellar was in high dudgeon. Other exchanges during the hearing were equally combative:

McKELLAR: Your attitude here is one of sullenness, and one of disrespect to this committee because of the way you talk about it. And when you say that you have views on it, which you are loath to express, why, we understand exactly what you mean. You mean you have no respect for this committee. . . . I think you owe this committee an apology. You have no business talking in the manner you have been talking here this afternoon.

SMITH: Well, I am sorry, Senator McKellar, if I have offended anyone. But I have been trying to answer some questions, and I certainly do not want you to put words in my mouth. (319)

A few minutes later:

SMITH: Senator McKellar, I feel a little uneasy, and I do not want to leave feeling that you may believe that I have deliberately given offense.

McKELLAR: I think you have been exceedingly discourteous.

SMITH: I did not intend to be.

McKELLAR: If you say you did not intend to be, that is all right.

SMITH: I am very sorry.

McKELLAR: That is all right.

SMITH: Because I want to get before this committee the information we have, and I am perfectly willing to come up here any time and answer your questions, and you can pummel me as much as you want.

McKELLAR: I am not pummeling you.

SMITH: I do not believe many people have had cause to accuse me of a lack of frankness.

McKELLAR: That is the way I looked at it. I am a very direct man, and I expect others to be direct with me; especially other officers of the Government. (321)

Smith felt that "in general, the hearing was even more difficult than last year."[39] Smith then had the unpleasant duty of calling McKellar the next day and asking permission to edit some of his testimony before the hearing record was published. Smith said he merely wanted to strike out some comments "in the interest of clarity." McKellar would not agree. At most, he would let Smith indicate changes in the margins of the stenographic record and then would consider accepting them. Apparently listening in, at least on Smith's side of the conversation, Smith's secretary noted that "at first the Senator was steamy about Mr. Smith's call, but he later calmed down."[40] The worst was yet to come. The other shoe dropped in mid-March, when the Senate Appropriations Committee released its report on the Independent Offices bill. McKellar had cut BOB's budget from $2.6 million in FY 1945 to $2 million for FY 1946.[41] Smith quickly asked for a meeting with FDR. They met on March 12 (the first time since January 19). Roosevelt recalled some of his earlier conflicts with McKellar when he felt McKellar had "misrepresented" compromises they had agreed to.[42] FDR was supportive of Smith. Shortly after this meeting Roosevelt talked to Senator Lister Hill (D-AL) about McKellar's attacks on BOB. Hill, usually an ally of the New Deal and FDR, could not promise much because he was preoccupied fighting off McKellar's incessant and longtime war on the TVA.[43] Roosevelt also invited E. H. Crump, the political boss of Memphis (and politically influential throughout Tennessee), to meet with him. Crump had largely supported McKellar in the past and his help had been a major boost to McKellar's electoral victories. Crump came to the White House on March 21.[44] FDR told Crump about some of the major problems he was having with McKellar. As he related the conversation to Smith, he asked Crump "if he could get McKellar a little more in line." Crump promised to try.[45] Smith focused on lobbying the House conferees and leaders to reject the Senate cuts. He talked to Woodrum, who "was not too hopeful, but he finally said it wouldn't do any harm to talk to Wigglesworth," a leading Republican on the committee.[46] Smith also had a phone conversation with Majority Leader John McCormack (D-MA), who suggested that Smith come and brief him and Speaker Rayburn (D-TX) about it.[47] Roosevelt suggested that when Smith met with the two leaders, he emphasize FDR's strict practice of never tinkering with Congress's own annual budget proposal for legislative branch spending (which was routinely conveyed to a president for incorporation into the president's annual budget plan to be submitted to Congress). Roosevelt argued that it was reasonable for him to expect reciprocity by Congress vis-à-vis the budget for his Executive Office.[48]

Smith, increasingly concerned, talked to Roosevelt again on March 23. Roosevelt agreed to sign a letter to Woodrum, hoping to influence the conference committee. Smith submitted a draft on March 28.[49] FDR approved it without change and it was sent on March 31.[50] The letter ("Dear Cliff:") made the argument that a president must have an effective BOB to fulfill his executive duties. It ended on a strong note: "If the Congress persists in this matter I am left with no alternative but to send a special message and a request for a supplemental estimate, in order to make my position clear. . . . I greatly regret that this issue has arisen. However, since it endangers good administration, I cannot do otherwise than make clear my position in the matter."[51] (After Roosevelt's death, Congress passed the Independent Offices bill in May. Woodrum told Smith that he had fought McKellar and got "about 99–99/100 per cent on our budget." It included a net increase of $40,000 and retention of funding for the War Projects unit, for a total of about $2.5 million to BOB. However, McKellar refused to consider adding any more field offices and Woodrum settled for keeping open the current four.[52] It was a pretty good outcome, considering.[53])

Manager-in-Chief of the Executive Branch

Smith continued the pattern of practices he had developed to manage the executive branch, both before and during the war. For example, he convened a summit meeting for all agencies to coordinate the financing of civilian supplies in Europe. It included high-level representatives from FEA, the State Department, the War Department, and the army.[54] On matters of organization, Smith was very concerned about bureaucratic and political maneuvering already occurring for control of the postwar structures for intelligence, science, and planning. On March 2, he memoed the president that "there seems to be a tug-of-war going on between some of the agencies" and enclosed several articles on the subject that were leaked to advance one agency's agenda over another. Smith was particularly "concerned about incomplete and ex parte reports being sent to the White House by advocates." He urged FDR not to make any decisions and to refer any plans he received to BOB, which was already in the midst of conducting a study of postwar organization of intelligence.[55] There was particularly intense lobbying about control over federally funded scientific research. Smith felt the issue "is becoming an acute problem because of the proposed action of Vannevar Bush and the Office of Scientific Research and Development [OSRD] crowd in general."[56] Early in the war, Smith had tried to assert BOB's jurisdiction over science research budgets (except the Manhattan Project), but Vannevar Bush, head of OSRD, "stonewalled, invoking secrecy and scientific unpredictability" (Owens 1994, 534). In anticipation of an even more consequential fight, Smith asked the Navy to detail Don Price to BOB to conduct a study of how to organize science after the war.[57] Smith then raised the subject with FDR at their (last) meeting on March 23. He told Roosevelt he was concerned because, at Bush's request, FDR had signed a letter to Bush asking Bush to conduct a study of the performance of his own organization. "The President seemed unaware that he had done this." Smith emphasized the importance of a postwar organization and policy to protect the government's interests in the research it funded and to retain control, through organization, over policymaking. Smith implored Roosevelt. "If the crowd came to him he would push them into our laps so that we could see that the Government was properly protected and so we could avoid more of these piecemeal approaches to the subject which would certainly get us into trouble." At the end of the conversation, Smith recalled, "The president *seemed* to agree with my thesis on the matter. Apparently, he had quite forgotten having signed any communication asking Bush to make a study."[58] A week later,

Smith decided to intervene more aggressively. In a letter to James Conant, chair of the committee overseeing Bush's agency, Smith stated his views:

> How research in the Government is controlled is to me of paramount importance. I am sure that I cannot agree that a matter so important should have its locus on the periphery of Government. My philosophy concerning democracy does not permit me to accept such a view. . . . It must be subjected to the impact of the same democratic controls as any other activity of the Government. From my point of view, it is undesirable to leave research entirely in the hands of the scientists.[59]

Smith sent a copy of his letter to FDR. In his cover memo, he said, "The battle lines are being drawn over the organization of research in the Government. . . . This crowd is trying to take a step in the wrong direction, and I am trying to keep them from doing so."[60] A few days after that, a navy officer called Smith "about the proposed Executive Order pertaining to setting up a control committee to handle the release of certain scientific information." Smith explained his views. The officer asked for copy of Smith's letter to Conant so he could share it with the secretary.[61]

Planning continued being a dirty word on Capitol Hill and for the conservative coalition. Smith, in his congressional testimonies, always said unequivocally that BOB did not engage in planning. (He considered economic projections for budgeting purposes a wholly different enterprise.) However, liberal senator Robert Wagner (D-NY) was drafting a bill to give the federal government the responsibility for full employment after the war. In preparation, he asked BOB for its plans for the postwar economy.[62] In response, Smith submitted two memos to Wagner. The first, probably prepared by the Fiscal Division, presented how BOB could—if the bill passed—engage in the economic planning that the bill anticipated. The second, probably prepared by the Statistical Standards Division, summarized the current absence of comprehensive collection of statistics on the economy by the federal government. There was a distinct "sparsity of direct forecasts" of macro-economic projections, Smith said. "A considerable improvement of statistical information is needed" if reliable economic forecasts were necessary to underpin federal implementation of the bill.[63] On March 14, Smith memoed FDR about Wagner's initiative. The policy goals of the legislation would require economic planning. That meant "the importance of [the president's] settling upon the location of the over-all planning function" in the executive branch. Reflecting on his entire public service career, he said, "For 25 years I have watched the up's and down's [*sic*] of planning in this country, and I feel keenly that it is time for a new administrative approach. At the moment, the Bureau of the Budget is in the anomalous position of approving funds for departmental planning projects but having little or no funds to coordinate these plans for the Government as a whole."[64] Clearly, he was hoping Roosevelt would designate BOB as the coordinator of executive branch economic planning in the same way that BOB already had jurisdiction over statistical collection, government questionnaires, and mapping. Byrnes quickly heard about the memo and reacted by saying that there were "really two planning groups" in the president's official family, OWMR and BOB.[65] He did not sound happy about BOB's effort at achieving supremacy.

Meanwhile, there was a typical Washington kerfuffle that drew in BOB. In a front-page story, Kluttz reported that the Census Bureau had just released a 265-page report on women at a cost of $2 million.[66] In a next-day story, Kluttz seemed to backtrack, quoting the Census Bureau as saying the cost of printing the report was $2,000 and that it was based on statistics the bureau had routinely collected previously. No new research or expenditure was involved. Nonetheless, there was the predictable reaction on the Hill, with the chair of the House Commerce Committee saying he would "call upon the Census and the Budget Bureau for an explanation," particularly because of the wartime shortage of newsprint for newspapers and magazines.[67] Smith coolly replied several weeks later that the report was not a questionnaire and therefore not subject to BOB's proactive control. He also noted that in 1944 all federal agencies, including the military, used less than half a percent of the entire supply of newsprint in the US. That put in context conservative complaints that this census report could have had *any* significant impact on commercial printing supplies.[68] A few days later, in another front-page story, a different *Post* reporter gave Smith an opportunity to provide extensive details and statistics about the significant savings of paper that BOB had accomplished during the war.[69] It was practically a knockdown of Kluttz's original report.

Management Improvement Campaign

The previous year, Smith and Stone began modifying their strategy for promoting management improvements. The Administrative Management Division shifted to producing visually engaging and popularized guides for managers (chap. 7). Smith explained the change to House appropriators: "I conceive of [it] as a kind of mass approach to the great procedural problems of the Federal Government" (US House 1945, 1304). The campaign came to full flowering in early 1945. In rapid succession, BOB released four issues of its *Management Bulletin* series with a focus on the coming postwar reconversion. They were on *Fiscal Records and Controls* (nine pages), *Personnel Records and Controls* (five pages), *Property Records and Controls* (five pages), and *Records Retirement and Controls* (five pages, with illustrations). They all had the same subtitle: *A Check List for Periodic Evaluation and Improvement*. The checklist approach was intended to be easy for midlevel managers and even frontline supervisors to use. BOB further adapted its approach by publishing five training guides for its work simplification campaign. They were heavy with entertaining graphics and cartoons. Instead of the usual black on white GPO publication, the text and figures were in black and blue, hence enhancing their visual appeal. Smith explained that successful management improvement hinged on "teaching line supervisors to analyze and improve methods" (1945c). The training guides were *Specifications for an Agency Work Simplification Program* (three pages) and four how-to booklets: *Trainer's Guide to the Work Simplification Training Sessions, Supervisor's Guide to the Work Distribution Chart, Supervisor's Guide to the Process Chart,* and *Supervisor's Guide to the Work Count* (each seven pages). The focus on trainers and supervisors reflected BOB's realization that management reforms had to begin at the lower (hierarchical) units and had to have buy-in by participants. BOB wanted to make this fun, or at least concrete and tangible.

Stone, the former director of Public Administration Service, then arranged for his former organization to publish a compilation of the pamphlets. PAS gave it the cumbersome title of *Work Simplification: As Exemplified by the Work Simplification Program of the U.S. Bureau of the Budget.* In his foreword, Smith hoped that the materials "may prove useful to state and local agencies in meeting their own needs for reducing costs and plugging time-loss loopholes" (1945c). The publication also included an addendum of all the graphics used in the series, apparently to facilitate reproducing them in other management improvement campaigns (43–48), and a bibliography of published materials and films that could also be used to undergird such efforts (49). Management theorist J. M. Juran reviewed the publication in *PAR*.[70] He lauded the graphics and layout as "living, virile things" rather than the usual turgid federal documents. "There are well-designed, arresting cartoons. There are vivid analogies. There is a sincere effort to explain something by using the other fellow's language." Juran acknowledged that the information and techniques were well known to industrial engineers in the business sector, but were largely unknown in government. Therefore, "here is something to warm the hearts of those who yearn for streamlining and for efficiency in government. The federal Bureau of the Budget, utilizing to good effect the management training experience of the wartime government" (1946, 79).

Promoting Public Administration

Public Relations

In January, Stone was invited to deliver a guest lecture to public administration students at the University of Alabama.[71] Speaking on the role and methods of a governmental executive, Stone included "external affairs" as one of the major areas that a successful public manager needed to spend time on and pay attention to. An administrator should be active at

> influencing the outside environment. It is the executive's job to cultivate relations with . . . private institutions, and with the public, so that his staff will have a favorable climate within which to function. In this way he can increase his awareness of the way in which programs and ideas must be carried out if they are to be accepted. The job of running interference for his organization is one that only the executive can do, and the effectiveness with which it is done will be a significant determinant of what his organization can accomplish. (Stone 1945, 57–58)

Given how close Smith and Stone were, there is little doubt that Smith shared Stone's views on the importance of public relations in public administration. Smith's behavior throughout his years at BOB (and before) reflected that perspective. Smith continued to do so in the spring of 1945. In early March, Smith participated in a radio interview program hosted by Barnet Nover. They spoke about the federal budget and its importance.[72] Later that month, he participated in the CBS network series *Congress Speaks* for an episode on "Paperwork and Teamwork."[73] Along with Senator Murray (D-MT) and the chair of BOB's questionnaire advisory committee, Smith talked about BOB's regulation of questionnaires and its effort to reduce unnecessary ones. He said that "perhaps three-quarters of the questionnaires that might have gone out have been stopped." Murray reacted by saying, "Those are gratifying results."[74] Marsh also continued to be active behind the scenes drafting BOB press releases, coordinating with the White House press office, advising when not to react to critical publicity, and briefing reporters off-the-record.[75]

The Profession

As its immediate past president, Smith was active in ASPA in 1945. The annual conference had been scheduled for January. However, during the winter, Byrnes had made a public appeal that all conventions of over fifty people be canceled to relieve the congestion on the transportation system that was hampering war-related travel. Smith and Gulick agreed that the ASPA conference should be canceled.[76] A few weeks later, he met with Gulick and Brownlow to discuss the plans for the association given the lack of the annual meeting.[77] Smith also continued encouraging his staff to write for *PAR*. In the first half of the year, four of them published articles (Collett 1945; Laves 1945; May 1945; Pincus 1945) and two wrote book reviews (Leiserson 1945; Morrison 1945). Smith persisted in promoting his vision of a closer relationship between the professions of public and business administration. He continued trying to persuade academic leaders to support his idea for merging schools of business and public administration. He met with longtime acquaintance Joseph Harris, who was about to leave public service and return to the University of California (Berkeley). Harris was interested in "revitalizing public administration teaching" there and told Smith that perhaps "some steps" to bring the public and business administration programs on campus closer together might be helpful.[78] Smith also met with the dean of Dartmouth's Amos Tuck School of Business Administration who was serving as president of the national association of business schools. He, too, expressed an interest in exploring Smith's idea.[79]

Smith's 1945 Book

Smith's most prominent effort to promote public administration was to write a book on *The Management of Your Government* (Smith 1945a). It was an effort to reach a lay audience about the importance of public administration and BOB's work. The idea began germinating in the fall of 1944, when Marsh and BOB staffer S. McKee Rosen came up with the idea to compile some of Smith's speeches, statements, and congressional testimonies into book form. They suggested that the compilation would be "a substantial contribution to the literature on public administration" for the public at large, rather than a more technical work aimed at university students taking courses in public administration and budgeting.[80] That the book was oriented to a lay audience was later confirmed when it was reviewed in mass media outlets, including the *Detroit News*, *New York Times*, and *New Republic*. The publisher also paid for ads touting the book in two issues of the Sunday *New York Times Book Review*.[81] In March 1945, McGraw-Hill publishing house sent Smith a signed contract.[82] At variance with its boiler plate contract, the publisher agreed to Smith's insistence that any revisions in the manuscript "shall be subject to the *approval* of the author" (instead of the more ambiguous "pass upon"), deleted an obligation of the author to revise the manuscript for later editions, and deleted the duty of an author not to write or publish anything "that might interfere with or injure the sales of said book." He countersigned the contract and returned it on April 11.[83] Smith signed off on the manuscript in mid-May, saying he "was pleased with the result."[84] Even though the source materials had been created by federal employees and by Smith himself on office time, the royalties were to be paid to Smith. It is possible that one of Smith's motivations was to earn extra income, similar to his goal for the farm.

The book was formally published in December.[85] It started with two oddities, one political, one editorial. The former was a foreword written by Eric Johnston, president of the US Chamber of Commerce.[86] As a bastion of pro-business advocacy, his willingness to write a foreword is a tribute to Smith's efforts to build bridges to all constituencies when it came to better management. Johnston praised Smith as "one of our most competent and devoted public servants." Furthermore, Smith "has established an enviable record for efficiency in his own organization and has contributed hugely to efficiency in all other departments and agencies" (Smith 1945a, vi). The editorial oddity was the introduction. Its author, the implied editor of the book, was only identified as "S. McK. R." (xiii). His full name, S. McKee Rosen, was not listed, nor was his employment at BOB. That was only hinted at in the last sentence of the introduction: "One hardly needs to add that the publication of this volume on his part comes largely as a result of continued urging by his associates in the Bureau of the Budget" (xiii). Nor does the introduction admit that the bulk of the text came from previous writings and speeches by Smith. Rosen obliquely hints at it by saying, "The chapters which follow are based on papers that were prepared for varied audiences" (x–xi). A more explicit acknowledgment was buried in chapter 8 on the impact of the war on local government. Smith introduces long passages from earlier speeches with the phrase, "I quote excerpts from material which I made public during the war period" (106).[87] The final chapter pivoted to discuss America's postwar future with some new text, but it largely repeated themes from earlier chapters. The book ended with an exhortation: "The democracies have proved that they can effectively mobilize all their resources for war. They must also prove that they can organize to solve the problems of peace. In this they will succeed only if individual freedom is blended with social responsibility. The management of democratic government must be imbued with both individual freedom and social responsibility in order to master its peacetime task" (179).

Reviews in lay publications were generally positive. The *Detroit News* suggested the book would be "of interest to all intelligent citizens."[88] According to a quote from the *Chicago Sun* that McGraw-Hill used in its advertising, the book "hits a gratifying level of simplicity, insight and intelligence."[89] The *Times* reviewer found it "well-organized and well-written," with Smith "concisely and clearly" making his points. However, the review concluded that the book would most likely interest those seeking a future in government management, rather than the public at large.[90] In the *New Republic*, reviewer J. Donald Kingsley said the book made a "notable contribution" and contained "wise and significant observations." However, "the book exhibits some of the usual defects of collected papers written on diverse subjects at different times." Regarding the role of the president vis-à-vis Congress, especially regarding a postwar full employment policy, he wished "that Mr. Smith had more fully developed this argument."[91]

The book was reviewed in the publications of several nonacademic professional associations. In *National Municipal Review* (of the National Municipal League), budget specialist A. E. Buck give it a mixed review. He said it was "easy to read" and "the casual reader may find the contents of the book quite satisfying." However, specialists in public administration and budgeting would be "disappointed" because Smith did not provide any in-depth discussion. For the specialized reader, the most interesting part was the table placing the federal budget in the context of the macro-economy, which had been published in January 1945 as part of FDR's annual budget message. Otherwise, "the chapters are loosely put together and continuity is poor. . . . It is to be regretted that Mr. Smith did not take the time to rewrite the text." Also, "parts of it are exceedingly sketchy, [and] sometimes repetitious."[92] Brownlow reviewed it in *Public Personnel Review*, published by the Civil Service Assembly. He commended the book, saying "thoughtful

Americans should read him." However, he noted that the book was a collection of speeches. Therefore, it was "lacking, perforce, a schematic or
systematic organization, since the pieces of it were written at different times
and for different purposes."[93] The monthly newsletter of the Council of
State Governments briefly reviewed it. The book "should interest all persons
engaged in agriculture, business, or labor" as well as government officials and
students.[94] Similarly, a monthly for social welfare professionals in Alabama
said government management was "interestingly discussed" in the book.[95]
Several academic journals also reviewed the book, although many of the
reviewers were not orthodox academics and some had undisclosed links
to Smith. In *APSR*, Charles Ascher, who knew Smith well from PACH
in Chicago,[96] recommended the book for "the average intelligent citizen-
taxpayer," but that "a more systematic exposition based on his uniquely rich
experience must probably wait" until Smith retired.[97] *PAR* presented a review
of the book as an essay on administrative evaluation. The reviewer, Charles
Aikin, was a professor at the University of California (and had worked at
OPA during the war). Aikin praised the book as "a significant beginning"
that "will assist its readers in their appraisal of the changes the nation has
so recently experienced." However, he too was disappointed at the lack
of in-depth of discussion and hoped that Smith would follow up with a
second volume that would provide a more detailed analysis of government
management.[98] In *Political Science Quarterly*, the reviewer liked the book as
a "lucid volume," noting that "every chapter offers its dividends." Coming
from "one of our ablest public administrators," the book would be valuable
to students in public administration "and the citizen who wants direct light
on how the public business is managed."[99] However, the reviewer, John A.
Vieg, then at Pomona College, had worked in BOB during the war and,
while there, had written a book review for *PAR* (Vieg 1944). The journal
did not disclose this possible lack of objectivity by the reviewer. Professor
James W. Martin sparingly praised the book, but also noted that the contents
of the book were "previously presented in addresses." Therefore, there was
"some duplication and some lack of articulation" between chapters. Nonetheless, "the material is attractively edited and presented."[100] In the initial
postwar decades, the 1945 book was often cited in public administration
and budgeting textbooks and excerpts from it often included in public
administration readers. However, it gradually faded from attention, if only
due to the increasing datedness of the discussion. According to WorldCat/
OCLC, about 250 public and university libraries had it in their collections.

Also, as its copyright expired and it was in the public domain, the book was on the Hathi Trust website.

April 12, 1945

As recounted by his secretary, here is how Smith got the news of FDR's death:

> At 5:45 the flash concerning the death of President Roosevelt came over the news ticker. The Director was already on his way to the court [yard of the building] to get his car and drive home. Miss Johnston, putting on her hat, saw the ticker item and dashed across the hall to Donald Stone's office, shouting [out the window] to the Director—who was in the court by that time—to return to the office. When Mr. Smith returned, Miss Johnston handed him the ticker tape. In a few moments, the Director called [former assistant director] Wayne Coy at the *Washington Post*, then left the office shortly afterward.[101]

The first call Smith made the next morning was to Brownlow "to discuss the tragic death of the President." Commerce Secretary Wallace called "just to check in."[102] Later that day, Smith sent a memo to all BOB staff:

> We in the Bureau of the Budget have had the rare opportunity of working directly for President Roosevelt, who has occupied the most important office in the world. Our close appreciation of him makes our sorrow the deeper with his passing.
>
> Yet, the tasks that were dropped remain to be completed. President Truman has been suddenly called upon to assume the gravest responsibilities in this tragic period of world history. We must now turn the best of our abilities and our energies to performing the tasks required of us by our new President.[103]

On Saturday afternoon, April 14, Mr. and Mrs. Smith went to the White House for the funeral services. His secretaries closed his office suite when he departed, noting, "Government offices generally were closed at one o'clock in respect for President Roosevelt."[104] In one of the few hints about how hard Smith took FDR's death, after their first lunch a few weeks later, Ickes said in his diary, "I do not think that Smith has much heart in staying."[105]

After FDR, April 1945–January 1947

Dutifully, Smith offered to stay on with the new president. Truman accepted. With VE-Day in May and VJ-Day in August, Smith's leading managerial responsibilities were to undo the wartime infrastructure he had created under FDR and to shrink the budget. It was like running a movie backward. Executive orders quickly abolished many of the emergency civilian agencies. At Smith's suggestion, Truman seized on the offers of cooperation to the new president from Capitol Hill by requesting renewing (prewar) presidential reorganization powers. Finally passed in December, Smith was then able to prepare three plans. Two passed and one was vetoed by Congress. Smith was also actively involved in promoting the principles of good management in congressional consideration of postwar bills relating to an agency for science research, control of atomic power, and sales of surplus merchant ships. Given his FDR-era involvement in fiscal policy, he also testified in favor of various full employment bills that would assign to the federal government the duty to enact macro-economic policies to create jobs for returning vets. In parallel, he urged state and local governments to use the surpluses they had accumulated during the war (to soak up discretionary consumer buying power) on public works.

However, his enthusiasm for the job was fading, his health was increasingly fragile, and he was just plain worn out from his FDR years. In June 1946, he resigned from BOB to take a more lucrative position as vice president of the new World Bank, saying he needed to earn more money. But it was not a good fit and in December, he announced he would depart once a successor was in place. While still at the bank, he gave a speech to the Council of State Governments in Chicago in January 1947. In retrospect, it was his swan song, calling for improved intergovernmental relations and professionalized public administration (Smith 1947). He died six days later.

Death and Tributes

A week after his Chicago speech, Smith took a few days off to work on the farm. On Thursday, January 23, "he was pitching hay high into a rick to feed the horses when his aorta split" (L. Smith 2003, 17).[106] He was found by a "family servant," but died of the heart attack before any medical help could arrive. Without contradicting these medical details, Sherwood suggested quite forcefully that Smith died "from sheer exhaustion" (1950, 211). Similarly, Dimock and Dimock stated that Smith's death "was unquestionably hastened by the rigors of his wartime post" (1953, 209). When he heard the news, Professor Merriam recalled that Smith "had been in bad shape for many years and it was inevitable that some collapse like this would occur. He was really too ill to go on with his work, but by the same logic, he was too ill to stop and take the necessary rest."[107] On the other hand, longtime colleague Frank Bane (then at the Council for State Governments) told Mrs. Smith he was shocked by Smith's death even though he knew about Smith's ongoing health problems. Bane had attended Smith's speech in Chicago and told her that Smith "never looked better."[108]

Encomiums for his public service poured in. President Truman was at an event of the American Newspaper Women's Club when he got the news. He said he was "terribly shocked." He described Smith as "one of the ablest servants in the public service. The country needs the services of men like Harold Smith."[109] The AP story similarly described Smith as "one of the ablest career men in Federal government."[110] Columnist Drew Pearson described him as "a great public servant."[111] He also noted that the family, reflecting Smith's personal modesty and focus on the public interest, requested donations to cancer research in lieu of flowers. Several papers editorialized about him. According to the *Post*, "He was admired even by the men whose budgets he was constantly trimming, for he was known to be impartial and progressive and uniquely knowledgeable about Government practice."[112] The *Star* noted, "Few officials labored as prodigiously or as earnestly. Members of both parties in Congress respected him. . . . Politics was out of his line. His business, his enthusiasm, his career, centered on economy and efficiency."[113] As a longtime resident of Michigan, the *Detroit Free Press* proudly recalled the (not quite) hometown boy: "The Nation has lost an able and distinguished public servant, who wore himself out and shortened his years in unselfish labor for it."[114] In the fall, the *Ladies Home Journal* explored the difficulties of federal service, using as a jumping-off point Smith's public observations on low government salaries when he resigned from BOB (Smith 1946a). The article described him as "one of the most distinguished officials in the whole executive department."[115] A few years later, financial columnist Sylvia Porter described him as "a brilliant public servant."[116]

Reminiscences and tributes from his academic and professional colleagues also came quickly. Brownlow wrote a four-page obit in *APSR*, saying that Smith "understood the new significance of public administration in our constitutional system" and worked to integrate it into the older system of government (1947, 329). Brownlow acknowledged that Smith was "so deliberate that sometimes he seemed to be slow. . . . His gait, too, seemed slow; but if one attempted to walk with him the ordinary person had almost to run to keep up with what may only be described as his loping gait." Lightheartedly, Brownlow also acknowledged, "He had one great fault. He never learned to loaf. He was always working." Overall, he described Smith as "one of the greatest public administrators in the history" of the US (330).

The spring 1947 issue of *Public Administration Review* led off with two tributes that balanced Smith's contributions to the profession, one by a person who only knew him at BOB and the other by someone who knew him only before BOB. Smith's last deputy director, Appleby (by then dean of Syracuse's Maxwell School), praised Smith's judgment, such as intuiting in 1939 what a restructured BOB should look like and his hiring decisions to staff the reorganized bureau. In particular, he praised his *political* acumen. "A successful man in a high level of public administration needs more. He needs political sense. He needs a sense of both strategy and tactics. He needs to know when not to move, when not to fight, when and where to advance, when to stand firm, when to retreat, when to fight. In this area, we come close to mysticism"—and Smith had it (1947, 79). Appleby also noted Smith's deference to the office of president while never being shy to indicate when he thought the president was making a mistake. He regretted that "the amount of general managerial work performed by the bureau has never been widely known" (80). However, Appleby was not sycophantic. He identified Smith's "faults as an administrator. His method was slow. . . . He couldn't often give clear and incisive directions." Overall, "he was almost painfully conscientious, a thoroughly devoted believer in and practitioner of democratic ways. He was a great public administrator. He was strong, and peculiarly free from vulnerability in a scene where practically everyone in high place[s] is almost always vulnerable" (81).[117] The second tribute in *PAR* was from Herbert Olson, who worked at the Michigan Municipal League when Smith headed it and then was Smith's successor there. Olson had known Smith beginning in WWI, when both were naval cadets at a unit stationed at Lawrence (KS). Olson described how Smith led MML. "When he came to Michigan, he was, literally, unimportant, unknown and unimpressive; therefore in everything he undertook he had to depend on facts rather than personal status. Those facts became his and the league's fortune. . . . The status he gradually acquired was based on this reputation for solid honesty. Lawmakers got in the habit of taking his word for it when he told them that the effect of such-and-such a bill would be thus-and-so" (1947, 82–83). Then, as state budget director, he "helped pioneer the translation of modern budget theory into active governmental practice" (84). Olson praised Smith's personal qualities, including that "his steady, fearless sincerity was leavened not only by heart and sympathy but by a wonderful sense of humor. I never once saw him lose his temper." Above all, Olson recalled how hard Smith worked, remembering finding him at his MML office on Thanksgiving. Linking that anecdote with Smith's premature death, Olson honored Smith "for wearing himself out with overwork" (84). In a public finance journal, BOB staffer I. M. Labovitz described Smith as both working hard and "thinking hard" about the issues facing the government. He praised Smith for "his preoccupation with the relationships between means and ends" and his focus on program planning and fiscal policy (1947, 135). Smith's reputation lasted in the media through the 1950s and '60s, with reporters occasionally referring to him and how he had made BOB such a strong and central institution.[118]

Figure 5. Smith headstone as a veteran. Credit: Arlington National Cemetery.

Figure 6. Smith headstone as Bureau of the Budget director. Credit: Arlington National Cemetery.

Smith's gravesite at Arlington National Cemetery has a two-sided headstone, one summarizing his WWI military service (Apprentice Seaman, US Naval Reserve Force), the other his federal service. The latter reads:

S M I T H

DIRECTOR

U.S. BUREAU OF THE BUDGET

1939–1946

He was 48 when he died.

Conclusion

FDR's *Other* Assistant President

This inquiry into Harold D. Smith's record as Franklin Roosevelt's budget director used several prisms and themes to explore and evaluate his work. As the cofounder and second president of ASPA, he actively participated in the development of norms and values for the nascent profession of public administration. Some of its central tenets emerging in that era included the separation of administration from politics, the distinction between staff roles (advising) from line duties (managing), the separation of policymaking from budgeting, the need for professionals to obtain specialized training in public administration from institutions of higher education, a qualitative distinction between business administration and public administration, public reporting as an ongoing duty for public managers, and a (relative) passion for anonymity. Smith professed and advanced nearly all these dogmas as part of his work.

Nonetheless, his behind-the-scenes record also indicated some deviations from these doctrines. He was modestly involved in politics, whether giving the president political advice about Congress or occasionally in direct contact with candidates and election campaigns. He insisted that he was only an advisor to the president but emerged both before and during the war as FDR's manager-in-chief of the entire executive branch. He repeatedly testified before Congress that he was not involved in policymaking, yet his work inevitably led to participation in policymaking, policy development, policy reevaluation, and policy coordination. He was strongly supportive of the development of university-based degrees and training in public administration, yet sometimes called for broad-based liberal arts education and critical thinking for future managers. Contrary to the rest of his professional peers and colleagues, he insisted that there was a strong overlap and similarity between public and business administration. He urged the merging of training programs for both careers and also called for silo-crossing opportunities between the two. His implementation of public reporting veered away from annual print reports, which were often the central reporting venue in the new profession. Rather, he was actively involved in public speaking, writing, and radio appearances as ways to report on BOB's work to specialized audiences as well as to the public at large. He had a much higher public profile than most White House aides and he viewed his public role as including vigorous advocacy for the president's goals and objectives. In sum, Harold Smith was both an orthodox practitioner and role model for public administration of the times, while simultaneously something of a dissident from those same values.

How FDR Viewed Smith:
Nicknames and Humor as Job Descriptions

President Roosevelt was master of memorable phrases, including nicknames. One of his most famous was when, during WWII, he referred to himself as changing from "Dr. New Deal" to "Dr. Win-the-War." He occasionally used that talent for humorous nicknames for Smith. These lighthearted quips help convey FDR's assessment of Smith's work and character. When Smith took the oath of office in 1939, Roosevelt turned to the media witnessing the event and said they might want to refer to Smith as "the Great Reorganizer" because that was his first major assignment from the president.[1] A few years later, when the Roosevelt saw Smith and Assistant Director Blandford walking into his office carrying thick files for their final meeting about the president's annual budget plan, FDR said, "Oh Lord, here come the heavenly twins."[2]

On another occasion, Smith and Treasury Secretary Morgenthau were fighting about federal anti-inflation policy. Roosevelt nicknamed him "Battling Smith" because of Smith's indefatigable willingness to fight for a position that he was convinced was right (Rosenman 1952, 357). For the same reason, when Morgenthau complained to FDR about Smith's persistence, Roosevelt metaphorically sighed and conveyed there was nothing he could do about it. Smith's character was a fixed element of the administration's political landscape and even a president couldn't change that. "Smith was a very stick-to-it person," FDR said (Blum 1967, 38). Brownlow recounted a meeting with the president and Smith when Roosevelt spun something of a parable to differentiate the two Harolds of his administration, Ickes and

Smith. He lightheartedly turned to Smith and called him "dishonest Harold" to make a point about "honest Harold" Ickes. FDR regarded Ickes as self-righteously pious to the point of exculpating himself when his behavior reflected a double standard (chap. 1). Smith understood the point of the appellation and took the nickname in good humor, if only because Ickes was the butt of the joke.

In mid-1940, Smith was conferring with Roosevelt about cutting civilian spending to help offset increases in military spending. Roosevelt recounted how carmaker Henry Ford had boasted he could manufacture a thousand planes a day if only the government would just stop interfering in how he did his work. When Ford's son, Edsel, was asked about that claim, he said his father often made extravagant claims and then delegated their (impossible) implementation to Edsel. Edsel said he always tried his best, but often could not fully attain his father's promises. FDR turned to Smith and said, "Edsel Smith, carry this program out!"[3] Again, Smith did not take offense at the nickname. He understood the president's point was that he should try his best, but not to worry if he, as "Edsel Smith," could not literally accomplish whatever commitment Roosevelt had made.[4] These colorful nicknames are amusing and Smith tried to take them in the spirit in which they were offered. However, given that many a truth is said in jest, FDR's good opinion of Smith comes through quite clearly. It also was evident from other prosaic interactions.

In 1942, Roosevelt referred a matter to Smith with the one-word directive: "Unscramble." He knew that Smith would handle it, that he would not drop the ball or let it fall between the cracks.[5] Roosevelt also often sent packets of paper to Smith with a cover note, "see me," or "talk to me" about it.[6] Slightly differently, at a meeting, when FDR was somewhat at a loss over a fight between State and the FCC, he asked Smith "to look into the matter."[7] For Roosevelt, handling matters in that way was easier than dictating a long message. It also helped him empty his in-box and, if it was a touchy subject, avoided a paper trail of his views. At one point, when Smith felt he was falling behind on these assignments, he welcomed a relatively leisurely meeting with Roosevelt in the White House library on a Saturday afternoon. "I had accumulated many notes from him over the last month, in which he had asked me to speak to him about a point, but his time had heretofore been so taken up that I had not been able to get around to this material."[8] Smith was conscientious about always following up on assignments from the president. In the same vein, when Smith called himself FDR's "Mr. Fix-it," he was also capturing the trust that Roosevelt had in him (chap. 6).

Smith's Image as Apolitical, Non-policymaking, and Anonymous

As presented in the introduction, Smith's normative philosophy of successful government budgeting included being apolitical, not being involved in
policymaking, and having a low public profile. They were, largely, inaccurate.

Politics

Smith was involved in lowercase politics and upper-case Politics. For the
former, he offered his advice about the political mood on Capitol Hill. For
example, he urged FDR to act on a reorganization of federal PR agencies
before it became a major political controversy, being careful not to let Senator
Byrd use him in Byrd's so-called investigations of federal operations, declining to testify in the investigation of the FCC, and later advising Truman to
submit quickly a request to Congress to renew presidential reorganization
powers to take advantage of the goodwill and offers of cooperation he was
receiving from senators and members of Congress upon becoming president.
However, Smith also was quietly involved in outside politics. For example,
he looked into the political situation in Michigan in 1940 and reported
back to the president on it, favored FDR's reelection in 1944, tried his best
to be responsive to the public works projects and other favors requested by
FDR's allies on the Hill, and sought to scrounge up good news for FDR to
announce at press conferences and in press releases from the White House
press secretary. In particular, many of Smith's public speeches were implicit
endorsements of FDR's presidency, thereby providing justification for public
opinion to generally view FDR favorably and particularly in run-ups to
elections. These included praising FDR's defense mobilization, justifications
for federal deficit spending, explaining quasi-Keynesian fiscal policy, and saying after the war that Truman's goal for a balanced budget was reasonable.

   In trying to square the reality of Smith's political role with his
insistence on BOB as serving the institutionalized presidency rather than
the individual politician in the White House, Dickinson and Rudalevige
gently suggested that Smith had a "dual-hatted" role and that he kept his
political role mostly to private and one-on-one meetings with FDR and
separate from BOB's professional duties (2007). They understated his role.
Whatever the explanation, Smith was neither a technocrat nor an automa-
ton. He had political opinions. In Michigan, he may have been viewed as
an apolitical budgeteer, equally respected and happy professionally to work
for a Democratic governor and then for the Republican who defeated him.

However, his service to Governor Murphy's Republican successors was for an extremely brief period of January–April 1939. It is impossible to imagine Smith being equally happy professionally working for a President Hoover or Reagan or Trump. He served Truman, in part because Truman's policies were largely a continuation of FDR's. As for the hyperbolic test of the professional paradigm of neutral competence, Smith never would have worked for Hitler. Smith frequently referred to the democratic basis of American public administration, even though many of the other cofounders of the profession rarely mentioned it or only paid it lip service.

Policy

Despite Smith's oft-repeated claims that he was not a policymaker, he most definitely was. If only based on a narrow definition of BOB's budgeting duty, he was involved in *everything* because everything government did involved spending money and, inextricably, prioritizing how to spend it. Beyond that, he was involved in policy due to BOB's roles in legislative clearance, coordination, and reorganizations. These were policymaking by another name. In public, during Roosevelt's presidency, he openly offered his advice to Congress on such non-budgeting matters as economics and military unification. He continued this pattern under Truman, such as testifying before Congress on organizing federal activity in science, atomic energy, and reorganizing Congress itself. In all those cases, he was pronouncing his preferences and recommendations about federal policy, even if slightly veiled as input on organization and management. In private, he even more strongly advocated for policies in multiple areas. Examples included fighting inflation, veterans, the size of the navy, farm policy, moving agencies out of Washington, Pentagon construction, and major appointments (which often were fights about policy in disguise).

Publicity

Smith dedicated major efforts to public relations, an inherent element of good public administration. His public speeches, radio appearances, writings, and accessibility to reporters were substantial investments of his time and effort. In the abstract, he understood the democratic imperative for public administrators to be accountable to the public at large. However, most of his PR was more closely related to his BOB responsibilities and desire to generate support for the president's factual record (such as reductions in

non-war expenditures) and priorities. When talking publicly about public
policy (and, impliedly, politics), he carefully crafted his words to depoliticize
them and make seemingly logical and low-key points. For example, when he
advocated for postwar fiscal policies, he presented the national debt in the
context of the macro-economy, thereby reducing its supposedly scary size.
When he advocated reconversion policies that were comprehensive and well
planned, he specifically identified the social and economic problems that
would emerge after winning the war unless they were dealt with proactively.
Another signal of how important he thought public relations was: in 1941 he
hired Howard Marsh as BOB's full-time information officer. Marsh drafted
speeches and articles, wrote press releases, and attended presidential press
conferences. He frequently met with Smith and was his lunch or dinner
companion. When Marsh resigned, Smith quickly hired a replacement. This,
again, indicated his view of the agency's need for institutionalizing its PR.
Another signal of Smith's commitment to PR was that BOB had a numbered
press release *series*, often differentiated by the particular division that the
material originated from, such as administrative management or estimates.

The most notable, even odd, example of Smith's involvement in a
subject combining the seemingly verboten trifecta of politics, policy, and
publicity was his support for creating a Jewish army to help fight Nazi
Germany. It was promoted by Peter Bergson, a Zionist activist who was
on the ideological right (Breitman and Lichtman 2013, 217, 244, 322).
Smith signed a public petition circulated by the Committee for a Jewish
Army of Stateless and Palestinian Jews that urged the UK to create a Jewish brigade. Smith's endorsement, identified by name and his BOB title,
was first reported in the *Times* as one of several dozen prominent people
supporting the initiative.[9] After that came some paid advertisements from
the committee in 1943, which continued listing his name. One ad was
full page in the *Times*.[10] Smith was later again identified in a news story
in the *Baltimore Sun* about the cause.[11] The background on the issue was
that the UK, then controlling Palestine under a post-WWI mandate from
the League of Nations, was resisting efforts to create a separate military
unit for Jewish soldiers. Given the tensions in Palestine between Arabs and
Jews, the British government did not think it should train and arm men
who would likely turn on it after WWII to fight for Jewish independence
in Palestine. Confusingly, what was opaque to the public at large about this
issue and the committee was where it was located on the ideological spectrum of Zionist politics. The committee was associated with the right wing
of Zionism (later led by Menachem Begin) and was in political opposition

to the more moderate establishment politics of the Zionist left (associated with David Ben Gurion, Golda Meir, and the labor party). Presumably, this internal political fight was invisible to most Americans, not clearly being able to identify the committee's ideological politics or its vehement efforts to undermine Great Britain's hold on Palestine.

There is no clear explanation for what prompted Smith to engage in such a public activity that was inherently critical of an ally in the war effort. It could well have been motivated by his personal abhorrence of the horrible news that was starting to seep out about the fate of Jews under Nazism. Another potential explanation (that is not mutually exclusive) is that the suggestion for involvement may have come from BOB staffer and friend Louis K. Friedman. Smith had hired him to work in the Director's Office in 1942 on special projects. They became friendly on a personal level, with Friedman occasionally joining Smith for lunch and the two socializing at the end of the workday. Specifically, Friedman had occasionally talked to Smith about Jewish issues, including the situation in Palestine and the cause of creating a Jewish homeland there.[12] Whether from Freidman or other sources, Smith eventually realized the internecine politics associated with the group he had publicly endorsed. The organizer of that committee, now working for the same cause but under the name of a different organization, contacted him in 1944 for an appointment to discuss ideas "to help the Jewish people of Europe." Smith declined to meet or get involved, referring him to the War Refugee Board. Smith wanted to be sure he was conveying how strongly he now intended to distance himself from that activist. The reply letter declining the request for an appointment was from Smith's secretary, not from Smith himself.[13]

∾

Looking at Smith's record and performance overall, perhaps the enigma of his professional success was that he was able overcome the inherent internal contradictions of government budgeting. He figured out a way to square the circle of administration, policy, and politics. Outwardly, he presented a persona of a budgeteer who was strictly interested in the value-free world of good government and modern management. He repeatedly said publicly that he did not make policy (let alone participate in politics). To the media and to Congress, he insisted that he sought to improve government management by increasing the efficiency and effectiveness of the bureaucracy. Yet, internally, he was deeply involved in policy and even politics, if only through his occasional public acknowledgment that he was a supporter of FDR's program. Sometimes he talked politics with the president and the inner circle of advisors by expressing views on strategy and goals. There was no politics/administration dichotomy in his daily work.

Smith shrewdly was able to tiptoe through this minefield of the nexus of administration, policy, and politics. That was likely why his tenure was so impressive, part of the "golden period" of BOB/OMB (Dickinson and Rudalevige 2004–2005).[14] His successors, gradually, were unable to pull it off. When Congress insisted during Nixon's second term that budget directors must be confirmed by the Senate, it was acknowledging the policy and political importance of the role. After that, the associate and assistant directors of OMB took on an even more obvious political hew, as members of the president's team who needed to be in agreement with the administration's goals. This evolution was inevitable because it gradually brought into harmony the image and reality of government budgeting. Smith's impressive record was the exception, not the rule. As a cofounder of ASPA and its second president, Smith presented himself as a role model of neutral competence. He advocated for a particular culture, ethics, and ethos for the new profession that kept it separate from politics. In the retrospect of the twenty-first century, this was an ideal. However, it was more idyllic myth and normative vessel than day-to-day reality.

FDR's Manager-in-Chief: Staff *and* Line

Traditional public administration differentiated between two distinct managerial roles: line and staff. A line administrator was in charge of an entity and responsible for delivering a government product or service. He or she was in the hierarchical chain of command. On the other hand, a staff person provided an ancillary service to assist the line administrator in doing her or his job. Budgeting was the prototypical staff activity. Smith insisted that he was an advisor to the president and that BOB's capabilities assisted the president manage the executive branch. For that reason, for example, Smith had a strict policy that BOB employees would not serve on committees, boards, councils, or task forces formed by executive branch departments and agencies. As voting members of such bodies, they would be put in the position of expressing views on issues (chap. 2). When those matters eventually reached the White House, BOB had already taken sides and its views ostensibly already baked in the recommendation to the president. That would be, in his eyes, verboten. The role of BOB was to advise the president on matters that reached his desk. BOB needed to be unencumbered until the matter reached that final presidential stage. This strict policy was one way for Smith to convey that his budgeting role was staff, not line. His hands should not be tied before BOB advised the president.

However, Smith's strict insistence that budgeting was a staff activity was largely incompatible with the actual details of his record as the de facto general manager of the federal executive branch. Managers manage! The preceding chapters provided many examples of Smith's activities in this managerial role. Whether he was helping coordinate something, developing a common policy, breaking bottlenecks, brokering compromises, reorganizing, preparing executive orders, or declaring positions on legislation, Smith was engaging in the totality of activities that encompass public administration. Cutting these Gordian knots before, during, and after the war encompassed much more that a quiet staff activity of advising the president. Smith was a problem solver and did so as part of his largely unacknowledged line management of the executive branch. He was in the role of a hierarchical boss, way up near the top of the federal pyramid. While violating this basic tenet of orthodox public administration separating line and staff roles, Smith was inherently pragmatic and expedient. *Someone* needed to do these things, especially for a president like Roosevelt who was involved in so much and responsible for so many vital and strategic decisions during the war. In particular, Smith was confronting the inherent centrifugal nature of the federal executive branch. That bureaus, agencies, and departments sought autonomy was part of the dynamics of the executive branch. They did not want any outsiders supposedly meddling in their work and direction. *They* knew what was best. Smith and BOB were practically the only venue for centripetal countermeasures. Smith understood the levers of power at BOB's disposal and made the most of them, whether they be budgeting, release of apportioned funds, release of discretionary presidential funds, moving agency offices, reorganizations, executive orders, or legislative clearance. He zealously protected and enhanced these bureau jurisdictions and used them to the hilt. No one wanted to be at war with BOB given that Smith had so many ways to push back.

In the *Time* magazine cover story in mid-1943, Smith estimated that Roosevelt approved about 60 percent of his recommendations and that he felt this was a very good batting average. He repeated that estimate in a *Newsweek* profile two years later.[15] But at other times, Smith volunteered higher batting averages. For example, early in 1943, he claimed to a columnist that FDR accepted 90 percent of his recommendations.[16] Whether he was exaggerating or poormouthing given the particular time he offered up these stats to reporters, few department and agency heads wanted to go toe-to-toe with him lest they end up on the wrong side of that percentage. Smith's de facto line management role was exactly what the Brownlow Committee was hoping for. With its famous phrase, "the president needs help," it was referring to more than just permitting a handful of administrative assistants to do staff work in the White House. A bit indirectly, the phrase also referred to its central theme, namely, that a president needed additional administrative *management* powers to lead, direct, and run the executive branch. Hence, one of its central recommendations was that there should be an executive office with fuller capability to herd the autonomy-seeking entities of the executive branch. In particular, the committee and FDR viewed the functions of budgeting, planning, and personnel as the three central management devices necessary for effective governing. Their push for presidential powers in the areas of planning and personnel management did not work out, largely due to opposition from the conservative coalition in Congress. However, enhancing the role of central presidential budgeting largely fulfilled their original expectations—and then some. Smith's predecessors placed budget cutting and role modeling such cuts to the rest of the executive branch as a top priority. Smith expanded BOB's staffing and duties to manage the government in so many more respects than a narrow definition of the inherent staff role of budgeting. For him, budgeting and management were practically synonyms. He conveyed this with the title of his book. It was not *The Budgeting of Your Government*. Rather, it was *The **Management** of Your Government*. Professor Leonard White was one of the few to catch this shift from staff to line, or at least Smith's successfully transcending these supposedly mutually exclusive roles. In the 1948 edition of his textbook, White said that Smith had developed BOB "into the principle *staff* agency of the Federal government" (1948, 62, emphasis added). In the fourth (and last) edition of his textbook, White described Smith as transforming BOB's role into "the most influential central *management* agency of the federal government" (1955, 62, emphasis added).

Smith's rocky relations with Byrnes hint at Smith's broad view of BOB as having a monopoly on central coordination of just about everything relating to the federal government. Whether the issue was budgetary, staffing, policy, or program delivery, Smith claimed BOB was the venue for dealing with it. When Byrnes emerged as the "assistant president," Smith was quietly quite miffed (Somers 1969, 67–68). That was supposed to be his job! Coy told Somers that Smith "refused to take official recognition of Byrnes as a Presidential spokesman. He dealt with Byrnes on an austere formal basis. He stubbornly resisted visiting Byrnes. He tried to follow the practice of simply writing memos to Mr. Byrnes."[17]

Smith also displayed a few lesser known, but sharper, edges in other instances that stood out in contrast to his image of anonymity and impassiveness. He was no martinet, saluting when he got an order from the president, clicking his heels, and then implementing it in a mindless come-hell-or-high-water way. For example, when he thought FDR was wrong, he often argued with the president. A prominent example related to draft deferments for federal employees (chap. 5). Another example was a "personal and confidential" memo he wrote to FDR about a pending decision on WMC. He submitted a four-and-a-half-page memo outlining why he thought the president was leaning in the wrong direction and assumed it was too late to affect the outcome. Nonetheless, Smith recalled, "I felt that I would not be fair to you as Chief Executive or to my own conscience if I did not set forth rather fully and completely what I know and think about the current manpower situation."[18] To Smith's surprise, it was not too late and he had convinced FDR to change his mind.[19] Another incident not only contradicts the image of a robotic presidential technocrat, but also showed Smith jockeying for power and presidential favor by criticizing to FDR a potential rival. After FDR appointed Wayne Coy as the liaison officer for the Office for Emergency Management (OEM), FDR also asked Isadore Lubin (of the Bureau of Labor Statistics) to report to him directly with some armament production statistics, thus bypassing Coy's official role. Coy protested to FDR (Lee 2018, 149–51). Smith, who was close to Coy, then sent, on his own initiative, a memo to FDR supporting Coy. Smith was sticking his neck out and meddling in something that was not directly his business. He began with the conventional managerial argument that Lubin's role would undercut Coy's power vis-à-vis OEM's constituent agencies. Smith then engaged in a scathing attack on Lubin personally. "As to Mr. Lubin's characteristics, I can hardly conceive of a person more ill-adapted to the job. . . . He has emotional slants that blind him to a complete [i.e., objective] view of the subject. He has been accused on more than one occasion of twisting his statistics to suit his purpose. He is ambitious for power, and, in my judgment, this alone disqualifies him."[20] It was a flat-out attack on a potential rival, practically demonizing Lubin. Smith realized how far beyond his usual role this memo had gone, concluding with the suggestion, "when you have read it, I hope you will see fit to destroy it." FDR was nonplussed. In fact, he sometimes seemed to promote a form of competitive administration by giving overlapping assignments to multiple people. He thrived on conflict within his administration rather than shying away from it because conflict guaranteed the subject would have to rise to him to resolve. In a soothing reply to Smith, Roosevelt claimed that his request to Lubin was not in competition with Coy's role. However, he made a point of telling Smith, "I, of course, have known Lubin for many years and have great confidence in his ability and integrity." Nonetheless, FDR reassured Smith. "I appreciate your thoughtfulness in writing me as frankly as you did, and I hope I have relieved your mind of any misconception you have had of his work here."[21]

Notwithstanding his frustrations with FDR's seemingly loose and erratic style of management, decision-making, and policymaking, Smith never came close to breaking with the president (chaps. 6–7). Only after FDR's death and the end of the war, with time and distance to reflect, he came to a very different conclusion about Roosevelt's executive style. "Now, I can see in perspective the . . . unbelievably skillful organization and direction. . . . Roosevelt must have been one of the greatest geniuses as an administrator that ever lived. What we couldn't appreciate at the time was the fact that he was a real *artist* in government" (Sherwood 1950, 73, emphasis in original).

Building on his experience as federal manager at the highest levels of the executive branch, Smith gradually evolved into something of a management theorist, albeit with some non-mainstream views. For example, he became a consistent advocate of merging business and public administration training on college campuses (chaps. 6 and 8). Despite his standing as former ASPA president, his views were largely out of step with the emerging public administration consensus that the qualitative differences between the two made them distinctly different.[22] Smith also became committed to experimenting with new ways of delivering federal services on a local level. He wanted to integrate the services of multiple agencies and all levels of government at the grassroots. He worked hard to obtain a substantial grant from one of the Rockefeller funds to finance the program. However, the Council on Intergovernmental Relations had not yet concluded its experiment when he died in 1947. That his last speech was on the subject demonstrates how important it was to him as a long-term goal (chap. 8). However, the long gestation period and the modest results shown from the early pilot projects were likely signals of the difficulty of pulling it off. For politicians and government managers, getting public credit for something was the coin of the realm. Subsuming "their" services and separate identity

CONCLUSION 299

into a one-stop shop was something that needed to be avoided strenuously. The status quo is very hard to change, even with Smith at the wheel and Rockefeller money backing him.

FDR's Czars and Byrnes as his Only Assistant President

Political science literature has explored the emergence of czars as part of the modern presidency beginning with FDR. These have been senior officials to whom the president has assigned major powers, usually to coordinate broad swaths of federal operations in a relatively specific policy era that cut across departmental and agency boundaries (Villalobos and Vaughn 2015; Sollenberger and Rozell 2012; Relyea 2011; 2002). Such discussions in the academic literature about czars during FDR's presidency are not neologisms. Rather, usage of the term was commonplace at the time. Some headlines from those years include "Price Czar Henderson Puts on Exciting Show,"[23] "Roosevelt Makes Ickes Defense Fuel Czar,"[24] "President Gives Nelson Full Power of Czar,"[25] "Land Made Czar of War Shipping,"[26] "Wallace Expected to Replace Jones as Import 'Czar,' "[27] "Roosevelt's Press Conference: He Will Announce Rubber Czar Monday,"[28] "Manpower Czar,"[29] and "Food Czar Davis."[30] While Smith was powerful, he was no czar, whether based on the academic usage or the informal media lingo of the time. When *Time* magazine selected Smith for its cover, it sought to convey his importance with the cover's subtitle declaring that he was *more* important than any run-of-the-mill presidential czar: "Czars may come and czars may go, but he goes on forever."[31] If Smith was more powerful than a czar, then what was he and where was he in the hierarchy of power?

Based on academic and lay usage, the person who was more powerful than a czar during FDR's presidency was James Byrnes, OWMR director. He was commonly referred to as the assistant president. Before his appointment, the media had toyed with the term for others. Before Pearl Harbor, the *Times* wondered if VP Wallace deserved that moniker due to the direct line managerial assignments FDR had given him, unprecedented in the history of the roles of VPs.[32] In mid-1942, another *Times* profile suggested that perhaps Harry Hopkins should be called the assistant president.[33] However, none of those media labels stuck. Only Byrnes was widely referred to as assistant president, initially after his appointment as director of economic stabilization in October 1942 and more universally after becoming the director of war mobilization in May 1943.[34] FDR did not particularly like the term (Somers 1969, 54), though he used it himself on occasion (Ferrell 1994, 5). Giving Byrnes the de facto appellation of assistant president was reasonable because Byrnes had full powers over all domestic policy, including all the departments and agencies sans the military. The most indicative signal of his power was that *there could be no appeal of his decisions to Roosevelt*, the habitual behavior of all cabinet secretaries and agency heads from 1933 until Byrnes's appointment. Now, the buck truly stopped with Byrnes. That made him a stand in for the president, an assistant president. The only difficulty of applying that informal title to Byrnes was that he was only interested in *policy*. He implicitly yielded everything else, especially routine public administration (Lee 2018, 237–39, 256). In that case, history should probably retitle him as Assistant President for Domestic Policy or Assistant President for Civilian Policy.[35]

This review of Smith's work responsibilities documented several parallels to Byrnes's unappealable power. In 1943, as FDR was preparing to leave for the Teheran summit with Stalin, he delegated to Smith full power and final authority to prepare the president's FY 1945 budget for submission to Congress as well as the budget message to accompany it (chap. 6). This was even more so for Smith's budgeting work in late 1944, both for the FY 1946 budget and the annual budget message (chap. 7). In early 1944 and 1945, Smith led the annual budget seminar for the White House press corps, something FDR had always done previously. In terms of getting decisions from the president on other issues, Smith only saw Roosevelt eight times in 1944 and five times in 1945. Essentially, he was on his own for all matters within BOB's jurisdiction. That covered a lot of territory, including executive orders and legislative clearance. Essentially, Smith's decisions were similarly as unappealable as Byrnes's.

If it is roughly right to describe Byrnes as the assistant president for domestic policy, then Smith could similarly be viewed as Byrnes's counterpart, in charge of just about everything Byrnes did not want to get involved in. In that case, history could consider Smith to be FDR's Assistant President for Management.[36] He most certainly did not treat Byrnes as his boss, with Smith even apparently viewing Byrnes as usurping his own managerial powers. Another possible approach to capturing Smith's standing would be to follow the pattern of titles used in the executive branch in the first half of the twentieth century. It was common to designate officers below cabinet rank by number. The numbering generally reflected importance, rank, and hierarchal power within that department. For example, in 1923, the State Department had an assistant secretary of state, a second assistant secretary, and a third assistant secretary.[37] In 1943, the Labor Department had, besides an assistant secretary, also a second assistant secretary.[38] In the most elaborate of such an organizational structure, the Post Office Department had a first assistant postmaster general, second assistant postmaster general, third assistant postmaster general, and fourth assistant postmaster general.[39] Following that nomenclature, then Byrnes could be seen retroactively as FDR's first assistant president, while Smith was Roosevelt's de facto second assistant president.

If viewing Smith as FDR's other assistant president is too much of a stretch, then perhaps a plan formulated by Coy would be less controversial historically but would make the same point a bit more softly. During the war, FDR invited Coy to suggest how to reorganize the president's management of the war effort. In response, Coy suggested that FDR promote Smith to Chief of Staff of the Executive Office of the President, hence with explicit line power over everything that EOP did (Lee 2018, 230–31). Impliedly, this included all the temporary wartime agencies subsumed under the Office for Emergency Management, sans any policy matters that Byrnes wanted to control. The scope of such a position would have covered the entire production effort, price control, rationing, priorities for raw materials, transportation, and housing. FDR never formally adopted Coy's plan, but Smith's authoritative roles as the war went on suggest that he had quietly evolved into the de facto director of the entirety of EOP or, in Coy's nomenclature, as EOP's chief of staff.

In conclusion, this close examination of Smith's day-to-day record as FDR's budgeteer and manager-in-chief documented that he justly earned his high standing in the historical and budgeting literature. He was a pioneer in the advancement of public administration as a field of practice in the United States, particularly that of government budgeting. He set a very high bar for budgeteers to aspire to, even if he was not always quite as apolitical, removed from policymaking, or as anonymous as he often claimed. Budgeting and central management simply cannot be separated from politics in a democracy.

Notes

Preface

1. In 1972, President Nixon did not bother to wait for members of his administration to do this. The morning after his reelection, he convened a cabinet meeting and had his chief of staff brusquely demand it from all of them.

2. Letter from FDR to Smith, December 9, 1944, File 10: Miscellaneous, Box 4, HSDP. For a reproduction of the letter, see L. Smith 2003, 15.

3. Letter from FDR to Smith, April 21, 1942, File 10: Miscellaneous, Box 4.

Introduction

1. *Time*, June 14, 1943, cover.

2. June 8, 1941: "Today's Radio Highlights: War Discussions Vie with Music and Comedy," *WP*, June 8, 1941, L-5; "On the Radio This Week: Leading Events of the Week," *NYT*, X-9.

3. *WS*: January 10, 1941, A-1; January 19, 1942, A-1; January 7, 1943, A-1; November 30, 1943, A-1. *CT*: August 5, 1943, 12.

4. July 16, 1943, DR, File 7, Box 2, HDSP, FDR Library.

5. "The Roosevelt Party," *Life*, October 26, 1942, 103; "Mr. Smith Stays in Town," *Newsweek*, August 13, 1945, 29.

6. For example, coverage of a 1946 speech in Chicago: June 7, 1946: "Budget Director Says Federal Budget Will Be Balanced in 1947," *WSJ*, 5; "Budget Chief Asks Economy, High Tax Level," *CT*, 35; "Smith Says U.S. Budget Must Produce a Surplus," *NYHT*, 33; AP, "Balanced Budget in 1947 Hoped For," *LAT*, 1. Smith's speech continued to be referred to in the media days later: F. A. Korsmeyer, "Review and Outlook," *WSJ*, June 8, 1946, 1; Frank Kelley, "Credit Curb, No Tax Cuts Urged on U.S.," *NYHT*, June 17, 1946, 1; Raymond Moley, "Fiscal Prospects" (syndicated column), *LAT*, June 27, 1946, A-4.

7. Joseph Alsop and Robert Kintner, "The Capital Parade" (syndicated column), *Atlanta Constitution*, March 8, 1941, 4; Ernest Lindley, "The Men Around the President" (column), *WP*, March 9, 1941, B-5; Hermann Hagedorn, "The Heart of the Nation," *Woman's Home Companion* 68, no. 12 (December 1941): 10.

8. "Budget Chief: A Quiet Power in National Issues," *United States News*, December 28, 1945, 65.

9. Results of a search in ProQuest Historical Newspapers.

10. Results of a search in ProQuest Historical Newspapers. The feature was suspended in February 1942, due to security concerns about providing information on FDR's whereabouts.

11. Frederick Shelton, "Management's Washington Letter" (column), *Nation's Business* 30, no. 5 (May 1942): 33.

12. "Our Form of Government," part 5 of "The United States in a New World," Supplement to *Fortune* 28, no. 5 (November 1943): 6.

13. April 25, 1945, DR, File 9, Box 2.

14. "Management vs. Dictatorship" (editorial) and "Contributors in Review," *National Municipal Review* 31, no. 9 (October 1942): 474, 503.

15. *Time*, June 14, 1943, 24. The other two were professional training and an unemotional approach to success, regardless of personal prestige, friendship, and loyalties.

16. Hagedorn, "Heart of the Nation," 10.

17. "Budget Chief Smith Figures in Other Big Official Planning Too," *WSJ*, January 11, 1943, 1.

18. Baukhage, "Bureau of Budget Assumes New Legislative Importance" ("Washington Digest" column), *Midland [Rising Sun, MD] Journal*, January 22, 1943, 2. This columnist, a longtime reporter, only used his last name as his byline.

19. Blair Moody, "Mr. Smith Doubles for Roosevelt," *Saturday Evening Post*, March 27, 1943, 24.

20. Pipeline Pete, "Intercepted Letter," *DFP*, June 23, 1946, 4.

21. AP, "Hopes to Help States," *NYHT*, March 9, 1939, 11.

22. Frank I. Weller, AP, "Budget Director Smith Keeps Tab on Government Billions," *New Orleans [LA] Times-Picayune*, November 1, 1943.

23. AP, "Smith's Boss of U.S. Budget, but Wife Is Banker at Home," *WP*, January 6, 1941, 3.

24. North American Newspaper Alliance, "Plain Talk to Kansas," *Kansas City Star*, May 25, 1941, 4-A.

25. Shelton, "Management's Washington Letter" (column).

26. Weller, "Budget Director Smith."

27. Pfiffner and Smith were casual acquaintances. For example, Pfiffner came to Smith's office in 1945 for a short visit. August 8, 1945, DR, File 9, Box 2.

28. Lepawsky had a casual acquaintance with Smith. Both addressed a conference at the University of Alabama and both were on a University of Chicago radio round table (Smith 1941b; 1941e).

29. Similarly, there is an absence of historical examinations of the professional contributions and records of other major figures in the early professionalization of public administration, including Brownlow, Gulick, Leonard D. White, William Mosher, Donald Stone, Paul Appleby, Herbert Emmerich, and Frederick Davenport.

30. For example, see the cover note to Smith from one of his office assistants detailing how she parceled out different sections of the summary of a presidential meeting to appropriate BOB staff. Note from nkg (Nita K. Gavaris) to Smith, July 22, 1942. Attached to meeting of July 21, 1942 (drafted by Coy), CwP 1942, File 4, Box 3.

31. February 6, 1941, CwP 1941, File 3, Box 3.

32. October 14, 1941, CwP 1941, File 3, Box 3.

33. December 18, 1941, CwP 1941, File 3, Box 3. There are two summaries of the meeting. Blandford dictated a relatively lengthy one and then Smith supplemented it with dictation about a few issues that Blandford did not cover.

34. June 3, 1943, CwP 1943–45, File 5, Box 3.

35. January 7, 1944, CwP 1943–45, File 5, Box 3.

36. September 4, 1939 (Labor Day), DM September 1939, File 5, Box 1.

37. During the period that Smith dictated DMs, the typewriters used for DMs and CwPs were different. This suggests that different secretaries handled these duties separately, which enhances the reliability of the documents they prepared.

38. Very rare examples of handwritten notes taken by the assistant director *during* a presidential meeting are for June 28, 1940. Blandford then used his notes as a basis for dictating his summary of the meeting. "June 28," BOB File 2 of 5, Box 4, Subject File, Blandford Papers, Truman Library.

39. CwP 1941, File 3, Box 3.

40. Morgenthau Diary, 1939: April 20, Book 183, 14; May 15, Book 189, 336; May 23, Book 183, 114.

41. January 20, 1945, DR, File 9, Box 2.

42. For example, "Notes on telephone conversation between Cong. Barden and Director Smith" and "Notes on telephone conversation between Cong. Ramspeck and Director Smith," November 20, 1945, DR, File 9, Box 2.

43. December 14, 1945, DR, File 9, Box 2.

44. December 19, 1941, DR, File 4, Box 2.

45. May 20, 1946, DR, File 10, Box 2.

46. Emails from Susan Halpert, Public Services, Houghton Library, Harvard University, December 21, 2018, and Jessica Becker, Public Services, Manuscripts and Archives, Yale University Library, February 12, 2019.

Chapter 1: FDR's "Great Reorganizer," April–July 1939

1. 42 *Stat.* 20.

2. "No Comment by Douglas," *NYT*, September 2, 1934, 2.

3. "Douglas Offers to Assist Bell," *NYT*, September 3, 1934, 16. FDR continued thinking well of Douglas, in part because of the way he behaved when he resigned. After leaving, Douglas was true to his conservative economic principles. He supported Landon against FDR in the 1936 election and campaigned for Willkie in 1940. After Pearl Harbor, Douglas asked to play a role in the war effort and FDR approved it, not something he always did vis-à-vis political enemies he felt had crossed a line of honorable conduct (Lee 2018a, 113–16). For example, FDR vetoed any official federal role for Charles Lindbergh in the war. Douglas served as the deputy director of the War Shipping Administration during the war. Truman then appointed him ambassador to Great Britain. He lost an eye in a hunting accident there and had to wear an eyepatch. A revisionist history of those times suggested he was the role model for the famous ad campaign by Hathaway shirts featuring a man wearing an eyepatch. Derek Leebaert, *Grand Improvisation: America Confronts the British Superpower, 1945–1957* (New York: Farrar, Straus and Giroux, 2018), 277–78, 551n56.

4. The Budgeting Act of 1921 placed BOB in the Treasury Department, but under the direct supervision of a president. Confusingly, there was another Daniel Bell at BOB during the Kennedy administration: Daniel *E.* Bell.

5. In the 1970s, Congress was missing the June 30 deadline so routinely that a budget reform bill bumped the federal fiscal year forward by a quarter to give Congress more time to deal with the annual appropriations bills. That changed the federal fiscal year to October 1–September 30. The added time was for Congress's benefit. Presidents would continue to submit their budgets at the beginning of the calendar year. It didn't help. Congress kept missing deadlines.

6. A somewhat similar situation arose when FDR wanted to appoint another Treasury civil servant, William McReynolds, as one of his administrative assistants (AAs). McReynolds, who was nearing retirement age, wanted to keep his civil service status. FDR obliged him (Lee 2016a, 73, 168n57).

7. Elsewhere, I have presented the reorganization origins of three of the original six agencies of the Executive Office of the President (EOP): emergency management, personnel management, and public reporting (Lee 2018a, chap. 1; 2016a, chaps. 2–3; 2005, chaps. 3–5).

8. 52 *Stat.* 1149.

9. "Tangle of Federal Burocracy [*sic*] Calls for New Budget Machine," *CT*, November 20, 1938, A-9.

10. FDR Day by Day: http://www.fdrlibrary.marist.edu/daybyday/. Talking to Smith in the fall of 1939, Bell guessed he routinely saw the president about once a week, except during the budgeting season (the fourth quarter of the calendar year) when he saw FDR about twice a week. September 7, 1939, DM September 1939, File 5, Box 1.

11. Herbert Corey, "Lost: Two Treasury Watchdogs," *Nation's Business* 27, no. 5 (May 1939): 62. The US Chamber of Commerce was the publisher of this monthly.

12. 53 *Stat.* 561–65.

13. Congress granted most subsequent presidents similar reorganization powers. However, in 1983, the Supreme Court ruled in the *Chada* case that a legislative veto was unconstitutional because it reversed the Constitution's process of lawmaking. Only Congress could enact legislation and only a president could exercise a veto. As a result, these special presidential reorganization powers ended.

14. Smith said he had been under the impression that Roosevelt had appointed an informal *committee* to search for a new BOB director and that a passive FDR had merely "acquiesced" to the committee's recommendation to appoint him. However, even six years later, Smith recounts, "I had never been quite able to put my fingers on the membership of the committee and I had, therefore, begun to suspect that the members were not altogether willing to accept responsibility for their recommendation" in case FDR quickly became dissatisfied with Smith. April 18, 1945, CwP 1945, File 6, Box 3.

15. Jones later worked for Smith as an assistant BOB director, beginning in 1941.

16. Transcript of Morgenthau phone conversation with Murphy, January 17, 1939, Morgenthau Diary, Book 160, 217–20.

17. Blair Moody, "Mr. Smith Doubles for Roosevelt," *Saturday Evening Post*, March 27, 1943, 24.

18. North American Newspaper Alliance (news syndicate), "Mr. Smith in Washington," *Kansas City (MO) Star*, February 21, 1942. "Smith, Harold D.," Clippings, Vertical Files, Kansas State Library.

19. FDR Day by Day, February 1, 1939. Murphy might have been there in part because he was to have lunch with FDR immediately after Smith's swearing in.

20. North American Newspaper Alliance, "Mr. Smith in Washington," *Kansas City (MO) Star*, February 21, 1942. This irresistible story was subsequently published in a few slightly different versions. In mid-1943, Smith drafted a biographical sketch and described it in the third person: "He told the President he was reluctant to take the job, having too many bridges to burn in Michigan. The President picked up a packet of matches and handed them to Smith. 'Start burning your bridges,' he said." "Current Biography, July 1943," File 10: Miscellaneous, Box 4. The 1999 edition of *Current Biography* had it slightly differently: "Roosevelt handed him a match and commanded, 'Burn them'" (Blumberg 1999). There was also a postscript to the story. In late 1944 and early 1945, there were rumors in the capital that FDR was about to appoint Smith as czar over federal loan and credit agencies. When asked about it, Smith reportedly said, "If F.D.R. wants me to take it, match sticks won't do; he'll have to club me." "Mr. Smith Stays in Town," *Newsweek*, August 13, 1945, 29.

21. Lee Carson, "Mr. Smith: He Can Handle U.S. Purse, Wife Handles His," *WP*, February 14, 1943, B-4.

22. Transcript of Morgenthau phone conversation with Bell, February 3, 1939, Morgenthau Diary, Book 163, 127–29.

23. AP, "Budget Post Offered to Murphy Protege [*sic*]," *NYT*, March 7, 1939, 5.

24. AP, "Murphy Will Pick Michigan Men as Washington Aides," *(Benton Harbor, MI) News-Palladium*, February 22, 1939, 7.

25. AP, "Confirms Being Offered Federal Budget Post," *BS*, March 7, 1939, 6.

26. J. Russell Young, "H.D. Smith to succeed Bell as Budget Chief Next Month," *WS*, March 8, 1939, 1.

27. "Smith Named Federal Budget Head," *Michigan Daily*, March 9, 1939. File: Smith, Harold Dewey, Necrology Files, Alumni Records, University of Michigan. The *Daily* was the university's student newspaper.

28. AP, "Hopes to Help States," *NYHT*, March 9, 1939, 11.

29. James McMullin, "National Whirligig" (syndicated column), *(Danville, VA) Bee*, March 25, 1939, 4.

30. Transcript of Morgenthau staff meeting, "Re: Tax Statement," April 11, 1939, Morgenthau Diary, Book 177, 314.

31. Corey, "Lost: Two Treasury Watchdogs," 62.

32. "Quotations," *Wilkes-Barre (PA) Times Leader/Evening News*, April 22, 1939, 11.

33. Emmerich also attended the ceremony.

34. April 16, 1939: "Budget Director Sworn In," *NYT*, 30. Photos only: *WP*, 16; *WS*, A-4.

35. April 25, 1939, DM April–May 1939, File 1, Box 1. A month later, Congressman Keller called Smith again to push the purchase. By now, Smith felt "not at all certain of Mr. Keller's impartiality in this matter." May 20, 1939, DM April–May 1939, File 1, Box 1. Keller kept lobbying Smith. Indicating an understanding of the political need for good legislative relations, Smith even agreed to tour the site personally with Keller. July 29, 1939, DM July 1939, File 3, Box 1.

36. "Name-Only Agency Affected by Reorganization Plan," *WS*, April 26, 1939, A-3.

37. Smith's aide made that point expressly later that year when presenting the FY 1941 EOP budget to the House Appropriations Committee. US House 1939f, 8.

38. For additional discussion of the importance of this seemingly minor detail, see Lee 2005, 67–79. Conservatives finally vanquished NRPB by defunding (rather than deauthorizing) it in 1943 in the FY 1944 annual appropriations bill that funded EOP. 57 *Stat.* 170.

39. April 19, 1939, CwP 1939, File 1, Box 3. At this early meeting, Smith also demonstrated how quickly he was mastering the details of federal operations. In response to the president's request for statistics on relief spending for American Indians, Smith asked if the figure should include payments of tribal claims against the federal government. Smith lightheartedly said it seemed to him there were only a handful of lawyers who handled these claims. Maybe their legal fees were a form of tribal relief, too? FDR enjoyed the byplay, but said not to include those amounts.

40. April 26, 1939, CwP 1939, File 1, Box 3.

41. May 31, 1939, CwP 1939, File 1, Box 3. Smith was also impressed by FDR's work ethic. In August, he observed that "the boss is getting a little temperamental and needs a vacation more than anything else. He works like a slave." August 2, 1939, CwP 1939, File 1, Box 3. Another hilarious example of FDR's interest in detail occurred a few years later. He rejected the estimate for funding a highway in Nicaragua. He said it was "too high" and suggested redesigning it as a one-lane highway. "He even drafted a little diagram to show that a roadbed for a narrow, single-lane highway was bound to be less expensive. . . . The President maintained that a single-lane highway would do the trick and that people could pass at intervals by driving off the slab." June 6, 1942, CwP 1942, File 4, Box 3.

42. April 28, 1939, DM April–May 1939, File 1, Box 1.

43. August 2, 1939, DM August 1939, File 4, Box 1.

44. April 20, 1939, CwP 1939, File 1, Box 3; April 23, 1939, DM April–May 1939, File 1, Box 1.

45. Three years later, Smith concluded that "the Works Agency has really never worked for various and sundry reasons." April 16, 1942, CwP 1942, File 4, Box 3.

46. "Taber Forces Showdown on Reorganization," *NYHT*, April 27, 1939, 13.

47. 53 *Stat*. 1423–30.

48. May 3, 1939. DM April–May 1939, File 1, Box 1.

49. April 26, 1939, CwP 1939, File 1, Box 3.

50. "New Order Is Near in Reorganization," *NYT*, May 7, 1939, 4. One of the frequent attendees at White House reorganization meetings was Newman A. Townsend of the Justice Department. A former judge in North Carolina, Townsend was routinely referred to as Judge Townsend by federal officials. He specialized in preparing formal legal documents (such as executive orders and reorganization plans), was considered an expert drafter, and—most importantly—he had FDR's confidence. Other midcareer civil servants who had FDR's esteem were USDA's Milton Eisenhower, brother of army officer and future president Eisenhower (Lee 2005, 150–53) and Treasury's William H. McReynolds (Lee 2016a, 70–72).

51. May 8, 1939, CwP 1939, File 1, Box 3.

52. May 8, 1939, DM April–May 1939, File 1, Box 1.

53. "New Order Is Near in Reorganization," *NYT*, May 7, 1939, 4.

54. April 27, 1939, DM April–May 1939, File 1, Box 1.

55. May 6, ibid.

56. April 21, ibid.

57. May 4, ibid.

58. 53 *Stat*. 1431–36.

59. "Roosevelt Seeking 'Teeth' for Federal Economy Program," *WS*, July 20, 1939, A-2; Robert C. Albright, "Roosevelt Orders Savings in Government," *WP*, August 10, 1939, 1, 6.

60. July 19, 1939, DM July 1939, File 3, Box 1.

61. June 3, 1939, DM June 1939, File 2, Box 1.

62. June 22 and July 21, 1939, CwP 1939, File 1, Box 3.

63. August 7, ibid.

64. He eventually succeeded. AP, "Blandford Appointed Assistant Budget Chief," *WS*, September 23, 1939, A-3.

65. May 12, 1939, CwP 1939, File 1, Box 3. Smith sometimes referred to BOB as the "Budget Office."

66. Memo from Smith to BOB staff, May 18, 1939, DM April–May 1939, File 1, Box 1; June 7, 1939, DM June 1939, File 2, Box 1.

67. August 12, 1939, DM August 1939, File 4, Box 1; AP, "Appointed to Federal Board" [CSC examination and selection board for BOB vacancies], *BS*, September 8, 1939, 11. Notwithstanding the bureaucratic and lumbering CSC he was dealing with, Smith retained his strong commitment to the good government principle of a merit system. For example, Secretary of War Woodring called Smith about a BOB secretary who was a friend of a friend. She felt she was undercompensated and therefore had requested that a cabinet secretary personally intervene on her behalf. Smith was disgusted by the call because her work performance was routine at best and she did not deserve a pay raise or promotion. "If there is anything I detest is the attitude of [government] employees that they must attempt to secure advancement through influence rather than merit," he commented in his diary. July 24, 1939, DM July 1939, File 3, Box 1.

68. August 17, 1939, DM August 1939, File 4, Box 1.

69. July 31, 1939, DM July 1939, File 3, Box 1.

70. At the time, all budget examiners and other professionals were men. That was one of the reasons they were sometimes referred to as "the budget boys." The major exception to the male culture were BOB's library professionals who were mostly women (Lee 2016b).

71. July 11, 1939, DM July 1939, File 3, Box 1.

72. August 12, 1939, DM August 1939, File 4, Box 1.

73. For a profile of Gladieux a few years later, see Jane McBaine, "Post Profile: Bernard L. Gladieux Has One of the Toughest Jobs Here; Knows It," *WP*, February 14, 1943, S-5. For his obituary, see "Bernard L. Gladieux, Management Consultant" (obit), *WP*, May 20, 1997, B-6.

74. May 25, 1939, DM April–May 1939, File 1, Box 1.

75. May 31, 1939, CwP 1939, File 1, Box 3.

76. June 16, 1939, DM June 1939, File 2, Box 1.

77. May 12, 1939, DM April–May 1939, File 1, Box 1.

78. May 15, 1939, 336–64, part 2, Book 189; May 23, 114–48, and May 25, 157ff., Book 183, Morgenthau Diary. Amusingly, Morgenthau's stenographer still did not know Smith's correct name, listing him as "Donald C. Smith."

79. June 6, 1939, CwP 1939, File 1, Box 3.

80. Morgenthau's ostensible abandonment of fiscal conservatism was considered important news. Joseph Alsop and Robert Kintner, "Self-Liquidating Spending to Replace Outright Pump-Priming" (Capital Parade syndicated column), *Boston Globe*,

June 20, 1939, 1, 15. While not wanting to disagree with FDR publicly, he none-theless continued a behind-closed-doors rearguard battle to hold down the deficit.

81. May 24, 1939, DM April–May 1939, File 1, Box 1.

82. AP, "Budget Director Suggests Unit to Map New Deal Spending," *WS*, June 8, 1939, A-15.

83. June 12, 1939, DM June 1939, File 2, Box 1.

84. June 13, ibid.

85. June 30, 1939, CwP 1939, File 1, Box 3.

86. May 29, 1939, DM April–May 1939, File 1, Box 1.

87. AP, "Farm Parity Payment Tax Put Up to Senate Again," *NYHT*, May 31, 1939, 35.

88. August 7, 1939, CwP 1939, File 1, Box 3.

89. AP, "Budget Boosted $260,937,376 by Congress, Report Shows," *Boston Globe*, August 8, 1939, 1, 6. Using the same AP story, the conservative *LA Times* slightly reframed the blame away from Congress: "Ten Billions in Appropriations Reported by Budget Bureau," August 8, 1939, 6.

90. "U.S. Ends Ban on Shifts without Supervisors' O.K.," *WS*, May 3, 1939, A-2.

91. "D.C. Welfare Budget Sent to Senate," *WP*, May 17, 1939, 17.

92. AP, "Asks Aides for Hopkins," *NYT*, May 18, 1939, 17.

93. Don S. Warren, "Employer Tax Cut Faces Fight in Congress," *WS*, June 10, 1939, A-20.

94. AP, "Nicaragua Canal Survey Fund Asked," *LAT*, June 21, 1939, 12.

95. "Zimmerman Put on Staff of Personnel Unit," *WP*, June 28, 1939, 3.

96. "Bureau Approves Changes in Lunacy Detention Law," *WP*, July 1, 1939, 1–2.

97. July 24, 1939, DM July 1939, File 3, Box 1.

98. July 31, ibid.

99. April 26, 1939, DM April–May 1939, File 1, Box 1. Later, Wheeler was one of the leading isolationists opposing any role for the US in the European war.

100. May 3, ibid.

101. May 8, ibid.

102. May 11, ibid.

103. May 16, ibid.

104. May 20, ibid.

105. June 5, 1939, DM June 1939, File 2, Box 1.

106. June 7, ibid. Smith called him the next day to tell him that BOB was recommending passage of that bill. June 8, ibid.

107. June 8, ibid.

108. June 10, ibid.

109. June 15, ibid.

110. June 17, ibid.

111. June 20, 21, 22, ibid.

112. June 24, ibid.

113. June 15, ibid., emphasis added.

114. April 27, 1939, DM April–May 1939, File 1, Box 1. There were two federal agencies with the same initials, the other being the Federal Security Agency that had been created by Reorganization Plan I.

115. May 9, ibid.

116. May 12, ibid.

117. July 13, 1939, DM July 1939, File 3, Box 1.

118. July 14, ibid.

119. June 19, DM June 1939, File 2, Box 1.

120. May 6, 1939, DM April–May 1939, File 1, Box 1.

121. May 3, ibid.

122. May 5, ibid.

123. May 19, ibid.

124. May 20, ibid.

125. May 25, ibid.

126. May 31, ibid.

127. June 19, 1939, DM June 1939, File 2, Box 1.

128. June 29, ibid.

129. June 30, ibid. Lewis was later a major political enemy of FDR's.

130. July 20, 1939, DM July 1939, File 3, Box 1.

131. August 18, 1939, DM August 1939, File 4, Box 1. Fesler had served on the PCAM staff to investigate federal field operations (Lee 2007). Years later, he chaired Yale's political science department and was a leader in both the American Political Science Association and the American Society for Public Administration.

132. August 25, ibid.

133. June 23, 1939, DM June 1939, File 2, Box 2.

134. June 25, 1939, Ickes Diary, 3524.

135. July 2, 1939, Ickes Diary, 3536.

136. June 26, 1939, DM June 1939, File 2, Box 1.

137. July 19, 1939, DM July 1939, File 3, Box 1.

138. August 10, 1939, DM August 1939, File 4, Box 1.

139. July 24, 1939, Ickes Diary, 3600.

140. August 12, 1939, Ickes Diary, 3631.

141. June 12, 1939, DM June 1939, File 2, Box 1.

142. May 23, 1939, DM April–May 1939, File 1, Box 1.

Chapter 2: War in Europe, Empowering BOB, and First Budget, July–December 1939

1. Memo (summarizing meeting), April 27, 1939, DM April–May 1939, File 1, Box 1.

2. May 12, 1939, CwP 1939, File 1, Box 3.

3. June 8, 1939, DM June 1939, File 2, Box 1. The War Department had just moved into its new building when the US entered the war. Then FDR ordered the construction of the Pentagon. While it was awkward politically, Secretary of War Stimson decided nonetheless that the department must vacate its new office building and move to the Pentagon so that its offices would be next to the Army's.

4. May 31, 1939, CwP 1939, File 1, Box 3.

5. AP, "$25,000,000 to Be Asked for Strategic War Goods," *WS*, June 16, 1939, A-4. Congress eventually appropriated $10 million.

6. June 16, 1939, CwP 1939, File 1, Box 3.

7. June 30, ibid.

8. August 24, 1939, DM August 1939, File 4, Box 1.

9. June 22, 1939, CwP 1939, File 1, Box 3.

10. June 21, 1939, DM June 1939, File 2, Box 1.

11. July 5, 1939, CwP 1939, File 1, Box 3.

12. August 26, 1939, DM August 1939, File 4, Box 1.

13. July 13, 1939, DM July 1939, File 3, Box 1; August 7 and 10, 1939, DM July 1939, File 4, Box 1.

14. August 25, 1939, DM August 1939, File 4, Box 1.

15. August 22, ibid.

16. There was also the seemingly minor detail of *where* EOP agencies would be located. FDR wanted the offices of the three management agencies (budgeting, personnel, and planning) to be in arm's reach. He decided he wanted them in the State, War, and Navy Building that was immediately west of the White House proper, also on the south side of Pennsylvania Avenue and just across a narrow alley. The State Department resisted giving up any space *at all*. Finally, FDR had to inspect the building personally and decide what departmental activities did not have to be there, such as the passport office and old files. Smith, who accompanied FDR on that inspection tour, hilariously described what it was like (Lee 2016a, 74–75). On the day that Smith's office moved there from the Treasury building, Roosevelt "said he was very glad to hear this so that I would be where he could get at me more quickly." September 7, 1939, DM September 1939, File 5, Box 1.

17. Emmerich was present when FDR briefed congressional leaders at the White House in January 1937 about the comprehensive reorganization bill he was about to send Congress based on PCAM's report. His notes of the meeting are the only known record of it (1971, appendix 1). In 1941, Brownlow and Smith recruited Emmerich to be the executive secretary of the Office of Production Management (OPM). They hoped he could improve the management of this ungainly and strife-ridden agency.

18. July 28, 1939, DM July 1939, File 3, Box 1.

19. Memo from Smith to FDR, August 10, 1939, WHM 1939–40, File 1, Box 4.

20. August 29, 1939, CwP 1939, File 1, Box 3.

21. In his diary, Smith made the point that, notwithstanding its packaging for the news media and the public, the executive order had not been prepared in reaction to the outbreak of the world war: "It may be of some significance on this fateful day in world history that the Orders we were working on were arranged for several day ago." September 3, 1939, DM September 1939, File 5, Box 1.

22. August 24, 1939, CwP 1939, File 1, Box 3. He signed it on September 7, DM September 1939, File 5, Box 1.

23. The abridged historical narrative has it that from the start, FDR wanted to enter the war to fight Germany. This is an oversimplification that telescopes developments. In part, it reflects a tendency to impose retroactively what happened later onto preceding events. In 1939, 1940, and even 1941, the president was hoping that military and financial aid to the UK and USSR would be enough to defeat the Nazis. Ideally, the US could stay out of the war as a combatant nation. For example, he told Smith in early September that the reorganization he had in mind was part of his larger desire to strengthen defense and, at the same time, "tend to keep it [the US] neutral and from becoming involved in the European war." September 7, 1939, DM September 1939, File 5, Box 1. Two months later, when friends in Michigan complained to Smith that it looked like FDR wanted to get in the war, he told them that based on his personal interactions with Roosevelt, "the President was adopting strategy calculated to keep this country out of war. His position is pretty clear to me." November 3, 1939, DM November 1939, File 7, Box 1. In that context, Roosevelt's reelection campaign pledge in 1940 that he would "not send American boys into any foreign wars" can be interpreted as having some element of good faith. As late as August 1941, when FDR had his first summit meeting with Churchill off the coast of Newfoundland, he declined Churchill's persistent request that the US enter the war. The best Churchill could get was the Atlantic Charter issued at the conclusion of the meeting. Even at that point, Roosevelt continued to hope that the US could avoid becoming a combatant nation (Lee 2018a, 282n40).

24. July 5 and 6, 1939, CwP 1939, File 1, Box 3.

25. August 29, ibid.

26. August 28, 1939, DM August 1939, File 4, Box 1.

27. August 30, ibid.

28. September 4, 1939, CwP 1939, File 1, Box 3.

29. FDR's concerns were well founded. When Brownlow met with Roosevelt to discuss some reorganization, emergency management, and executive order issues, Roosevelt told Brownlow to prepare documents implementing their conversation, but not to discuss the matter with *anyone*, including the president's personal staff. When Brownlow came back to show FDR the papers he had prepared, White House appointments secretary (and army general) "Pa" Watson told Brownlow that the president was not feeling well and that Brownlow should leave the papers with Watson. Brownlow, flustered, did. September 5, 1939, DM September 1939, File

5, Box 1. Evidently, Watson promptly read the documents and tipped off the Army about what FDR was contemplating regarding emergency management. It contradicted the Army's support for a powerful business-dominated War Resources Board.

30. Smith thought the accusation was laughable, that the opposite was the case regarding executive management. In his opinion, "in the field of administration, his position is amazingly weak." March 1, 1940, DM March 1940, File 11, Box 1.

31. Felix Belair, Jr., "100,000 More Men," *NYT*, September 9, 1939, 1, 6.

32. Being careful about attacks on making BOB too powerful, this section declared that these roles were "in accordance with past practice."

33. Again, to reduce attacks, this section noted that this role was "in accordance with the provisions" of a 1936 executive order, hence simply old-hat stuff predating the reorganization fight.

34. AP, "Roosevelt Drops Brain Trust in Revising Staff for Emergency," *WP*, September 10, 1939, 1. FDR quickly denied it, but Early nonetheless stood by his original comment. "President Labels Brain Trust Ghost," *NYT*, September 12, 1939, 26.

35. The Neutrality Act that was in effect in September 1939 prohibited all arms sales and other overt actions to any combatants in a war. During the Spanish Civil War, American supporters of the Republican side complained that the Neutrality Act had a non-neutral effect. It rewarded the aggressors (Franco's Fascists) by refusing to help the legitimate and elected Republican government (which included Socialists and Communists). On September 21, 1939, Roosevelt addressed a special joint session of Congress on the European war. He included a request to amend the Neutrality Act so that the US could differentiate between belligerent nations who were aggressors and those who were being attacked. Without saying it explicitly, he was calling for sales of military materiel to the UK and France while embargoing sales to Germany and Russia. Congress declined to act (although eventually permitting cash and carry sales to the UK). This was the beginning of the eighteen-month public debate on American isolationism and the legal limits on the president's ability to help the European democracies. After long and emotional arguments, Congress finally yielded and passed the Lend-Lease Act in March 1941. By then, the UK was on the verge of bankruptcy and facing the prospect of not being able to pay for arms and food.

36. December 30, 1939, DM December 1939, File 8, Box 1.

37. Another issue was lurking in the background. Morgenthau was still smarting over losing BOB to the new EOP. As long as it was organizationally in Treasury (although, the 1921 budget law placed it under the president's direct supervision), he could treat the budget director as a bureau chief subject to Morgenthau's (slight) oversight. When convening meetings, he could invite the budget director and expect him to attend. That had become his expectation during the many years when Bell wore two hats, as acting budget director and Treasury official. When Smith moved from the Treasury building to the State Department building, it was a tangible reminder to Morgenthau that the budget director was no longer at his beck and call.

38. December 24, 1939, 4038, Ickes Diary.

39. During the Red Scare after WWII, Currie was accused of passing on information to Soviet agents in the US. While Currie was living in Colombia in 1954, the State Department (led by John Foster Dulles, who sought to be tougher on Communists than the red hunters in Congress) refused to renew his passport and he could not return to the US. These accusations were eventually documented by historians as largely credible. On the mitigating side, a reminder that the USSR was an ally of the US during the war and those who passed information on did not think they were engaging in treason.

40. January 1, 1940, DM January 1940, File 9, Box 1.

41. September 4, 1939, DM September 1939, File 5, Box 1.

42. October 21, 1939, DM October 1939, File 6, Box 1.

43. November 24, 1939, DM November 1939, File 7, Box 1.

44. September 9, 1939, DM September 1939, File 5, Box 1.

45. September 8, ibid.

46. November 15, 1939, DM November 1939, File 7, Box 1.

47. September 23, 1939, DM September 1939, File 5, Box 1.

48. December 15, 1939, DM December 1939, File 8, Box 1.

49. November 15, 1939, DM November 1939, File 7, Box 1.

50. Box 1: July 7, 1939, DM July 1939, File 3; December 6, 20, and 28, 1939, DM December 1939, File 8. This initiative would continue through the 1940s and culminate in the Rockefeller-funded Council on Intergovernmental Relations, which Smith chaired.

51. Ickes had used his new studio for an experiment in a radio version of the department's annual public report (Lee 2018c). Other federal information offices were using radio programming extensively and creatively to report to the public, including fictional plays and dramatizations to make public policy issues more tangible and relevant to rank-and-file citizens (Lee 2012, 95, 122–23).

52. October 3 and 19, 1939, DM October 1939, File 6, Box 1.

53. October 26, ibid.

54. October 14, ibid.

55. September 27, 1939, DM September 1939, File 5, Box 1.

56. October 31, 1939, DM October 1939, File 6, Box 1.

57. December 6, 1939, DM December 1939, File 8, Box 1. The subject was FDR's idea for building a federal museum row in DC and that it should include a museum for the historically significant collections held by the Army's medical library, including old books, documents, and artifacts. November 30, 1939, DM November 1939, File 7, Box 1.

58. September 7, 1939, DM September 1939, File 5, Box 1. This document is a summary of a conference with FDR. Apparently, it was misfiled and placed in Smith's Daily Memoranda for September 1939 instead of in the folder on 1939 Conferences with the President.

59. October 3, 1939, CwP 1939, File 1, Box 3.

60. October 13, 1939, ibid.

61. October 25, 1939, ibid.

62. November 6 and 16, 1939, DM November 1939, File 7, Box 1; November 20, 1939, CwP 1939, File 1, Box 3.

63. November 20, 1939, CwP 1939, File 1, Box 3.

64. December 14, ibid.

65. FDR gradually came to see the importance of this distinction. When AA James Rowe asked him for money to hire an assistant, FDR declined. If Rowe needed an assistant, then Rowe was going beyond what an AA should do, he told Rowe (Lee 2016a, 85). Roosevelt made an exception for McReynolds because he wore two hats: AA and head of the small Liaison Office for Personnel Management, a separate EOP agency.

66. September 28 and October 3, 1939, CwP 1939, File 1, Box 3.

67. November 18 and 29, 1939, DM November 1939, File 7, Box 1.

68. November 29, ibid.

69. October 13, 1939, DM October 1939, File 5, Box 1.

70. The organization was created in 1936 by a merger of the Taylor Society (named after Frederick Taylor and founded in 1912) and the Society of Industrial Engineers. Both were interested in how managers of large organizations could promote efficiency.

71. Alfred Friendly, "Imaginary Federal Agency to Purge Old Demon Graft" (Federal Diary daily column), *WP*, October 16, 1939, 2; Clarke Beach, AP, "One Bureau in Jam at Washington," *HC*, October 29, 1939, A-16; November 29, 1939, DM November 1939, File 7, Box 1.

72. October 13, 1939, DM October 1939, File 6, Box 1.

73. May 23, 1939, DM April May 1939, File 1, Box 1.

74. Even though Smith did not attend the 1939 GRA conference, current and future BOB staffers Donald Stone, Bernard Gladieux, and John Blandford presented papers there: *Governmental Research and Citizen Control of Government; Proceedings of the Twenty-Eighth Conference* (Detroit: GRA, 1940).

75. Box 1: November 14, 1939, DM November 1939, File 7; December 11, 1939, DM December 1939, File 8.

76. "Budget Director Asks Closer Co-operation from Congress," *WS*, December 28, 1939, B-2. December 29, 1939: "Budget Bureau Head Deplores Gulf between His Unit and Congress," *WSJ*, 2; "Using What They Have," *DFP*, 4.

77. AP, "Society to Promote Civic Administration," *NYT*, December 25, 1939, 32; "Administrators Launch New Society Here," *WS*, December 27, 1939, B-1; "At political science meeting" (photo), *WS*, December 29, 1939, A-4.

78. December 28, 1939, DM December 1939, File 8, Box 1.

79. "WPA Head Says U.S. Unemployment Still Acute," *WSJ*, November 3, 1939, 6. I was unable to locate the text of Smith's speech.

80. "Warns War Boom Won't Employ All," *NYT*, November 3, 1939, 11; "Cities Told to Use Research of State League and Save Cost," *CSM*, November 10, 1939, 3; Earl D. Mallery, "Relief and Planning Discussed at AMA Conference," *Public Management* 21, no. 12 (December 1939): 369.

81. The same AP story on November 11, 1939, had several distinctly different headlines: "Budget Chief Raps Huge 'War' Outlays," *Atlanta Constitution*, 4; "Budget Director Makes Plea for 'Common Sense,'" *CT*, 14; "War Spending Plan Assailed," *LAT*, 5. A few days later, an editorial declared "it is a cause of satisfaction" to know of Smith's cautious stance. "How Big an Army?" (editorial), *CSM*, November 13, 1939, 24.

82. Richard L. Strout, "New Deal Cash Is So Low It Is Real Problem," *CSM*, November 27, 1939, 1, 6.

83. November 22, 1939: *NYT*, 1; AP, *DFP*, 10.

84. AP, "Plan Studied to Cut Deficit to 2½ Billion," *WS*, November 21, 1939, 1.

85. "Smith Refuses Comment," *NYT*, November 27, 1939, 1.

86. AP, "Budget Director Goes to Warm Springs to See Roosevelt," *WS*, November 27, 1939, A-2.

87. Bruce Pinter, "Budget Director and Roosevelt Discuss Saving," *NYHT*, November 28, 1939, 13.

88. "Twenty News Questions: Who's Who? What's What?," *NYT*, December 3, 1939, 2-E. The news quiz was a regular feature in the Sunday section titled "News of the Week in Review." That day's edition also had an article by Delbert Clark on "New Budget Takes Form after Months of Testing," 6-E. It had no quotes from Smith, but featured his picture with the title "Busy on budget."

89. Box 1: November 13, 1939, DM November 1939, File 7; December 7, 1939, DM December 1939, File 8.

90. Sigrid Arne, AP Feature Service, "Our Mr. Smith Goes to Washington," *Grand Rapids (MI) Herald*, December 24, 1939. The reporter was a woman. This reflected the gender roles in journalism of the time. Hard news was a man's job, while soft features were for women. There were, of course, occasional exceptions, such as news columnist Dorothy Thompson.

91. December 7, 1939, DM December 1939, File 8, Box 1. The comment should probably be interpreted as sincere and authentic (rather than the fake humility common with politicians) because Smith dictated it for an in-house and private document that was not intended to become public.

92. Sigrid Arne, op. cit.

93. The quotes come from a slightly different version published in the *(Manhattan, KS) Morning Chronicle*, December 23, 1939, 1. It was common for newspapers to edit wire service stories based on space and interest.

94. December 30, 1939, CwP 1939, File 1, Box 3.

Chapter 3: Spending, Reorganization, Defense, and Third Term Campaign, 1940

1. January 3, 1940, CwP 1940, File 2, Box 3.

2. December 30, 1939, DM December 1939, File 8, Box 1.

3. In the 1950s, management theorist C. Northcote Parkinson called this his Law of Triviality: "The time spent on any item of the agenda will be in inverse proportion to the sum [of money] involved" (1957, 24).

4. March 1, 1940, DM March 1940, File 11, Box 1.

5. February 28, 1940, DM February 1940, File 10, Box 1.

6. *CR* 86, no. 1 (January 18, 1940): 455. This bill echoed the earlier opposition on Capitol Hill to the good government reformers who promoted the benefits of executive-centered budgeting over legislative-centered budgeting. Public administration strongly supported the former. This position prevailed in the 1921 budget bill establishing BOB in the executive branch. Senator Davis was trying to redo history, a very difficult thing to accomplish in government and politics.

7. February 10, 1940, CwP 1940, File 2, Box 3.

8. *CR* 86, no. 19 (Index): 672.

9. However, the logic of Congress having its own independent source of budgetary expertise and analysis was institutionally compelling and probably inevitable. The Congressional Budget Office (CBO) was created thirty-four years later, as part of the 1974 Congressional Budget and Impoundment Act. The law was triggered by Nixon's claim at the beginning of his second term that he could impound (i.e., not spend) money that Congress had appropriated and that he had signed into law. Nixon's overreach in early 1973 was followed by his gradual political weakening due to Watergate. Indicating how much political power he had lost by mid-1974 was his decision to sign the bill on July 12, 1974, even though its intent was to rein in his own actions and budgeting powers. Four weeks later, he resigned.

10. December 19, 1939, DM December 1939, File 8, Box 1.

11. March 19, 1940, CwP 1940, File 2, Box 3.

12. March 8, 1940, DM March 1940, File 11, Box 1.

13. March 11, ibid.

14. January 6, 1940, DM January 1940, File 9, Box 1. After WWII, as chair of the Senate Foreign Relations Committee, Vandenberg famously switched to being an internationalist and advocate for a bipartisan foreign policy. He played a key role in getting Truman's Marshall Plan approved by the Senate.

15. January 19, 1940, DM January 1940, File 9, Box 1.

16. February 27, 1940, DM February 1940, File 10, Box 1.

17. February 7, 1940, CwP 1940, File 2, Box 3.

18. Memo from Smith to FDR, January 29, 1940, WHM 1939–40, File 1, Box 4.

19. "Third Reorganization Plan White House Parley Topic," *WS*, February 7, 1940, A-3.

20. "Reorganization Plans May Be Divided into Two More Orders," *WS*, February 8, 1940, A-3.

21. March 16, 1940, DM March 1940, File 11, Box 1.

22. March 28, 1940, CwP 1940, File 2, Box 3.

23. John C. Henry, "Roosevelt, Pleased at Trade Pact Victory, Rests at Hyde Park," *WS*, April 7, 1940, A-2.

24. 54 *Stat.* 1231–34.

25. BOB's early draft of the plan included transferring to BOB the Census Bureau's office that produced the annual *Statistical Abstract of the United States.* The rationale was that BOB's central statistical coordination powers should include responsibility for the *Abstract.* However, the proposal was deleted from the final plan that FDR sent to Congress. "Reorganization Plan No. IV," Master Copy, 3rd Draft, 4/5/40. BOB Folder 2 of 5, Box 4, Subject File, Blandford Papers.

26. *CR* 86, no. 15 (May 8, 1940): 2783–84.

27. Arthur Krock, "Election-Year Politics Eclipses Statesmanship," *NYT*, May 5, 1940, E-3. Krock, a southerner, was initially friendly toward FDR in the first term and often wrote supportive columns. By now, he was becoming a relatively consistent conservative critic and his writings took on an increasingly acid tone toward Roosevelt (Lee 2005, 38, 76, 129; 2012, 253n2).

28. Reflecting that, the Las Vegas airport is named after him.

29. *NYT*: "An Independent CAA" (editorial), May 9, 1940, 21; "Budget Bureau's Plan on Aeronautics Transfer," May 4, 1940, 8. The leak was of an early draft of the proposal. The White House was on the verge of releasing a later version of the plan to the press to defend its CAA reorganization proposal, but Smith felt that would not be a good idea. There would be political accusations that the later draft was changed after the leak and was therefore of dubious credibility. After coordinating with the White House press secretary, Smith then released a copy of the same early draft published by the *Times* to AP and UP. May 4, 1940, DR, File 2, Box 2.

30. Joseph Alsop and Robert Kintner, Capital Parade syndicated column, *Boston Globe*, April 17, 1940, 17.

31. *NYT*, May 1, 1940, 18.

32. UP, *NYHT*, May 4, 1940, 7.

33. Felix Cotten, *WP*, May 5, 1940, B-3.

34. *NYT*, May 8, 1940, 13.

35. The fight on Capitol Hill from 1937 to 1939 over the implementation of the Brownlow Committee report occurred in a slightly different context. Instead of it being between public administration and politics, it was between Brownlovian public administration and Congress's conservative, but equal, public administration experts from the Brookings Institution.

36. *CR* 86, no. 15 (May 6, 1940): 2688.

37. Ibid., 2690 and 2716.

38. Indicating the importance of these documents to lawyers involved in the aviation industry, the *Journal of Air Law and Commerce* published them in full. "Official Interpretations of Reorganization Plan IV," 11, no. 3 (July 1940): 281–89.

39. After WWII, Smith's successor, Paul Appleby, was convinced that this distinction was impossible. He argued that public administration encompassed policy and administration—just not politics.

40. May 10, 1940: "Senators Hear Plan for C.A.A. Shift Defended," *NYHT*, 14; "Senate Sets Test on CAA for Monday," *NYT*, 16.

41. Chesly Manley, "Hearings Delay Senate Vote on Air Rule Shift," *CT*, May 10, 1940, 14.

42. May 10, 1940: "Listening to Defense of C.A.A. Reorganization Plan," *NYHT*, 14; "How They Reacted to Smith's Defense of Reorganization," *DFP*, 20.

43. Barkley was Truman's vice president, 1949–1953.

44. Charles W. Hurd, "Senate Approves Transfer of CAA," *NYT*, May 15, 1940, 20.

45. AP, "Senate Vote Upholding Reorganization Order," *NYT*, May 15, 1940, 20.

46. May 14, 1940, DM May 1940, File 12, Box 1.

47. 54 *Stat.* 1234–38.

48. May 21 and 22, 1940, CwP 1940, File 2, Box 3. When Roosevelt reviewed the draft message on May 22, he noticed a split infinitive and kidded Smith about it. Smith parried by saying that "liberal and modern grammarians were not so concerned about split infinitives where there was some gain in inferences."

49. This public rationale for the transfer also helped mute the predictable complaints by Labor Secretary Perkins that her department was continuing to be denuded. Bureaucratic politics and policy priorities were at the heart of the move. Perkins was a lone champion in the cabinet of opening up the US to war refugees from Europe, who were predominantly Jewish. State Department officials (some explicitly anti-Semitic) opposed any bending of immigration rules. FDR's decision to transfer the unit to Justice indicated a shifting of his policy perspectives. He had been modestly in favor of letting more Jewish refugees in, short of doing it publicly or needing congressional action. Now, with the war in Europe, national security became the dominant policy perspective, in this case the rationale of the need for even stricter screenings to block German spies from entering the US under the guise of being political refugees (Breitman and Lichtman 2013, 71–73, 162–63).

50. May 21, 1940, DM May 1940, File 12, Box 1.

51. 54 *Stat.* 230–31.

52. 54 *Stat.* 1238.

53. June 24, 28, 29 and July 10, 1940, DR, File 2, Box 2.

54. July 5, ibid.

55. July 15, ibid.

56. Memorandum of Interview, Harold D. Smith, by Guy Moffett, Spelman Fund, August 19, 1940. Folder 223, Box 5, Council on Intergovernmental Relations, Series 4, Spelman Fund.

57. *WS*: "New D.C. Budget Plan Shifts Load from Bureau," August 7, 1940, A-1; "Commissioners Hail New Budget Policy in Letter to Smith," August 9, 1940, B-1.

58. January 18, 1940, DM January 1940, File 9, Box 1. A few weeks later, he took ten days off, February 16–26. February 15, 1940, DM February 1940, File 10, Box 1. In late summer, Smith also took a series of short vacations.

59. June 8, 1940, DM June–December 1940, File 13, Box 1.

60. Box 1: March 20, 1940, DM March 1940, File 11; May 29, 1940, DM May 1940, File 12.

61. Memorandum of Interview, Harold D. Smith, by Guy Moffett, Spelman Fund, August 19, 1940.

62. June 10, 1940, DM June–December 1940, File 13, Box 1.

63. November 22, 1940, DR, File 2, Box 2.

64. "Kemp Named Budget Counsel by Roosevelt," *WP*, March 26, 1940, 6. Kemp and Smith knew each other because both had worked for Michigan governor Frank Murphy and then both eventually followed Murphy to Washington.

65. "Personnel Changes: Bureau of the Budget," *Personnel Administration* 3, no. 1 (September 1940): 11.

66. May 25, 1940, DM May 1940, File 12, Box 1.

67. June 6, 1940, DM June–December 1940, File 13, Box 1.

68. September 27, 1940, DR, File 2, Box 2.

69. March 11, 1940, DM March 1940, File 11, Box 1. During this meeting, they also talked about the need to revise the routine annual federal schedule for budget preparation and submission. In passing, Roosevelt made an unusual comment about his health and possibly dying in office. He said to Smith: "If his cold should develop into pneumonia and he were to kick off within the course of a week or so the Vice-President, Mr. Garner, would be sworn in as President, and he should have the opportunity of revising the Budget. The President said, 'God knows what he would do with it, but aside from that it should be his prerogative anyway to make such revisions as he saw fit.'" March 11, 1940, CwP 1940, File 2, Box 3. The political context of the comment was that the two-term vice president was a conservative and was breaking with the liberal administration. Garner was planning to run for president that year regardless of the possibility that Roosevelt would seek an unprecedented third term.

70. May 31, 1940, DM May 1940, File 12, Box 1.

71. October 18, 1940, DR, File 2, Box 2.

72. August 13, ibid.

73. John H. Crider, "Roosevelt Orders Reform on Budget," *NYT*, August 14, 1940, 11. The article mistakenly referred to Smith as "Dr. Smith."

74. AP, "President Orders Changes in Federal Budgetary Procedure," *WSJ*, August 14, 1940, 6.

75. BOB Administrative Bulletin No. 5, "Improvement of Budgetary Administration and Financial Reporting," August 29, 1940. Reprinted in Catheryn Seckler-Hudson, ed., *Execution of the Federal Budget and Fiscal Accountability*, unit [volume] 6 in *Budgeting: An Instrument of Planning and Management* (Washington, DC: School of Social Sciences and Public Affairs, American University, 1944), 54–58.

76. *CR* 34, no. 1 (February 17, 1942): 1307–08.

77. June 1, 1940, DM June–December 1940, File 13, Box 1.

78. June 5, ibid.

79. June 13, 1940, DR, File 2, Box 2.

80. July 29, ibid.

81. October 2, ibid.

82. February 9, 1940, DM February 1940, File 10, Box 1.

83. February 13, ibid.

84. March 6, 1940, DM March 1940, File 11, Box 1.

85. May 27, 1940, DM May 1940, File 12, Box 1.

86. October 11, 1940, DR, File 2, Box 2.

87. Stone, "In Defense of the Budget," presented at GRA conference, September 6, 1940, Princeton, NJ, 6. Copy located in the collection of the National Agricultural Library.

88. Ibid., 17.

89. Ibid., 18.

90. January 15, 1940, DM January 1940, File 9, Box 1.

91. Ralph G. Coulter, "Budget Chief Offers a Plan: Suggests Citizen Council to Stimulate, Unify Small Groups," *Flint (MI) Journal*, April 5, 1940, 1. I was unable to locate the text of the speech in Smith's papers.

92. AP, April 12, 1940: "Budget Head Sees Deficit Justified," *CSM*, 3; "Budget Chief Advocates Cyclical Balance," *WS*, B-13.

93. "H.D. Smith Says U.S. Payroll Not Major Part of Budget," *WSJ*, April 30, 1940, 2.

94. Often forgotten, the *Daily News* was a Scripps-Howard afternoon newspaper. It was popular with federal employees because its first edition came out in time for their lunch break. As an intern at the US Geological Survey in the summer of 1970, I recall seeing Interior employees sitting outside with their sandwiches and reading the *Daily News*. Some of its other outstanding reporters were Lowell Mellett (Lee 2005), Robert Horton (Lee 2012), Richard Scholz (Lee 2018a, 77–78), Ernie Pyle, and Ruth Finney (one of the first women to cover hard news in DC).

95. June 21, 1940, DR, File 2, Box 2.

96. August 1, ibid.

97. AP, "President Asks Funds for Refugee Children," *HC*, August 2, 1940, 2.

98. August 26, 1940, DR, File 2, Box 2.

99. AP, "F.D. Allocates $10,000,000 for Defense Workers," *Boston Globe*, August 27, 1940, 7.

100. AP, *Ironwood (MI) Daily Globe*, January 10, 1940, 1. The precise number was 5,006. Earlier that month, Senator Robert Taft (R-OH), a conservative and isolationist, had written Smith to ask for the amount. January 6, 1940, DM January 1940, File 9, Box 1. Taft then used the reply as the basis for an attack on the administration and the media turned to Smith for a rejoinder.

101. UP, *NYT*, January 11, 1940, 39.

102. AP, *LAT*, January 15, 1940, 7.

103. AP, *WS*, January 17, 1940, A-2.

104. August 7, 1940, DR, File 2, Box 2.

105. July 31, ibid. Before WWII, the State Department Building, where Smith's office was located, was open to the public (Lee 2018a, 146).

106. July 11, ibid.

107. October 22, ibid.

108. Joseph Alsop and Robert Kintner, "System of Reports on U.S. Defense Started to Give Officials Clear View of Progress Being Made" (Capital Parade syndicated column), *Boston Globe*, October 27, 1940, B-9.

109. May 13, 1940, CwP 1940, File 2, Box 3.

110. May 15, ibid.

111. "Roosevelt Asks Billion Fund, 50,000 Planes," *NYT*, May 17, 1940, 1.

112. May 16 and 18, 1940, DR, File 2, Box 2.

113. May 19, 23, 25, CwP 1940, File 2, Box 3; May 19, 22, 24, DM May 1940, File 12, Box 1; May 24, 1940, DR, File 2, Box 2.

114. May 30, 1940, DM May 1940, File 12, Box 1.

115. June 3 and 4, 1940, CwP 1940, File 2, Box 3; June 4, 1940, DM June 1940, File 13, Box 1; June 26 and October 16, 1940, DR, File 2, Box 2.

116. FDR had hinted to Smith his good opinion of Knox as early as November 1939. Then, in May 1940, he permitted Brownlow to share only with Smith and Merriam the president's thinking about a coalition government. June 20, 1940, DM June–December 1940, File 13, Box 1.

117. "45 New Navy Ships Ordered in a Day," *NYT*, July 2, 1940, 1.

118. July 30 and September 24, 1940, CwP 1940, File 2, Box 2. Oddly, he (not Blandford) prepared a detailed summary of the other meetings with Roosevelt in the summer and fall. Instead, these meeting were listed in his daily record, with an occasional brief elaboration: August 22, 24, September 5, 12 (lunch), 14, October 18, 1940, DR, File 2, Box 2. It is possible that these were brief meetings and not particularly important for other BOB staffers to read about. It is also possible that

some of these meetings related to relatively political matters that touched BOB and that Smith did not want an extensive record about them, even if kept in-house.

119. August 30, 1940, DR, File 2, Box 2.

120. October 3 and 16, 1940, DR, File 2, Box 2. Smith also tried to attend the first draft lottery on October 29, but by the time he got there, the auditorium was full and he could not get in. October 29, 1940, DR, File 2, Box 2. Roosevelt attended and gave a short talk about the significance of the event. It was broadcast nationally on the radio.

121. September 24, 1940, CwP 1940, File 2, Box 2.

122. Even after that, Roosevelt insisted that some of his public events were nonpolitical, such as dedicating the new campus of the National Institute of Health in Bethesda (MD) on October 31, a week before the election (Lee 2018a, 58).

123. October 18, 1940, DR, File 2, Box 2.

124. June 12, ibid.

125. "Willkie Predicts Six-Ballot Choice," *NYT*, June 13, 1940, 10.

126. August 24, 1940, DR, File 2, Box 2.

127. July 9, ibid.

128. August 2, ibid. A month later, Wallace resigned as USDA secretary to be a full-time candidate. Roosevelt quickly appointed Under Secretary Claude Wickard to replace him.

129. Memo to FDR, September 18, 1940, WHM 1939–40, File 1, Box 4. A copy of the clipping was not included in the archival file.

130. Letter to Smith from Van Wagoner, October 7, 1940, WHM 1939–40, File 1, Box 4. Smith replied on October 14, but a copy was not in this file.

131. October 18, 1940, DR, File 2, Box 2.

132. October 19, ibid.

133. Memo from Smith to Hopkins, October 17, 1940, WHM 1939–40, File 1, Box 4.

134. Memo from Smith to FDR, October 21, ibid.

135. October 22, 1940, DR, File 2, Box 2.

136. Ibid. Smith's daily record indicates that he took Larned "to the White House." It is unclear if that was a reference to McIntyre's office. It is also possible that McIntyre squeezed in a quick, off-the-books meeting for Larned with FDR so he could hear it for himself. The president's daily calendar does not list meeting with Larned, but sometimes political or other discreet matters were kept off his formal appointment calendar (Lee 2016a, 179n46).

137. October 18, 1940, DR, File 2, Box 2.

138. For example, Puerto Rico governor Leahy and the commandant of the Annapolis Naval Academy dropped by Smith's office to say hello after their budget hearings. October 17 and 28, 1940, DR, File 2, Box 2.

139. November 5, ibid.

140. November 12, ibid.

141. November 13, ibid.

142. November 20, ibid.

143. November 27, ibid.

144. AP, "Federal Revenue to Cover All Needs Except Defense Seen," *WS*, November 22, 1940, A-23.

145. December 17, 1940, CwP 1940, File 2, Box 3.

146. John C. Henry, "Roosevelt Summons Smith for Conference on 1942 Budget," *WS*, December 17, 1940, A-2.

147. AP, "Budget for Defense Next Year Forecast at $10,000,000,000," *WS*, December 27, 1940, A-21.

148. AP, "17 Billion Budget Drafted; Defense Takes 10 Billions," *NYT*, December 28, 1940, 1, 7.

149. December 27, 1940, DR, File 2, Box 2.

150. Joseph P. Harris et al., "Relations of Political Scientists with Public Officials: Report of a Committee," *APSR* 35, no. 2 (April 1941): 333–43.

151. Kenneth Colegrove, "Thirty-Sixth Annual Meeting," *APSR* 35, no. 1 (February 1941): 121.

152. "News of the Society," *PAR* 1, no. 2 (Winter 1941): 222.

Chapter 4: Neither War nor Peace, plus Business as Usual, 1941

1. This chapter covers events in 1941 until the bombing of Pearl Harbor on December 7.

2. November 30, 1940, CwP 1940, File 2, Box 3.

3. December 1, 1940, DR, File 2, Box 2.

4. December 2, ibid. When Roosevelt traveled by train (his special car was called the *Ferdinand Magellan*), it usually parked at the railroad siding near the Bureau of Engraving close to the White House. It is unclear why he used Union Station for this trip.

5. December 18, 1940, CwP 1940, File 2, Box 3.

6. December 20, ibid.

7. December 20, 1940, DR, File 2, Box 2.

8. The FDR Library was unable to locate the organization chart in its holdings. Email from Patrick F. Fahy to the author, July 26, 2019, author's files.

9. Drew Pearson and Robert S. Allen, "FDR Defense Plan Was Surprise to Commission" (Washington Merry-Go-Round syndicated column), *Washington Times-Herald*, December 26, 1940.

10. December 26, 1940, DR, File 2, Box 2.

11. December 31, ibid.

12. "Knudsen Receives Broad Powers in Tentative Executive Order in Defense Set-Up," *WSJ*, December 31, 1940, 1. So unhappy about that leak, Smith even met with the paper's reporter, Eugene Duffield. Smith told him he was checking up on Duffield's story because he was concerned that some people at NDAC were "becoming careless" about confidential information. Duffield said no one person was his source. He justified the story as newsworthy because there was so much obvious difficulty getting agreement on the order and implied he wrote the story without ever seeing the draft. He also said that, unlike most reporters, he usually was willing to identify his sources, but not in this case because "he would not want to get anyone into trouble." January 10, 1941, DR, File 3, Box 2.

13. "New Defense Plan Advances Knudsen," *NYT*, January 1, 1941, 9.

14. "Capital Parade" (syndicated column), *NYHT*, January 6, 1941, 4.

15. December 21, 26, and 31, 1940, DR, File 2, Box 2; January 2, 3, 4, 5, and 6, 1941, DR, File 3, Box 2. During this drawn-out planning process, Smith tinkered slightly with the name, changing it from the title FDR used at his December 20 press conference, the Office *for* Production Management, to Office *of* Production Management.

16. December 31, 1940, CwP 1940, File 2, Box 3.

17. January 3, 1941, CwP 1941, File 3, Box 3.

18. For example, on Sunday January 4, Smith and three BOB staffers went to Secretary Knox's office for a long discussion of the draft. January 5, 1941, DR, File 3, Box 3.

19. January 6, 1941, CwP 1941, File 3, Box 3. A reminder that administrative orders were a short-lived Roosevelt and Smith invention that served as a subset to executive orders (chap. 3). They were not numbered, only dated.

20. January 7, 1941, DR, File 3, Box 2; "Conferences with the President—Not Dictated (1941)," CwP 1941, File 3, Box 3.

21. Smith attended the press conference. At one point, as Roosevelt was reading the executive order to the press and explaining it, he turned to Smith to clarify why there was a certain cross-reference in the text. Smith said it was about the federal power to take over a production facility (Roosevelt 1972, 17: 56). The two orders Smith drafted for the Council of National Defense were moving NDAC into OEM and restructuring the Priorities Board (17: 62–63).

22. January 9, 1941, DR, File 3, Box 2.

23. In New York, mayors were elected on a partisan basis. La Guardia was a Republican.

24. EO 8757, May 20, 1941.

25. January 2, 3, and 4, 1941, CwP 1941, File 3, Box 3.

26. No title, *WS*, January 10, 1941, 1, emphasis in original.

27. 55 *Stat.* 93.

28. January 8, 1941, DR, File 3, Box 2.

29. *CR* 87, no. 1 (January 30, 1941): 407–408.

30. March 15, 1941, DR, File 3, Box 2.

31. Harold B. Hinton, "7 Billion Aid Bill Wins Its First Test," *NYT*, March 16, 1941, 1.

32. "Testify on British Aid Bill" (photo), *WS*, March 21, 1941, 2-X; "How to Spend $7,000,000,000" (photo), *LAT*, March 22, 1941, 5. As Smith and Knudsen were both from Michigan, the *Detroit Free Press* also published it.

33. EO 8751, May 2, 1941.

34. In mid-1941, Administrative Management staffer James Sundquist suggested that the internal record-keeping of the division needed to be reformed so that it could operate more as a learning organization. He feared that most of the division's studies and reports were one-offs that did not generate a growing body of knowledge and principles that other staffers could apply as generalizations in similar situations. Memo from Sundquist to Stone, "Proposal for a Record System Organizing Division Experiences by Problem Areas," August 5, 1941. File: BOB, Box 2, Sundquist Papers.

35. February 25, 1941, DR, File 3, Box 2.

36. March 18, 1941, CwP 1941, File 3, Box 3.

37. Memo from Smith to FDR, April 9, 1941, WHM 1941, File 2, Box 4.

38. "Vote Likely Monday on 6 New Buildings in or Near District," *WS*, March 29, 1941, A-20.

39. "Arlington Entering Greatest Expansion Period in History," *WS*, March 30,1941, B-1.

40. April 11, 1941, CwP 1941, File 3, Box 3.

41. November 12, 1941, WHM 1941, File 2, Box 4.

42. Robert De Vore, "Roosevelt Calls for $6,500,000 to Build Offices in Suburbs," *WP*, July 16, 1941, 1, 5.

43. "War Department 'Dream' Building," *WP*, July 25, 1941, 17.

44. For a comprehensive chronicling of the fight over the Pentagon's site and size, see part 1 of Steve Vogel, *The Pentagon: A History* (New York: Random House, 2007).

45. July 30, August 11 and 27, DR, File 4, Box 2; August 19 and 27, 1941, CwP 1941, File 3, Box 3.

46. July 24, 1941, DR, File 4, Box 2.

47. August 19, 20, 25, WHM 1941, File 2, Box 4.

48. August 29, 1941, DR, File 4, Box 2.

49. "Army Refuses to Yield on Arlington Site," *Washington Times-Herald*, August 27, 1941. Located in DR—Clippings (1941–43), File 1, Box 2.

50. "President Gets New War Unit Plans Today," *WP*, August 29, 1941, 19.

51. Jerry Kluttz, "The Federal Diary" (daily column for federal employees), *WP*, April 10, 1941, 17; "Talk of Moving ICC to Chicago Stirs Up Storm," *CT*, June 14, 1941, 5.

52. April 18, 1941, DR, File 3, Box 2.

53. "Loan Bank Board Will Move Here," *NYT*, July 4, 1941, 24.

54. *WS*: "Miss Perkins, Aides Oppose Taking Units Away from Capital," December 3, 1941, B-1; "Randolph Protests Moving U.S. Bureaus to Crowded Cities," December 4, 1941, A-2.

55. "Four Agencies Fight Removal from Capital," *WP*, December 3, 1941, 9.

56. "Plan to Shift U.S. Agencies Hit at Hearing," *WS*, December 2, 1941, B-1.

57. March 18, 1941, DR, File 3, Box 2; "U.S. Staggers Hours of 75,000 Workers to Relieve District Traffic Congestion," *WS*, March 19, 1941, A-1, A-12; Howard F. Wentworth, "New Work Hours Win Wide Favor," *WP*, March 20, 1941, 1, 7.

58. November 24, 1941, DR, File 4, Box 2.

59. Kluttz, "Federal Diary," *WP*, March 13, 1941, 17.

60. Kluttz, "Federal Diary," *WP*, July 22, 1941, 15.

61. September 29, 1941, DR, File 4, Box 2.

62. Kluttz, "60,000 Here Will Get U.S. Pay Increases," *WP*, November 5, 1941, 1, 10.

63. March 31 and May 5, 1941, DR, File 3, Box 2.

64. May 12, ibid.

65. May 20, 1941, DR, File 3, Box 2.

66. Memo from Gardiner G. Means to J. Weldon Jones, "Persons Invited to Production Conference," May 19, 1941, DR, File 3, Box 2.

67. Memo from Smith to FDR, "Developing an Anti-Inflation Program," July 23, 1941. WHM 1941, File 2, Box 4.

68. August 12, 1941, DR, File 4, Box 2.

69. Warren B. Francis, *LAT*, October 19, 1941, A5.

70. "Speech Echoes in a Hushed City as Radios Go in Homes, on Streets," *NYT*, May 28, 1941, 21.

71. Proclamation 2487, May 27, 1941 (Roosevelt 1969, 1941: 194–95).

72. EO 8802, June 25, 1941.

73. EO 8807, June 28, 1941.

74. This was by presidential order rather than an executive order so the details of its scope and operations would be as secret as possible. Roosevelt 1969, 1941: 264.

75. EO 8839, July 30, 1941.

76. EO 8840, July 30, 1941.

77. EO 8875, August 28, 1941.

78. EO 8890, September 3, 1941.

79. EO 8922, October 24, 1941.

80. EO 8926, October 28, 1941. It replaced the Division of Defense Aid Reports.

81. October 27, 1941, DR, File 4, Box 2; "President Requests Plans Be Drawn to Merge CCC and NYA," *Women's Wear Daily*, October 28, 1941, 9.

82. November 19, 1941, DR, File 4, Box 2; UP, "NYA Funds Are Impounded," *NYT*, November 19, 1941, 19; "C.C.C.'s Withheld Fund Called Still Available," *WS*, November 21, 1941, A-1.

83. November 13 and 17, 1941, DR, File 4, Box 2.

84. EO 8773, June 9, 1941.

85. EO 8785, June 14, 1941.

86. EO 8832, July 26, 1941.

87. 53 *Stat.* 564.

88. October 15, 1941, CwP 1941, File 3, Box 3.

89. June 3 and 27, 1941, DR, File 4, Box 2.

90. Washington was about a thousand miles from Kansas. That meant Smith drove about an additional thousand miles for side trips and on-site inspections that were not on his direct route.

91. AP, "Defense Cost to Soar to Billion Monthly, Budget Head Says," *WS*, July 6, 1941, A-9.

92. Dictated on Saturday July 5, 1941, Reel 4, Ickes Diary, 5688–89.

93. A different wing of the revived conservative coalition focused on the anti-business thrust of the New Deal. It emphasized the imperative of unleashing the private sector to help with the national mobilization. That meant giving control over NDAC/OPM to business executives who knew how to do this compared to New Deal ideologues who knew nothing about business administration. They also argued that the defense emergency required setting aside pro-union labor rights that were allegedly harming the all-out production effort. Managers should solely be in charge. The social reforms of the New Deal would have to be rolled back and then postponed indefinitely until after the threats to American security were defeated, they said.

94. 55 *Stat.* 726.

95. September 15, 1941, CwP 1941, File 3, Box 3.

96. DR, File 4, Box 2.

97. October 14, 1941, CwP 1941, File 3, Box 3.

98. BOB, "Report on Non-Defense Expenditures in the 1942 Budget," October 15, 1941, Morgenthau Diary, Book 452, 141–69. The cover page of the typescript report in Morgenthau's papers had a handwritten note: "Hold for release, Saturday, noon, October 18, 1941."

99. October 15, 1941, DR, File 4, Box 2.

100. One article stated that the report "was made public yesterday by the Senate Finance Committee." Robert De Vore, "2-Billion Cut in Nondefense Costs Outlined," *WP*, October 19, 1941, 1.

101. October 16, 1941, DR, File 4, Box 2. Perlmeter also called back the next day, presumably to clarify a few details. October 17, 1941, DR, File 4, Box 2. On Saturday, Blair Moody of the *Detroit News* called, probably for the Sunday paper. October 18, DR, File 4, Box 2.

102. AP, "Three Economy Plans Offered to Congress," *WS*, October 18, 1941, 1. Afternoon papers usually published their Sunday edition in the morning.

103. AP, "Possible Cuts in Spending Suggested," *HC*, October 19, 1941, 17.

104. October 19, 1941: Robert De Vore, "2-Billion Cut in Nondefense Costs Outlined," *WP*, 1, 5; Henry N. Dorris, "Lists Way to Cut Non-arms Costs" and "Possible Non-defense Cuts" (chart), *NYT*, 39; Paul W. Ward, "Bureau of Budget Maps Paring Plan," *BS*, 18.

105. "Budget Revision—The First Step" (editorial), *NYHT*, October 20, 1941, 10. It misidentified him as "Harold L. Smith."

106. "How to Save Two Billions," *Time* magazine, October 27, 1941, 22.

107. "Byrd for Deep Cuts in Civil Outlays," *NYT*, October 30, 1941, 20.

108. Memo from Smith to FDR, November 1, 1941, WHM 1941, File 2, Box 4.

109. November 14, 18, and 28, December 1, 2, and 4, 1941, DR, File 4, Box 2. He also came to the Hill for a committee meeting on November 25, but when no members from the appropriations committees turned up, Byrd canceled it.

110. Byrd released the report for publication in newspapers on the day after Christmas, a traditionally slow news day (even in a war). December 26 was on Friday, which helped the committee's report dominate coverage over the weekend.

111. "Marsh Accepts Post," *San Bernardino County (CA) Sun*, July 29, 1941, 12. Marsh had been the editor of a small newspaper in Michigan and then a successful pulp fiction writer, sometimes in his own name, sometimes as Ivan Marsh. In the summer, he lived in the family cottage in rural Michigan and in the winter in Redlands (CA). Marsh moved to DC in 1935 to work for the National Emergency Council, which was the New Deal's de facto PR agency (Lee 2005, chap. 2). In 1939, as part of Reorganization Plan I that Smith worked on, it became EOP's Office of Government Reports. Kemp, whom Smith hired in 1940 to be BOB's legal counsel, had been Marsh's fraternity brother at the University of Michigan. It is likely that Kemp introduced Marsh to Smith, leading to Smith hiring him.

112. Smith was ahead of his time. About fifty years later, the accounting profession developed the concept of "popular reporting." The Government Finance Officers Association then established an annual award for financial reports that were in plain English and understandable to the lay public.

113. In August 1941, Smith's secretary described Marsh as "doing special writing jobs for the Bureau." August 28, 1941, DR, File 4, Box 2. That odd wording implied he might have originally been hired as a consultant or temporary staffer. Another oddity was that, when she listed in Smith's daily calendar the names of staffers with whom he met, she routinely inserted a parenthetical identification of their divisional affiliation. She did not do that for Marsh, even though he met frequently with Smith in 1941 and after. A few years later, she began identifying him as in "DO," meaning the Director's Office.

114. In the 1942 movie *Casablanca*, the police chief, a regular gambler at the casino, suddenly says, "I am shocked, shocked to find that gambling is going on in here." The line was so funny and immediately memorable because the audience was already cynically aware of how public officials would try to pretend away something from their past record, no matter how recent.

115. Memo from Smith to FDR, January 30, 1941, WHM 1941, File 2, Box 4.

116. AP, "Budget Head Says Bankruptcy Talk Is 'Sheer Nonsense,'" *CSM*, February 1, 1941, 15. Later that year, the Council of State Governments reprinted the last paragraph of Smith's speech as a frontispiece in its monthly publication. "A Vital Democracy," *State Government* 14, no. 9 (September 1941).

117. *CR* 87, no. 10 (February 18, 1941): A716–19.

118. Ernest K. Lindley, "Federal Budgeting" (column), *WP*, February 10, 1941, 7. Lindley had been a political correspondent for the *New York Herald Tribune* until 1937, then moved to *Newsweek*. In 1938, he also began writing a thrice-weekly syndicated column. The *Washington Post* ran it on Wednesday, Friday, and Sunday. Placing Lindley in the big Sunday paper instantaneously signaled his importance and influence. In a front-page announcement, *Post* publisher Eugene Meyer explained that Lindley "is generally recognized as a well-informed and sympathetic interpreter of the Administration's program and point of view," that is, he would counterbalance the abundance of conservative syndicated columnists then dominating the punditocracy. "An Announcement," *WP*, July 18, 1938, X-1.

119. "The Presidency," *Time*, March 31, 1941, 9.

120. "New Managers?," *Time*, May 19, 1941, 16.

121. "Budget Bureau, with Many New Duties, Becomes a Key U.S. Agency," *WSJ*, April 28, 1941, 3.

122. Blair Moody, "The Low-Down on Washington," *Detroit News*, May 4, 1941. File: Personal Data, Box 3, OFHDS. As a reporter for a Hearst paper, Moody's profile would likely have been distributed to all Hearst newspapers in the US through the company's in-house news service.

123. May 8, 1941: AP, "Budget Head Urges Local Governments to Reduce Spending," *CSM*, 21; "State and Municipal Budget Cuts Sought," *LAT*, 14.

124. June 1, 1941: Sandor S. Klein, UP, "Revision of Estimates Puts U.S. Budget at 22 Billions, with 9.4 Billions Income Forecast," *WP*, 8; John Fisher, "War Sends U.S. Budget for '42 Past 22 Billion," *CT*, 1, 2; "3½ Billion Jump in Deficit Likely," *NYT*, 29; "Budget Boosted to 22 Billions, Topping '18–'19," *NYHT*, 1-A; AP, "1942 Budget Estimates Boosted to 22 Billion," *WS*, A-18.

125. July 5, 1941, DR, File 4, Box 2. Also, it was the long weekend after the Fourth of July, so there was little governmental news to compete with.

126. July 6, 1941: John H. Crider, "Billion Monthly Defense Outlay Seen by Fall," *WP*, 4; Paul W. Ward, "Defense Production Stepup of 16 Per Cent. Is Forecast," *BS*, 3; "Defense Outlay Seen at Billion a Month by Fall," *NYHT*, 18-A. July 7, 1941: AP, "U.S. Spending Rate Billion Monthly Soon," *CSM*, 18.

127. Seventy-Fifth Anniversary Diamond Jubilee, June 5–9, 1941 (program); *University of Kansas Newsletter* (Spring 1941). University Archives, Kenneth Spencer Research Libraries, University of Kansas.

128. Smith's use of the term "Battle of the Atlantic" in mid-1941 is a reminder that this was an active naval war well before the US declared war half a year later.

129. June 8, 1941: "Today's Radio Highlights: War Discussions Vie with Music and Comedy," *WP*, L-5; "On the Radio This Week: Leading Events of the Week," *NYT*, X-9.

130. UP, "Blood, Sweat, Tears in U.S.? Patterson, Smith Talk," *WP*, June 9, 1941, 9; AP, "75th Anniversary Observed by 'K.U.,'" *CSM*, June 10, 1941, 6.

131. AP, "Allays Debt Fear," *Kansas City Times*, June 10, 1941. Source: Vertical files, Kansas State Library.

132. "Longing to See Old Farm Played Big Part in Bringing Harold D. Smith to Kansas," *Topeka (KS) Capital*, June 10, 1941. Vertical files, Kansas State Library. It was no longer in the family. His father had died when Smith was interning at the Detroit Bureau of Governmental Research as part of his graduate studies at University of Michigan and his mother had moved to Michigan when Smith settled there.

133. July 30 and 31, 1941, DR, File 4, Box 2.

134. August 4, 1941, DR, File 4, Box 2. After the broadcast, he stayed at the University of Chicago radio studio to record remarks related to the University of Kansas's seventy-fifth anniversary. It was intended for time capsules to be opened in 1966 and 2066 (August 3, ibid.). The Archives of the University of Kansas could locate neither that recording nor the audio record of Smith's speech at the university's commencement in June. Email to the author from Kathy A. Lafferty, University Archives, University of Kansas, February 18, 2019.

135. AP, "32-Billion Budget Seen Next Year, with 19-Billion Deficit," *WS*, September 16, 1941, A-4. Although it did not like being beaten to a story by the *Star*, the news was considered important enough that the *Post* reprinted the AP story the next day. AP, "32 Billion Hinted as Budget Figure," *WP*, September 17, 1941, 14.

136. October 4, 1941, DR, File 4, Box 2.

137. October 5, 1941: Turner Catledge, "Arms Budget Put 7 Billions Higher," *NYT*, 1, 42; AP, "Defense to Cost Two Billions Monthly in '42," *WP*, 1–2; AP, "Defense Spending to Reach 2 Billions Monthly by Spring," *WS*, 1, 3; Clifford A. Prevost, "Defense Cost Tops Budget by 31 Billion," *DFP*, 1, 4.

138. October 25, 1941: Ralph W. Cessna, "Cities Found Well Prepared to Meet Crises," *CSM*, 3; "Budget Director Opposes Cuts in City Taxes," *WSJ*, 7; AP, "Budget Director Asks Cost Cuts," *Wilmington (NC) Morning Star*, 6.

139. For example: AP, "Budget Head Bans Bronze to Mark Soldier Graves," *WS*, November 18, 1941, A-13; November 19, 1941: "Bronze Markers Barred on Graves of Soldiers," *WP*, 4; "U.S. Bars Bronze on Vets' Graves to Aid 'Defense,'" *CT*, 9; "Bronze Markers on Graves Banned," *LAT*, 6; "Bronze Markers Banned from Soldiers' Graves," *BS*, 17.

140. *WP*, January 6, 1941, 3. The story ran in the hard news section, not in the women's section.

141. "Budget Director Thrift Fiend," *Kansas City (MO) Times*, December 16, 1941. Vertical Files, Kansas State Library. (This article noted it was excerpted from a Smith profile in *American Magazine*, but I was unable to locate the original source.) Malvina Stephenson, Central Press, *(Uniontown, PA) Morning Herald*, June 10, 1941, 3. Kiplinger 1942, 447. Lee Carson, INS, "Mr. Smith: He Can Handle U.S. Purse, Wife Handles His," *WP*, February 14, 1943, B-4. Frank I. Weller, AP, "Budget Director Smith Keeps Tab on Government Billions," *New Orleans Times-Picayune*, November 1, 1943. Larson Dawn Farrar, "The Man Behind the Budget," *Taxes: The Tax Magazine* 24, no. 1 (January 1946): 84. "Budget Chief: A Quiet Power in National Issues," *United States News*, December 28, 1946, 66. Sidney Shalett, "Capital Portrait," *NYT Sunday Magazine*, May 19, 1946, SM-16. Kluttz, "Uncle's Low Pay Forced Out Smith of Budget," *WP*, June 23, 1946, B-3.

142. September 10, 1941, DR, File 4, Box 2.

143. Inga Arvad, "Did You Happen to See—Harold Dewey Smith?," *Washington Times-Herald*, September 15, 1941. File: Personal Data, Box 3, OFHDS. Arvad was from Denmark and had been Hitler's guest at the 1936 Olympics in Berlin. Then she moved to Washington to become a journalist. FBI chief J. Edgar Hoover was convinced she was a Nazi spy and had her followed and wiretapped. That led to finding out she was sleeping with a young navy officer, John F. Kennedy, who was then stationed in DC. Navy intelligence officials quickly reassigned him out of the capital.

144. Hermann Hagedorn, "The Heart of the Nation," *Woman's Home Companion* 68, no. 12 (December 1941): 10. The magazine published the issue before Pearl Harbor.

145. Joseph Alsop and Robert Kintner, "The Capital Parade" (syndicated column), *Atlanta Constitution*, March 8, 1941, 4.

146. Ernest Lindley, "The Men around the President" (column), *WP*, March 9, 1941, B-5.

147. Edson Blair, "Washington: Both Sides of the Curtain," *Barron's* 21, no. 36 (September 8, 1941): 4.

148. September 24, 1941, DR, File 4, Box 2.

149. November 7, ibid.

150. *Key West (FL) Citizen*, June 6, 1941, 2.

151. March 4, 1941, CwP 1941, File 3, Box 3.

152. "Group Meeting," April 21, 1941, Morgenthau Diary, Book 390, 85–86.

153. May 1, 1941, WHM 1941, File 2, Box 4.

154. At the top of the original Smith's secretary typed, "THIS MEMORANDUM WAS NOT SENT," ibid.

155. That was a reference to WPA's Howard Hunter: "Assails Economy League," *NYT*, November 25, 1941, 15.

156. Bell, "Conference in the Secretary's Office at 9 a.m., May 13, 1941," Morgenthau Diary, Book 397, 207–09.

157. Bell, "Conference in the Secretary's Office at 9:00 a.m., May 22, 1941, with the Director of the Bureau of the Budget and Mr. Bell," Morgenthau Diary, Book 401, 16–19.

158. "Group Meeting," October 27, 1941, Morgenthau Diary, Book 454, 187–88.

159. November 30, 1941, Ickes Diary, 6079.

160. November 24, 1941, DR, File 4, Box 2. It never happened. On December 22, Smith and Brownlow talked on the phone about Morgenthau possibly canceling. Smith depicted Morgenthau as apparently backing away from it because he "is fearful of undercutting the Budget Message" (DR, File 4, Box 2). That sounds like a weak excuse, at least the way Smith framed it. Given the context (post–Pearl Harbor) as well as the antipathy between the two, Smith seemed to be implying to Brownlow that Morgenthau had suddenly decided to play hard to get and wanted to force Smith to beg him to do it. He wouldn't. Around the same time, Smith also consulted with Emmerich about this. Then, the next day, Morgenthau called Smith and said he was canceling. It was an elliptical conversation, ostensibly about the speech, but their comments could just as well have been about their ongoing fight over the revenue section of the president's Budget Message for FY 1943 (chap. 5). Smith insisted that Morgenthau be the one to cancel the arrangements ASPA had made for a live radio network broadcast of his speech. If someone was going to look bad after all the trouble it took to arrange it, Smith wanted the onus to be on Morgenthau. Transcript of phone call from Morgenthau to Smith, December 23, 1941, Book 477, 63–64. Perhaps Morgenthau canceled because of his hectic workload immediately after Pearl Harbor, perhaps in pique at Smith, probably both.

161. October 6, 1941, DR, File 4, Box 2. Walker's predecessor was James Farley, longtime political strategist for FDR. However, Farley broke with FDR over seeking a third term in 1940 and ran as a candidate for the Democratic nomination to succeed Roosevelt. He came in second and resigned as postmaster general.

162. November 3, ibid.

163. November 6, 12, and 26, ibid.

164. November 11, 1941, CwP 1941, File 3, Box 3.

165. November 17, 24, and 28, ibid.

166. "Roosevelt Sees Smith about 1942 budget," WS, December 6, 1942, 2-X.

167. December 6, 1941, CwP 1941, File 3, Box 3. Blandford dictated the FY 1943 aspects of the meeting. The detail about the call from Knox was dictated by Smith after Pearl Harbor and added to the summary.

168. Ibid.

169. Summary, File 1941, Box 1, Office for Emergency Management, Official Files 4240, FDR Library.

170. Voorhis was defeated for reelection in 1946 by newcomer Richard Nixon.

171. December 6, 1941, DR, File 4, Box 2. I did not locate the text of the speech in Smith's files nor was it published in MFOA's quarterly.

172. Lawton, Smith's AA, testified at a congressional hearing on December 2 that BOB now employed 270 permanent staffers and an additional 85 in the (temporary) defense unit. "Plan to Shift U.S. Agencies Hit at Hearing," *WS*, December 2, 1941, B-1.

Chapter 5: The First Year of the War, 1942

1. December 7, 1941, DR, File 4, Box 2.

2. December 10, 17, and 22, ibid.

3. December 26, ibid.

4. December 15, 18, and 19, ibid.

5. December 18, 1941, CwP 1941, File 3, Box 3.

6. AP, "150 Billion Seen Cost of Victory Program Doubling Arms Output," *WS*, December 9, 1941, A-7.

7. Memo from Smith to FDR, December 13, 1941, WHM 1941, File 2, Box 4.

8. Memo from Smith to FDR, December 17, ibid.

9. Ibid.

10. December 18, 1941, CwP 1941, File 3, Box 3.

11. Memo from FDR to Morgenthau, December 19, 1941, Morgenthau Diary, Book 475, 33.

12. Transcript of phone call from Smith to Morgenthau, December 19, 1941, Morgenthau Diary, Book 475, 35–36.

13. "Group Meeting," December 20, 1941, Morgenthau Diary, Book 475, 164–75.

14. "Re President's Budget Message," December 23, 1941, Morgenthau Diary, Book 477, 51–68.

15. By October, the reality of the cost of the war had sunk in. By then, taxes were only covering about 20 percent, leaving the rest for indebtedness. John MacCormac, "6 Billions Monthly for War," *NYT*, October 11, 1942, E-6.

16. December 30, 1941, DR, File 4, Box 2. Uncharacteristically, neither Smith nor Blandford wrote up a summary of the meeting. "Conferences with the President—Not Dictated (1941)," CwP 1941, File 3, Box 3.

17. "Group Meeting," December 31, 1941, Morgenthau Diary, Book 480, 176.

18. December 21, 1941, Ickes Diary, 6143.

19. August 27, 1941, DR, File 4, Box 2.

20. In September 1940, as a staffer at PACH, Sundquist wrote a report for the AMA and the Civil Service Assembly on "Emergency Personnel Policies: A Check List of Items Which Might Be Considered by State and Local Governments"

(File: OCD, Box 9, Sundquist Papers). Sundquist's MPA thesis, "British Cities at War," was on the impact of WWII on municipal government in the UK (before Pearl Harbor). Sundquist met Stone at Syracuse when Stone was briefly a visiting professor there. Sundquist's thesis was published in 1941 by Public Administration Service (which Donald Stone had headed before moving to BOB). Stone brought Sundquist to BOB.

21. July 1 and August 28, 1941, DR, File 4, Box 2.

22. October 16, 1941, DR, File 4, Box 2. OCD had just been established in May, so in October it was still trying to construct a fully staffed organization.

23. BOB, "Memorandum on Program and Organization, Office of Civilian Defense," November 6, 1941. File: OCD, Box 9, Sundquist Papers. Sundquist also drafted a "Manual of Field Operations" for use by OCD. November 26, 1941, File: BOB, Box 2, Sundquist Papers.

24. December 2 and 3, 1941, DR, File 4, Box 2.

25. December 19, 1941, CwP 1941, File 3, Box 3.

26. After BOB, Sundquist had a storied career, including speech-writing for President Truman and as deputy under secretary of USDA during the Johnson administration. He then became a political science scholar at the Brookings Institution, writing several impressive studies about the federal government, politics, and public policy. I got to know him when I was a guest scholar there in 1972–1974. He was very friendly to the junior staff in the Governmental Studies Division, always open to conversation, and loved talking politics. At the time, I didn't know much about his background because he never said, "and then I told the president . . . ," the stock phrase old hands in Washington used to try to impress outsiders and newcomers.

27. Memo to FDR, December 13, 1941. File: Roosevelt (1941), Box 13, Coy Papers, FDR Library.

28. December 15, 1941, CwP 1941, File 3, Box 3.

29. Memo from Smith to FDR, "Unification of Home Defense Agencies," December 31, 1941. File: OCD 1941, Box 2, Liaison Officer for Emergency Management—General Records, OEM, RG 214.

30. All quotes from December 19, 1941, CwP 1941, File 3, Box 3. When dictating his summary of the meeting, Smith added, "Although I did not say this, I confess I felt he could not handle the job on any basis."

31. December 21, 1941, Ickes Diary, 6143–44. That Smith didn't fall for the political bait of "I promise to do X, but only *after* you do Y . . ." demonstrates his lack of naïveté when dealing with politicians. In this kind of political transaction, one must insist that the paired commitments are delivered simultaneously.

32. January 2, 1942, CwP 1942, File 4, Box 3.

33. The need for housing was, too. In December, Smith recommended a new appropriation of $300 million for defense housing. "Congress speeds bills for huge war effort," *NYT*, December 17, 1941, 7. The housing shortage in DC was lightheartedly depicted in the 1943 movie *The More the Merrier*.

34. December 19, 1941, DR, File 4, Box 2.

35. "Cities Clamor for U.S. Agencies Being Removed from Washington," *DFP*, December 21, 1941, 4.

36. "Pension Board Moved to Chicago," *Railway Age* 111, no. 26 (December 27, 1941): 1091, 1095.

37. Jack Stinnett, "Washington Daybook" (syndicated column), *Wilmington (NC) Morning Star*, December 31, 1941, 4.

38. Respectively: EO 8989, December 18, 1941; EO 8985 on December 19, 1941.

39. EO 9001, December 27, 1941.

40. December 18, 1941, CwP 1941, File 3, Box 3. A reminder that those powers had expired in January 1941.

41. For example, he met with Robert Page, the secretary-treasurer, February 13 and April 3; Charles Ascher, March 3; and a luncheon with "junior" members of ASPA, April 2, 1941, DR, File 3, Box 2. Later in the year, when he was in Chicago, he conferred with many of the association's leadership and staff based at PACH, August 4, 1941, DR, File 4, Box 2. He also hosted many routine business meetings in his office, including coordinating the ASPA and APSA conference programs, August 19, 1941; Brownlow, September 4, 1941; Harvard professor Arthur Holcombe about the conference program, September 10, 1941; phone call from Vice President Luther Gulick, September 11, 1941; planning meetings on the conference program, September 15 and December 13; and asking people to serve on a nominating committee for the 1942 slate of officers, December 17, 1941, DR, File 4, Box 2.

42. "Open Shop Is Urged for War Duration," *NYT*, December 30, 1941, 12.

43. Smith, "Management in a Democracy," *National Municipal Review* 31, no. 9 (October 1942): 476–80.

44. January 2, 1942, DR, File 5, Box 2.

45. January 3, 1942, CwP 1942, File 4, Box 3.

46. January 4, 1942, DR, File 5, Box 2.

47. January 4, 1942, CwP 1942, File 4, Box 3.

48. Strout, a good reporter, claimed in a column that FDR referred to Smith as "Harry" at the budget briefing. Richard L. Strout, "Intimate Message: Washington" (column), *CSM*, January 9, 1942, 13. However, the transcript of the press conference has Roosevelt calling him "Harold."

49. January 7, 1942, DR, File 5, Box 2.

50. George B. Bryant, Jr., "Nine Billion Tax Proposal Jolts Congress; Leaders See Good Deal of Trouble Ahead," *WSJ*, January 8, 1942, 1, 9.

51. Smith submitted this study to Congress in late January. Ben H. Miller, "Propaganda by Government Costs More than $30,000,000," *BS*, February 14, 1942, 7.

52. May 7, 1942: Hal Foust, "U.S. Officials Urge Auto and Tire Seizures," *CT*, 1; UP, "Rubber Situation 'Perilous,' Senate Group Told," *WSJ*, 6.

53. F. R. Kent, Jr., "Agencies Must Turn In Rubber," *BS*, July 1, 1942, 1, 11.

54. Kluttz, "Federal Diary," *WP*, January 21, 1942, 17.

55. March 4, 1942, CwP 1942, File 4, Box 3.

56. March 10, ibid.

57. January 12, ibid.

58. January 13, ibid., emphasis added.

59. Ibid.

60. "Statement by the President," press release, January 13, 1941. A copy of the press release is attached to Smith's summary of his January 13 conference with the president, ibid.

61. EO 9024, January 16, 1942.

62. EO 9040, January 24, 1942.

63. EO 9125, April 7, 1942.

64. EO 9017, January 12, 1942.

65. EO 9054, February 7, 1942.

66. EO 9070, February 24, 1942.

67. EO 9095, March 11, 1942.

68. EO 9102, March 18, 1942. This was not the infamous EO 9066 of February 19, 1942, that authorized forcibly moving Japanese and Japanese Americans in western states into concentration camps. Smith apparently played no major role in it nor is there any archival record in his papers or office files of either objecting to or supporting it. The request for that order came directly to FDR from the Army. BOB would likely have had only a glancing (if any) role in the preparation of the order because it did not directly relate significantly to its hegemony over executive orders impacting budgets, organization, coordination, and management. This subsequent EO 9102 related to the organizational creation of the War Relocation Authority to implement the policy. Smith is only mentioned briefly in the literature on the subject of the concentration camps, for example, a quote of correspondence from Milton Eisenhower (deputy director of the relocation authority) to Smith on wage policy (J. Smith 2003, 88).

69. EO 9139, April 18, 1942.

70. EO 9163, May 15, 1942. Later renamed the Women's Army Corps.

71. EO 9182, June 13, 1942. For a detailed discussion, see Lee 2005 (chap. 9); 2012 (180–83).

72. Military Order, June 13, 1942. This was a reorganization of the office of the Coordinator of Information, which FDR had created in 1941.

73. EO 9205, July 25, 1942.

74. EO 9246, September 17, 1942. The rubber director was placed within WPB, so subject to Nelson's oversight. The executive order was, in part, an attempt

to deflate any congressional effort to overturn FDR's veto of a bill to create a separate and independent Rubber Supply Agency headed by a director of rubber supplies. Roosevelt's veto message emphasized the public administration principle of having a "unified, integrated, and efficient" production program that considered all needs, instead of a structure that put one goal above others (Roosevelt 1969, 1942: 312).

75. EO 9250, October 3, 1942.

76. EO 9276, December 2, 1942. Ickes, again.

77. EO 9280, December 5, 1942. These specified powers were assigned to the USDA secretary, making him "two-hatted."

78. EO 9285, December 24, 1942.

79. EO 9082, February 28, 1942; EO 9096, March 12, 1942.

80. EO 9142, April 21, 1942.

81. Memo from Coy to FDR, July 11, 1942, WHM 1942, File 3, Box 4.

82. EO 9245, September 16, 1942.

83. EO 9247, September 17, 1942.

84. EO 9279, December 5, 1942.

85. EO 9256, October 13, 1942.

86. EO 9094, March 10, 1942.

87. EO 9183, June 15, 1942.

88. US Bureau of the Budget, "Organization Nomenclature in the Federal Government" (mimeo), January 21, 1942. The EOP library has this publication in its collection.

89. EO 9128, April 13, 1942. Hinting at the pragmatist approach Smith took to reorganization, he told FDR that "while this Order may not go as far as is desirable, it is definitely a step in the right direction." Memo from Smith to FDR, April 13, 1942, WHM 1942, File 3, Box 4. This executive order was the subject of a column by Arthur Krock, "The Executive Order as a Deadly Weapon" (In the Nation column), *NYT*, May 22, 1942, 20.

90. EO 9165, May 19, 1942.

91. Presidential Statement, May 20, 1942 (Roosevelt 1969, 1942: 242–45).

92. EO 9193, July 6, 1942.

93. EO 9112, March 26, 1941. Phil Graham, then a lawyer working for OEM's Wayne Coy, prepared the first draft of the order (Memo from Coy to Smith, March 20, 1942, File: Roosevelt (1942), Box 13, Coy Papers). He married Katharine Meyer, daughter of the owner of the *Washington Post*. When his father-in-law died, he became the publisher of the paper.

94. "President Orders War-Plant Audits," *NYT*, April 11, 1942, 7.

95. June 21, 1942, Ickes Diary, 6729–30.

96. Krock, "The Executive Order as a Deadly Weapon."

97. "Our 'Kitchen Congress': Real Wielders of Power," *United States News* 13, no. 24 (December 11, 1942): 13–14.

98. Memo from F. J. Bailey to Marsh, December 10, 1942. File: Legislative Reference, Box 1, Office of Information (OOI) 1941–1951, Central Files, RG 51.

99. One of the principles of statutory interpretation was that if a later law contradicted a preceding law, then the later law prevailed because it impliedly repealed the earlier one.

100. Oliver McKee, "Housing Shortages in Other Cities Face Shifted Workers," *WS*, February 1, 1942, A-5.

101. "Immigration-Naturalization Unit Will Move to Philadelphia," *WP*, January 2, 1942, 1.

102. February 3, 1942: AP, "Washington Shifts Nondefense Staffs," *CSM*, 8; "Agriculture Transfer Will Send 3,848 Workers from D.C.," *WS*, A-1. February 4, 1942: Kluttz, "Federal Diary," *WP*, 19; James M. Minifie, "Capital Exodus to Move 3,850 Farm Staff," *NYHT*, 7.

103. James M. Fisher, "Alien Property Offices Going to Chicago," *Washington Times-Herald*, March 13, 1942. Copy in CwP 1942, File 4, Box 3.

104. "Most in F.D.I.C. Leave about June 15 for Chicago," *WS*, April 17, 1942, 1-X; Kluttz, "Federal Diary," *WP*, April 18, 1942, 17.

105. AP, "Shift Part of Veterans Bureau," *NYT*, April 21, 1942, 13.

106. "Security Unit Wins Dispute for Offices," *BS*, April 24, 1942, 30. The *Chicago Tribune* was delighted to have additional federal employees moved to Chicago, trumpeting "Personnel Shift Sends More U.S. Aids [*sic*] to Chicago," April 24, 1942, 29.

107. Kluttz, "Federal Diary," *WP*, April 25, 1942, 17.

108. Kluttz, "Federal Diary," *WP*, June 19, 1942, 23.

109. AP, "Cleveland to Get a Navy Bureau," *DFP*, October 27, 1942, 2.

110. "Send 3,150 U.S. Workers to Chicago," *CT*, December 29, 1942, 1.

111. No title, *WS*, January 19, 1942, A-1.

112. Kluttz, "Federal Diary," *WP*, January 18, 1942, 13.

113. January 2, 1942, DR, File 5, Box 2. Robertson was the father of Pat Robertson, a prominent Christian evangelist in the 1980s who founded a successful religious TV network as well as Regent University. He ran for president in 1988, coming in second in the Iowa caucuses, ahead of then vice president Bush (but behind Senator Bob Dole [KS]).

114. "Senators Summon Budget Aides to Quiz on Bureau Shifts," *WS*, January 8, 1942, 1-X.

115. Charles Mercer, "Parley Seen on Shifting of Agencies," *WP*, January 10, 1942, 15.

116. "President Says Agencies Must Move," *WP*, January 14, 1942, 1, 7.

117. Senate Resolution 216, 77th Congress, 2nd sess.

118. Charles Mercer, "Foes of Moving U.S. Agencies Give Up the Fight," *WP*, January 15, 1942, 1, 15.

119. *CR* 88, no. 1 (January 14, 1942): 322–45.

120. January 28, 1942, DR, File 5, Box 2.

121. William Strand, "Move to Speed Bureau Shifts Out of Capital," *CT*, January 7, 1942, 25.

122. January 26 and February 3, 1942, DR, File 5, Box 2.

123. March 3 and April 24, ibid.

124. April 21, ibid.

125. "Traffic Court Move Planned," *DFP*, December 31, 1941, 3.

126. May 5, 1942, DR, File 5, Box 2.

127. February 4, ibid.

128. January 18, 1942: Gerald G. Gross, "Quarter Million More Coming to Live in Washington Area," *WP*, 1, 13; J. A. Fox, "Population Rise of 250,000 Seen Here This Year," *WS*, A-1, A-10.

129. February 26, 1942: "U.S. to Free Apts. Now Used as Offices," *WP*, 17; J. A. Fox, "Further Shifts of Agencies Mapped," *WS*, B-1.

130. February 11, 1942, CwP 1942, File 4, Box 3; "President Studies Plan for Still More Temporary Offices," *WS*, February 11, 1942, B-1.

131. February 13, 1942, DR, File 5, Box 2.

132. EO 9067, February 20, 1942.

133. "List of Government Agencies in the Order of Priority for Employes [*sic*]," *WP*, February 27, 1942, 16.

134. "Priorities Set in War Shifts of Personnel," *WS*, February 27, 1942, B-1.

135. AP, "Army Assumes Control of CCC Camp Equipment," *CT*, March 22, 1942, 17; "W.P.B. Checks on N.Y.A. Machine Tool Supply Disclosures," *LAT*, March 22, 1942, 10; EO 9133, April 14, 1942.

136. Memo from Smith to FDR, March 16, 1942, WHM 1942, File 3, Box 4. FDR's reply was then typed onto the file copy.

137. Memo from Smith to FDR, March 26, ibid.

138. "Sunday, March 29 in the *Sunday Star*" (ad), *WS*, March 28, 1942, A-9.

139. "Sunday's *Free Press*" (ad), *DFP*, March 28, 1942, 16. Also, Friday, March 27, 8.

140. April 1, 1942, CwP 1942, File 4, Box 3.

141. April 4, ibid.

142. W. H. Lawrence, "President Plans a Broad Campaign against Inflation," *NYT*, April 11, 1942, 1.

143. Richard L. Strout, "Threat to Inflation Effort Seen in Compromise on Taxes," *CSM*, April 30, 1942, 8.

144. Memo from Smith to FDR, April 20, 1942, WHM 1942, File 3, Box 4.

145. "Conference on Information Aspects of the President's Economic Program," April 29, 1942. File: Steering Committee—Information Coordination, Box 2, OOI.

146. "Air Views," *BS*, June 28, 1942, SM-9.

147. July 2, 1942: UP, "Inflation Still a Danger, Budget Chief Warns," *DFP*, 1; Robert De Vote, "Crack in Price Ceiling Blamed on Congress," *WP*, 1, 4; "Declares Inflation Still Threatens U.S. despite OPA Ceilings," *Women's Wear Daily* 65, no. 2, 5.

148. UP, "Henderson, Congress Fight over His Policies," *WSJ*, July 3, 1942, 3.

149. J. S. Armstrong, "Puncturing of Ceilings Seen as Inflation Threat," *BS*, July 12, 1942, 5.

150. "Writing on the Wall" (editorial), *WP*, July 3, 1942, 14; " 'Education' Is Not Enough" (editorial), *NYHT*, July 4, 1942, 10.

151. September 26, 1942, Ickes Diary, 7011. So did influential columnist Walter Lippmann, "Weakness of Seven Point Program," *Boston Globe*, April 30, 1942, 16.

152. EO 9250, October 3, 1942.

153. October 19, 1942, DR, File 6, Box 2.

154. Kluttz, "Federal Diary," *WP*, October 20, 1942, B-1.

155. Letter from FDR to Smith, April 21, 1942, File 10: Miscellaneous, Box 4.

156. February 7, 1942, CwP 1942, File 4, Box 3.

157. Frederick Shelton, "Management's Washington Letter" (monthly column), *Nation's Business* 30, no. 5 (May 1942): 33.

158. Letter from Smith to Early, March 12, 1942, WHM 1942, File 3, Box 4.

159. It was also a way to ease out OEM's housing director without firing him (Lee 2018a, 312n10; 2012, 107–08, 161).

160. February 14, 1942, CwP 1942, File 4, Box 3.

161. March 6, 1942, DR, File 5, Box 2.

162. March 14, 1942, CwP 1942, File 4, Box 3.

163. 56 *Stat.* 234. Scant evidence suggests it was Senator McKellar (D-TN) who slickly torpedoed Smith's raise while pretending to support it. When Senator Mead (D-NY) asked McKellar, chair of the subcommittee handling the legislation, to permit Smith's raise to be added to the bill, McKellar gave him a mildly favorable answer (Memo from Coy to FDR, April 22, 1942, File: BOB 1942, Box 2, RG 214). Smith's raise was in the Senate-passed version of the bill. Then, when the House and Senate conferees met, they "agreed to keep Budget Director Harold Smith's salary at $10,000 rather than to raise it to $12,000" (Kluttz, "Federal Diary," *WP*, June 9, 1942, 17). That means McKellar quickly yielded to the House conferees who did not like it on principle because it had not been in their version of the bill. He gave them a win and that earned him the right to ask them to yield on something in his version that he truly cared about. With this maneuver, he could claim to Mead and FDR that he had done everything he could. McKellar, he of long knives and longer memory, always focused on getting his way or getting even (chaps. 6–8; Lee 2016a, 113–14, 181n99; 2005, chaps. 8–9).

164. January 8, 1942, DR, File 5, Box 2.

165. February 5, ibid.

166. February 11, ibid.

167. March 6, ibid.

168. March 2, ibid.

169. March 23, ibid.

170. April 11, 1942, Ickes Diary, 6524.

171. April 15, 1942, DR, File 5, Box 2.

172. Letter from Smith to James C. Rettie, NRPB Regional Office, Juneau, AK, May 13, 1942. File: Alaska, Box 1, OFHDS.

173. Memo from FDR to Smith, December 19, 1942, "I think a million dollars would be worth spending," File: Smith, Harold D.—Director—Misc., Box 3, OFHDS; December 24, 1942, DR, File 6, Box 2.

174. Kluttz, "Federal Diary," *WP*, November 19, 1942, B-1.

175. November 18, 1942, DR, File 6, Box 2.

176. Memo from Smith to FDR, November 18, 1942, WHM 1942, File 3, Box 4.

177. Memo from Roosevelt to Smith, November 19, 1942, ibid.

178. December 30, 1942, DR, File 6, Box 2.

179. Kluttz, "Federal Diary," February 8, 1943, B-1. Agency heads sometimes only asked for a one-time postponement of the conscription date, rather than a permanent deferment. That was somewhat easier to obtain.

180. My father, Jack H. Lee, was caught in the web of this policy. As a recently minted lawyer, he applied to be a special agent of the FBI and was accepted. The no-exceptions policy Roosevelt announced would have stripped the FBI of all its draft-aged special agents, a very large number. Eventually, the compromise FBI director Hoover accomplished was that they would continue to serve in the FBI as essential to the war effort and automatically qualified for draft deferments. However, being an FBI agent was not considered as the *equivalent* of being drafted. Instead, if/when they were no longer in the FBI, they would become eligible for the draft. During the war, my dad was assigned to Latin America as a counterintelligence agent, seeking to identify Nazi spies. Sometimes he had diplomatic cover, but oftentimes posed as a businessman. He served in the FBI through 1946 and therefore was never subject to the wartime draft.

181. Memo from Smith to FDR, November 23, 1942, WHM 1942, File 3, Box 4; Kotlowski 2015, 350–51.

182. Memo from Smith to Marvin McIntyre, Secretary to the President, March 5, 1942, WHM 1942, File 3, Box 4. Roosevelt announced it at a press conference on March 6, 1942.

183. Memo from Smith to Stephen Early, Press Secretary, March 12, 1942, WHM 1942, File 3, Box 4.

184. "Budget Bureau Tells Government Agencies to Cut Use of Paper," *WS*, April 6, 1942, A-10.

185. UP, "Federal Bureaus to Give Up Scrap," *LAT*, July 1, 1942, 1, 9.

186. "Federal Automobiles Will Be Cut to Two Oil Changes Yearly," *WS*, August 28, 1942, A-7.

187. Memo from Roosevelt to heads of departments and agencies, August 31, 1942. File: Est. [Estimates Division]—Surplus Supplies and Equipment, Box 1, OOI.

188. EO 9235, August 31, 1942. In part, the order requested all agencies to use standardized categories and uniform nomenclature for equipment and supplies. "Use of Standards Helps Win the War," *NYT*, January 3, 1943, A-59.

189. "Agencies Told to Swap for Typewriter Needs," *WS*, December 11, 1942, B-19.

190. US BOB, *Standardized Government Travel Regulations as of January 30, 1942* (Washington, DC: GPO, 1942). WorldCat/OCLC No. 54977953.

191. EO 9084, March 3, 1942.

192. February 7, 1942, DR, File 5, Box 2.

193. February 6, ibid.

194. In the 1950s and '60s, Catton became a popular historian of the Civil War. His books won awards and were bestsellers.

195. Frederick Shelton, "Management's Washington Letter" (monthly column), *Nation's Business* 30, no. 5 (May 1942): 33.

196. Childs also wrote something of a puff piece profiling Smith in May: "Superman of the Budget: Harold D. Smith, Director, Has Herculean Task," *WS*, May 3, 1942, B-1. A friendly congressman inserted it in the *Congressional Record* 88, no. 9 (May 6, 1942): A1655–66.

197. The organization and management of the war effort *looked* so complicated because it necessarily *was* so complicated. The American free market economy was very decentralized, the opposite of a command and control marketplace. Bringing the business sector under control and into coordination involved many moving parts. Inevitably, there were unintended consequences, mistakes, and complaints by those on the losing side of a policy decision (Lee 2012, 204).

198. BOB press release, April 24, 1942. File: Receipts and Expenditures, Box 3, OFHDS.

199. April 25, 1942: John MacCormac, "Year's Outlay on War Rated at 70 Billions after June 30," *NYT*, 1, 6; Samuel W. Bell, "Budget Head Sees '43 deficit of 49 Billion," *NYHT*, 4; Willard Edwards, "Places 2 Year U.S. Spending at 113 Billions," *CT*, 23, 25.

200. W. H. Lawrence, "United Nations Surpass Axis Arms Production," *NYT*, April 26, 1942, E-6.

201. "Raising our Sights" (editorial), *WS*, April 26, 1942, B-2.

202. "The Budget Tells the Story of War Production" (editorial), *BS*, April 26, 1942, 10.

203. Ernest K. Lindley, "Cost of the War" (column), *WP*, April 27, 1942, 9.

204. May 9, 1942: "Fiscal Unity Urged for U.S., States," *NYT*, 19; "Head of Budget Opposes City, State Tax Cuts," *NYHT*, 12. A few weeks later, the Catholic weekly *America* commented on his speech (67, no. 7 [May 23, 1942]: 171).

205. May 16, 1942: "Keep Local Tax Rates Up, Urges U.S. Budget Chief," *CT*, 14; "Urges States Keep Fiscal Houses in Order," *WSJ*, 3. May 18, 1942: AP, "States Are Urged to Resist Demands to Reduce Taxes," *CSM*, 16.

206. AP, "State's Mayors Advised Not to Reduce Taxes," *NYHT*, June 10, 1942, 13. The conservative *WSJ* opposed his suggestion of keeping tax levels higher than absolutely necessary. "As to 'Popular Pressure'" (editorial), June 11, 1942, 4.

207. James C. Hagerty, "Landis Outlines Defense for Cities," *NYT*, June 10, 1942, 42. After the speech, Smith hurried back to DC to attend the funeral of Brian Bell, AP's Washington Bureau chief and a personal friend. Indicating the friendship, he was named one of the honorary pallbearers. However, his plane was grounded in Philadelphia and by the time he got to DC by train, he had missed the funeral. June 10, 1942, DR, File 6, Box 2; "Brian Bell Funeral Is Held in Virginia," *NYT*, June 11, 1942, 23.

208. October 31, 1942: AP: "Budget Director Says U.S. Is Doing 'Great Job,'" *NYHT*, 6; "Says Japan Ended Joy-Ride for U.S.," *BS*, 2.

209. Irving Perlmeter, "December Sets Record in U.S. Costs," *DFP*, January 3, 1942, 15.

210. Perlmeter, World Wide News, "Jobs for Ex-soldiers," *WS*, January 4, 1942, B-5.

211. Memo from Marsh to Smith, "Federal-State-Local Fiscal Cooperation," January 22, 1942. File: Fiscal, Box 1, OOI.

212. AP, "Roosevelt Requests $11,000,000,000 More for Navy," *WS*, January 18, 1942, A-1, A-5.

213. AP, "Indian Treaties Force Stretching of Priorities," *WP*, February 2, 1942, 10.

214. AP, "One of Every 102 in U.S. Soon to Be on Civil Pay Roll, *WS*, January 22, 1942, A-6; AP, "War Outlay Nears a Billion a Week," *NYT*, June 19, 1942, 7.

215. August 28, 1942, DR, File 6, Box 2; AP, "Steps Taken to Free President of Routine," *WP*, August 31, 1942, 1, 4; "President as Clerk" (editorial), *NYT*, September 1, 1942, 18.

216. "Federal Diary," *WP*, July 8, 1942, 19.

217. August 27 (note to Smith from Miss Gavaris with long phone message from Kluttz about the contest) and September 1, 1942, DR, File 6, Box 2.

218. Kluttz, *WP*: "Judges Chosen for the Post's Federal Workers Contest," September 20, 1942, 1, 6; "Navy Personnel Assistant Wins $100 War Bond for Suggestion," October 18, 1942, 1, 12; "Federal Diary's War on Waste Applauded by Magazine [*Newsweek*]," October 24, 1942, 1-B; "Federal Diary," December 8, 1942, B-1. The contest continued into 1943.

219. Lindley, "Wayne Coy, in the Slot" (column), *WP*, April 28, 1941, 9.

220. DR, Files 5 and 6, Box 2.

221. "Japan Agreed Not to Fortify Pacific Isles," *WP*, February 2, 1942, 2.

222. Robert De Vore, "Senators Pin War Losses on Smugness of Americans," *WP*, February 4, 1942, 1, 4.

223. February 4, 1942, DR, File 5, Box 2.

224. Lindley, "Defense and Security" (column), *WP*, February 22, 1942, B-7.

225. BOB, Press Release OD [Office of the Director]-4, "Revision of Federal Budget Estimates," for release October 7, 1942.

226. Jack Beall, "'43 War Budget Estimate Rises to 78 Billions," *NYHT*, October 7, 1942, 24; AP, "War Spending Up 25 Billion," *LAT*, October 8, 1942, 8; John MacCormac, "6 Billions Monthly for War," *NYT*, October 11, 1942, E-6.

227. Memo from Smith to FDR, October 7, 1942, WHM 1942, File 3, Box 4.

228. "The Roosevelt Party," *Life*, October 26, 1942, 103.

229. Ibid., 105. On September 18, 1942, Smith had sat for an interview and photo shoot with a *Time-Life* reporter and photographer (DR, File 6, Box 2). He, of course, did not know what the angle of the coverage would be.

230. Donald MacGregor, "The Belligerent Mr. Byrd," *This Week* (Sunday magazine), *NYHT*, May 31, 1942, 12–13; "Harry Byrd Wages a Nine-Year War on Waste," *BS*, SM-1.

231. "Senator Byrd's Axe" (editorial), *WP*, July 31, 1942, 12.

232. The conservative Tydings was one of the legislators FDR had tried to purge in 1938. He withstood the attack and returned as an even-more committed anti-FDR conservative. In 1950, he was successfully purged, but from his right. Senator Joseph McCarthy (R-WI) circulated a doctored photo supposedly showing Tydings being friendly to the head of the American Communist Party. Tydings lost to his largely unknown Republican opponent, making most of his ex-colleagues on the Hill very afraid of McCarthy.

233. *CR* 88, no. 1 (February 17, 1942): 1311.

234. *CR* 88, no. 5 (August 27, 1942): 6974.

235. "Navy's Red Tape Slash Praised by President," *WS*, June 12, 1942, A-1.

236. June 12, 1942, DR, File 6, Box 2.

237. June 13, 1942: AP, "7,500,000 Pounds Paper Collected in Campaign," *Wilmington (NC) Morning Star*, 2; Kluttz, "Federal Diary," *WP*, 19.

238. F. R. Kent, "Government to Cut Red Tape; Hopes to Save $1,250,000," *BS*, June 13, 1942, 11.

239. *CR* 88, no. 9 (June 23, 1942): A2391–92.

240. Kluttz, "Federal Diary," *WP*, June 29, 1942, 13.

241. AP, "92 Per Cent of U.S. Funds Go for War," *HC*, October 17, 1942, 4.

242. Louis M. Lyons, "War Takes 95¢ of Every Dollar in U.S. Budget" (column), *Boston Globe*, November 16, 1942, 15. Lyons should not be confused with the better-known gossip columnist Leonard Lyons.

243. AP, "Congress Plans Budget Talks with U.S. Agency Heads in Move to Slash Next Year's Non-war Expenditures," *WSJ*, October 31, 1942, 3.

244. There was some modest positive news that year, such as the Doolittle Raid over Tokyo (in April) and the Battle of Midway (in June).

245. The US invasion of North Africa occurred five days after the election. Had it occurred a week earlier the results of the election may well have been different.

246. "Questionnaires Strangle Business and Bring Demand for an Inquiry," *NYT*, December 2, 1942, 1, 20.

247. "1-1071-PLOF-5-NOBU-COSA-WP Is Explained," *WS*, December 3, 1942, 1-X.

248. "U.S. Will Limit Calls for Data from Industry," *NYHT*, December 20, 1942, 10; AP, "Censorship to Curb Questionnaires Sent to U.S. Businessmen," *CSM*, December 22, 1942, 15.

249. "President Hits Critics of Gain in U.S. Workers," *WS*, December 8, 1942, 1-X; "Roosevelt Hits Rumors about Soft U.S. Jobs," *WP*, December 9, 1942, 1, 16.

250. "FDR Debunks Byrd Figures," *(New York) PM*, December 9, 1942. File: Byrd Report, Box 1, OOI.

251. Bruce Boissat, "Sen. Byrd to Press Battle for Slash in U.S. Spending," *Washington Times-Herald*, December 10, 1942. Ibid.

252. "President Misled, Byrd Maintains," *NYT*, December 10, 1942, 20.

253. Frank R. Kent, "President Declared Overlooking Facts in Defense of Swollen U.S. Payrolls" (Great Game of Politics syndicated column), *WS*, December 16, 1942, A-11.

254. Memo from Smith to White House Secretary McIntyre, December 9, 1942, File 1942, Box 6, OF 79: BOB, FDR Library.

255. BOB, "Saves $3,000,000 and Time of 2,000 Employees," Press Release AM [Administrative Management] No. 7, December 10, 1942. File 1942, Box 6, OF 79: BOB.

256. December 20, 1942: "Budget Director Reports on Reclaimed Equipment," *WS*, A-21; "U.S. Reclaims $250,000 Worth of Idle Equipment," *WP*, 12; "Unused Equipment," *WSJ*, 11.

257. "President Signs Federal Pay Raise," *NYT*, December 25, 1942, 23. On December 21, 1942, the Administrative Management Division prepared a draft press release on this initiative, but it apparently was not issued. File: Administrative Management, Box 1, OOI.

258. March 24–26, and 30, April 6–7, 9, 13–15, 23, and 28, June 12, July 23, September 16, October 6 and 26, November 9–11 and 13, December 18–19, 22, 26, and 28, 1942, DR, Files 5–6, Box 2. Due to the war, Brownlow decided to cancel ASPA's annual conference, which had been tentatively scheduled for late December 1942 in Chicago. November 28, 1942, DR, File 6, Box 2.

259. May 2, June 13, and December 16, 1942, DR, Files 5–6, Box 2.

260. February 26, March 19, and March 28, 1942, DR, File 5, Box 2.

261. June 3, June 15, July 30, October 27, and November 18, 26, DR, File 6, Box 2.

262. February 12 and October 20, 1942, DR, Files 5–6, Box 2.

263. April 27 and May 1, 1942, DR, File 5, Box 2. The committee was funded by the Social Science Research Council. Strictly speaking, it was a *sub*committee of the Committee on Public Administration, a group that Smith had belonged to when he had been in Michigan.

264. November 9, 1942, DR, File 6, Box 2. The project culminated in multiple volumes issued by individual agencies as part of the series titled Historical Reports on War Administration. BOB's volume, released in 1946, focused on the development and management of the war effort (US BOB 1972). Smith was unusually attuned to history. Over lunch, Ickes had recounted to him some maneuverings about the idea of a grand shakeup of the cabinet, including appointing Ickes as both secretary of labor and head of WMC. Smith "suggested that he [Ickes] write them up, inasmuch as I [Smith] did not have the time to do so. . . . Since he will write all of this up for the benefit of historians, I am saved the task." December 4, 1942, CwP 1942, File 4, Box 3.

265. June 3, 1942, DR, File 6, Box 2.

266. October 1, ibid.

267. March 7 and November 10, 1942, DR, Files 5–6, Box 2.

268. November 11, 1942, DR, File 6, Box 2.

269. Memo from Professor Catheryn Seckler-Hudson, Chair, Department of Public Administration, American University, to the AU Budget Committee, Subject: Progress Report on the Project in "Budgeting," May 22, 1944. File: Budget and Budgeting, Box 1, OFHDS.

270. Memo from Smith to FDR, November 24, 1942, WHM 1942, File 3, Box 4.

271. December 4, 1942, CwP 1942, File 4, Box 3.

272. "Harold D. Smith Is Given Doctor's Degree," *(Pocomoke City, MD) Worcester Democrat*, June 12, 1942, 5.

273. November 18 and 20, 1942, DR, File 6, Box 2.

274. October 12, ibid.

275. Memo from Smith to FDR, November 5, 1942, WHM 1942, File 3, Box 4.

276. November 10, 1942, CwP 1942, File 4, Box 3.

277. DR, File 6, Box 2; Roosevelt Day-by-Day, FDRL. Smith's papers do not include memos summarizing these conferences with the president.

278. December 18, 1942, CwP 1942, File 4, Box 3.

279. Perlmeter, AP, "'44 Budget May Top All in World History," *WP*, December 2, 1942, B-10. The *Star* scooped the *Post* by running the AP story on its front page the day before, but it did not give Perlmeter a byline: "100-Billion-Dollar Budget Seen for Next Year," *WS*, December 1, 1942, A-1. Smith and Perlmeter talked on November 28, 1942. DR, File 6, Box 2.

280. December 18, 1942, CwP 1942, File 4, Box 3.

281. Memo from FDR to Secretary of Treasury and Director of Economic Stabilization (Byrnes), December 8, 1942. Morgenthau Diary, Book 594, 210. Morgenthau called it "a most peculiar note." He claimed Smith said AA Currie was the source of the previous year's leak. December 14, 1942, Book 596, 70–71.

282. "Morgenthau, Administration Officials Discuss New Tax Legislation and Inflation Controls," *WP*, December 11, 1942, B-7.

283. June 19, 1942, DR, File 6, Box 2.

284. Memo from Smith to FDR, July 16, 1942, WHM 1942, File 3, Box 4.

285. September 26, 1942, Ickes Diary, 7011.

286. Kluttz, "Federal Diary," *WP*, July 8, 1942, 19, ellipses in original.

287. Memo from Smith to FDR, July 16, 1942.

288. June 1942: out all day: 20, 22, 25, and 30; short days: 23, 24, and 29. July 1942: out all day: 7, 9–13, 15, 17–22, 24, and 29; short days: on 8, 14, 16, 23, and 31. August 1942: out all day: 1–12, 15, 20, 22, 27, and 29; short days: 13, 14, and 26. DR, File 6, Box 2.

289. "Mrs. Harold Smith Takes Golf Honors," *WP*, June 7, 1941, 18. As a full-time homemaker, when she signed up as a volunteer in the Office for Civilian Defense "she gave golf as her principal skill." "Mrs. Roosevelt Signs as Leaders Volunteer for Defense Service," *WS*, June 11, 1941, A-1.

290. September 26, 1942, Ickes Diary.

291. September 22, 1942, DR, File 6, Box 2.

292. October 7, ibid.

293. Out of the office all day: Saturday, October 24, and Monday, December 21, 1942. Golf: Thursday, November 19, and Friday, December 11, 1942. DR, File 6, Box 2.

Chapter 6: The Second Year of the War, 1943

1. February 16, 1944, CwP 1943–45, File 5, Box 3.

2. Memo from Smith to FDR, August 26, 1943, WHM 1943, File 4, Box 4.

3. February 13, 1943, Ickes Diary, 7435.

4. July 20, 1943, Ickes Diary, 7989.

5. August 29, 1943, Ickes Diary, 8115.

6. January 1, 1944, Ickes Diary, 8499. While dictated on New Year's Day, their lunch was on December 27, 1943.

7. January 1, 1943, DR, File 7, Box 2.

8. Memo from Bell to Morgenthau, January 2, 1943. Morgenthau Diary, Book 601, 91–92.

9. January 6, 1943, CwP, File 5, Box 3.

10. AP, "1,000-page Budget Will Be Ready for Congress Monday," *WS*, January 6, 1943, B-5.

11. Barryman, no title (cartoon), *WS*, January 7, 1943, A-1. Giegengack received the original from the cartoonist and gave it to Smith. January 18, 1943, DR, File 7, Box 2.

12. 57 *Stat.* 170.

13. "U.S. Agencies Told to Give Up Surplus Tires," *WP*, February 7, 1943, 11.

14. *CR* 89, no. 3 (April 8, 1943): 3138. *CSM* had republished the item from the *World Telegram*.

15. Memo from Howard Stone to Miss Gavaris, "Christian Science Monitor Article: 'The Swollen White House Budget,'" April 24, 1943. File: White House Budget, Box 4, OFHDS.

16. "U.S. Purchase of 28 Office Items Barred," *WP*, May 26, 1943, 2.

17. Morgenthau refused to sign it until Byrd agreed to delete from the report "certain caustic adjectives" criticizing the administration. "300,000 Cut in U.S. Pay Roll Asked," *CSM*, June 17, 1943, 9.

18. Sol Taishoff, "House Probe Claims FCC a War Hindrance," *Broadcasting* 25, no. 1 (July 5, 1943): 9–10, 45–48.

19. Note the oddity of the request not coming, as would be expected, from the chair of the committee, but rather from a minority party member. This indicates the unusually large role of the House Republican minority in pursuing the investigation.

20. Memo from Smith to FDR, June 26, 1943, WHM 1943, File 4, Box 4.

21. July 10, 1943: Winifred Mallon, "President Bars Data for Inquiry," *NYT*, 1, 7; William Moore, "F.D.R. Gag Edict Balks Congress Inquiry into FCC," *CT*, 10.

22. "Cox Probe to Charge Fly with Contempt," *Broadcasting* 25, no. 11 (September 13, 1943): 9.

23. Drew Pearson, "Washington Merry-Go-Round" (syndicated column), *WP*, November 24, 1943, B-7.

24. October 30, 1943: Samuel B. Bledsoe, "Eccles Offers Tax of $13,800,000,000," *NYT*, 1; AP, "Wartime Supertax Plan Killed by House Group," *LAT*, 5.

25. November 28, 1943: Mary Spargo, "Senate Seen Holding Tax at 2 Billion," *WP*, 1, 12; J. A. Fox, "Budget Chief Smith Denies Army Can Effect Savings of 13 Billion," *WS*, A-1, A-18. The *Star* reported that Smith's explanations were so confusing that after his testimony he felt compelled to issue a "clarifying statement."

26. "The Mystery of the Missing 13 Billion Dollars" (cartoon), *WS*, November 30, 1943, A-1.

27. 58 *Stat.* 21-94.

28. The committee established Truman's political image. The investigation was not flamboyant, did not make wild charges, and avoided any hint of partisan or ideological bias. While often critical of individual projects and waste, Truman did not use the investigation as an anti-FDR PR machine. Instead, he was largely methodical, fact-based, and focused on wasteful spending—all the while carefully avoiding interfering in strictly military operations.

29. AP, "Ickes Would 'Junk' Army Oil Project," *WP*, November 23, 1943, 1.

30. "The Canol Project" (editorial), *HC*, November 30, 1943, 10.

31. "Randolph Asks Action to Put Capital Garage on Economical Basis," *WS*, November 24, 1943, B-1.

32. Anne Hagner, "Budget Chief Calls Garage Setup Sound," *WP*, November 25, 1943, B-1.

33. Historically, there is only a short line between Taber's request for names and congressional Republicans demanding that the Truman administration identify the diplomats who "lost" China.

34. Samuel W. Bell, "U.S. Agencies' Funds Cut 82% in Committee," *NYHT*, November 5, 1943, 1.

35. AP, "Budget Bureau Is Told Not to Ask Extra Money," *Atlanta Constitution*, December 5, 1943, 4-A.

36. *CR* 89, no. 8 (December 7, 1943): 10355.

37. Memo re Senator Hayden's conversation, December 1, 1943, DR, File 7, Box 2.

38. *CR* 89, no. 8 (December 7, 1943): 10362.

39. "Senate Votes Curb on Excess Funds," *NYT*, December 9, 1943, 23. For the text of the Senate-approved amendment, see *CR* 89, no. 8 (December 16, 1943): 10780.

40. December 10, 1943, DR, File 7, Box 2.

41. "Notes on Congressional Contacts," December 11, 1943, DR, File 7, Box 2.

42. Ibid.

43. *CR* 89, no. 8 (December 16, 1943): 10780–81. The large number of members not voting (128) reflected the routine custom of skipping floor debates on amendments.

44. 57 *Stat.* 613.

45. EO 9294, January 4, 1943.

46. EO 9341, May 13, 1943.

47. EO 9412, December 27, 1943. For a more detailed explanation, see Roosevelt 1969, 1943: 567–69.

48. EO 9300, February 5, 1943.

49. These statistics do not cover cases that agencies handled internally or hiring applications rejected by the CSC. For examples of cases that did not rise to the level of the Interdepartmental Committee, see Lee 2018a (183–88, 212–14, 227–28).

50. EO 9312, March 9, 1943.

51. EO 9332, April 19, 1943.

52. EO 9346, May 27, 1943.

53. EO 9357, June 30, 1943.

54. EO 9350, June 10, 1943.

55. EO 9363, July 23, 1943.

56. February 23 and 25, March 2, May 20, 1943, DR, File 7, Box 2.

57. Kluttz, "Federal Diary," *WP*, July 21, 1943, B-1.

58. Drew Pearson, "Washington Merry-Go-Round" (syndicated column), *WP*, July 22, 1943, 8.

59. EO 9361, July 15, 1943.

60. EO 9380, September 25, 1943.

61. "Notes on Navy Organization, Covering November 2–3 Meetings," DR, File 7, Box 2.

62. EO 9347, May 27, 1943.

63. Somers interviewed Smith on August 12, 1946 (1969, 49n3). However, his notes from the interview are missing from the Somers Papers at Yale. Email from Jessica Becker, Public Services, Manuscripts and Archives, Yale University Library, February 2, 2019. Author's files.

64. Somers interview with Wayne Coy, August 12, 1946, Somers Papers, Yale University Library.

65. August 29, 1943, Ickes Diary, 8115.

66. November 4, 1943, DR, File 7, Box 2.

67. Memo from Smith to Justice Byrnes, November 5, 1943, WHM 1943, File 4, Box 4.

68. Letter from Smith to Byrnes, November 8, 1943, ibid.

69. November 9, 1943, DR, File 7, Box 2.

70. John H. Crider, "Byrnes Assumes Charge of Framing New Tax Policy," *NYT*, June 10, 1943, 1, 15.

71. "Byrnes Calls Conference on Tax Strategy," *WP*, June 10, 1942, 4.

72. John H. Crider, "Pay-as-You-Go Tax Is Signed into Law," *NYT*, June 11, 1943, 17.

73. "360 War Dept. Jobs Shift to Philadelphia," *WP*, January 2, 1943, B-1.

74. "5000 Houses Released by Removal Plan," *WP*, January 3, 1943, 12.

75. "Shift Veterans' Offices," *NYT*, May 1, 1943, 16.

76. Kluttz, "Federal Diary," *WP*, May 10, 1943, B-1. Kluttz did not attribute his source, but it likely was Smith or Marsh.

77. Blair Moody, "Mr. Smith Doubles for Roosevelt," *Saturday Evening Post*, March 27, 1943, 58.

78. "The Institutional Presidency: Questions/Discussion" (transcript), 53. Conference on the Institutional Presidency, April 11–13, 1974, National Academy of Public Administration (typescript, spiral-bound). Daniel E. Bell Papers, Kennedy Presidential Library. Jones did not provide any dates of those conversations, except that they occurred after he left BOB and was in military service.

79. North American Newspaper Alliance (news service), "Brown to Remake the OPA Command," *NYT*, June 17, 1943, 9.

80. July 22 and 24, 1943, DR, File 7, Box 2. In part, this related to social and recreational facilities provided in congested production areas (discussed later).

81. October 18, ibid.

82. EO 9301, February 9, 1943.

83. EO 9384, October 4, 1943. Reprinted in *CR* 90, no. 8 (March 2, 1944): A1045.

84. EO 9404, December 17, 1943.

85. EO 9411, December 23, 1943.

86. "Summary of Director's Remarks at Staff Meeting, Room 474, State Department Building, 4:00 PM," January 27, 1943, DR, File 7, Box 2.

87. May 11, 1939, DM April–May 1939, File 1, Box 1. For narrative simplicity, this section covers the story of the field service when Smith headed BOB, instead of limiting it to events in 1943.

88. It was relatively common at the time for other federal agencies to use the Fed's districts for their own field and regional offices (Lee 2012, 126, 131).

89. 58 *Stat.* 362.

90. 59 *Stat.* 107.

91. FY 1947: 60 *Stat.* 61; FY 1948: 61 *Stat.* 586.

92. For narrative simplicity, this section covers the full story of the committee's work, instead of limiting it to events in 1943.

93. Moses started out his career in the 1920s as a good-government activist and civil service reformer. By WWII, he was New York City's park commissioner. Moses's later negative reputation as the construction czar for multiple state and municipal public authorities was recounted in Robert Caro's 1974 *The Power Broker: Robert Moses and the Fall of New York*. Caro contrasted the public administration theory that independent authorities were ideal because they would be free from politics with Moses's arrogant disregard for the public interest, secret favors and deals with politicians and powerful interests, and the lack of accountability for his actions.

94. February 23, March 15, 24, and 30, April 2, 1943, DR, File 7, Box 2.

95. Memo from Smith to FDR, April 6, 1943, WHM 1943, File 4, Box 4.

96. EO 9327, April 7, 1943, emphasis added.

97. "Board Created for War-Congested Districts," *WP*, April 15, 1943, 3.

98. AP, "Board Is Set Up by Roosevelt to Aid War on Vice," *NYHT*, April 9, 1943, 20.

99. "Agency to Clear Way for Building," Real Estate and Industry Section, *LAT*, April 25, 1943, 16.

100. Frank R. Kent, "Great Game of Politics" (syndicated column), *WSJ*, June 3, 1943, 6.

101. April 13, 1943, DR, File 7, Box 2.

102. AP, "Gill, Former WPA Aide, to Assist Budget Chief," *WS*, May 6, 1943, B-1.

103. Smith had known him at least since the mid-thirties. For example, Smith arranged for Gill to address MML's 1934 annual conference. Gill briefed them on new federal relief programs and how they could help municipalities facing enormous welfare costs. At the time, the agency was called the Federal Emergency Relief

Administration (FERA), later renamed WPA. Gill, "The Federal Relief Problem," *Proceedings of the Michigan Municipal League Thirty-Sixth Annual Convention, Held at St. Joseph-Benton Harbor, Michigan, October 3, 4, and 15, 1934*, 16–22 (Ann Arbor: MML).

104. Memo from Smith to FDR, May 17, 1943, WHM 1943, File 4, Box 4.

105. Joseph H. Short, "Federal Group Seeks to Speed Relief to War-Crowded Areas," *BS*, June 20, 1943, 13.

106. For example: May 15, June 4, July 22, August 9, September 8, October 4, November 19, and December 16, 1943, DR, File 7, Box 2.

107. In June, there had been major racial violence in Detroit (mostly Whites against Blacks), requiring federal troops to restore order.

108. "Conference with John Ballenger, Detroit Commissioner of Public Welfare, October 11, 1943, in Detroit," DR, File 7, Box 2. Smith probably knew him from when he headed MML and then as state budget director.

109. "Conference with Sherry Reeder, Federal Public Housing Authority Office in Detroit, October 11, 1943, in Detroit," ibid.

110. *NYT*: "Says Norfolk Jam is War-Long Crisis," December 22, 1943, 13; C. P. Trussell, "Neglect Charged in Coast War Area," December 31, 1943, 7.

111. "Congested Areas Committee Helps Meet Many Needs," *National Municipal Review* 33, no. 3 (March 1944): 139–40.

112. 58 *Stat.* 535. It was a provision in the National War Agency Appropriation Act of 1945, signed on June 28, 1944. To give context to the political environment on the Hill, two weeks later Roosevelt confirmed that he would run for a fourth term.

113. For a pro-FDR summary of the committee's work that was written by Sam Rosenman, his outside advisor, see Roosevelt 1969, 1943: 146–48.

114. November 10, 1943, DR, File 7, Box 2.

115. Division of Administrative Management, BOB, "Organization and Responsibility for Personnel Administration," *[Public] Personnel Administration* 5, no. 9 (April 1943): 3–5.

116. Donald C. Stone, "Administrative Aspects of World Organization," paper presented at the fourth conference on Science, Philosophy, and Religion, New York, September 12, 1943. File: Administrative Management, Box 1, OOI.

117. Memo from F. J. Lawton, Administrative Assistant [to the Director], to All Staff Members, "Clearance of Articles and Speeches," September 1943 [draft]. File: Speech Clearance, Box 1, OOI.

118. February 16 and November 17, 1943, DR, File 7, Box 2.

119. February 16 and October 19, ibid.

120. Brownlow: January 12, February 18, April 6 and 17, September 29, December 14, 1943. Gulick: February 16, March 4, August 31, 1943, ibid.

121. July 6, ibid. This summary of his talk was likely prepared by his secretary, who must have been in the room.

122. His opinion was not a one-off or throwaway line. In 1944, he talked to Harvard professor Pendleton Herring urging that Harvard consider doing this. December 29, 1944, DR, File 8, Box 2.

123. Eleanor Roosevelt, "My Day" (syndicated column), *DFP*, July 23, 1943, 9.

124. AP, "Burdens of World War I Dwarfed by Those of II," *(Adrian, MI) Daily Telegram*, October 9, 1943, 1; AP, "Budget Director Says U.S. War Output Is Greatest in History," *WS*, October 8, 1943, A-11.

125. Memo from Marsh to Smith, "Article for the Chilean Scientific Congress," October 1, 1943. File: Smith, Harold D.—Director—Misc., Box 3, OFHDS. The previous year, Smith had been one of the honored guests at a luncheon hosted by Chile's ambassador to the US ("Chileans to Fete Van Wagoners at Luncheon," *WP*, January 22, 1942, 14). It is possible that this modest interaction contributed to a positive disposition to accept the invitation to submit a paper for the conference.

126. John H. Crider, "Roosevelt Asks More War Taxes, Savings, or Both," August 1, 1943, 1, 30; Robert C. Albright, "100-Billion War Budget Emphasizes Navy Needs," *WP*, August 1, 1943, 1, 9; "President Renews Demand for More 'Taxes, Savings, or Both' to Help Stabilize Nation's Cost of Living," *WSJ*, August 2, 1943, 3.

127. August 1, 1943: "Text of the President's Statement on Summation of the 1944 Federal Budget," *NYT*, 30; "President Submits Summation of 1944 Budget, Explaining War Estimates," *WP*, 9.

128. "Army Studies Veterans' Care after War," *WP*, April 8, 1943, 19.

129. "Year's War Cost to Be Cut 8 Billion, Budget Head Says," *NYT*, November 28, 1943, 1, 28.

130. Memo from Marsh to Smith, "Newspaper Release on Personnel Ceilings," December 27, 1943. File: Personnel Ceilings, Box 2, OOI. December 31, 1943: "Federal Civilian Jobs 197,512 Fewer Today than on June 30," *WS*, B-1; Paul W. Ward, "90,373 Lose Overtime Pay," *BS*, 3.

131. AP, "Tax Conferees to Hear Plan of Budget Director," *NYHT*, February 9, 1943, 16. It was probably written by Perlmeter, who had called Smith the day before. February 8, 1943, DR, File 7, Box 2.

132. "Our Form of Government," part 5 of "The United States in a New World," Supplement to *Fortune* 28 (November 1943), 6.

133. The idea of making personnel management an executive duty similar to budgeting, instead of the responsibility of an apolitical and independent commission, dated back to President Taft's Commission on Economy and Efficiency. FDR sought to include it in the bill implementing the Brownlow Committee report, but was defeated in the House of Representatives in 1938 by a vote of 204–196 (Lee 2016a, 58).

134. The reporter had shared a draft of his report with Smith in early October. Smith quickly protested the idea of reverting back to Treasury, but to no

avail. Letter from Smith to Hubert Kay, *Fortune* magazine, October 4, 1943. File: Fortune Magazine, Box 2, OFHDS.

135. "Budget Chief Smith Figures in Other Big Official Planning Too," *WSJ*, January 11, 1943, 1, 5.

136. Blair Moody, "Mr. Smith Doubles for Roosevelt," *Saturday Evening Post*, March 27, 1943, 24.

137. The photographer for the piece was Ollie Atkins, years later the official White House photographer for President Nixon.

138. Moody strained to make Smith's work more tangible to readers and to come up with stories that captured his activities. When preparing the piece, he "requested more anecdotes to illustrate the points made." November 7, 1942, DR, File 6, Box 2.

139. Moody, "Smith Doubles for Roosevelt," 58.

140. "The General Manager," *Time*, June 14, 1943, 23–24.

141. July 16, 1943, DR, File 7, Box 2.

142. Walter Lippmann, "And Then" (Today and Tomorrow syndicated column), *WP*, July 17, 1943, 5.

143. Baukhage, "Bureau of the Budget Assumes New Legislative Importance" (Washington Digest syndicated column), *(Rising Sun, MD) Midland Journal*, January 22, 1943, 2. He only used his last name for his byline, a common practice in journalism earlier in the century. His full name was Hilmar Robert Baukhage.

144. Lee Carson, International News Services, "Wife Gives Spending Money to Director of U.S. Budget, Who Operates in Billions," *Cincinnati Enquirer*, February 14, 1943, 40.

145. Jay Franklin, "F.D.R. and His Friends," *Cosmopolitan* 114, no. 5 (May 1943): 97. Franklin was one of the few columnists and feature writers who was favorable to FDR.

146. James Thrasher, "Washington Column" (syndicated column), *Wilmington (NC) Morning Star*, September 29, 1943, 4.

147. Frank I. Weller, AP, "Budget Director Smith Keeps Tab on Government Billions," *New Orleans Times-Picayune*, November 1, 1943. Located in University of Michigan Alumni Records' Necrology Files.

148. Edwin Cox, "Private Lives" (syndicated feature), *Winnipeg (MB) Tribune*, May 22, 1943, 35, underlining in original.

149. "Test Your Facts," *CT*, June 21, 1943, 6, 33. The question was probably a bit harder than usual given that Coy was BOB's assistant director.

150. [J. L.] Parrish, *CT*, August 5, 1943, 12. The others were Coy, Frankfurter, Cohen (identified as "Benny the Brain"), Rosenman, and Hopkins. Oddly, Smith was identified as "Dewey Smith." Dewey was indeed his middle name, but he never used it, always signing letters and documents as Harold D. Smith.

151. January 2, 1943, DR, File 7, Box 2.

152. January 7, ibid.

153. February 6, ibid.

154. March 1, ibid.

155. April 4, ibid.

156. May 18, ibid.

157. August 26, ibid.

158. December 27, ibid.

159. April 9, ibid. See next chapter for a review of the kinds of comments Marsh included in his print summaries of FDR's press conferences.

160. September 14, ibid.

161. Lunches: February 26 (at Marsh's home), March 12, April 3, 14, and 21, July 9 and 22, October 29 (at Marsh's), November 29, and December 20, 1943. Dinners: January 1, March 15, July 6 and August 18 (at Marsh's), November 17, and December 29, 1943 (including Mrs. Marsh). Also, the last entry in Smith's schedule for May 8 lists an opaque "Left the office and went out to call on Howard Marsh." Perhaps Marsh had been ill and confined to bed. DR, File 7, Box 2.

162. Respectively: April 9 and 14, ibid.

163. September 16, ibid.

164. March 18 and 29, 1943, DR, File 7, Box 2.

165. April 23, ibid.

166. July 20, 1943, Ickes Diary, 7989.

167. August 30, 1943, DR, File 7, Box 2. Vitamin B_1 comes from eating meat, nuts, and whole grains. If his doctors had diagnosed that he needed this supplement, it hints at deficiencies in Smith's routine diet. Symptoms from a B_1 deficiency can include fatigue, irritability, and changes in heart rate.

168. September 23, ibid. The next year, FDR's White House doctor asked Bruenn to examine Roosevelt's seemingly never-ending ill health. Bruenn quickly diagnosed the president's very severe heart condition and prescribed treatments to try to bring him back from the brink. From that point, Bruenn attended to FDR full-time through to his death, including traveling with him to Yalta.

169. November 9, ibid.

170. November 29, ibid.

171. December 9, ibid.

172. August 29, 1943, Ickes Diary, 8115.

173. That Smith liked Coy personally as well as professionally was demonstrated when both occasionally took the afternoon off to play golf. September 16, November 18, 1943, DR, File 7, Box 2.

174. May 18, ibid.

175. Kluttz, "Federal Diary," WP, August 11, 1943, B-1.

176. May 17 and October 4, 1943, DR, File 7, Box 2.

177. December 20, ibid.

178. April 9, 1943, CwP 1943–45, File 5, Box 3.

179. Smith's salary of $10,000 was relatively high for a senior federal official. But he had four children and was facing the costs of sending them to college. When he resigned from BOB in mid-1946, he said explicitly he needed a position with a higher salary. After leaving government, he wrote an article in the *NYT Sunday Magazine* on the problem of (relatively) low salaries for senior officials (Smith 1946a).

180. "Farm as a Laboratory: Harold D. Smith, Who Was Born in Kansas, to Test His Theories of Scientific Management in Historic Area," *Kansas City (KS) Star*, June 25, 1943, 23; Sidney Shalett, "Capital Portrait," *NYT Sunday Magazine*, May 19, 1946, SM-16.

181. April 24, 1943, DR, File 7, Box 2.

182. May 9, 1943, Ickes Diary, 7732.

183. June 3, 1943, CwP 1943–45, File 5, Box 3.

184. AP, "Differences in Rationing Worked Out," *HC*, July 11, 1943, 12. The feature was a grab bag of minor new tidbits from all of AP's Washington staff. Presumably, this came from Perlmeter.

185. DR, File 7, Box 2.

186. For a photo of Smith with Gypsy King, see L. Smith 2003, 16.

187. September 3, 1943, DR, File 7, Box 2. Two weeks later, he was still thinking about it and talked to the owner over the phone. September 17, ibid.

188. November 5, ibid.

189. November 20, ibid.

190. November 8, ibid.

191. November 15, ibid.

192. November 19, ibid.

193. November 24, ibid.

194. November 8, ibid.

195. April 10 and May 12, ibid.

196. April 5, 17, ibid. The council was an independent nonprofit funded by the Rockefellers to experiment with ways to consolidate delivery of all government services at the local level. Smith chaired the council while at BOB and after.

197. April 8, 17, ibid.

198. August 17, ibid.

199. April 24, ibid.

200. June 22, ibid.

201. September 13, 14, 18, 21, November 18, December 13, ibid.

202. November 16, ibid.

203. November 4, 1943, CwP 1943–45, File 5, Box 3.

204. November 11, ibid.

205. In the retrospect of history, this was perhaps an early indication of FDR's gradually diminishing energy due to his health. Hamilton (2016; 2019), however, argued that FDR was simply keeping his focus on the major strategic policy decisions necessary to win the war. These included keeping D-Day on track

for spring 1944 by fending off Churchill's seemingly endless opposition (masked as concerns), resisting any further major military adventures in the Mediterranean despite Churchill's repeated unorthodox schemes, and keeping Stalin in the alliance to prevent a sudden separate peace deal with Hitler and to maintain Stalin's promise to declare war on Japan after Germany surrendered.

206. December 31, 1943, DR, File 7, Box 2.

207. December 27, ibid.

208. December 28, ibid.

209. December 27, ibid.

Chapter 7: The Third Year of the War and Fourth Term-Campaign, 1944

1. November 4, 1943, CwP 1943–45, File 5, Box 3.

2. January 7, 1944, ibid. A biographer cited Smith's account because it so tangibly conveyed Roosevelt's decline (Hamilton 2019, 204).

3. Ibid.

4. Stenographic record of phone call from Morgenthau to Smith, January 8, 1944, Morgenthau Diary, Book 692, 165–67.

5. Stenographic record of phone call from Morgenthau to Ted Gamble, ibid., 192–93.

6. January 12, 1944, DR, File 8, Box 2.

7. J. A. Fox, "Congress Meets; Message to Be Sent Tomorrow," *WS*, January 10, 1944, A-1; C. P. Trussell, "Congress Returns from Home Front," *NYT*, January 11, 1944, 17.

8. January 11, 1944: Paul W. Ward, "President's Message to Be by Proxy," *BS*, 1; Don Cook, "Roosevelt's Message to Be Wide in Scope," *NYHT*, 1.

9. July 13, 1944, CwP 1943–45, File 5, Box 3. Smith held a press conference on August 1 to release the budget summation.

10. November 27, ibid.

11. CwP 1943–45, File 5, Box 3.

12. This was not make-work. For example, at a press conference in August, FDR talked about wanting to improve education for youth in the military. Smith quickly asked the White House for the verbatim transcript to be sure he knew exactly what FDR had said. August 22, 1944, DR, File 8, Box 2. Then he sent a memo to FDR filling him in on what BOB was already doing about it based on the president's May request. Memo from Smith to FDR, "Education and Military Training," August 24, 1944, WHM 1944, File 5, Box 4.

13. File: White House Press Conferences, Box 4, OFHDS.

14. August 6, 1944, Ickes Diary, 9150, emphasis added.

15. September 24, ibid., 9233.

16. October 6, ibid., 9276.

17. *CR* 90, no. 2 (March 16, 1944): 2654.

18. Memo from Smith to FDR, "Subject for Discussion with Congressional Leaders," May 26, 1944. WHM 1944, File 5, Box 4.

19. *CR* 90, no. 5 (June 15, 1944): 5969; 58 *Stat.* 362.

20. EO 9417, January 22, 1944.

21. EO 9425, February 19, 1944; EO 9427, February 24, 1944.

22. June 29, 1944, DR, File 8, Box 2.

23. Memo from Smith to Rosenman, June 30, 1944, WHM 1944, File 5, Box 4.

24. 58 *Stat.* 649–71.

25. Mary Spargo, "Wadsworth Urges Army, Navy Merger as Hearings Recess," *WP*, May 20, 1944, 1, 2; "Preparedness" (editorial), *WP*, May 25, 1944, 8; AP, "Bill Asks Merger of Armed Forces," *NYT*, May 29, 1944, 1; AP, "Woodrum Warns against Hasty Move for Military Merger," *WS*, May 29, 1944, A-2. When the question became more pressing after the end of the war, *Congressional Digest* reprinted Smith's 1944 testimony as a cogent statement of the "pro" side of the debate (24, no. 12 [December 1945]: 308–12).

26. May 19, 1944, DR, File 8, Box 2.

27. The published committee hearing has a typo in the title of Smith's statement, practically a political Freudian slip by his conservative opponents: "Governing Panning [*sic*] for a High Level of Employment in the Post-War Period" (US House 1944d, 407).

28. May 31, 1944, DR, File 8, Box 2; "Planning Employment" (editorial), *WP*, July 5, 1944, 6.

29. BOB staff debated in-house whether to publicize the brochure with a press release consisting of a public letter to the president from Smith. They apparently decided not to recommend it. Memo from E. B. Young to Marsh, January 22, 1944. File: Administrative Management, Box 1, OOI.

30. Memo from Smith to FDR, March 17, 1944, WHM 1944, File 5, Box 4.

31. Letter from Marsh to Jack Durham, News Desk, OWI, April 7, 1944. File: OWI—Correspondence, Box 2, OOI.

32. John F. Cramer, "Budget Bureau Tries to Establish Better Management Methods" ("9 to 4:30" daily column), *Washington Daily News*, n.d. (probably late March or early April 1944), ibid.

33. July 19, 1944, DR, File 8, Box 2.

34. November 7, ibid.

35. On the other hand, Marsh recommended proceeding carefully. He reminded Stone, "We have both seen graphic work put out by agencies which is ridiculed by the press and the public." Memo from Marsh to Stone, "Selling Bureau Wares," September 7, 1944. File: Administrative Management, Box 1, OOI.

36. November 3, 1944, DR, File 8, Box 2.

37. November 10, ibid.

38. November 17, ibid.

39. 58 *Stat.* 854.

40. July 13, November 16 and 27, 1944, CwP 1943–45, File 5, Box 3.

41. February 16, ibid.; February 14–17, 1944, DR, File 8, Box 2. In March, Marsh drafted a press release to promote BOB's pro-planning position, but concluded that "the Bureau's good work could possibly be twisted by opponents." He urged caution. Given that "we would have no control over the final form of the publicity, the reasons for it [the press release] should be quite strong if the risks are to be incurred." Memo from Marsh to AA Lawton, "Budget Bureau Policy on Missouri River," March 11, 1944, File: Speech Clearance, Box 1, OOI.

42. Letter from FDR to Congressman Mansfield, February 22, 1944. File: WHM 1944, File 5, Box 4.

43. June 6 and 16, 1944, DR, File 8, Box 2.

44. March 13, 1944, CwP 1943–45, File 5, Box 3.

45. April 26, 1944, DR, File 8, Box 2.

46. Memo from Smith to FDR, April 27, 1944, WHM 1944, File 5, Box 4.

47. May 2, 1944, DR, File 8, Box 2.

48. July 13, 1944, CwP 1943–45, File 5, Box 3.

49. January 10 and 11, 1944, DR, File 8, Box 2.

50. January 13 and 14, ibid.

51. "Listeners Choice," *CT*, January 16, 1944, SW-5.

52. "Washington Reports on Rationing" (ad), January 16, 1944: *WP*, S-13; *WS*, C-10.

53. Letter (on *Newsweek* stationery) from Lindley to Smith, January 19, 1944. File: Articles and Speeches by the Director, Box 1, OFHDS.

54. December 31, 1943, DR, File 7, Box 2.

55. January 10, 1944, DR, File 8, Box 2.

56. January 11, ibid.

57. November 16, ibid.

58. February 2, 1944: AP, "States Asked to Plan for Public Works," *CSM*, 16. February 3, 1944: "Public Works Role after War Defined," *NYT*, 20; UP, "U.S. Won't Finance Any Unsound Public Works, Budget Head Promises," *WSJ*, 1.

59. "More Planning Is Urged in the President's Office," *NYHT*, February 18, 1944, 17.

60. File: Articles and Speeches by the Director, Box 1, OFHDS.

61. Indicating the significance of Smith's theme to the academic discipline, Waldo included it in his 1953 reader (308–17).

62. February 23, 1944, DR, File 8, Box 2.

63. "Radio Today," *NYT*, August 1, 1944, 29.

64. Letter from Marsh to OWI, July 22, 1944, File: Speech Clearance, Box 1, OOI.

65. July 12, 1944, DR, File 8, Box 2.

66. September 1 and December 6, ibid.

67. December 29, ibid.

68. March 20–June 29, 1944, File: Speech Clearance, Box 1, OOI.

69. Memo from Marsh to Thomas E. Blake, White House Press Office, "Ticker Tape Announcement," July 31, 1944. File: Speech Clearance, Box 1, OOI.

70. "Partial list of press present at conference," August 1, 1944, DR, File 8, Box 2.

71. J. A. Fox, "Revised Budget Based on Early Nazi Defeat, Longer War on Japs," WS, August 2, 1944, A-1, A-4. August 3, 1944: Lansing Warren, "War Successes Cut Budget 3 Billions," NYT, 1, 4 (with the full text of the BOB report on p. 5); Don Cook, "5 Billion Added to Estimates of U.S. Receipts," NYHT, 1-A, 8-A (with the full text of the BOB report on p. 8-A); UP, "Budget Bureau Forecasts $3 Billion Cut in Year's War Costs on Hope of Beating Nazis by Next Summer," WSJ, 4; AP, "This Year's War Bill Placed at 90 Billion," Atlanta Constitution, 11.

72. "Revised Budget Estimates" (editorial), NYHT, August 9, 1944, 18.

73. "A Smaller Budget" (editorial), HC, August 4, 1944, 10.

74. "The Spenders Take Over" (editorial), CT, August 12, 1944, 8.

75. September 11, 1944, DR, File 8, Box 2.

76. Herbert Corey, "Man Who Holds the Purse Strings," Nation's Business 32, no. 11 (November 1944): 36, 39–42.

77. Paul Ford, "Private Lives" (syndicated feature), WS, September 23, 1944, B-9.

78. April 18, 1944, DR, File 8, Box 2. Ickes framed it differently. He agreed with Smith that if Smith sent the Ickes proposal to the president for approval, then "the President would start it on a round of the agencies interested, which might mean serious trouble." April 23, 1944, Ickes Diary, 8804.

79. Memo from Smith to FDR, May 2, 1944, "Personal and Confidential," WHM 1944, File 5, Box 4. It is hard to tell if the memo was intended to be humorous or, even though worded lightheartedly, was a serious suggestion. (Willkie died in October.) FDR quickly nominated Under Secretary James Forrestal as secretary. Although a Wall Street financier, he was a Democrat.

80. May 9, 1944, CwP 1943–45, File 5, Box 3.

81. July 13, ibid.

82. July 14, 1944, DR, File 8, Box 2.

83. Memo from Marsh to Curran, June 29, 1944. File: Speech Clearance, Box 1, OOI.

84. July 16, 1944, Ickes Diary, 9084.

85. August 6, ibid., 9150.

86. September 24, ibid., 9233.

87. Memo from Marsh to Appleby, August 28, 1944. File: Speech Clearance, Box 1, OOI.

88. August 30, 1944: "Census of '44 Industry Ordered by Roosevelt to Cover War Peak," *NYHT*, 1, 23; "President Orders Economic Census," *NYT*, 18; "Reconversion Census Desired by Roosevelt," *WP*, 4; George B. Bryant, Jr., "Roosevelt Orders Budget Bureau to Make Economic Survey for Post-war Planning," *WSJ*, 2.

89. C. P. Trussell, "President Orders Survey to Plan War Agency Cuts," *NYT*, September 20, 1944, 1, 17. Some other examples of coverage: UP, "Roosevelt Orders Budget Bureau Plan Civil Worker Demobilization," *(Long Island, NY) Newsday*, September 19, 1944, 28; AP, "War Agencies Warned to Plan for Liquidation," *Atlanta Constitution*, September 20, 1944, 2; "Budget Bureau Asks Agencies to Submit Plans to Cut Personnel, Appropriations Now and at V-E Day," *WSJ*, September 25, 1944, 8.

90. "Byrd Attacks F.D.R. Delay in Pay Roll Cuts," *CT*, September 20, 1944, 33.

91. August 31, 1944, CwP 1943–45, File 5, Box 3.

92. Cover memo from Smith to Rosenman, October 11, 1944, WHM 1944, File 5, Box 4.

93. Memo from Smith to Rosenman, October 26, 1944. Attachment: "Draft of statement, 'Postwar Employment' (Strictly Confidential)," October 9, 1944. One-page summary entitled, "Summary of Postwar Employment Report." WHM 1944, File 5, Box 4.

94. "Governor Dewey's Address in Minneapolis on Forging Policy Harmony" (text of speech), *NYT*, October 25, 1944, 14.

95. Cover memo from Appleby to Rosenman, October 26, 1944, and attached draft statement (no author, title, or date). File: White House—Misc., Box 4, OFHDS.

96. October 26, 1944, DR, File 8, Box 2.

97. October 27, 1944: "White House 'Refutes' Dewey on Budget," *WP*, 10; "White House Lets Hannegan Reply to Dewey; Budget Bureau Assails Report on War Slash," *NYT*, 13; AP, "Dewey Ignored 800% Boost in War Budget, White House Says," *WS*, A-15.

98. Perhaps political hyperbole, but it was a very large crowd. According to the *Times*, 110,000 people were in Soldier Field and 150,000 more outside, listening on loudspeakers. C. P. Trussell, "President Offers Post-war Program for Aiding Business," *NYT*, October 29, 1944, 1.

99. October 30, 1944, CwP 1943–45, File 5, Box 3.

100. Letter from Smith to FDR, November 9, 1944, WHM 1944, File 5, Box 4.

101. November 10, 1944, DR, File 8, Box 2.

102. "Notes on Wisconsin—Chicago trip, July 1944," ibid.

103. July 20 and 22, ibid.

104. January 20, ibid.

105. January 22, ibid.

106. January 30, 1945, DR, File 9, Box 2.

107. Notwithstanding the title of the HR organization, it was for *public* personnel officers and mostly those based in DC.

108. September 26 and 27, 1944, DR, File 8, Box 2.

109. Kluttz, "Federal Diary," *WP*, January 19, 1945, 7.

110. "Outline for Discussion on Improvement of Budget Justifications," February 1947; "Report of the Committee on Work Measurement and Its Practical Application in Budget Presentation," December 1947. Both documents are in the collection of the National Agricultural Library. See also Virginia L. Fisher, "Conference Training in Federal Budgeting," *PAR* 9, no. 4 (Autumn 1949): 267. (Fisher worked in the Division of Administrative Management.)

111. In the 1970s, the conference helped found a successor organization, the American Association for Budget and Program Analysis.

112. January 19, April 13 and 25, 1944, DR, File 8, Box 2. The April 13 appointment was made at the last minute, likely due to something that unexpectedly became pressing, perhaps overnight. Smith's secretary noted that he called her at 9:45 a.m. and told her he was at the hospital and would be there "for a while in the morning."

113. November 13, ibid.

114. November 20–21, ibid.

115. April 23 and May 20, 1944, Ickes Diary, 8804, 8913.

116. July 16, ibid., 9083.

117. February 28, 1944, DR, File 8, Box 2.

118. For example: February 26–28 (Saturday–Monday), March 26 (Saturday), April 1 (Saturday), April 20–23 (Thursday–Sunday), May 27 (Saturday), June 20 (Tuesday), August 26 (Saturday), October 5–9 (Thursday–Monday), November 4 (Saturday), and December 2 (Saturday), 1944, ibid.

119. March 13, 1944, CwP 1943–45, File 5, Box 3.

120. July 16, 1944, Ickes Diary, 9083.

121. April 4, June 1, 1944, DR, File 8, Box 2.

122. Corey, "Man Who Holds the Purse Strings."

123. January 24, 1944, DR, File 8, Box 2.

124. January 26, ibid.

125. April 26, ibid.

126. September 11, ibid.

127. October 4 and 11, ibid.

128. November 3, ibid.

129. March 2, ibid.

130. March 29, ibid.

131. April 5, ibid.

132. April 12, ibid.

133. May 26, ibid.

134. October 27, ibid.

135. February 9, ibid.

136. February 25, ibid.

137. September 20, ibid.

138. October 30, 1944, CwP 1943–45, File 5, Box 3. Appleby became vice president of the Queen City Broadcasting Company in Seattle.

139. Appleby's last day on the payroll was December 1, but with his eye already on the door, Smith needed to be the senior official at all the boards, even before Appleby left.

140. November 27, 1944, CwP 1943–45, File 5, Box 3. Smith repeated the presidential "one hundred per cent" delegation of authority for the FY 1946 budget in his first meeting with President Truman. April 18, 1945, CwP 1945, File 6, Box 3.

141. December 20, 1944, DR, File 8, Box 2.

142. December 22, ibid.

143. December 21, 1944, CwP 1943–45, File 5, Box 3.

144. Letter from FDR to Smith, December 9, 1944, File 10: Miscellaneous, Box 4. The letter misstates the date of Smith's resignation letter. It was November 9, not 19. It is possible that FDR's secretary simply misheard him when he was dictating the letter. Smith and his family cherished this letter. When his son, Larry, wrote a short reminiscence of his father in ASPA's newsletter, he included a reproduction of it (L. Smith 2003, 15).

145. Whether due to lack of energy or other reasons, when planning his administration for the fourth term, "he wanted it to be as little different as possible from the old one" (Lelyveld 2016, 243). He asked Ickes, now seventy-one, to stay, said the same to Stimson (seventy-seven), as well as Labor Secretary Perkins, who had been with him since the beginning. The only changes he made were the ones that he could not finesse. He had to replace Secretary of State Cordell Hull, who was very ill and in the hospital, and he had to keep his promise to give VP Wallace just about any position he asked for in appreciation for going quietly. For a liberal who often was critical of business, Wallace surprisingly asked to replace Jesse Jones at Commerce.

Chapter 8: FDR's Fourth Term, 1945

1. January 1, 1945, CwP 1943–45, File 5, Box 3.

2. Memo from Smith to Judge Rosenman, January 2, 1945, WHM January–April 1945, File 6, Box 4.

3. January 2, 1945, DR, File 9, Box 2.

4. Letter from Morgenthau to FDR, January 2, 1945, Morgenthau Diary, Book 806, 238. Oddly, the transcript of the phone conversation with Smith is not in the Morgenthau Diary. Treasury promptly leaked Morgenthau's complaint about

Byrnes. International News Service, "Treasury Repudiates Byrnes," *Washington Times-Herald*, January 2, 1945. Book 806, 242.

5. January 4, 1945, CwP 1943–45, File 5, Box 3.

6. Memo from Smith to FDR, January 5, 1945, WHM January–April 1945, File 6, Box 4. The long gap between Jones's appeal to the president and Roosevelt's request that Smith draft a reply probably reflected, in part, how little work FDR engaged in while at Warm Springs. It is also possible that, knowing he would be replacing Jones with Wallace on January 20, FDR could blithely disregard complaints from a lame duck secretary (who had heard probably heard the rumors, too, but had not yet been told for sure until January 21).

7. January 4, 1945, CwP 1943–45, File 5, Box 3.

8. Memo from FDR for the Director of the Budget, January 8, 1945, WHM January–April 1945, File 6, Box 4. Roosevelt's plan for the postwar use of the Pentagon, of course, did not come to pass. However, the thick floors (to carry the weight of paper records) that FDR had insisted on when planning the building was a lifesaver more than a half-century later. During the airplane terrorist attacks on 9/11, the unusual solidity of the building slowed down the momentum of the plane that crashed into the Pentagon. This largely forgotten structural feature discernably reduced the plane's penetration into the building and the damage from collapsing floors. The attack would have been much deadlier without this FDR detail. Steve Vogel, *The Pentagon: A History* (New York: Random House, 2007).

9. January 19, 1945, CwP 1943–45, File 5, Box 3, 4.

10. March 12, 1945, ibid., emphasis added.

11. File: White House Press Conferences, Box 4, OFHDS.

12. He did not sign such an executive order before he died. The reason may have been his fading energies and focus. On the other hand, he was well aware of the pro-USDA forces on Capitol Hill who, for example, had successfully prevented him from even proposing moving the Forest Service from Agriculture to Interior. Roosevelt may have made a political decision not to sign the executive order because it might trigger a major fight.

13. March 23, 1945, CwP 1943–45, File 5, Box 3.

14. March 31, 1945, Ickes Diary, 9630.

15. April 7, ibid., 9652.

16. File 10: Miscellaneous, Box 4. The memo in Smith's file was handwritten, presumably as a precaution by Smith's secretary to keep it secret by preventing any carbon copies from circulating.

17. Based on the timing and the context, the likely subject was the Navy's maneuvering to use the war as an excuse to build more ships. Given the long lead time necessary for shipbuilding, they would not be ready for use in the war, even if fighting went on into 1946 or even '47. Smith and Byrnes agreed that it was important to stop the unnecessary spending. Smith talked to the president about this on March 12 and FDR said he opposed any additional ship construction (CwP

1943–45, File 5, Box 3). The next day, Byrnes called Smith about the latest Navy tactics to get the new ships authorized. They agreed to try to stop it ("No more ships," March 13, 1945, DR, File 9, Box 2). Smith was nonetheless pessimistic they could stop it, in part because such construction contracts were politically popular on the Hill as pork barrel spending. Byrnes probably sent a memo to FDR in early April raising concerns about the latest Navy efforts to circumvent the obstacles he and Smith were putting up. This fight continued into Truman's presidency.

18. January 19, 1945, CwP 1943–45, File 5, Box 3.

19. John H. Crider, "Wartime Severity to Open 4th Term without Fanfare," *NYT*, January 20, 1945, 1.

20. "Luncheon with Vice President Wallace, Friday, January 19, 1945," DR, File 9, Box 2.

21. He opted for a quiet lunch upstairs with his devoted and apolitical cousin, Daisy Suckley.

22. January 19, 20, and 21, 1945, DR, File 9, Box 2.

23. 59 *Stat.* 5–6.

24. March 2, 1945, DR, File 9, Box 2.

25. AP, "Vinson Confirmed Swiftly by Senate," *NYT*, March 7, 1945, 1. Vinson had been Byrnes's successor at the Office for Economic Stabilization when Byrnes moved up to be the director of war mobilization.

26. Paul W. Ward, "Four Agencies Seen on Way to Wallace," *BS*, March 5, 1945. Reprinted in *CR* 91, no. 2 (March 8, 1945): 1892.

27. AP, "Byrd Says FDR Has Power to Turn Over Agencies to Wallace," *(Hagerstown, MD) Daily Mail*, March 9, 1945, 3.

28. March 5, 1945, DR, File 9, Box 2.

29. Conveying the intense preparation for the seminar, BOB staff submitted to Smith fifty-nine questions likely to come up. Marsh mischievously added a sixtieth question: "In what year will the Brave New World begin?" "Director's Budget Seminar: Possible Questions," January 5, 1945, File: Budget and Budgeting, Box 1, OFHDS. Aldous Huxley's novel of that title had been published in 1932.

30. January 8, 1945, DR, File 9, Box 2.

31. Misleadingly, FDR's papers backdated the budget to January 3 (Roosevelt 1969, 1944–1945: 457). This reflected Rosenman's recurring annual concern about legally complying with the statutory requirement when the budget was to be submitted to Congress.

32. A staffer at the White House press office later told Smith that radio commentator Morgan Beatty broke the embargo. Therefore, Beatty "would be properly spanked by the proper authority," he promised Smith. January 11, 1945, DR, File 9, Box 2.

33. John H. Crider, "70 Billion for War," *NYT*, January 10, 1945, 1.

34. Crider, "Budget Shows Extent of Nation's War Effort," *NYT*, January 14, 1945, B-7.

35. AP, "Budget Drop of 17 Billion in Estimate," *HC*, January 10, 1945, 1.

36. UP, "$83,760,000,000 'Play Safe' Budget Sent to Congress by President," *Atlanta Constitution*, January 10, 1945, 5.

37. The two major weekly newsmagazines (Lindley on behalf of *Newsweek* and Ed Lockett for *Time*) asked Smith to permit them to see the budget message before the seminar (and release date) because of the early deadline for the next issue. They argued that by the time the issue would reach the public, it would be after the president sent the budget to Congress. Smith declined. January 6, 1945, DR, File 9, Box 2.

38. Lindley, "New Budget: Tabular Report" (syndicated column), *WP*, January 10, 1945, 7.

39. February 28, 1945, DR, File 9, Box 2. The traumatic experience reverberated throughout BOB. About a year later, when Sundquist (of the Administrative Management Division) was drafting Smith's cover letter to the secretary of state with a departmental reorganization plan, he lightheartedly suggested a paragraph explaining why the plan omitted dealing with the organization of the department's congressional relations: "You will note that nothing has been mentioned in the report on Congressional relations. If you will refer to the Senate Appropriations Committee Hearings for [FY] 1946 containing my dialogue with Senator McKellar, you will understand my earnest conviction that any advice I have to offer on Congressional relations would be better left unheeded." Sundquist, "Letter of Transmittal to the Secretary of State" (draft), no date (probably early 1946), File: BOB, Box 2, Sundquist Papers.

40. March 1, 1945, DR, File 9, Box 2.

41. March 12, ibid.

42. One instance was a 1942 fight over funding OGR (*after* it had been authorized by law). Then-justice Byrnes volunteered to mediate between FDR and McKellar. It led to an exchange of letters agreeing to a compromise to keep OGR's funding at about its current level. However, McKellar never agreed on any specific amount. Then, when the appropriations committee released its report on the bill, McKellar had broken his promise and instead cut its funding significantly (Lee 2005, 132–34).

43. March 12, 1945, CwP 1943–45, File 5, Box 3.

44. FDR Day-by-Day.

45. March 23, 1945, CwP 1943–45, File 5, Box 3. FDR's personal intervention to protect BOB from McKellar (talking to Senator Hill, inviting Crump to the White House) needs to be seen in the context of his health, lassitude, memory, and focus. Here, three weeks before he died, he invited a Tennessee political boss to meet with him in order to bring political pressure on McKellar. Roosevelt even suggested that Crump hint to McKellar that McKellar might have a primary opponent when he ran for reelection in 1946. According to FDR, Crump replied "that this was possible," hinting he was open to not supporting McKellar in the next

election. FDR's behavior demonstrates an ongoing interest and involvement in the day-to-day problems of his administration. It is quite at odds with a perception or historical expectation that by this time his medical condition was so severe that he was an AWOL president.

46. March 20, 1945, DR, File 9, Box 2.

47. Ibid.

48. March 23, 1945, CwP 1943–45, File 5, Box 3. Roosevelt and Smith had tried the same argument in 1940 to get funding from Congress for EOP's Office of Government Reports. It did not work (Lee 2005, 69).

49. Memo from Smith to FDR, March 28, 1945, WHM January–April 1945, File 6, Box 4.

50. He was only at the White House on March 29 (between returning from Hyde Park and departing for Warm Springs). Presumably, he approved it then, but the retyped letter (signed on his behalf) did not go out until the 31st, when he was already in Georgia.

51. Letter from FDR (drafted by Smith) to Representative Woodrum, March 31, 1945, WHM January–April 1945, File 6, Box 4.

52. April 20, 1945, DR, File 9, Box 2.

53. 59 *Stat.* 106–07.

54. February 20, 1945, DR, File 9, Box 2.

55. Memo from Smith to FDR, March 2, 1945, WHM, File 6, Box 4.

56. March 19, 1945, DR, File 9, Box 2.

57. Ibid.

58. March 23, 1945, CwP 1943–45, File 5, Box 3, emphasis added.

59. Letter from Smith to Conant, March 30, 1945, WHM January–April 1945, File 6, Box 4.

60. Memo from Smith to FDR, March 30, 1945, ibid.

61. April 3, 1945, DR, File 9, Box 2.

62. Letter from Wagner to Smith, March 3, 1945, WHM January–April 1945, File 6, Box 4.

63. John H. Crider, "Forecast Studied to Meet Full Jobs," *NYT*, April 13, 1945, 21. Presumably, Crider had filed his story on the afternoon of April 12, before the public announcement of FDR's death at 5:45 p.m.

64. Memo from Smith to FDR, March 14, 1945, WHM January–April 1945, File 6, Box 4.

65. April 13, 1945, DR, File 9, Box 2.

66. Kluttz, "Census Bureau Tells about Women—in $2,000,000 Volume," *WP*, March 5, 1945, 1.

67. Kluttz, "Federal Diary," *WP*, March 6, 1945, 3.

68. AP, "Denies Waste of Paper," *NYT*, March 24, 1945, 19.

69. Fred Brandeis, "Government Doing Its Bit in Paper Drive," *WP*, March 28, 1945, 1, 4. It is possible that Coy, now at the *Post*, worked behind the scenes to encourage such an article.

70. Juran started out as an efficiency expert in the private sector, worked for the federal government in WWII, and then became a professor and consultant. He was best known for his focus on quality improvement. His work influenced Japan's post-WWII reindustrialization toward high-quality products. (Separately, W. E. Deming, also influential in Japan, focused on *statistical* process control.) Juran was active in the Washington chapter of the Society for the Advancement of Management during the war (Lee 2018, 258n11).

71. His lecture, along with those of five other leaders in the discipline, was then published by University of Alabama Press as a symposium. It was the first volume in a long-running series of annual lectures on public administration that were then published as books.

72. March 2, 1945, DR, File 9, Box 2. I did not locate the script.

73. Sonia Stein, "Final Radio Auditions for 'Met' Singers Listed," *WP*, March 18, 1945, S6; "Radio Today," *NYT*, March 20, 1945, 35. I did not locate the script.

74. Brandeis, "Government Doing Its Bit in Paper Drive."

75. File: Correspondence—1945—Office of the Director, Box 2, OFHDS.

76. January 10, 1945, DR, File 9, Box 2.

77. January 30, ibid.

78. March 21, ibid.

79. January 30, ibid.

80. Memo from Marsh to Smith, October 11, 1944. File: Smith, Harold D.—Director—Personal Data, Box 3, OFHDS.

81. *NYT Book Review*: January 27, 1946, 13; February 24, 1946, 9. McGraw-Hill also marketed it for introductory courses in political science. An ad in *APSR* said the book was written "in simple, understandable fashion" and would be of "timely interest" (Back Matter, 39, no. 5 [October 1945]).

82. "Memorandum of Agreement" (book contract), File 10: Miscellaneous, Box 4.

83. Memo from Marsh to Rosen, "Contract for Harold D. Smith's Book," April 11, 1945, ibid.

84. Memo from Marsh to Rosen, "Manuscript, 'The Management of Your Government,'" May 16, 1945. File: Correspondence—1945—Office of the Director, Box 2, OFHSD.

85. "Books published today," *NYT*, December 3, 1945, 15.

86. In mid-1945, Smith had asked Johnston if he would write a foreword and he reacted positively. However, Smith did not get back to Johnston to obtain the draft until the fall. So much time had passed that Johnston began wondering if perhaps the entire project had been canceled. October 5, 1945, DR, File 9, Box 2.

87. As Smith's book was largely a compilation of his speeches and addresses, the book's contents were discussed in preceding chapters.

88. William F. Pyper, "Timely Book by Harold D. Smith Explains Budget," *Detroit News*, December 31, 1945. File: Smith, Harold D., Necrology Files, Alumni Records, University of Michigan.

89. Quoted in publisher's ad for the book, *NYT Book Review*, January 27, 1945, 13.

90. Luther Huston, "For an Efficient Government," *NYT Book Review*, February 3, 1946, 10.

91. J. Donald Kingsley, "Your Bureaucracy," *New Republic* 114, no. 11 (March 18, 1946): 388–89. Kingsley coauthored an early textbook on public personnel management with William Mosher. Before WWII, he was a professor at Antioch College. During the war, he worked at WMC and then OWM. It is likely that he had at least a casual acquaintance with Smith.

92. A. E. Buck, *National Municipal Review* 35, no. 4 (April 1946): 218–19. Fifteen years earlier, Smith had written a positive review of a book by Buck, also in *NMR*.

93. Brownlow, "The Bookshelf," *Public Personnel Review* 7, no. 3 (July 1946): 169–70. Before submitting his review for publication, Brownlow first shared it with Smith and asked "if it was all right" with him. It was. May 17, 1946, DR, File 10, Box 2.

94. "News and Views of Books," *State Government* 19, no. 5 (May 1946): 146. The *Public Policy Digest* of the National Planning Association neutrally summarized the contents of the book, but without any recommendation (nos. 65–66 [May–June 1946]: 6).

95. "Book Notes," *Alabama Social Welfare* 11, no. 7 (July 1946): 6.

96. Ascher was "a personal friend" of Smith's. July 31, 1945, DR, File 9, Box 2.

97. Charles S. Ascher, "Book Reviews and Notices," *APSR* 40, no. 2 (April 1946): 361–62.

98. Charles Aikin, "Toward Administrative Evaluation," *PAR* 6, no. 3 (Summer 1946): 261–66.

99. John A. Vieg, "Reviews," *Political Science Quarterly* 61, no. 4 (December 1946): 618–20. Vieg's review explicitly identified the book's editor as BOB's S. McKee Rosen.

100. James W. Martin, "Book Reviews," *Southern Economic Journal* 13, no. 1 (July 1946): 79–80. The Martin School of Public Policy and Administration at the University of Kentucky is named after him.

101. April 12, 1945, DR, File 9, Box 2.

102. April 13, ibid.

103. Memo from Smith to the Staff, April 13, 1945, WHM April 13–December 31, 1945, File 7, Box 4.

104. April 14, 1945, DR, File 9, Box 2.

105. April 29, 1945, Ickes Diary, 9679.

106. Somewhat more bucolically, a wire service story said, "Smith was stricken while in a pasture looking over his prize cows." UP, "Harold D. Smith Dies; Bank

Head," *Waukesha (WI) Freeman*, January 24, 1947, 3. The version by Smith's son is likely more accurate.

107. Letter from Merriam to John O. Walker, Director, Council on Inter-governmental Relations, January 28, 1947. Merriam Papers, University of Chicago.

108. Telegram from Bane to Mrs. Lillian Smith, January 24, 1947. File: Correspondence, Box 6, Bane Papers.

109. UP, "Harold D. Smith Dies."

110. AP, "Harold D. Smith Dies; Executive of World Bank," *NYHT*, January 24, 1947, 16.

111. Drew Pearson, "Washington Merry-Go-Round" (syndicated column), *DFP*, March 22, 1947, 4. The delay between Smith's death and this column is likely because columnists sometimes saved minor items that were not time sensitive until needed to fill out a column.

112. "Harold D. Smith" (editorial), *WP*, January 25, 1947, 6.

113. "Harold D. Smith" (editorial), *WS*, January 25, 1947, A-6.

114. "Harold D. Smith" (editorial), *DFP*, January 25, 1947, 4.

115. Henry F. and Katharine Pringle, "It's Hard to Work for Uncle Sam," *Ladies Home Journal* 64, no. 10 (October 1947): 52.

116. Sylvia F. Porter, "How to Put Brains in Government," *Cosmopolitan* 132, no. 1 (January 1952): 100.

117. In 2000, Appleby's tribute to Smith was republished in a reader for public administration students (Holzer, chap. 2).

118. Paul R. Leach, "A Deficit Again, but . . . ," *DFP*, January 16, 1955, B-5; Don Oberdorfer, "Budget Bureau: Unloved," *Philadelphia Inquirer*, July 20, 1959, 13; Frank C. Porter, "A Bookkeeper's Paradise," *WP*, June 6, 1965, E-1.

Conclusion: FDR's *Other* Assistant President

1. "Budget Director Sworn," *NYT*, April 16, 1939, 30.

2. AP, "Smith's Boss of U.S. Budget, but Wife Is Banker at Home," *WP*, January 6, 1941, 3.

3. June 3, 1940, CwP 1940, File 2, Box 3.

4. A reporter evocatively described Smith arriving at the White House for a meeting with the president carrying "his bulging briefcase." Lee Carson, INS, "Roosevelt's Prayers Start Tenth Year," *WP*, March 5, 1942, 5.

5. February 7, 1942, CwP 1942, File 4, Box 3.

6. For example: memos from FDR to Smith, April 3, 11, and 27, 1942, File: Smith, Harold D.—Director—Misc., Box 3, OFHDS; June 13, 1942, CwP 1942, File 4, Box 3.

7. April 16, 1942, CwP 1942, File 4, Box 3.

8. June 13, ibid.

9. "1,521 Sign Appeal for Jewish Army," *NYT*, November 17, 1942, 23.

10. *NYT*: "What is the shocking TRUTH about saving the lives of the European Jews" (ad), April 13, 1943, 19. The committee also ran an ad one column short of a full page: "The people have spoken" (ad), March 10, 1943, 10.

11. Paul W. Ward, "Conference Critics Hit," *BS*, May 7, 1943, 11.

12. DR, Box 2: April 27, 1944, File 8, Box 2; May 30, 1945, File 9. Later in the war, Friedman moved to Pittsburgh.

13. Letter from Nita Gavaris, Secretary to the Director, to Peter H. Bergson, Co-Chairman, Emergency Committee to Save the Jewish People of Europe, February 2, 1944. File: General Files A-Z, Box 2, OFHDS.

14. Sundquist, the former BOB staffer, read the article and then wrote the authors of his reactions. In his view, BOB's effectiveness was not primarily because of neutral competence, rather the opposite. He recalled that most BOB staffers were New Dealers and therefore a good fit for working with White House staff. Letter from Sundquist to Dickinson and Rudalevige, August 2, 2005. File: BOB, Box 2, Sundquist Papers. He died in 2016 at age one hundred.

15. "Mr. Smith Stays in Town," *Newsweek*, August 13, 1945, 29.

16. Baukhage, "Washington Digest" (syndicated column), *(Rising Sun, MD) Midland Journal*, January 22, 1943, 2.

17. Coy interview with Somers, 1946, Papers of Herman Miles Somers, Yale University Library.

18. Memo from Smith to FDR, November 23, 1942, WHM 1942, File 3, Box 4.

19. December 4, 1942, CwP 1942, File 4, Box 3. As part of his dictation, Smith said he had trouble "restraining my emotions" when FDR told him how much his memo had reversed a major presidential decision.

20. Smith memo to FDR, May 15, 1941. WHM 1941, File 2, Box 4.

21. Letter from FDR to Smith, May 20, 1941. WHM 1941, File 2, Box 4. FDR also told Smith, "As you have requested, I have destroyed" Smith's memo to him.

22. The preference for separate academic disciplines may have been driven by faculty politics. Public administration faculty probably wanted the prestige and independent identity from having their own schools, journals, and professional associations. They probably also feared, rightly, being subsumed under the larger and more dominant business faculty in a merged school. This separatist dogma was pithily captured by Wallace Sayre's quip that "business and public administration are alike only in all unimportant respects" (*PAR* 18, no. 3 [Summer 1958]: 245).

23. *WP*, August 24, 1941, B-4.

24. *WSJ*, November 8, 1941, 2.

25. UP, *LAT*, January 17, 1942, 1.

26. James G. Simonds, *WP*, February 10, 1942, 7.

27. UP, *WP*, April 14, 1942, 24.

28. *WSJ*, September 12, 1942, 2.

29. Editorial, *WP*, December 7, 1942, 14.

30. Ernest K. Lindley, column, *WP*, March 29, 1943, 9.

31. *Time*, June 14, 1943, cover page.

32. James B. Reston, "The 'Assistant President,'" *NYT*, October 12, 1941, SM-3.

33. Frank L. Kluckhohn, "Washington Success Story," *NYT*, July 26, 1942, SM-6.

34. Hamilton went further, declaring that Byrnes was the "de facto domestic *deputy* president" (2016, 262, emphasis added). Hamilton's phrase was a promotion for Byrnes, because in federal hierarchical parlance a deputy secretary is higher up in the departmental chain of command than an assistant secretary.

35. The "for policy" appellation has become relatively common in the federal government: Under Secretary of Defense for Policy, Assistant Secretary of Treasury for Economic Policy, Assistant Secretary of Labor for Policy, and Under Secretary of Transportation for Policy.

36. The "for management" term in titles is now common: Under Secretary of State for Management, Assistant Secretary of Treasury for Management, and Assistant Secretary of Labor for Administration and Management.

37. *Congressional Directory*, 68th Cong., 1st sess., 1st ed., December 1923, 277.

38. The title Second Assistant Secretary of Labor was set by law, 42 *Stat.* 766 (P.L. 260, 1922).

39. *US Government Manual*, 1943, 257, 413.

Bibliography

Archival Sources

Bane, Frank, Papers of. MSS 7280, Albert and Shirley Small Special Collections, University of Virginia Library, Charlottesville.

Bell, Daniel E., Personal Papers (#25). Series 3.1: Conferences, Box 35. Kennedy Presidential Library, Boston.

Blandford, John B., Papers of. Harry S Truman Presidential Library, Independence, MO.

Brownlow, Louis, Diary. Special Collections Research Center, Regenstein Library, University of Chicago.

Bureau of the Budget. Official Files (OF) 79 Roosevelt Presidential Library, Hyde Park, NY.

Confidential Publications of the Bureau of the Budget (Library Materials), 1940–1942. Records of the Office of Management and Budget, Record Group (RG) 51, National Archives II (NA II), College Park, MD.

Council on Intergovernmental Relations. Series 4, Spelman Fund of New York, Rockefeller Archives Center, Sleepy Hollow, NY.

Coy, Wayne, Papers of. FDRL.

Coy, Wayne. Interview with H. M. Somers, August 12, 1946. Folder 4, Box 31-a, Series IV, Papers of Herman Miles Somers, Collection ID MS 1238, Manuscripts and Archives, Yale University Library, New Haven, CT.

Ickes, Harold L., Diaries. March 5, 1933–December 27, 1951 (unpublished long version). Washington, DC: Photoduplication Service, Library of Congress, 1978. (Original in the Manuscript Division, Library of Congress.)

Jones, Roger W., Oral history interview, 1969, Truman Library. Accessed March 1, 2021: https://www.trumanlibrary.gov/library/oral-histories/jonesrw.

Liaison Officer for Emergency Management—General Records. Office for Emergency Management, RG 214, NA II.

Merriam, Charles E., Papers of. Folder 10, Box 61, Special Collections Research Center, Regenstein Library, University of Chicago.

Morgenthau, Henry, Jr., Diaries. FDRL. Accessed March 1, 2021: http://www.
    fdrlibrary.marist.edu/archives/collections/franklin/index.php?p=collections/
    findingaid&id=535.
Morrison, Donald H., Papers of. MS-822, Rauner Special Collections Library,
    Dartmouth College, Dartmouth, NH.
Office of Information, Bureau of the Budget, 1941–1951. Series 39.27c, Central
    Files, Records of the Office of Management and Budget, RG 51, NA II.
Seventy-Fifth Anniversary Diamond Jubilee, June 5–9, 1941, and *University of Kan-
    sas Newsletter* (Spring 1941). University Archives, Kenneth Spencer Research
    Libraries, University of Kansas, Lawrence.
Sherwood Robert E., Papers of. MS Am 1947 (1517–1518), Houghton Library,
    Harvard University, Cambridge, MA.
Smith, Harold D., Papers of. FDRL.
———, Office Files: 1939–1946. Series 39.24a, Central Files, Records of the Office
    of Management and Budget, RG 51, NA II.
———. Clippings: Vertical Files, Kansas State Library, Topeka.
Smith, Harold Dewey. Necrology Files, Alumni Records, Bentley Historical Library,
    University of Michigan, Ann Arbor.
Sundquist, James L., Papers. Truman Library.

Federal Publications

US Bureau of the Budget. 1942 (October 23). *Bureau of the Budget—Development
    and Organization* (mimeo). Washington, DC: US BOB.
———. 1943. *Budget Circulars: In Effect August 1, 1943* (mimeo). Washington,
    DC: US BOB.
———, Committee of Records of War Administration. (1946) 1972. *The United
    States at War: Development and Administration of the War Program by the
    Federal Government*, No. 1. New York: Da Capo.
———, Field Service. 1945. *Management Techniques: Field Service Training Institute,
    January 25–February 3, 1945, Chicago* (mimeo). Washington, DC: BOB.
US Civilian Production Administration. 1946. *Minutes of the Supply Priorities and
    Allocations Board, September 2, 1941, to January 15, 1942*, Documentary
    Publication No. 3, Historical Reports on War Administration. Washington,
    DC: GPO. (*Note*: The Civilian Production Administration was the postwar
    successor to the War Production Board.)
US Committee for Congested Production Areas. 1944. *Final Report, December 1944*.
    Washington, DC: GPO.
US Congress. 1941a. Joint Committee on Reduction of Nonessential Federal
    Expenditures. *Reduction of Nonessential Federal Expenditures*, public hearings.
    77th Cong., 1st sess.

———. 1941b. Joint Committee on Reduction of Nonessential Federal Expenditures. *Reduction of Nonessential Federal Expenditures; Preliminary Report.* 77th Cong., 1st sess., S. Doc. 152.

———. 1942. Joint Committee on Reduction of Nonessential Federal Expenditures. *Issuance of Questionnaires by Governmental Agencies,* public hearings. 77th Cong., 2nd sess.

———. 1943a. Joint Committee on Reduction of Nonessential Federal Expenditures. *Reduction of Nonessential Federal Expenditures: Additional Report.* 78th Cong., 1st sess., S. Doc. 5.

———. 1943b. Joint Committee on Reduction of Nonessential Federal Expenditures. *Reduction of Nonessential Federal Expenditures: Travel and Communications in the Federal Government.* 78th Cong., 1st sess., S. Doc. 57.

———. 1943c. Joint Committee on Reduction of Nonessential Federal Expenditures. *Reduction of Nonessential Federal Expenditures: Federal Personnel.* 78th Cong., 1st sess., S. Doc. 66.

———. 1943d. Joint Committee on Reduction of Nonessential Federal Expenditures. *Reduction of Nonessential Federal Expenditures: Progress Report.* 78th Cong., 1st sess., S. Doc. 140.

———. 1945. Joint Committee on the Organization of Congress. *Organization of Congress,* part 3, public hearings. 79th Cong., 1st sess.

US Coordinator of Inter-American Affairs. 1947. *History of the Office of the Coordinator of Inter-American Affairs,* Historical Reports on War Administration (series). Washington, DC: GPO.

US House. 1938a. *Supplemental Estimate of Appropriation for the Bureau of the Budget, Fiscal Year 1939,* Message from the President. 75th Cong., 3rd sess., H. Doc. 615.

———. 1938b. Committee on Appropriations. *Second Deficiency Appropriation Bill, Fiscal Year 1938.* 75th Cong., 3rd sess., H. Rep. 2614.

———. 1939a. Committee on Appropriations. *Treasury Department Appropriation Bill for 1940,* public hearings. 76th Cong., 1st sess.

———. 1939b. Committee on Appropriations. *Treasury and Post Office Departments Appropriation Bill, Fiscal Year 1940.* 76th Cong., 1st sess., H. Rep. 98.

———. 1939c. *First Plan on Government Reorganization,* Message from the President. 76th Cong., 1st sess., H. Doc. 262.

———. 1939d. *Second Plan on Government Reorganization,* Message from the President. 76th Cong., 1st sess., H. Doc. 288.

———. 1939e. *Draft of Proposed Provision Pertaining to Existing Appropriation, Bureau of the Budget,* Message from the President. 76th Cong., 1st sess. H. Doc. 355.

———. 1939f. Committee on Appropriations, Subcommittee on Independent Offices. *Independent Offices Appropriation Bill for 1941,* part 1, public hearings. 76th Cong., 3rd sess.

———. 1940a. *The Budget of the United States Government for the Fiscal Year Ending June 30, 1941*. 76th Cong., 3rd sess., H. Doc. 529.

———. 1940b. Committee on Appropriations. *Independent Offices Appropriation Bill, 1941*. 76th Cong., 3rd sess., H. Rep. 1515.

———. 1940c. Committee on Appropriations, Subcommittee on Independent Offices. *Independent Offices Appropriation Bill for 1942*, part 1, public hearings. 77th Cong., 1st sess.

———. 1940d. *Third Plan on Government Reorganization*, Message from the President. 76th Congress, 3rd sess., H. Doc. 681.

———. 1940e. *Fourth Plan on Government Reorganization*, Message from the President. 76th Congress, 3rd sess., H. Doc. 692.

———. 1940f. *Fifth Plan on Government Reorganization*, Message from the President. 76th Congress, 3rd sess., H. Doc. 784.

———. 1940g. *Supplemental Appropriation for 1941*, Message from the President. 76th Congress, 3rd sess., H. Doc. 807.

———. 1940h. Committee on Appropriations, Subcommittee on Deficiencies. *Second Deficiency Appropriation Bill for 1940*, public hearings. 76th Cong., 3rd sess.

———. 1940i. Committee on Appropriations. *A Salary Advancement Plan for the Federal Service; Letter from the Director of the Budget*. 76th Cong., 3rd sess., Committee Print.

———. 1941a. *Independent Offices Appropriation Bill, 1942*. 77th Cong., 1st sess., H. Rep. 15.

———. 1941b. Committee on Appropriations, Subcommittee on Deficiencies. *Defense Aid Supplemental Appropriation Bill, 1941*, hearings. 77th Cong., 1st sess.

———. 1941c. Committee on the Civil Service. *Uniform Salary Increases*, public hearings. 77th Cong., 1st sess.

———. 1941d. *Amending the Classification Act of 1923, as Amended*. 77th Cong., 1st sess., H. Rep. 533.

———. 1942a. Committee on Appropriations, Subcommittee on Independent Offices. *Independent Offices Appropriation Bill for 1943*, part 1, public hearings. 77th Cong., 2nd sess.

———. 1942b. *Trends in Nonwar Federal Expenditures*, Message from the President. 77th Cong., 2nd sess., H. Doc. 870.

———. 1943a. Committee on Appropriations, Subcommittee on Independent Offices. *Independent Offices Appropriation Bill for 1944*, public hearings. 78th Cong., 1st sess.

———. 1943b. Committee on the Civil Service. *Investigation of Civilian Employment*, part 2, public hearings. 78th Cong., 1st sess.

———. 1943c. Committee on the Civil Service. *Investigation of Civilian Employment: Interim Report*. 78th Cong., 1st sess., H. Rep. 766.

———. 1943d. Select Committee to Investigate the Federal Communications Commission. *Study and Investigation of the Federal Communications Commission*, public hearings. 78th Cong., 1st sess.

———. 1943e. *Supplemental Estimate of Appropriation for the Executive Office of the President, Bureau of the Budget*, Message from the President. 78th Cong., 1st sess., H. Doc. 326.

———. 1943f. Committee on Appropriations, Subcommittee on Deficiencies. *First Supplemental National Defense Appropriation Bill for 1944*, public hearings. 78th Cong., 1st sess.

———. 1944a. Committee on the Civil Service. *Investigation of Civilian Employment: Report.* 78th Cong., 2nd sess., H. Rep. 2084.

———. 1944b. Committee on Appropriations, Subcommittee on Independent Offices. *Independent Offices Appropriation Bill for 1945*, public hearings. 78th Cong., 2nd sess.

———. 1944c. Select Committee on Post-War Military Policy. *Proposal to Establish a Single Department of Armed Forces*, Part 1, public hearings. 78th Cong., 2nd sess.

———. 1944d. Special Committee on Post-War Economic Policy and Planning. *Economic Problems of the Transition Period*, part 2, public hearings. 78th Cong., 2nd sess.

———. 1945. Committee on Appropriations, Subcommittee on Independent Offices. *Independent Offices Appropriation Bill for 1946*, public hearings. 79th Cong., 1st sess.

US Senate. 1937a. *Reorganization of the Executive Departments*, Message from the President. 75th Cong., 1st sess., S. Doc. 8.

———. 1937b. Select Committee to Investigate the Executive Agencies of the Government. *Investigation of Executive Agencies of the Government.* 75th Cong., 1st sess., S. Rep. 1275.

———. 1940a. *Independent Offices Appropriation Bill, 1941.* 76th Cong., 3rd sess., S. Rep. 1177.

———. 1940b. Committee on Appropriations, subcommittee (no title). *Independent Offices Appropriation Bill for 1941*, public hearing. 76th Cong., 3rd sess.

———. 1940c. Select Committee on Government Organization. *Fourth Plan on Government Reorganization*, public hearings. 76th Cong., 3rd sess.

———. 1941a. Committee on Appropriations, subcommittee (no title). *Defense Aid Supplemental Appropriation Bill, 1941*, hearings. 77th Cong., 1st sess.

———. 1941b. *Amending the Classification Act of 1923, as Amended.* 77th Cong., 1st sess., S. Rep. 503.

———. 1941c. Committee on Finance. *Report on Nondefense Expenditures in the 1942 Budget.* 77th Cong., 1st sess., Committee Print.

———. 1941d. *The Revenue Bill of 1941.* 77th Cong., 1st sess., S. Rep. 673, pt. 1.

———. 1942a. Committee on Military Affairs. *Motor Vehicles*. Unpublished executive session, ProQuest Congressional ID: HRG-1942-MAS-0064. 77th Cong., 2nd sess.

———. 1942b. Committee on Appropriations, Subcommittee on S. Res. 223. *Transfer of Employees, Conserving Office Space, Relief in Housing Conditions, and Promotion of Economy and Efficiency*. 77th Cong., 2nd sess., S. Rep. 1554.

———. 1943a. Committee on Appropriations, subcommittee (no title). *Independent Offices Appropriation Bill for 1944*, public hearings. 78th Cong., 1st sess.

———. 1943b. Special Committee Investigating the National Defense Program. *Investigation of the National Defense Program*, part 22: *The Canol Project*, hearings. 78th Cong., 1st sess.

———. 1943c. Committee on Appropriations, subcommittee (no title). *First Supplemental National Defense Appropriation Bill for 1944*, public hearings. 78th Cong., 1st sess.

———. 1944. Committee on Appropriations, subcommittee (no title). *Independent Offices Appropriation Bill for 1945*, public hearings. 78th Cong., 2nd sess.

———. 1945. Committee on Appropriations, subcommittee (no title). *Independent Offices Appropriation Bill for 1946*, public hearings. 79th Cong., 1st sess.

Smith Bibliography (1939–1945)

Note: A few of the following entries were not cited in the text but are included in the interest of comprehensiveness. This section also includes a few key post-FDR writings. Smith's appearances at congressional hearings are included in the preceding section.

1939. "The Role of the Bureau of the Budget in Federal Administration" (mimeo). Speech to joint conference of APSA and ASPA, Washington, DC, December 28. Washington, DC: BOB.

1940a. "The Budget in Transition," April 11. In *Allegheny College Business Lectures: No. 8 of a Series of Ten Lectures as Part of the 125th Anniversary Program of Allegheny College*, edited by L. J. Long and J. L. Fisher, 135–48. Meadville, PA: Allegheny College. Wayne and Sally Merrick Historic Archival Center, Pelletier Library, Allegheny College.

1940b. "Some Budget Problems" (mimeo). Address to Economic Club of Detroit, MI, April 29. Washington, DC: BOB. File: Articles and Speeches by the Director, Box 1, OFHDS.

1941a. "The Bureau of the Budget." *PAR* 1, no. 2 (Winter): 106–115. Based on "The Bureau of the Budget as an Instrument of Management" (mimeo), speech to joint conference of APSA and ASPA, Chicago, December 29, 1940. Washington, DC: BOB.

1941b. "National Defense Spending: 1940 and Beyond." Address to Southwide Conference on the National Defense Program and State Finance, University of Alabama, January 31, 1941. In *National Defense and State Finance*, Publication no. 3, 88–101. Tuscaloosa: Bureau of Public Administration, University of Alabama.

1941c. "A Day in the Federal Budget Bureau." *Municipal Finance* 13, no. 3 (February): 7–10.

1941d. "Democracy on Trial" (mimeo). Speech to University of Kansas 69th annual commencement, Lawrence, June 8. Washington, DC: BOB.

1941e. "Defense: Who'll Pay the Piper?" *University of Chicago Round Table* (transcript of radio broadcast), no. 177, with Albert Lepawsky and Henri S. Bloch. August 3. Chicago: University of Chicago.

1941f. "Cities Face the Emergency." *Addresses Delivered at the 18th Annual Conference of the American Municipal Association*, October 24, Series AM Report no. 24, 96–106. Chicago: American Municipal Association. For a slightly edited version, see "Cities Focal Point in Defense Program," *Michigan Municipal Review* 14, no. 1 (December 1941): 145–47. For an adaptation, see "To Improve Emergency Relationships Between Municipal and Federal Officials," *American City* 56, no. 11 (November 1941): 72–74.

1941g. "The Management of Government in a Democracy" (mimeo). Speech to joint conference of APSA and ASPA, New York, December 29. Washington, DC: BOB. For an adaptation, see "Management in a Democracy," *National Municipal Review* 31, no. 9 (October 1942): 476–80.

1942a. "With Financial Joy Ride Over, Headaches Start for U.S. Now" (nationally syndicated Sunday column). *WS*, March 29, B-1, B-3.

1942b. "Federal-State Fiscal Cooperation in Wartime" (mimeo). Council of State Governments conference on emergency fiscal problems, New York, May 8. Washington, DC: BOB. File: Articles and Speeches by the Director, Box 1, OFHDS. For a short excerpt, see "Suggestions for Harmonizing State with Federal Wartime Fiscal Policies," *State Government* 15, no. 6 (June 1942): 123.

1942c. "Wartime Unity for Our Government Fiscal Front." Speech to Council of State Governments conference on emergency fiscal problems, Chicago, May 15. *Kansas Government Journal* (June 1942): 8–9, 48, 50. For a condensed version, see "On Home Front: Unified Fiscal Policies," *Michigan Municipal Review* 15, no. 7 (July 1942): 82–84.

1942d. "Cities: Defenders of Democracy." Speech to New York state conference of mayors and other municipal officials, June 9, Syracuse. *Minnesota Municipalities* 27, no. 8 (August 1942): 281–86.

1942e. "A Call for Action: The President's Seven-Point Program" (text of radio broadcast), July 1. *Vital Speeches of the Day* 8, no. 20 (August 1): 639–40.

1942f. "The War and the Federal Budget." *Municipal Finance* 15, no. 1 (August): 3–5.

1942g. "Progress Toward Victory." Speech to Muskegon (MI) Chamber of Commerce and West Michigan Legislative Council, October 30. *CR* 88, no. 10 (November 12): A4046–48.

1943a. "The Wartime Challenge to Education" (mimeo). Address at Grinnell College (IA) commencement ceremony, May 23. Washington, DC: BOB.

1943b. "The Nation Discovers Itself" (excerpt). Speech to University of Michigan Press Club, 25th annual conference, Ann Arbor, October 7. In *Wartime Budgeting; Including Federal-State-Local Fiscal Problems,* unit [volume] 3 in *Budgeting: An Instrument of Planning and Management,* 1944, edited by Catheryn Seckler-Hudson, 92–94. Washington, DC: School of Social Sciences and Public Affairs, American University.

1943c. "Fiscal Policy and Budget Operations in War and Peace" (mimeo). Paper submitted on October 14 for the Tenth Chilean Scientific Congress, January 1944. Washington, DC: BOB.

1944a. "Washington Reports on Rationing" (transcript). Radio interview with *Newsweek*'s Ernest Lindley, January 16. File: Articles and Speeches by the Director, Box 1, OFHDS.

1944b. "Public Works and the National Welfare." Speech to conference of American Road Builders Association, Chicago, February 2. In *The Relationship of Budgeting to Planning and Management,* unit [volume] 4 in *Budgeting: An Instrument of Planning and Management,* 1945, edited by Catheryn Seckler-Hudson, 120–29. Washington, DC: School of Social Sciences and Public Affairs, American University.

1944c. "Administration and Planning" (excerpts from four-page text). Speech to Washington, DC, Chapter of the Society for the Advancement of Management, February 17, 1944. In *Administration: The Art and Science of Organization and Management,* edited by Albert Lepawsky, 493–94. New York: Alfred A. Knopf, 1949.

1944d. "The Budget as an Instrument of Legislative Control and Executive Management." Speech to Municipal Finance Officers Association, Cleveland, June 9. *PAR* 4, no. 3 (Summer): 181–88.

1944e. "The Need for New Perspectives in Education" (abridgement). Address to the annual Institute for Superintendents and Principals, University of Wisconsin, Madison, July 24. *Summer Cardinal,* July 25, 6.

1944f. "Improve Management—Now." Introduction to *Management Bulletin: Management Improvement Work Sheet* (mimeo), January. File: Administrative Management, Box 1, OOI.

1944g. (No title.) Introduction to *Management Bulletin: An Agency Management Program, A Guide for Self-Appraisal and Planning Economies in Operation,* March 2. [Washington, DC]: EOP, BOB.

1944h. "Opening Statement" (mimeo). Conference of Historical Officers, December 8, Committee on Records of War Administration, 1–3. Washington, DC: BOB.

1945a. *The Management of Your Government*. [Edited by S. McKee Rosen.] New York: McGraw-Hill.

1945b. Foreword to *Status of Geographic Projects* (mimeo), Bulletin no. 7, March 15, 1945. Washington, DC: BOB.

1945c. Foreword to *Work Simplification: As Exemplified by the Work Simplification Program of the U.S. Bureau of the Budget*, Publication no. 91, iii. Chicago: Public Administration Service.

1945d. "Our 300-Billion-Dollar Headache." *American Magazine*, June, 42–43, 114–17.

1946a. "Government Must Have and Pay for Good Men." *New York Times Sunday Magazine*, July 14, 9, 34–36.

1946b. "Trifles That Smother the President." *American Magazine*, June, 23, 121–26.

1947. *Intergovernmental Relations and Effective Government*. Address before the Eighth General Assembly of the States, Council of State Governments, Chicago, January 17. Washington, DC: International Bank for Reconstruction and Development.

Published Primary Sources (memoirs and reports)

American University. 1943. *The Director of the Bureau of the Budget, United States of America*, Governmental Portrait No. 1. Washington, DC: American University Press.

Brownlow, Louis. 1958. *A Passion for Anonymity: The Autobiography of Louis Brownlow; Second Half*. Chicago: University of Chicago Press.

Byrnes, James F. 1947. *Speaking Frankly*. New York: Harper & Brothers.

Catton, Bruce. (1948) 1969. *The War Lords of Washington*. New York: Greenwood.

Ickes, Harold L. 1954. *The Secret Diary of Harold L. Ickes; Vol. II: The Inside Struggle, 1936–1939*. New York: Simon and Schuster.

Nelson, Donald M. (1946) 1973. *Arsenal of Democracy: The Story of American War Production*. New York: Da Capo.

Roosevelt, Franklin D. (1938–1950) 1969. *Public Papers and Addresses of Franklin D. Roosevelt*, 13 vols. New York: Russell and Russell.

———. 1972. *Complete Presidential Press Conferences of Franklin D. Roosevelt*. 25 vols. New York: Da Capo.

Rosenman, Samuel I. 1952. *Working with Roosevelt*. New York: Harper & Brothers.

Smith, Larry. 2003. "Harold D. Smith: ASPA Founder and Trusted Advisor to FDR." *ASPA [American Society for Public Administration] Times* 26, no. 8 (August): 15–17. (L. Smith was Harold Smith's son.)

Wallace, Henry A. 1973. *The Price of Vision: The Diary of Henry A. Wallace, 1942–1946*. Edited by John Morton Blum. Boston: Houghton Mifflin.

Secondary Sources

Appleby, Paul H. 1946. "Organizing Around the Head of a Large Federal Department." *PAR* 6, no. 3 (Summer): 205–12.

———. 1947. "Harold D. Smith—Public Administrator." *PAR* 7, no. 2 (Spring): 77–81.

Arnold, Peri E. 1997. "Executive Reorganization and the Executive Office of the President." In *The Executive Office of the President: A Historical, Biographical, and Bibliographical Guide*, edited by Harold C. Relyea, chap. 11. Westport, CT: Greenwood.

———. 1998. *Making the Managerial Presidency: Comprehensive Reorganization Planning, 1905–1996*, 2nd ed. Lawrence: University Press of Kansas.

Berman, Larry. 1979. *The Office of Management and Budget and the Presidency, 1921–1979*. Princeton, NJ: Princeton University Press.

Blum, John Morton. 1965. *From the Morgenthau Diaries*, vol. 2: *Years of Urgency, 1938–1941*. Boston: Houghton Mifflin.

———. 1967. *From the Morgenthau Diaries*, vol. 3: *Years of War, 1941–1945*. Boston: Houghton Mifflin.

Blumberg, Barbara. 1999. "Smith, Harold Dewey." In *American National Biography*, vol. 20, edited by John A. Garraty and Mark C. Carnes, 195–96. New York: Oxford University Press.

Bose, Meena, and Andrew Rudalevige, eds. 2020. *Executive Policymaking: The Role of OMB in the Presidency*. Washington, DC: Brookings Institution Press.

Bouverie, Tim. 2019. *Appeasement: Chamberlain, Hitler, Churchill, and the Road to War*. New York: Tim Duggan.

Breitman, Richard, and Allan J. Lichtman. 2013. *FDR and the Jews*. Cambridge, MA: Belknap/Harvard University Press.

Brownlow, Louis. 1947. "Harold D. Smith." *APSR* 41, no. 2 (April): 327–30.

Burke, John P. 2000. *The Institutional Presidency: Organizing and Managing the White House from FDR to Clinton*, 2nd ed. Baltimore: Johns Hopkins University Press.

Burkhead, Jesse. 1956. *Government Budgeting*. New York: John Wiley & Sons.

Burns, James MacGregor. 1956. *Roosevelt: The Lion and the Fox*. New York: Harcourt, Brace.

———. 1970. *Roosevelt: The Soldier of Freedom*. New York: Harcourt Brace Jovanovich.

Carey, William D. 1944. "Central-Field Relationships in the War Production Board." *PAR* 4, no. 1 (Winter): 31–42.

———. 1946. "Control and Supervision of Field Offices." *PAR* 6, no. 1 (Winter): 20–24.

———. 1969. "Presidential Staffing in the Sixties and Seventies." *PAR* 29, no. 5 (September–October): 450–58.

Caro, Robert A. (2002) 2019. *Master of the Senate; The Years of Lyndon Johnson*, vol. 3. London: Bodley Head.

Childs, Marquis W. 1942. *I Write from Washington*. New York: Harper & Brothers.

Clawson, Marion. 1981. *New Deal Planning: The National Resources Planning Board*. Baltimore: Johns Hopkins University Press.

Collett, Merrill J. 1945. "The Role of Budget Planning and Personnel as Staff Services." *PAR* 5, no. 3 (Summer): 226–32.

Crider, John H. 1944. *The Bureaucrat*. Philadelphia: J. B. Lippincott.

Dame, Philip R., and Bernard H. Martin. 2009. *The Evolution of OMB*. [Charleston, SC?]: Philip Dame/Bernard Martin.

Daniels, Roger. 2016. *Franklin D. Roosevelt*, vol. 2: *The War Years, 1939–1945*. Urbana: University of Illinois Press.

Dickinson, Matthew J., and Andrew Rudalevige. 2004–2005. "Presidents, Responsiveness, and Competence: Revisiting the 'Golden Age' at the Bureau of the Budget." *Political Science Quarterly* 119, no. 4 (Winter): 633–54.

———. 2007. " 'Worked Out in Fractions': Neutral Competence, FDR, and the Bureau of the Budget." *Congress and the Presidency* 34, no. 1 (Spring): 8–26.

Dimock, Marshall Edward, and Gladys Ogden Dimock. 1953. *Public Administration*. New York: Rinehart.

Eller, Warren S., Brian J. Gerber, and Scott E. Robinson. 2013. *Public Administration Research Methods: Tools for Evaluation and Evidence-Based Practice*. New York: Routledge.

Emmerich, Herbert. 1971. *Federal Organization and Administrative Management*. Tuscaloosa: University of Alabama Press.

Ferrell, Robert H. 1994. *Choosing Truman: The Democratic Convention of 1944*. Columbia: University of Missouri Press.

Fine, Sidney. 1984. *Frank Murphy: The Washington Years*. Ann Arbor: University of Michigan Press.

Fleming, Thomas. 2001. *The New Dealers' War: Franklin D. Roosevelt and the War within World War II*. New York: Basic/Perseus.

Foner, Eric. 2019. *The Second Founding: How the Civil War and Reconstruction Remade the Constitution*. New York: W. W. Norton.

Gibson, Ed. 2003. "Tales of Two Cities: The Administrative Facade of Social Security." *Administration and Society* 35, no. 4 (September): 408–37.

Gibson, Frank. 1960. "A Bloody Tenet Washed and Made White: An Answer to a Proposal to Give Congress More Control over the Budget." *Midwest Journal of Political Science* 4, no. 1 (February): 76–82.

Gill, Corrington. 1945. "Federal-State-City Cooperation in Congested Production Areas." *PAR* 5, no. 1 (Winter): 28–33.

Gosling, James J. 1992. *Budgetary Politics in American Governments*. New York: Longman.

———. 2016. *Budgetary Politics in American Governments*, 6th ed. New York: Routledge.

Graham, George A. 1943. "Impartiality plus Integration" (book review). *PAR* 3, no. 2 (Spring): 172–74.

Graves, Thomas J., and William D. Carey. 1943. "The Copper Recovery Program." *PAR* 3, no. 3 (Summer): 205–12.

Grunes, Rodney A. 2011. "The Institutional Presidency." In *A Companion to Franklin D. Roosevelt*, edited by William D. Pederson, chap. 19. Chichester, UK: Wiley-Blackwell.

Guha, Ramachandra. 2018. *Gandhi*, vol. 2: *The Years That Changed the World, 1914–1948*. New York: Alfred A. Knopf.

Gulick, Luther. 1944. "War Organization of the Federal Government." *APSR* 38, no. 6 (December): 1166–79.

———. 1948. *Administrative Reflections from World War II*. Tuscaloosa: University of Alabama Press.

Hamilton, Nigel. 2016. *Commander in Chief: FDR's Battle with Churchill, 1943*. [Vol. 2 of FDR in WWII.] Boston: Houghton Mifflin Harcourt.

———. 2019. *War and Peace: FDR's Final Odyssey D-Day to Yalta, 1943–1945*. [Vol. 3 of FDR in WWII.] Boston: Houghton Mifflin Harcourt.

Harris, Joseph P. 1946. "Wartime Currents and Peacetime Trends." *APSR* 40, no. 6 (December): 1137–54.

Hart, James. 1943. "National Administration." *APSR* 37, no. 1 (February): 25–34.

Hess, Stephen, and James P. Pfiffner. 2021. *Organizing the Presidency*, 4th ed. Washington, DC: Brookings Institution Press.

Hobbs, Edward H. 1954. *Behind the President: A Study of Executive Office Agencies*. Washington, DC: Public Affairs.

Holzer, M., ed. (2000). *Public Service: Callings, Commitments, and Constraints*. Boulder, CO: Westview.

Juran, J. M. 1946. "Tools for Better Management in Government" (book review). *PAR* 6, no. 1 (Winter): 79–81.

Kahn, Jonathan. 1997. *Budgeting Democracy: State Building and Citizenship in America, 1890–1928*. Ithaca: Cornell University Press.

Kiplinger, M. W. 1942. *Washington Is Like That*. New York: Harper & Brothers.

Koistinen, Paul A. C. 2004. *Arsenal of World War II: The Political Economy of American Warfare, 1940–1945*. Lawrence: University Press of Kansas.

Kotlowski, Dean J. 2015. *Paul V. McNutt and the Age of FDR*. Bloomington: Indiana University Press.

Labovitz, I. M. 1947. "Harold Smith—Servant of the Public Interest." *Bulletin of the National Tax Association* 32, no. 5 (February): 135–38.

Latham, Earl. 1943. "The Technique of Administrative Reporting." *PAR* 3, no. 2 (Spring): 106–18.

———. 1945. "Executive Management and the Federal Field Service." *PAR* 5, no. 1 (Winter): 16–27.

Laves, Walter H. C. 1945. "The United Nations: Reorganizing the World's Governmental Institutions." *PAR* 5, no. 3 (Summer): 183–93.

Lee, Mordecai. 2003. "Is There Anything New Under the Sun? Herbert Simon's Contributions in the 1930s to Performance Measurement and Public Reporting." *Public Voices* 6, nos. 2–3: 73–82.

———. 2005. *The First Presidential Communications Agency: FDR's Office of Government Reports.* Albany: State University of New York Press.

———. 2006a. "The History of Municipal Public Reporting." *International Journal of Public Administration* 29, nos. 4–6 (April): 453–76.

———. 2006b. *Institutionalizing Congress and the Presidency: The U.S. Bureau of Efficiency, 1916–1933.* College Station: Texas A&M University Press.

———. 2007. "When Politics Overwhelms Administration: Historical Proofs for Fesler's Maxim against State-Based Federal Regions, 1934–1943." *Public Voices* 9, no. 2: 25–45.

———. 2010. *Nixon's Super-Secretaries: The Last Grand Presidential Reorganization Effort.* College Station: Texas A&M University Press.

———. 2011. *Congress vs. the Bureaucracy: Muzzling Agency Public Relations.* Norman: University of Oklahoma Press.

———. 2012. *Promoting the War Effort: Robert Horton and Federal Propaganda, 1938–1946.* Baton Rouge: Louisiana State University Press.

———. 2014. "Colluding to Create the American Society for Public Administration and the Consequent Collateral Damage." *Public Voices* 14, no. 1: 2–27.

———. 2016a. *A Presidential Civil Service: FDR's Liaison Office for Personnel Management.* Tuscaloosa: University of Alabama Press.

———. 2016b. "Information Is Power: Women as Information Providers to the President's Budgeting Men; A History of the Bureau of the Budget Library, 1940–1970." *Public Voices* 14, no. 2: 87–106.

———. 2017. "Trying to Professionalize Expert Knowledge, Part II: A Short History of Public Administration Service, 1933–2003." *Public Voices* 15, no. 1: 28–45.

———. 2018a. *Get Things Moving! FDR, Wayne Coy, and the Office for Emergency Management, 1941–1943.* Albany: State University of New York Press.

———. 2018b. "Guilt by Innuendo: GAO's *Political* Attack on Agency Training Programs, 1940." *Journal of Public and Nonprofit Affairs* 4, no. 3: 306–28.

———. 2018c. "Public Reporting in Public Administration, circa 1939: The Annual Report as Fictional Radio Stories." *Public Voices* 15, no. 2: 107–25.

———. 2019a. "Public Administration's First Training and Development Arm: The Origins and Pioneering Programs of the National Institute of Public Affairs, 1934–1985." *Public Voices* 16, no. 1: 63–83.

———. 2019b. "Historical Development of American Public Administration." In *Oxford Research Encyclopedia of Politics.* New York: Oxford University Press. DOI: 10.1093/acrefore/9780190228637.013.1441.

————. 2019c. "Revitalizing Historiography in Public Administration." In *Public Performance and Management Review*. Published ahead of print, October 16, 2019. https://doi.org/10.1080/15309576.2019.1677256.

————. 2020. "Harold D. Smith: From Central Kansas to FDR's White House." *Kansas History: A Journal of the Central Plains* 43, no. 3 (Autumn): 172–93.

————. 2021. "The Managerial Apprenticeship of FDR's Budget Director: Harold D. Smith and the Michigan Municipal League, 1928–1937." *Journal of Public and Nonprofit Affairs* 7, no. 1 (April): 46–67.

Lee, Robert D., Jr., and Ronald W. Johnson. 1973. *Public Budgeting Systems*. Baltimore: University Park Press.

————. 1977. *Public Budgeting Systems*, 2nd ed. Baltimore: University Park Press.

————. 1983. *Public Budgeting Systems*, 3rd ed. Baltimore: University Park Press.

Leiserson, Avery. 1945. "Politics in Administration—In Modern Dress" (book review). *PAR* 5, no. 2 (Spring): 168–72.

Lelyveld, Joseph. 2016. *His Final Battle: The Last Months of Franklin Roosevelt*. New York: Alfred A. Knopf.

Lepawsky, Albert. 1949. *Administration: The Art and Science of Organization and Management*. New York: Alfred A. Knopf.

Lynch, Thomas D. 1979. *Public Budgeting in America*. Englewood Cliffs, NJ: Prentice-Hall.

————, Jinping Sun, and Robert W. Smith. 2017. *Public Budgeting in America*, 6th ed. Irvine, CA: Melvin & Leigh.

May, Geoffrey. 1945. "Day Dreams of a Bureaucrat." *PAR* 5, no. 2 (Spring): 153–61.

McGee, Vernon A., and Ralph J. Burton. 1943. "The Assistant to the Administrator." *PAR* 3, no. 1 (Winter): 7–9.

McNabb, David E. 2018. *Research Methods for Public Administration and Nonprofit Management*, 4th ed. New York: Routledge.

————. 2021. *Research Methods for Political Science: Quantitative, Qualitative and Mixed Method Approaches*, 3rd ed. New York: Routledge.

Milton, George Fort. 1944. *The Use of Presidential Power, 1789–1943*. Boston: Little, Brown.

Mitchell, David, and Kurt Thurmaier. 2017. "Currents and Undercurrents in Budgeting Theory." In *Foundations of Public Administration*, edited by Jos C. N. Raadschelders and Richard J. Stillman II, chap. 12. Irvine, CA: Melvin & Leigh.

Moe, Gustave A. 1943. "The Bureau of the Budget and Governmental Budgeting in Wartime." *National Association of Cost Accountants Bulletin* 25, no. 2 (September 15): 43–62.

Moody, Blair. 1941. *Boom or Bust*. New York: Duell, Sloan and Pearce.

Morey, Lloyd. 1942. "Financial Reporting in the Federal Government." *Accounting Review* 17, no. 2 (April): 73–82.

Morrison, Donald. 1945. "Public Administration and the Art of Governance" (book review). *PAR* 5, no. 1 (Winter): 83–87.

Morstein Marx, Fritz. 1944. "Looking at Under-All Management" (book review).

PAR 4, no. 4 (Autumn): 368–71.

———. 1945. "The Bureau of the Budget: Its Evolution and Present Rôle, I." *APSR* 39, no. 4 (August): 653–84.

———. 1947. *The President and His Staff Services*, Publication no. 98. Chicago: Public Administration Service.

Mosher, Frederick C. 1984. *A Tale of Two Agencies: A Comparative Analysis of the General Accounting Office and the Office of Management and Budget*. Baton Rouge: Louisiana State University Press.

Neustadt, Richard E. 1954. "Presidency and Legislation: The Growth of Central Clearance." *APSR* 48, no. 3 (September): 641–71.

———. 1955. "Presidency and Legislation: Planning the President's Program." *APSR* 49, no. 4 (December): 980–1021.

Olson, Herbert A. 1947. "Harold D. Smith—What He Meant to State and Local Government." *PAR* 7, no. 2 (Spring): 82–84.

Owens, Larry. 1994. "The Counterproductive Management of Science in the Second World War: Vannevar Bush and the Office of Scientific Research and Development." *Business History Review* 68, no. 4 (Winter): 515–76.

Parkinson, C. Northcote. 1957. *Parkinson's Law, and Other Studies in Administration*. Boston: Houghton Mifflin.

Pearson, Norman N. 1943. "The Budgeting Function in the Department of Agriculture." *PAR* 3, no. 1 (Winter): 24–41.

Pemberton, William E. 1979. *Bureaucratic Politics: Executive Reorganization during the Truman Administration*. Columbia: University of Missouri Press.

Pfiffner, James P. 2020. "OMB, the Presidency, and the Federal Budget." In *Executive Policymaking: The Role of the OMB in the Presidency*, edited by Meena Bose and Andrew Rudalevige, chap. 2. Washington, DC: Brookings Institution Press.

Pfiffner, John M. 1946. *Public Administration*, rev. [2nd] ed. New York: Ronald.

Pincus, William. 1945. "Shall We Have More TVA's?" *PAR* 5, no. 2 (Spring): 148–52.

Polenberg, Richard. 1979. "Roosevelt, Carter, and Executive Reorganization: Lessons of the 1930s." *Presidential Studies Quarterly* 9, no. 1 (Winter): 35–46.

Relyea, Harold C. 2002. "Homeland Security: The Concept and the Presidential Coordination Office—First Assessment." *Presidential Studies Quarterly* 32, no. 2 (June): 397–411.

———. 2011. "The Coming of Presidential Czars and Their Accountability to Congress: The Initial Years: 1937–1945." *White House Studies* 11, no. 1: 1–20.

Roberts, Patrick S. 2014. "The Lessons of Civil Defense Federalism for the Homeland Security Era." *Journal of Policy History* 26, no. 3: 354–83.

Rubin, Irene S. 1994. "Early Budget Reformers: Democracy, Efficiency, and Budget Reforms." *American Review of Public Administration* 24, no. 3 (September): 229–52.

Seckler-Hudson, Catheryn, ed. 1944–1945. *Budgeting: An Instrument of Planning and Management*, 6 vols. (mimeo). Washington, DC: School of Social Sciences and Public Affairs, American University.

Seidman, Harold, and Louis E. Yavner. 1944. "Investigator and Investigatee." *PAR* 4, no. 3 (Summer): 234–37.

Sherwood, Robert E. 1950. *Roosevelt and Hopkins: An Intimate History*, rev. ed. New York: Harper & Brothers.

Smith, Jason Scott. 2003. "New Deal Public Works at War: The WPA and Japanese American Internment." *Pacific Historical Review* 72, no. 1 (February): 63–92.

Sollenberger, Mitchel A., and Mark J. Rozell. 2012. *The President's Czars: Undermining Congress and the Constitution.* Lawrence: University Press of Kansas.

Somers, Herman Miles. (1950) 1969. *Presidential Agency: OWMR, the Office of War Mobilization and Reconversion.* New York: Greenwood.

Stone, Donald C. 1943. "Federal Administrative Management 1932–1942." *Transactions of the American Society of Mechanical Engineers* 65 (April): 242–48.

———. 1945. "Notes on the Governmental Executive: His Role and His Methods." In *New Horizons in Public Administration: A Symposium*, edited by Roscoe C. Martin, chap. 3. Tuscaloosa: University of Alabama Press. Reprinted in *PAR* 5, no. 3 (Summer 1945): 210–25.

———, and Carl W. Tiller. 1943. "Use of Manuals of Financial Procedure by the Federal Government." *Municipal Finance* 16, no. 2 (November): 13–16.

Tomkin, Shelley Lynne. 1998. *Inside OMB: Politics and Process in the President's Budget Office.* Armonk, NY: M. E. Sharpe.

Vieg, John A. 1944. "Democracy and Bureaucracy" (book reviews). *PAR* 4, no. 3 (Summer): 247–52.

Villalobos, José D., and Justin S. Vaughn. 2015. *Czars in the White House: The Rise of Policy Czars as Presidential Management Tools.* Ann Arbor: University of Michigan Press.

Waldo, Dwight, ed. 1953. *Ideas and Issues in Public Administration.* New York: McGraw-Hill.

Wann, A. J. 1968. *The President as Chief Administrator: A Study of Franklin D. Roosevelt.* Washington, DC: Public Affairs.

White, Leonard D. 1948. *Introduction to the Study of Public Administration*, 3rd ed. New York: Macmillan.

———. 1955. *Introduction to the Study of Public Administration*, 4th ed. New York: Macmillan.

Williams, Arthur F., and Karl F. Johnson. 2000. "Race, Social Welfare, and the Decline of Postwar Liberalism: A New or Old Key?" *PAR* 60, no. 6 (November/December): 560–72.

Willoughby, Katherine G. 2014. *Public Budgeting in Context: Structure, Law, Reform and Results.* New York: Jossey-Bass/Wiley.

Zelizer, Julian E. 2012. *Governing America: The Revival of Political History.* Princeton, NJ: Princeton University Press.

Index

Note: Page numbers in *italics* indicate illustrations.

393

Marshall, George, 65, 91
Marshall Plan, 319n14
Martin, James W., 126, 280
Martin, L. C., 86, 191
Martin, Roscoe, 125–26
McCarran, Pat, 79, 81, 157–58
McCarthy, Joseph, 347n232
McCormack, John, 271
McIntire, Ross T., 229, 232
McIntyre, Marvin, 96
McKellar, Kenneth, 177, 189, 199–
    200, 234–35, 268–71, 369n45
McNary, Charles, 81
McNutt, Paul, 62, 167
McReynolds, William, 66–67, 306n6,
    317n65; on draft deferments, 167;
    at NDAC, 92, 101
Mead, James M., 343n163
Meir, Golda, 293
Mellett, Lowell, 87
merchant marine, 154, 267–68, 282
Merriam, Charles E., 19, 36, 41
methodology, 7–14
Meyer, Eugene, 332n118
Meyer, Katharine, 340n93
Michigan Municipal League, 23, 63,
    68, 284
Milton, George Fort, 185, 201
Missouri River public works, 240–41
Moffett, Guy, 63
Moody, Blair, 127, 357n138
Morgenthau, Henry, 11, 59, 315n37;
    Brownlow and, 335n160; budget
    message of, 183, 230; FDR on, 261,
    288; on inflation controls, 161–63;
    Smith's relationship with, 22–25,
    124, 134–38, 143–44, 149, 186–87;
    tax policies of, 35, 143; transcripts
    of, 14
Moses, Robert, 211–12, 354n93
Mosher, William, 2, 6, 252
Munich agreement, 47

Murphy, Frank, 22–23, 26, 29, 95,
    291

National Defense Advisory
    Commission (NDAC), 91–92, 98,
    101–6
National Defense Mediation Board,
    107
National Education Association, 265
National Housing Agency, 154
National Labor Relations Board
    (NLRB), 38
National Resources Planning Board
    (NRPB), 27–28, 35, 85; funding of,
    76, 308n38; postwar priorities of,
    179–80
National War Labor Board, 154
National Youth Administration (NYA),
    117, 123, 139, 142, 197
Native Americans. See American
    Indians
Navy. See Knox, Frank
Navy Department, 138, 154
Nelson, Donald, 102, 103, 153;
    memoirs of, 169; at War Production
    Board, 154
Neutrality Act, 51, 54, 315n35
New Deal policies, 18; Keynesian
    economics and, 44, 174; war critics
    and, 168, 174–76, 330n93
Nicaragua, 309n41
Nixon, Richard, 294, 303n1, 319n9,
    335n170
"nondefense expenditures," 122

Office for Emergency Management
    (OEM), 91, 92, 107–8, 115–16
Office of Alien Property Custodian,
    154, 157
Office of Censorship, 147
Office of Civilian Defense (OCD),
    144–46, 197

www.ingramcontent.com/pod-product-compliance
Lightning Source LLC
Chambersburg PA
CBHW030634270326
41929CB00007B/75